Guided Study

Surviving Chemistry

One Concept at a Time

A *Guided Study* and Workbook for High School Chemistry

2012 Revision

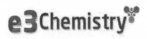

E3 Scholastic Publishing

Effiong Eyo

Surviving Chemistry Book Series

Student and Teacher Friendly HS Chemistry books that will:

☆ **excite** students to study

☆ **engage** students in learning

☆ **enhance** students understanding

For more information, preview and to order

e3chemistry.com
SurvivingChem.com

(877) 224 – 0484
info@e3chemistry.com

Surviving Chemistry One Concept at a Time
Guided Study Book – 2012 Revision

ISBN-13:   978-1478257868

ISBN-10:   1478257865

Printed in the United States of America

E3 Scholastic Publishing

Survivingchem.com
e3chemistry.com
(877) 224 - 0484

Now on
NYC DOE
Famis
E-catalog

New York City Teachers
Our books are now listed on
Famis E-catalog through Ingram

Vendor #: ING032000
Contract #: 7108108

Guided Study Book – 2012 Revision

Answer Booklet

Since this book is being used as classroom instructional material by teachers, the Answer Booklet is only available through the Publisher's website: e3chemistry.com.

Teachers: You can purchase the Answer Booklet directly from our website for $9.
Free Answer Booklets are only available to teachers who have made class order purchases. You can get up to four free copies with your class order.

Home-school parents and tutors: You can request an Answer Booklet by sending us a request-email to info@e3chemistry.com.
After reviewing your request, you will then be able to purchase the Answer Booklet for $7.

Students: If your school is not using this book in the classroom, and you had purchased this book for your own use, please send us an email requesting the answer booklet. After confirming that your school isn't using this book in the classroom, you will then be able to purchase the Answer Booklet for $9.

Versions of our books

Black and white version

The variation in print color that you will find in this book is due to the used of various color fonts. Some prints may appear darker or lighter than normal depending on the color font that was used. This book is also available in color paperback print.

Color print version.

This book is available in color paperback print. The colorful nature of the book enhances visual learning of chemistry. Comparisons are clearer and easier to see. Diagrams and graphs stand out more and convey the concepts better. Explanations and solutions to problems are easier to follow and understand. For the struggling students, the color print version can make all the difference.

Workbook.

A great companion to this study book is the workbook, which is sold separately. The workbook contains almost 5000 problems in four sections: Worksheets, multiple choices, constructed Response, and reference tables. Questions in the workbook are also separated into concept sets. This allows students to work on a group of questions of one or related concepts. By working on groups of questions related to the same concept, students will test their understanding of that concept.
Each concept covered in the study book has at least one set of questions in the workbook.
Please visit www.SurvivingChem.com to learn more about all of our Surviving Chemistry books.

Table of Contents

Table of Contents

Table of Contents

Topic 1 - Matter and Energy

Topic Outline

In this topic, you will learn the following concepts:

. Types of matter and their characteristics
. Phases of matter and their characteristics
. Phase changes and relationship to energy
. Phase change diagram

. Temperature
. Heat energy and heat calculations
. Properties of gases and the gas laws
. Physical and chemical properties and changes

Lesson 1: Types of Matter

Introduction

Chemistry is the study of matter: its composition, structure, properties, changes it undergoes, and the energy accompanying these changes.

Matter is anything that has mass and takes up space. Matter, in other words, is "stuff." Matter can be grouped and classified as pure substances or mixtures.

In this lesson you will learn about the different types of matter and their characteristics. You will also learn to recognize different types of matter by chemical symbols and diagrams.

1. Pure Substances

A **pure substance** is a type of matter in which every sample has:
. Definite and fixed composition
. Same unique sets of properties

Elements and *Compounds* are classified as chemical pure substances.

Examples of pure substances

Elements	*Compounds*
Na (sodium)	H_2O (water)
Al (aluminum)	CO_2 (carbon dioxide)
H_2 (hydrogen)	NH_3 (ammonia)
He (helium)	$C_6H_{12}O_6$ (sugar)

Practice 1
Carbon dioxide, CO_2, is classified as a pure substance because

1) Its composition can vary
2) Its composition is fixed
3) It cannot be separated
4) It can be separated

Practice 2
Which list consists only of chemical pure substances?

1) Soil and salt water
2) Air and water
3) Iron and sodium chloride
4) Sugar and concrete

2. Elements

An **element** is a pure substance that:
. Is composed (made up) of identical atoms with the same atomic number
. *Cannot* be decomposed (or broken down) into simpler substances by physical or chemical methods

Examples of elements

Mg (Magnesium) Br_2 (Bromine)   Au (gold)

There are more than 100 known elements. Names, symbols, and other important information for all the elements can be found on the Periodic Table.

LO**OO**KING Ahead ⟹ Topic 2 - Periodic Table , you will learn more about the elements.

Practice 3
Which cannot be decomposed by physical or chemical methods?

1) HBr   3) K_2O
2) Ni   4) CO

Practice 4
Lithium is classified as an element because it is composed of atoms that

1) have the same mass
2) have different masses
3) have the same atomic number
4) have different atomic numbers

3. Compounds

A **compound** is a pure substance that:
. Is composed of two or more different elements chemically combined
. Has a definite composition (fixed ratio) of atoms in all samples
. *Can be* decomposed into simpler substances by chemical methods
. Has the same unique set of properties in all of its samples
Note: Properties of a compound are different from those of the elements which it is composed.

Law of definite composition states that compounds contain two or more different atoms that are combined in a fixed ratio by mass. For example: The mass ratio in water, H_2O, is 8g of oxygen for every 1g of hydrogen. This ratio will be found in any sample of water.

Examples of compounds
H_2O (l) (Water) CO_2 (g) (Carbon dioxide)
NH_3 (g) (Ammonia)   NaCl (s) (Sodium chloride)

Similarities and differences between compounds and elements are noted below.

Compounds are similar to elements in that:
. Both are pure substances
. Both always have homogeneous properties
. Both have fixed and definite composition in all samples

Compounds are different from elements in that :
. Compounds can be broken down (decomposed) by chemical means
. Elements cannot be decomposed

Practice 5
Which list consists only of substances that can be chemically decomposed?
1) K(s) and KCl(aq)
2) CO(aq) and CO_2(g)
3) Co(s) and $CaCl_2$(s)
4) LiBr(s) and CCl_4 (l)

Practice 6
Which must occur for HF to form from its elements?
1) A physical change
2) A chemical change
3) A phase change
4) A nuclear change

Practice 7
MgO is different from Mg in that MgO
1) is a pure substance
2) has the same unique properties
3) can be chemically separated
4) can be physically separated

4. Mixtures

A **mixture** is a type of matter that:
. Is composed of two or more substances that are *physically* combined
. Has composition that can change (vary) from one sample to another
. Can be physically separated into its components
. Retains properties of the individual components

Examples of mixtures

NaCl (aq)   (salt water)
$C_6H_{12}O_6$(aq)   (sugar solution)
HCl (aq)   (hydrochloric acid solution)
Soil , concrete, and air are also mixtures

Similarities and differences between mixtures and compounds:

Mixtures are similar to compounds in that:
. Both are composed (made up) of two or more different substances
. Both can be separated into their components

Mixtures are different from compounds in that:
. Components of mixtures are *physically* combined , and the composition can change (vary)
    In compounds, they are *chemically* combined, and the composition is definite (fixed)
. Components of mixtures can be separated by *physical methods*
    In compounds, they can be separated by *chemical methods*
. Mixtures can be classified as homogenous or heterogeneous
    Compounds can only be homogenous.

Practice 8
Which is a mixture of substances?
1) Cl_2(g)   3) $MgCl_2$(s)
2) H_2O(l)   4) KNO_3 (aq)

Practice 9
Which is true of a KCl solution ?
1) It is composed of substances that are chemically combined
2) It is composed of substances that are physically combined
3) It is composed of substances with the same atomic number
4) It is a pure substance

5. Homogeneous and Heterogeneous Mixtures

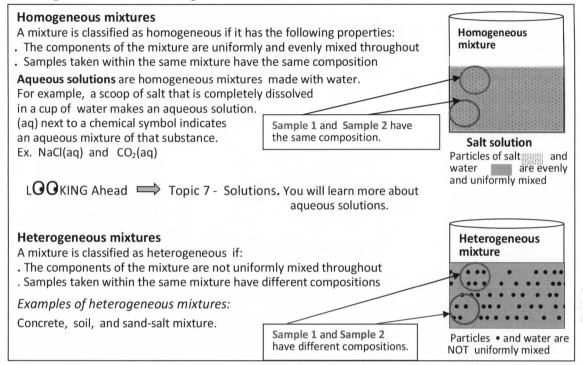

Homogeneous mixtures

A mixture is classified as homogeneous if it has the following properties:
. The components of the mixture are uniformly and evenly mixed throughout
. Samples taken within the same mixture have the same composition

Aqueous solutions are homogeneous mixtures made with water.
For example, a scoop of salt that is completely dissolved
in a cup of water makes an aqueous solution.
(aq) next to a chemical symbol indicates
an aqueous mixture of that substance.
Ex. $NaCl(aq)$ and $CO_2(aq)$

LOOKING Ahead ⟹ Topic 7 - Solutions. You will learn more about aqueous solutions.

Homogeneous mixture

Sample 1 and Sample 2 have the same composition.

Salt solution
Particles of salt and water are evenly and uniformly mixed

Heterogeneous mixtures

A mixture is classified as heterogeneous if:
. The components of the mixture are not uniformly mixed throughout
. Samples taken within the same mixture have different compositions

Examples of heterogeneous mixtures:

Concrete, soil, and sand-salt mixture.

Heterogeneous mixture

Sample 1 and Sample 2 have different compositions.

Particles • and water are NOT uniformly mixed

6   Classification of Matter: Summary diagram

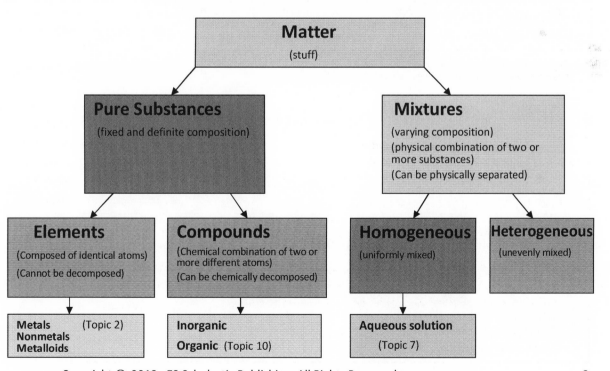

Matter
(stuff)

Pure Substances
(fixed and definite composition)

Mixtures
(varying composition)
(physical combination of two or more substances)
(Can be physically separated)

Elements
(Composed of identical atoms)
(Cannot be decomposed)

Compounds
(Chemical combination of two or more different atoms)
(Can be chemically decomposed)

Homogeneous
(uniformly mixed)

Heterogeneous
(unevenly mixed)

Metals   (Topic 2)
Nonmetals
Metalloids

Inorganic
Organic (Topic 10)

Aqueous solution
(Topic 7)

7. Separation of Mixtures

Substances that make up a mixture can be separated by various physical methods because the substances are physically combined, and each retains its physical properties. Methods of separation depend on physical characteristics of each substance in the mixture, as well as if the mixture is homogeneous or heterogeneous.

Separation of Homogeneous Mixtures

Distillation is a process of separating components of a homogeneous mixture (solution) by using differences in their boiling points. In a distillation process, a sample of a mixture is placed and heated in a distillation apparatus. As the *boiling point* of a substance in the mixture is reached, the substance will boil and evaporate out of the mixture. The substance with the lowest boiling point will boil and evaporate out first, and the substance with the highest boiling point will boil and evaporate out last. As each substance boils and evaporates out, it can be condensed back to liquid and collected in separate containers. Examples of mixtures that can be separated by distillation include: Water and alcohol mixture. A mixture of different hydrocarbon gases (methane, ethane, propane..etc). Salt and water mixture can be separated by boiling off the water and leaving the salt behind.

Chromatography is a process of separating substances of a homogeneous mixture by first dissolving the mixture in a solvent (mobile phase), and then allowing the substances in the mixture to move through some sort of a stationary phase.

In **gas chromatography,** a sample of a mixture is placed in equipment that vaporizes the components of the mixture and allows them to move through a series of columns packed with stationary phase chemicals. Components of the mixture will move through the columns at different speeds (rates), and can be detected and analyzed as they exit the columns. Gas chromatography is often used to analyze purity of a mixture.

In **paper chromatography**, a sample of a mixture is dissolved in a solvent (moving phase), and each component of the mixture will move up the chromatograph paper (stationary phase) at different rates. The height and other characteristics of each mark (blot) on the paper can be analyzed and used to identify the different components of the mixture. Pigment separation is often done by paper chromatography.

Separation of Heterogeneous Mixtures.

Decantation (pouring) is a simple process of separating a heterogeneous mixture in which the components have separated into layers. Each layer of the mixture can be poured out and collected one by one. Immiscible liquids (liquids that do not mixed well or evenly) are often separated by decantation. An oil and water mixture can be separated this way.

Filtration

Filtration is a process that can be used to separate a liquid mixture that is composed of substances with different particle sizes. A filter is equipment with holes that allows particles of a mixture that are smaller than the holes to pass through, while particles that are bigger than the holes are kept on the filter. A mixture of salt water and sand can be separated through using a filtration process. During filtration, the aqueous components (salt and water) will go through the filter paper because molecules of water and particles of salt are smaller than holes of a filter. The sand component of the mixture will stay on the filter because sand particles are generally larger than the holes of a filter paper.

Paper chromatography set up

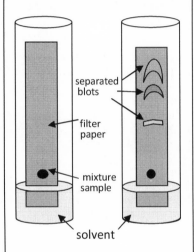

separated blots

filter paper

mixture sample

solvent

A filtration setup

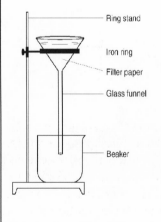

Ring stand

Iron ring

Filter paper

Glass funnel

Beaker

8. Types of Matter: Practice Questions

Practice 10
Which type of matter can be separated only by physical methods?
1) A mixture   2) An element   3) A pure substance   4) A compound

Practice 11
Which two types of matter are considered chemical pure substances?
1) Elements and compounds   3) Elements and mixtures
2) Solutions and compounds   4) Solutions and mixtures

Practice 12
Which type of matter is composed of two or more different elements chemically combined in a definite ratio?
1) A homogeneous mixture   2) A heterogeneous mixture   3) A compound   4) An element

Practice 13
The formula $N_2(g)$ is best classified as
1) A compound   2) A mixture   3) An element   4) A solution

Practice 14
When $NaNO_3$ salt is dissolved in water, the resulting solution is classifies as a
1) Heterogeneous compound   3) Heterogeneous mixture
2) Homogeneous compound   4) Homogeneous mixture

Practice 15
One similarity between all mixtures and compounds is that both
1) Are heterogeneous   3) Combine in definite ratio
2) Are homogeneous   4) Consist of two or more substances

Practice 16
Two substances, X and Y, are to be identified. Substance X cannot be broken down by a chemical change.
Substance Y can be broken down by a chemical change. What can be concluded about these substances?
1) X and Y are both elements   3) X is an element and Y is a compounds
2) X and Y are both compound   4) X is a compound and Y is an element

Practice 17
Bronze contains 90 to 95 percent copper and 5 to 10 percent tin. Because these percentages can vary,
bronze is classified as
1) A compound   2) A substance   3) An element   4) A mixture

Practice 18
When sample X is passed through a filter a white residue, Y, remains on the filter paper and a clear liquid, Z,
passes through. When liquid Z is vaporized, another white residue remains. Sample X is best classified as
1) A heterogeneous mixture   3) An element
2) A homogeneous mixture   4) A compound

Practice 19
A mixture of crystals of salt and sugar is added to water and stirred until all solids have dissolved. Which
statement best describes the resulting mixture.
1) The mixture is homogeneous and can be separated by filtration
2) The mixture is homogeneous and cannot be separated by filtration
3) The mixture is heterogeneous and can be separated by filtration
4) The mixture is heterogeneous and cannot be separated by filtration

9. Diagram Representations of Matter

Diagrams can also be used to show compositions of elements, compounds and mixtures
Examples are given below.

Concept Task: Be able to recognize a diagram that shows an element, a compound or a mixture.

Examples

Given the following symbols:

Atom X	Atom Y
O	●

Elements

The diagrams below represent elements because units in each diagram consist of identical atoms.

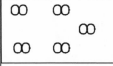

Diatomic element X

Monatomic element Y

Compounds

The diagrams below represent compounds because each consists of identical units, and each unit is composed of different atoms that are touching to show chemical bonding between the atoms.

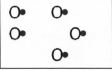

Compound composed of
one atom X and one atom Y
(Five identical units of O●)

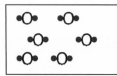

Compound composed of
two atoms Y and one atom X
(Six identical units of ●O●)

Mixtures

The diagrams below represent mixtures because each consists of a mix of two or more different units . One unit is not touching the other to show physical combination between the different units)

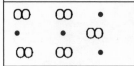

A mixture of diatomic element
X and monatomic element Y

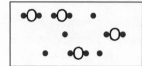

A mixture of compound XY
and atom Y

---

*Given diagrams A, B, and C below:
Answer practice questions 13 - 15
based on the diagrams.*

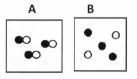

● = particle X
O = particle Y

Practice 20
Which diagram or diagrams represents a compound of X and Y

1) A and B
2) A and C
3) A only
4) B only

Practice 21
Which diagrams represent chemical pure substances?

1) A and B
2) B and C
3) A and C
4) A, B and C

Practice 22
Which best describes diagram B?

1) It is a mixture that is composed of substances physically combined

2) It is a mixture that is composed of substances chemically combined

3) It is a compound that is composed of substances physically combined

4) It is a compound that is composed of substances chemically combined

---

Topic 1 - Matter and Energy

Lesson 2 – Phases of Matter

Introduction

There are three phases of matter: solid, liquid, and gas. The fourth phase of matter, plasma, is not commonly discussed in high school chemistry.

The nature of a substance determines the phase in which the substance will exist under normal conditions. For example, gold will always be a solid at room temperature ($23^\circ C$). At the same room temperature, water will always exist as a liquid, and oxygen will always exist as a gas.

Most substances can change from one phase to another. The nature of a substance also determines the conditions (temperature and/or pressure) that the substance will change from one phase to another.

In this lesson, you will learn about the three phases of matter. You will also learn about phase changes and how they relate to temperature and energy.

10. Phases of Matter

The notes below define and summarize characteristics of substances in the three phases.
To the right are diagrams showing particle arrangements of water in each phase.

Solid (s) : A substance in the solid phase has the following characteristics:
. Definite volume and definite shape
. Particles arranged orderly in a *regular geometric pattern*
. Particles vibrating around a fixed point
. Particles with strong attractive forces to one another
. Particles that cannot be easily compressed (incompressible)

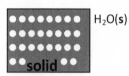

$H_2O(s)$

Orderly and regular geometric arrangement of particles in **solid** phase

Liquid (l) : A substance in the liquid phase has the following characteristics:
. Definite volume, but no definite shape (It takes the shape of its container)
. Particles that are less orderly arranged than those in the solid phase
. Particles with weaker attractive forces than those in the solid phase
. Particles that flow over each other
. Particles that cannot be easily compressed (incompressible)

$H_2O(l)$

Gas (g) : A substance in the gas phase has the following characteristics:
. No definite volume and no definite shape (it takes volume and shape of its container)
. Particles far less orderly arranged (most random)
. Particles that move fast and freely throughout the space of the container
. Particles with very weak attractive forces to each other
. Particles that can be easily compressed (compressible)

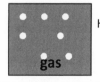

$H_2O(g)$

11. Phases of Matter: Practice problems

Practice 23
Which phase of matter is described as having a definite volume but no definite shape?

1) Aqueous   2) Solid   3) Liquid   4) Gas

Practice 24
Substance X is a gas and substance Y is a liquid. One similarity between substance X and substance Y is that

1) Both have definite shape
2) Both have definite volume
3) Both are compressible
4) Both take the shapes of their containers

Practice 25
Which of the following substances have particles that are arranged in regular geometric pattern?

1) Al(s)   3) $CCl_4(l)$
2) Ar(g)   4) $NH_3(aq)$

Practice 26
Which substance takes the space and shape of its container?

1) Gold   3) Water
2) Iron   4) Hydrogen

12. Phase Changes

During a phase change, a substance changes its form (or state) without changing its chemical compositions. Therefore, a phase change is a physical change. Any substance can change from one phase to another given the right conditions of temperature and/or pressure. Most substances require a large change in temperature to go through one phase change. Water is one of only a few chemical substances that can change through all three phases within a narrow range of temperature change.

Phase changes and example equations representing each change are given below.

Fusion (also known as melting) is a change from *solid* to *liquid*. $H_2O(s) ---------> H_2O(l)$

Freezing is a change of phase from *liquid* to *solid* $H_2O(l) ---------> H_2O(s)$

Evaporation is a change of phase from *liquid* to *gas* $C_2H_5OH(l) -------> C_2H_5OH(g)$

Condensation is a change of phase from *gas* to *liquid* $C_2H_5OH(g) ------> C_2HOH(l)$

Deposition is a change of phase from *gas* to *solid* $CO_2(g) ----------> CO_2(s)$

Sublimation is a change of phase from *solid* to *gas* $CO_2(s) ------------> CO_2(g)$

NOTE: **$CO_2(s)$** , *solid* carbon dioxide (also known as dry ice) , and **$I_2(s)$,** *solid* iodine, are two chemicals substances that readily sublime at room temperature because of the weak intermolecular forces holding their molecules together. Most substances do not sublime.

13. Phase Change and Energy

Each of the six phase changes defined above occurs when a substance has absorbed or released enough heat energy to rearrange its particles (atoms, ions or molecules) from one form to another. Some phase changes require a release of heat by a substance, while other phase changes require heat to be absorbed.

Endothermic describes a process that absorbs heat.

Fusion, evaporation and sublimation are endothermic phase changes.

Exothermic describes a process that releases heat.

Freezing, condensation and deposition are exothermic phase changes.

The diagram below summarizes phase changes and the relationship to energy.

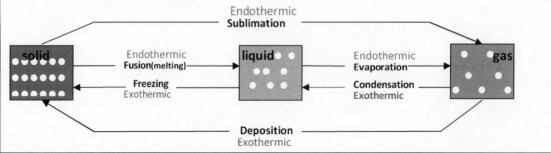

Topic 1 - Matter and Energy

14. Phase Change and Energy: Practice problems

Practice 27
Which phase change equation is exothermic?
1) $N_2(l)$ ---------- $> N_2(g)$ 3) $CH_4(g)$ -------- $> CH_4(l)$
2) $Hg(s)$ -------- $> Hg(l)$ 4) $I_2(s)$ ----------- $> I_2(g)$

Practice 28
Which equation is showing the sublimation of iodine?
1) $I_2(g)$ ---- -> $I_2(s)$ 3) $I_2(s)$ ------> $I_2(l)$
2) $I_2(s)$ -----> $I_2(g)$ 4) $I_2(g)$ ------> $I_2(l)$

Practice 29
The change $NH_3(g)$ --------> $NH_3(s)$ is best described as
1) Sublimation   3) Condensation
2) Evaporation   4) Deposition

Practice 30
Heat will be absorbed by a substance as it changes from
1) Solid to gas   3) Gas to solid
2) Liquid to solid   4) Gas to liquid

Practice 31
Which is true of ethanol as it changes from a liquid state to a gas state?

1) It absorbs heat as it condenses
2) It absorbs heat as it evaporates
3) It releases heat as it condenses
4) It releases heat as it evaporates

15. Temperature

Temperature is a measure of the average kinetic energy of particles in matter.

Kinetic energy is energy due to the movement of particles in a substance.
. The higher the temperature of a substance, the greater its kinetic energy
. As temperature increases, the average kinetic energy also increases

A **thermometer** is a piece of equipment that is used for measuring temperature.
Degree Celsius ($^{\circ}$C) and Kelvin (K) are the two most common units
for measuring temperature.. The mathematical relationship between
Celsius and Kelvin is given by the equation:

$$K = {^{\circ}C} + 273$$ See Reference Table T

According to this equation, the Kevin temperature value is always 273 higher
than the same temperature in Celsius.

Creating a thermometer scale of any unit requires two fixed reference points.
The freezing point ($0^{\circ}C$, 273K) and the *boiling point ($100^{\circ}C$, 373K)* of water
are often used as the two reference points in creating a thermometer scale. Once
the two reference points are marked on a thermometer, equal units are scaled
and marked between the two points.

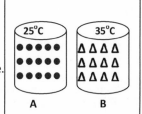

Since particles **Δ** in **B** are
at a higher temperature,
Δ will be moving faster
(higher kinetic energy)
than particles ● in A

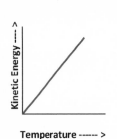

A graph showing a
direct relationship
between temperature
and kinetic energy

Important temperature points at normal pressure

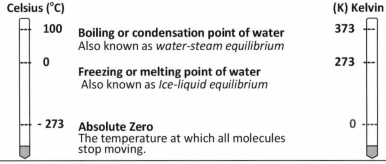

Celsius ($^{\circ}$C)

100 **Boiling or condensation point of water**
Also known as *water-steam equilibrium*

0 **Freezing or melting point of water**
Also known as *Ice-liquid equilibrium*

- 273 **Absolute Zero**
The temperature at which all molecules
stop moving.

(K) Kelvin

373

273

0

16. Temperature Conversion: Practice Problems

Concept Task: Be able to convert temperature between Celsius and Kelvin.

Recall: **K = °C + 273**

Practice 32
Which Celsius temperature is equivalent to +20 K?
1) -253   3) +253
2) -293   4) +293

Practice 33
The temperature of -30 °C is the same as
1) 30 K   3) 243 K
2) 303 K   4) 70 K

Practice 34
What is the equivalent of 546 K on a Celsius scale?
1) 273 °C   3) -273 °C
2) 818 °C   4) 546 °C

Practice 35
A liquid's freezing point is -38°C and its boiling point is 357°C. What is the number of Kelvin degrees between the boiling and the freezing point of the liquid?
1) 319   3) 592
2) 668   4) 395

Practice 36
Heat is being added to a given sample. Compared to the Celsius temperature of the sample, the Kelvin temperature will
1) Always be 273° lower
2) Always be 273° greater
3) Have the same reading at 273°C
4) Have the same reading at 0°C

17. Temperature and Kinetic Energy: Practice Problems

Concept Task: Be able to determine which temperature has the highest or lowest kinetic energy.

Recall:
The higher the temperature, the higher the kinetic energy

Practice 37
Which substance will contain particles with the highest average kinetic energy?
1) NO (g) at 40°C   2) NO₂ g) at 45°C   3) N₂O(g) at 30°C   4) N₂O₃(g) at 35°C

Practice 38
Which container contains water molecules with the lowest average kinetic energy?

 40°C
1)

 50°C
2)

300 K
3)

 320K
4)

Practice 39
Which change in temperature is accompanied by greatest increase in average kinetic energy of a substance?
1) -20°C to 15°C   2) 15°C to -20 °C   3) -25°C to 30°C   4) 30°C to -25°C

Practice 40
A sample of substance X can change from one temperature to another. Which change will result in the highest increase in the average kinetic energy of the molecules?
1) 250 K to -10°C   2) 300 K to 57°C   3) 400K to 100°C   4) 100K to -60°C

18. Phase Change Diagrams: Understanding phase change diagrams

A **phase change diagram** shows the relationship between temperature and phase changes of a substance over a period of time as the substance is heating or cooling.

A heating or cooling experiment of a substance can be conducted in a laboratory to see the change in temperature of the substance over time. Data of time and temperature from the experiment can be collected, plotted, and graphed to generate a phase change diagram.

The unique thing about all phase change data and diagrams is that temperature of the substance changes only at certain times. The temperature remains constant at other times even though heat is continuously being added to (or removed from) the substance at a constant rate. Your ability to explain this phenomenon depends on your understanding of the relationship between heat, temperature, kinetic energy, potential energy, and particles arrangement of a substance in different phases.

The two phase diagrams are the heating and cooling curves.

Heating curve:
. Shows changes of a substance starting with the substance in a more organized state (ex. from solid)
. Shows temperature changes of a substance as heat is being absorbed (endothermic process)

Cooling curve
. Shows changes of a substance starting with the substance in a less organized state (ex. from gas)
. Shows temperature changes of a substance as heat is being released (exothermic process)

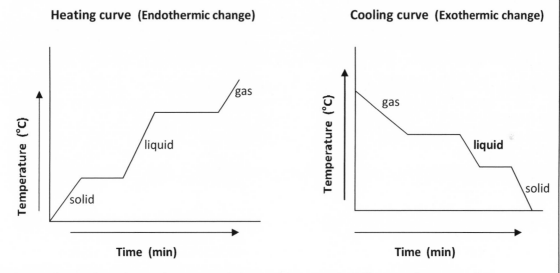

Understanding a phase change diagram can help you determine the following information about a substance:
    . Freezing , melting, and boiling points of a substance
    . When potential and kinetic energy are changing or remaining constant
    . When a substance is in one phase: solid, liquid, or gas phase
    . When a substance is in two phases: solid/liquid or liquid/gas mixture
    . The total time a substance stays in any phase
    . The total time it takes for a substance to go through any of the phase changes

The notes on the next section will show you how to determine the above information from any given phase change diagram. Follow the examples given when interpreting other phase change diagrams.

19. Phase Change Diagrams

Concept Task: Be able to identify and interpret segments of heating and cooling curves.

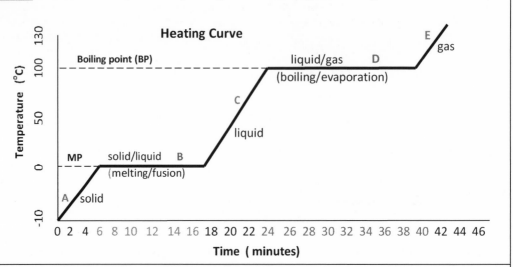

Some important information about the above heating curve .

Melting point / freezing point/ solid - liquid equilibrium occur at :	**0°C**
Boiling point / condensation point/ liquid-gas equilibrium occur at :	**100°C**
kinetic energy increases / potential energy remains constant during segments:	**A, C, and E**
The substance exists in one phase during segments:	**A, C, and E**
Potential energy increases / kinetic energy remains constant during segment:	**B and D**
The substance exists in two phases during segments:	**B and D**
Total time the substance goes through boiling (from 24 to 40 minutes) :	**16 minutes**

The substance is likely water because ice melts at 0°C and water boils at 100°C

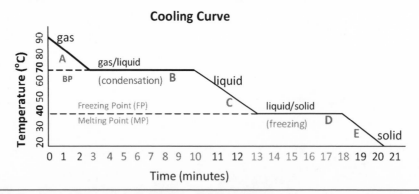

Some important information about the above cooling curve:

Melting point / freezing point/ liquid-solid equilibrium occur at :	**40°C**
Boiling point / condensation point/ gas-liquid equilibrium occur at :	**70°C**
kinetic energy decreases / potential energy remains constant during segments:	**A, C, and E**
Potential energy decreases / kinetic energy remains constant during segment:	**B and D**
Total time for substance to freeze (from 13 to 18 minutes) :	**5 minutes**

The substance is not water because the freezing and boiling points are different from those of water.

20. Phase Change Diagrams: Practice Problems

Concept Task: Be able to identify boiling, freezing, and melting points on phase change diagrams

Practice questions 41–43 are based on graph below, which represents a uniform heating of a substance, starting with the substance as a solid below its melting point.

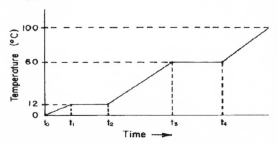

41. What is the melting point of this substance?
1) 0°C   3) 12°C
2) 60°C   4) 100°C

42. What is the boiling point of the substance?
1) 100°C   3) 60°C
2) 12°C   4) 0°C

43. The freezing point of the substance is
1) 100°C   3) 0°C
2) 60°C   4) 12°C

Concept Task: Be able to identify phase segments on phase change diagrams

Practice questions 44–46 are based on diagram below, which represents the relationship between temperature and time as heat is added at a constant rate to a substance, starting when the substance is a gas above its boiling point.

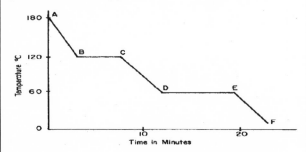

44. The liquid phase of the substance is represented by segment
1) BC   2) DE   3) CD   4) EF

45. Liquid/solid equilibrium of the substance is represented by which segment of the curve?
1) BC   2) AB   3) EF   4) DE

46. During which segment or segments does the substance exist in one phase?
1) AB only   3) AB and CD, only
2) BC only   4) AB, CD and EF, only

Concept Task: Be able to relate energy to phase change diagram

Practice questions 47-48 are based on graph below, which shows the uniform heating of a substance, starting with the substance as a solid below its melting point

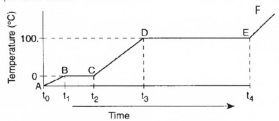

47. Which portions of the graph represent times when kinetic energy is increasing while potential energy remains constant?

1) AB, CD, and EF   3) BC and DE
2) AB, BC, and CD   4) CD and EF

48. Between which time intervals could the heat of fusion be determined?

1) t_0 and t_1 3) t_2 and t_4
2) t_1 and t_2 4) t_3 and t_4

Concept Task: Be able to interpret phase change data.

DATA TABLE	
Time (minutes)	Temperature (°C)
0	65
1	58
2	52
3	53
4	53
5	53
6	53
7	53
8	51
9	47
10	42

Practice questions 49 - 50 are based on data table below, which was collected as a substance in the liquid state cools.

49. Which temperature represents the freezing point of this substance?
1) 65°C   2) 42°C   3) 47°C   4) 53°C

50. Which is true of the kinetic energy and the potential energy of the substance from time 7 and 10 minute?
1) The kinetic energy is increasing and the potential energy is remaining constant
2) The kinetic energy is decreasing and the potential energy is remaining constant
3) The kinetic energy is remaining constant and the potential energy is decreasing
4) Both the kinetic energy and the potential energy are decreasing

Topic 1 - Matter and Energy

Lesson 3 – Heat (thermal) Energy and Heat Calculations

Introduction

Heat is a form of energy that can flow (or transfer) from one object to another. Heat (thermal) energy will always flow from an area or object of a higher temperature to an area or object of a lower temperature. During chemical and physical changes heat energy is either absorbed or released. The amount of heat energy absorbed or released can be determined using various methods. One of those methods (and the most convenience) is to take the temperature of the surrounding before and after a physical or chemical change. When other factors are known about the substance, the temperature difference can be used in a heat equation to calculate the amount of heat absorbed or released.

In this lesson, you will learn about heat and its relationship to temperature. You will also learn how to use heat equations to calculate heat absorbed or released during temperature and phase changes.

21. Heat

Heat is a form of energy that can flow from high to low temperature area. Below are some important information related to heat energy.

Joules and **calories** are the two most common units for measuring heat.

A **calorimeter** is a device used in measuring heat energy during physical and chemical changes.

Exothermic describes a process that releases (emits or loses) heat. As an object or a substance releases heat, its temperature decreases.

Endothermic describes a process that absorbs (takes in or gains) heat. As an object or a substance absorbs heat, its temperature increases.

Direction of heat flow

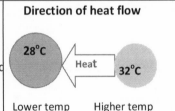

Lower temp   Higher temp

Heat will always flow from high temperature to lower temperature.

22. Heat Flow and Temperature: Practice problems

Concept Task: Be able to determine and describe direction of heat flow .

Practice 51

Object A and object B are placed next to each other. If object B is at 12°C, heat will flow from object A to object B when the temperature of object A is at

1) 6°C   2) 10°C   3) 12°C   4) 15°C

Practice 52

A solid material X is place in liquid Y. Heat will flow from Y to X when the temperature of

1) Y is 20°C and X is 30°C   3) Y is 15°C and X is 10°C
2) Y is 10°C and X is 20°C   4) Y is 30°C and X is 40°C

Practice 53

Given the diagrams

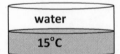

Which correctly describes the energy transfer when the metal object is dropped into the water?

1) Thermal energy will flow from the metal to water, and the water temperature will decrease
2) Thermal energy will flow from the metal to water, and the water temperature will increase
3) Chemical energy will flow from the metal to water, and the water temperature will decrease
4) Chemical energy will flow from the metal to water, and the water temperature will increase

23. Heat Constants and Equations

Amount of heat energy absorbed or released by a substance can be calculated using a heat equation.

There are three heat equations, and each heat equation contains a heat constant. The heat equations and heat constants for water are given on the Reference Tables.

Reference Table B Heat constants for water		Reference Table T Heat equations	
Specific Heat Capacity of $H_2O(l)$ (**C**)	4.18 J/g°K	$q = m \cdot C \cdot \Delta T$	*q is heat*
Heat of fusion (**H$_f$**)	334 J/g	$q = m \cdot H_f$	*m is mass*
Heat of Vaporization (**H$_v$**)	2260 J/g	$q = m \cdot H_v$	

The notes below explain more about the heat constants and equations.

24. Specific Heat Capacity

A substance can change from one temperature to another by either absorbing or releasing heat.
If heat is absorbed or gained, the temperature of the substance will increase.
If heat is released or lost, the temperature of the substance will decrease.

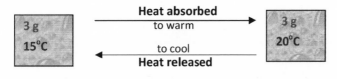

$$\text{Heat} = m \times C \times \Delta T$$

If the specific heat capacity and mass of a substance are known, the amount of heat absorbed or released by the substance to change from one temperature to another can be calculated using the equation below:

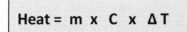

$$\textbf{Heat} = \textbf{m} \times \textbf{C} \times \mathbf{\Delta T}$$

m = mass of the substance (g)
C = specific heat capacity (J/g.°K)
ΔT = difference in temperature (°K)
(ΔT = High temp - Low temp)

The **specific heat capacity (C)** of a substance is the amount of heat needed to change the temperature of a one gram sample of a substance by just one degree Celsius or 1 Kelvin.

The specific heat capacity (C) for water = 4.18 J/g.°K   (See Reference Table B)

Interpretations:

It takes 4.18 joules (J) of heat energy to change the temperature of a one-gram (g) sample of water by just one Kelvin (1 K)
       Or
A one gram sample of water must absorb (or release) 4.18 Joules of heat energy to change its temperature by just one Kelvin.

In heat equations, the specific heat capacity (C) serves as a conversion factor that allows you to calculate the amount of heat absorbed (or released) by any given mass (grams) of a substance to change between any to two temperatures.

Note: Specific heat capacities of other substances are different from that of water.

25. Heat of Fusion

A substance can change between the solid and liquid phases by absorbing or releasing heat.
If heat is absorbed by a solid, the substance will change to its liquid state. This is called fusion (or melting).
If heat is released by a liquid, the substance will change to its solid state. This is called freezing.

If the heat of fusion and mass of a substance are known, the amount of heat absorbed or released by the substance to change between the solid an liquid states can be calculated using the heat equation below:

$$\text{Heat} = m \times H_f$$

m = mass of solid or liquid (g)
H_f = Heat of fusion (J/g)

The **heat of fusion (H_f)** of a substance is the amount of heat needed to melt a one-gram sample of a solid at a constant temperature.

The heat of fusion for water = 334 J/g   (See Reference Table B)

Interpretation:
It takes 334 joules of heat to melt or freeze a one gram sample of water at its melting point.

In the equation above, the heat of fusion (H_f) serves as a conversion factor that allows you to calculate the amount of heat absorbed or released by any given mass of a substance to melt or freeze.

Note: The heat of fusion of other substances are different from that of water.

26. Heat of Vaporization

A substance can change between the liquid and gas phase by absorbing or releasing heat.
If heat is absorbed by a liquid, the substance will change to its gaseous state. This is called vaporization.
If heat is released by a gas, the substance will change to its liquid state. This is called condensation.

If the heat of vaporization and mass of a substance are known, the amount of heat absorbed or released by the substance to change between the liquid and gas states can be calculated using the heat equation below:

$$\text{Heat} = m \times H_v$$

m = mass of the liquid or gas (g)
H_v = Heat of vaporization (J/g)

The **heat of vaporization (H_v)** of a substance is the amount of heat needed to vaporize a one-gram sample of a liquid at a constant temperature.

The heat of vaporization for water = 2260 J/g   (See Reference Table B)

Interpretation:

It takes 2260 joules of heat to vaporize or condense a one gram sample of water at its boiling point.

In the equation above, the heat of vaporization (H_v) serves as a conversion factor that allows you to calculate the amount of heat absorbed or released by any given mass of a substance to vaporize or condense.

Note: The heat of vaporization of other substances are different from that of water.

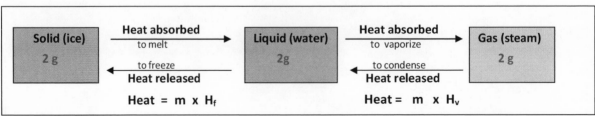

27. Heat Calculations: Examples and practice problems

Concept Task: Be able to use a heat equation to setup and calculate heat absorbed or released by a substance.

Heat equation for temperature change

$$\text{Heat} = m \times C \times \Delta T$$

Choose this equation if two different temperatures (or change in temp) are given in a heat problem.

Example

How much heat is released by a 3 gram sample of water to change its temperature from $15^{\circ}C$ to $10^{\circ}C$?
Show numerical setup and the calculated result

Step 1. Identify all known and unknown factors.

Known:	Unknown
Mass = 3 g	Heat = ?
ΔT = $15^{\circ}C - 10^{\circ}C = 5^{\circ}C$	
C = 4.18 J/g.$^{\circ}C$ *(for water – see Table B)*	

Step 2: Write equation, setup and solve

Heat = m x C x ΔT
Heat = 3 x 4.18 x 5 *numerical setup*

Heat = **62.7 Joules** *calculated result*

Heat equation for fusion phase change

$$\text{Heat} = m \times H_f$$

Choose this equation if a heat question has words or phrase such as *to melt, to freeze, solid to liquid.* or if the temperature is constant at $0^{\circ}C$.

Example

What is the number of joules needed to melt a 6-g sample of ice to water at $0^{\circ}C$?
Show numerical setup and the calculated result

Step 1: Identify all known and unknown factors.

Mass = 6 g   Heat = ?
H_f = 334 J/g *(for water – see Table B)*

Step 2: Write equation, setup and solve

Heat = m x H_f
Heat = 6 x 334 *numerical setup*
Heat = **2004 J** *calculated result*

Practice 54

How much heat is released by a 15-gram sample of water when it is cooled from $40.^{\circ}C$ to $30.^{\circ}C$?

1) 630 J   3) 63 J
2) 42 J   4) 130 J

Practice 55

What is the total amount of heat energy needed to change the temperature of a 65-gram sample of water from $25.^{\circ}C$ to $40^{\circ}C$?

1) 6.3×10^{-2} KJ   3) 1.1×10^{-1} KJ
2) 4.1×10^{0} KJ   4) 6.8×10^{1} KJ

Practice 56

What is the temperature change of a 5-gram sample of water that had absorbed 200 Joules of heat?
Show numerical setup and the calculated result.

Practice 57

The heat of fusion for an unknown substance is 220 J/g. How much heat is required to melt a 35-g sample of this substance at its melting point?

1) 255 J   3) 11690 J
2) 73480 J   4) 7700 J

Practice 58

1200 Joules is added to a sample of ice to change it to water at $0^{\circ}C$. What is the mass of the ice?

1) 3.6 g   3) 334 g
2) 0.27 g   4) 1.9 g

Practice 59

What is the heat of fusion of an unknown solid if 4.8 KJ of heat is required to completely melt a 10 gram sample of this solid?

28. Heat Calculations. Examples and Practice problems continue

Heat equation for vaporization phase change

$$\text{Heat} = m \times H_v$$

Choose this equation if a heat question has words or phrase such as *to boil, to vaporize, liquid to gas,* or if the temperature is constant at $100^{\circ}C$.

Example

Liquid ammonia has a heat of vaporization of 1.35 KJ/g. How many kilojoules of heat are needed to evaporate a 5-gram sample of ammonia at its boiling point?

Show numerical setup and the calculated result

Step 1: Identify all known and unknown factors.

Mass = 5 g   Heat = ?

H_v = 1.35 KJ/g *(NOT water, do not use Table B value)*

Step 2: Write equation, setup and solve

Heat = m × H_v

Heat = 5 × 1.35   *numerical setup*

Heat = **6.75 KJ**   *calculated result*

Practice 60

How much heat must be removed from a 2.5-g sample of steam to condense it to water at a constant temperature of $100^{\circ}C$?

1) 828.5 J   3) 250 J
2) 5650 J   4) 1050 J

Practice 61

How much heat must be added to an 11-g sample of water to change it to steam at a constant temperature?

1) 2.3 KJ   3) 25 KJ
2) 0.21 KJ   4) 2486 KJ

Practice 62

A 23 g sample of an unknown liquid substance absorbed 34 KJ of heat to change to gas at its boiling point. What is the heat of vaporization of the unknown liquid?
Show numerical setup and the calculated result

29. Heat Problems from Data Table

Practice 63
The following information was collected by a student from a calorimetric experiment.

Mass of calorimeter + water	48.0 g
Mass of calorimeter	37.0 g
Initial temperature of water	60.0 $^{\circ}C$
Final temperature of water	?

If the student determined that the water in the calorimeter had absorbed 400 Joules of heat, what would be the final temperature of the water?
Show numerical setup and the calculated result.

Practice 64
A student collected the following data from a calorimeter laboratory experiment

Mass of calorimeter + solid	72.5g
Mass of calorimeter	40.5 g
Heat absorbed by solid to melt	12736 J
Melting point of the solid	371 K

Based on the data collected by the student, what is the heat of fusion of the solid?

Show numerical setup and the calculated result.

Topic 1 - Matter and Energy

Lesson 4 – Characteristics of gases and gas laws

Introduction

Gas behavior is influenced by three key factors: volume (space), pressure and temperature. The relationships between these three factors are the basis for the gas laws and gas theories. These laws and theories attempt to explain how gases behave.

In this lesson you will learn about the kinetic molecular theory, gas laws, and gas law calculations.

30. Kinetic Molecular Theory (KMT) of an Ideal Gas

The **Kinetic Molecular Theory** of an ideal gas is a model (or properties) that is often used to explain the behavior of gases.

An **ideal gas** is a theoretical (or assumed) gas that has all the properties described below.

Concept Facts: Study to memorize the characteristics below.

Summary of Kinetic Molecular Theory of an ideal gas.

. Gases are composed of individual particles
. Distances between gas particles are large (far apart)
. Gas particles are in continuous, random, straight-line motion
. When two particles of a gas collide, energy is transferred from one particle to another
. Particles of a gas have no attraction to each other
. Individual gas particles have no volume (negligible or insignificant volume)

A **real gas** is a gas that we know to exist.

Examples of real gases: *oxygen, carbon dioxide, hydrogen, helium, etc.*

Since the kinetic molecular theory (summarized above) applies mainly to an ideal gas, the model cannot be used to predict the exact behavior of real gases. Therefore, real gases deviate from (do not behave exactly like) an ideal gas.

Reasons that real gases behave differently (deviate) from an ideal gas:
. Real gas particles do attract each other   (Ideal gas particles are assumed to have no attraction)
. Real gas particles do have volume   (Ideal gas particles are assumed to have no volume)

Types of gases that behave more like an ideal gas:
Real gases with small molecular masses behave more like an ideal gas.
Hydrogen (H) and Helium (He), the two smallest real gases by mass, will behave more like an ideal gas.

Temperature and Pressure conditions that real gases behave more like an ideal gas:

Real gases behave more like an ideal gas under
high temperature and low pressure

Real gases behave least like an ideal gas under
low temperature and high pressure

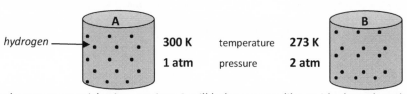

	A			temperature		B	
hydrogen		300 K		temperature	273 K		
		1 atm		pressure	2 atm		

The hydrogen gas particles in container **A** will behave more like an ideal gas than those in container **B** .

31. Kinetic Molecular Theory and Deviation: Practice problems

Practice 65
An ideal gas is made up of gas particles that
1) Have volume
2) Attract each other
3) Can be liquefied
4) Are in random motion

Practice 66
Real gases differ from an ideal gas because the molecules of real gases have
1) Some volume and no attraction for each other
2) Some volume and some attraction for each other
3) No volume and no attraction for each other
4) No volume and some attraction for each other

Practice 67
Under which two conditions do real gases behave least like an ideal gas?
1) High pressure and low temperature
2) Low pressure and high temperature
3) High pressure and high temperature
4) Low pressure and low temperature

Practice 68
The kinetic molecular theory assumes that the particles of ideal gas
1) Are in random, constant, straight line-motion
2) Are arranged in regular geometric pattern
3) Have strong attractive forces between them
4) Have collision that result in the system losing energy

Practice 69
At STP, which will behave most like an ideal gas?
1) Fluorine
2) Nitrogen
3) Oxygen
4) Chlorine

Practice 70
According to the Periodic Table, which of the following gases will behave least like an ideal gas?
1) Ar
2) Ne
3) Xe
4) Kr

Practice 71
Under which conditions of temperature and pressure would oxygen behaves most like an ideal gas?
1) $25^{\circ}C$ and 100 kPa
2) $35^{\circ}C$ and 100 kPa
3) $25^{\circ}C$ and 80 kPa
4) $35^{\circ}C$ and 80 kPa

Practice 72
A real gas will behave least like an ideal gas under which conditions of temperature and pressure?
1) $50^{\circ}C$ and 0.5 atm
2) $50^{\circ}C$ and 0.8 atm
3) 300 K and 0.5 atm
4) 300 K and 0.8 atm

32. Pressure, Volume, Temperature:

Behavior of gases is influenced by volume, pressure, and temperature of the gas.

Volume
Volume of a confined gas is a measure of the space in which the gas occupies.

  Units: milliliters (mL) or liters (L) $1 L = 1000 mL$

Pressure
Pressure of a gas is a measure of how much force the gas particles exert on the walls of its container. This pressure is equal but opposite in magnitude to the external pressure exerted on the gas.

  Units: atmosphere (atm) or Kilopascal (kPa) $1 atm = 101.3 kPa$

Temperature
Temperature of a gas is a measure of the average kinetic energy of the gas particles. As temperature increases the gas particles move faster, and their average kinetic energy increases.

  Units: degree Celsius ($^{\circ}C$) or Kelvin (K) $K = {^{\circ}C} + 273$

STP	Standard Temperature:	273 K or $0^{\circ}C$
	Standard Pressure:	1 atm or 101.3 kPa

Reference Table A

The relationships between these three factors of a gas are discussed in the next few pages.

Practice 73
Express 0.267 liters of O_2 in milliliters.

Practice 74
What is the equivalent of 3487.2 mL of He in liters?

Practice 75
What pressure, in kPa, is equivalent to 1.7 atm?

Practice 76
What is the pressure of 65 kPa in atm?

33. Avogadro's Law

Avogadro's Law states: Under the same conditions of temperature and pressure, gases of equal volume contain equal number of molecules (particles).

In the example below, container A contains helium gas and container B contains oxygen gas.

NOTE that both containers have the same volume , and are at the same temperature and pressure.

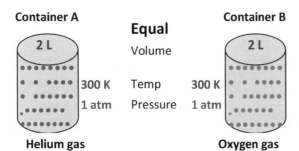

If the helium gas molecules are counted in Container A and the oxygen gas molecules are counted in Container B, you will find that:

The number of molecules of helium in A is *the same* as the number of molecules of oxygen in B.

Practice 77
At STP, a 1.0 L sample of $H_2(g)$ would have the same number of gas molecules as
1) 0.5 L of He   2) 1.0 L of CO   3) 2.0 L of Ne   4) 3.0 L of N_2

Practice 78
Under which conditions would a 0.2 L sample of O_2 has the same number of molecules as a 0.2 L sample of N_2 that is at STP?
1) 0 K and 1 atm   2) 0 K and 2 atm   3) 273 K and 1 atm   4) 273 K and 2 atm

Practice 79
The table below gives the temperature and pressure of four different gas samples, each in a 1.5 L container:

Gas sample	Temperature (K)	Pressure (atm)
SO_2	200	1.5
Ar	300	3.0
N_2	200	1.5
O_2	300	1.5

Which two gas samples contain the same number of molecules?
1) Ar and O_2 2) Ar and N_2 3) SO_2 and Ar   4) SO_2 and N_2

Practice 80
A sample of oxygen gas is sealed in container X. A sample of hydrogen gas is sealed in container Z. Both samples have the same volume, temperature, and pressure. Which statement is true?

1) Container X contains more gas molecules than container Z.
2) Container X contains fewer gas molecules than container Z.
3) Containers X and Z both contain the same number of gas molecules.
4) Containers X and Z both contain the same mass of gas.

34. Boyle's Law: Volume – Pressure relationship at constant temperature

Boyle's law describes the relationship between volume and pressure of a gas at constant temperature.

Concept Fact: Study to remember the following relationships.

At constant temperature, the *volume* of a set mass of a confined gas is *inversely proportional* to the *pressure* of the gas.

This fact can be expressed a few different ways:

As pressure is decreased on a gas, volume of the gas will increase proportionally.
. If pressure on a gas is halved, volume of the gas will double

As pressure is increased on a gas, volume of the gas will decrease by same factor.
. If pressure on a gas is doubled, volume of the gas will be half
(see diagram to the right)

The **Boyle's law equation** (below) can be used to calculate a new volume of a gas when the pressure on the gas is changed at constant temperature.

$$P_1 V_1 = P_2 V_2$$

P_1 = Initial pressure (atm or KPa)

P_2 = New pressure (atm of kPa)

V_1 = Initial volume (mL or L)

V_2 = New volume (mL or L)

According to Boyle's law:

At constant temperature, the product of the new pressure (P_2) and volume (V_2) will always be equal to the product of the initial pressure (P_1) and volume (V_1).

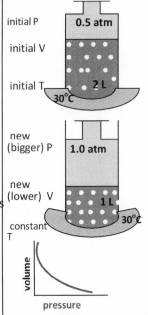

Diagrams and graph showing pressure-volume relationship of a gas at constant temperature.

35. Boyle's Law: Example and Practice problems

Concept Task: Be able to solve gas law problems at a constant temperature.

Example

At constant temperature, what is the new volume of a 3 L sample of oxygen gas if its pressure is changed from 0.5 atm to 0.25 atm?

Show numerical setup and the calculated result.

Step 1: Identify all known and unknown factors
$$V_1 = 3 \text{ L} \qquad V_2 = ? \text{ (unknown)}$$
$$P_1 = 0.5 \text{ atm} \qquad P_2 = 0.25 \text{ atm}$$

Step 2: *Write equation, setup, and solve*

$$P_1 V_1 \qquad = \qquad P_2 V_2$$

$$(0.5)(3) \qquad = \qquad (0.25)(V_2)$$

$$\frac{1.5}{0.25} \qquad = \qquad V_2$$

⎫ *numerical setup*

$$\boxed{6 \text{ L} = V_2} \qquad \textit{calculated result}$$

Practice 81
The volume of a CO_2(g) changes from 50 mL to 100 mL when pressure on the gas is changed to 0.6 atm. If the temperature of the gas is constant, what was the initial pressure on the gas?

1) 1.2 atm   3) 60 atm
2) 0.3 atm   4) 2 atm

Practice 82
A 0.8 L gas at STP had its pressure changed to 25.3 KPa. What is the new volume of the gas if the temperature is held constant?
Show numerical setup and the calculated result.

36. Charles' Law: Volume – Temperature relationship at constant pressure

Charles' law describes the relationship between volume and Kelvin temperature of a gas at constant pressure.

Concept Facts: Study to remember the following relationships.

At constant pressure, the *volume* of a set mass of a confined gas *is directly proportional* to the *Kelvin temperature.*

This fact can be expressed in a few different ways:

As temperature is increased on a gas, volume of the gas will also increase proportionally.
. If temperature of a gas is doubled, volume will also double

As temperature of a gas is decreased, volume of the gas will also decrease by same factor.
. If temperature of a gas is halved, volume will also be halved
                    (see diagram to the right)

The **Charles' law equation (**below) can be used to calculate a new volume of a gas when the temperature of the gas is changed at constant pressure.

$$\frac{V_1}{T_1} = \frac{V_2}{T_2}$$

V_1 = Initial volume (mL or L)
V_2 = New volume (mL or L)
T_1 = Initial Kelvin temperature (K)
T_2 = New Kelvin temperature (K)

According to Charles' law:

At constant pressure, the ratio of new volume (V_2) to Kelvin temperature (T_2) will always be equal to the ratio of initial volume (V_1) to Kelvin temperature (T_1).

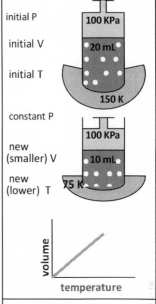

initial P   100 KPa
initial V   20 mL
initial T
     150 K

constant P
new (smaller) V   100 KPa   10 mL
new (lower) T   75 K

volume / temperature

Diagrams and graph showing temperature – volume relationship of a gas at constant pressure

37. Charles' Law: Example and practice problems

Concept Task: Be able to solve gas law problems at constant pressure.

Example

The volume of a confined gas is 25 mL at 280 K. At what temperature would the gas volume be 75 mL if the pressure is held constant?
Show numerical setup and the calculated result.

Step 1: *Identify all known and unknown factors*
     V_1 = 25 mL V_2 = 75 mL
     T_1 = 280 K T_2 = ? (unknown)

Step 2: *Write equation, setup, and solve*

$$\frac{V_1}{T_1} = \frac{V_2}{T_2}$$

$$\left.\frac{25}{280} = \frac{75}{T_2} \atop \frac{(75)(280)}{25} = T_2\right\} \text{numerical setup}$$

| 840 K | = | T_2 | *calculated result* |

Practice 83

A sample of oxygen gas has a volume of 150.mL at 300 K. If the pressure is held constant and the temperature is raised to 600 K, the new volume of the gas will be

1) 75.0 mL   3) 300 mL
2) 150 mL   4) 600 mL

Practice 84

A gas originally at STP has a volume of 0.8 L. If the pressure of the gas is held constant, at what temperature will the volume of the gas be decreased to 0. 6 L?
Show numerical setup and the calculated result.

38. Gay-Lussac's Law: Pressure – Temperature relationship at constant volume

Gay-Lussac's law describes the relationship between pressure and Kelvin temperature of a gas at constant volume.

Concept Facts: Study to remember the following facts:

At constant volume, the *pressure* of a set mass of a confined gas *is directly proportional to* the *Kelvin temperature* .

This fact can be expressed a few different ways:

As temperature of a gas is decreased, pressure of the gas will also decrease . If temperature of a gas is halved, pressure will also be halved

As temperature is increased on a gas, pressure of the gas will also increase . If temperature of a gas is doubled, pressure of the gas will also double.
(See diagram to the right)

The **Gay-Lussac's law equation** below can be used to calculate the new pressure of a gas when temperature of the gas is changed at constant volume.

$$\frac{P_1}{T_1} = \frac{P_2}{T_2}$$

P_1 = Initial pressure (atm or kPa)

P_2 = New pressure (atm or kPa)

T_1 = Initial Kelvin temperature (K)

T_2 = New Kelvin temperature (K)

According to Gay-Lussac's law:

At constant volume, the ratio of new pressure (P_2) to temperature (T_2) will always be equal to the ratio of initial pressure (P_1) to temperature (T_1).

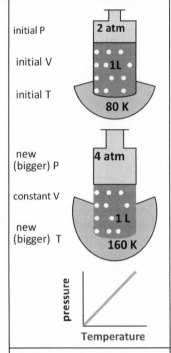

initial P

initial V

initial T

new (bigger) P

constant V

new (bigger) T

Diagrams and graph showing temperature-pressure relationship of a gas at constant volume

---

39. Gay-Lussac's Law: Example and practice problems

Concept Task: Be able to solve gas law problems at constant volume.

Example

Pressure on a gas changes from 20 kPa to 50 kPa when the temperature of the gas is changed to 30°C. If volume was held constant, calculate the initial temperature of the gas? *Show setup and the calculated result.*

Step 1: Identify all known and unknown factors

P_1 = 20 kPa P_2 = 50 kPa
T_1 = ? T_2 = 30°C (must be in Kelvin)
      T_2 = 30 + 273 = 303 K

Step 2: Write equation, setup, and solve

$$\frac{P_1}{T_1} = \frac{P_2}{T_2}$$

$$\frac{20}{T_1} = \frac{50}{303}$$ } *numerical setup*

$$T_1 = 121 \text{ K}$$ *calculated result*

Practice 85
A gas sample at 546 K has a pressure of 0.4 atm. If the volume of the gas sample is unchanged, what will be the new pressure of the gas if its temperature is changed to 136.5 K ?

1) 0.4 atm   3) 0.8 atm

2) 0.1 atm   4) 0.2 atm

Practice 86
A sample of CO_2 is at STP. If the volume of the CO_2 gas remains constant and its temperature is changed to 45°C, what will be the new pressure (in kilopascal) of the gas?
Show numerical setup and the calculated result.

40. Combined Gas Law

The **combined gas law** describes the relationship between all three factors : volume, pressure, and temperature: In the combined gas law, the only constant is the mass of the gas.

The combined gas law equation below is a combination of Boyle's, Charles' , and Gay-Lussac's law equations:

$$\frac{P_1 V_1}{T_1} = \frac{P_2 V_2}{T_2}$$

NOTE: In all gas law problems, mass and the number of particles of the gas are always constant.

See Reference Table T

Eliminating the constant from the combined gas law equation will give you the equation needed to solve any gas law problem.

41. Combined Gas Law: Example and practice problems

Concept Task: Be able to solve combined gas law problems

Example

Hydrogen gas has a volume of 100 mL at STP. If temperature and pressure are changed to 0.5 atm and 546 K respectively, what will be the new volume of the gas?
Show setup and the calculated result.

Step 1: Identify all known and unknown factors

$$\text{STP} \begin{cases} V_1 = 100 \text{ mL} \\ P_1 = 1 \text{ atm} \\ T_1 = 273 \text{ K} \end{cases} \quad \begin{array}{l} V_2 = \ ? \text{ (unknown)} \\ P_2 = 0.5 \text{ atm} \\ T_2 = 546 \text{ K} \end{array}$$

Step 2: Write out equation, setup, and solve

$$\frac{P_1 V_1}{T_1} = \frac{P_2 V_2}{T_2}$$

$$\left. \begin{array}{c} \dfrac{(1)(100)}{273} = \dfrac{(0.5)(V_2)}{546} \\[2mm] \dfrac{(1)(100)(546)}{(273)(0.5)} = V_2 \end{array} \right\} \begin{array}{l} numerical \\ setup \end{array}$$

$$\boxed{400 \text{ mL} \ = \ V_2} \quad \begin{array}{l} calculated \\ result \end{array}$$

Practice 87

A gas sample has a volume of 1.4 L at a temperature of 20.K and a pressure of 1.0 atm. What will be the new volume when the temperature is changed to 40.K and the pressure is changed to 0.50 atm ?
1) 0.35 L   3) 1.4 L
2) 0.75 L   4) 5.6 L

Practice 88

A gas occupies a volume of 3 L at 1.5 atm and 80°C. Calculate the new volume of the gas if the temperature is changed to 150°C and the pressure is dropped to 1.0 atm.
Show numerical setup and the calculated result.

Practice 89
The volume of a 1.0 mole sample of an ideal gas will increase when the
1) Pressure decreases and the temperature decreases
2) Pressure decreases and the temperature increases
3) Pressure increases and the temperature decreases
4) Pressure increases and the temperature increases

Practice 90
A gas is at STP, if the temperature of the gas is held constant while the volume of the gas is cut in half, the pressure of the gas will be
1) Double   3) Halve
2) Triple   4) Quadruple

Practice 91
The graph below shows a change in the volume of a gas sample as its temperature rises at constant pressure.

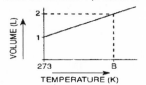

What temperature is represented by point B?
1) 546 K   2) 298 K   3) 273 K   4) 2 K

Lesson 5 – Physical and Chemical Properties and Changes

Introduction

Properties are sets of characteristics that can be used to identify and classify matter. Two types of properties of matter are physical and chemical properties.
In this lesson, you will learn the differences between physical and chemical properties as well as the differences between physical and chemical changes of matter.

42. Physical and Chemical Properties

Physical properties and changes

A **physical property** is a characteristic of a substance that can be observed or measured without changing chemical composition of the substance. Some properties of a substance depend on sample size or amount, others do not.

Examples:
Extensive properties depend on sample size or amount present. Mass, weight and volume are examples of *extensive properties.*

Intensive properties do not depend on sample size or amount. Melting, freezing and boiling points, density, solubility, color, odor, conductivity, luster, and hardness are *intensive properties.*

Differences in physical properties of substances make it possible to separate one substance from another in a mixture.

A **physical change** is a change of a substance from one form to another without changing its chemical composition.

Examples:

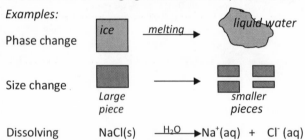

Phase change

Size change

Dissolving $NaCl(s) \xrightarrow{H_2O} Na^+(aq) + Cl^-(aq)$

Chemical properties and changes

A **chemical property** is a characteristic of a substance that is observed or measured through interaction with other substances.

Examples:
It burns, it combusts, it decomposes, it reacts with, it combines with, or it rusts are some of the phrases that can be used to describe chemical properties of a substance.

A **chemical change** is a change in composition and properties of one substance to those of other substances. **Chemical reactions** are ways by which chemical changes of substances occur.

Types of chemical reactions include *synthesis, decomposition, single replacement, and double replacement.*

L**OO**KING Ahead ⟹ Topic 5 – Formulas and Equations:
           You will learn more about these reactions.

Practice 92
Which best describes a chemical property of sodium?
1) It is a shiny metal
2) It is smooth
3) It reacts vigorously with water
4) It is a hard solid

Practice 93
A large sample of a solid calcium sulfate is crushed into smaller pieces. Which two physical properties are the same for both the large sample and one of the smaller pieces?
1) Mass and density
2) Mass and volume
3) Solubility and density
4) Solubility and volume

Practice 94
An example of a physical property of an element is the element's ability to
1) Form a compound
2) React with oxygen
3) React with an acid
4) Form an aqueous solution

Practice 95
During a chemical change, a substance changes its
1) Density   3) Solubility
2) Composition   4) Phase

Practice 96
Given the particle diagram representing four molecules of a substance.

Which particle diagram best represents this same substance after a physical change has

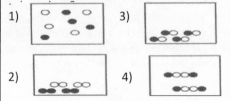

1)   3)

2)   4)

Topic 1 – Matter and Energy

Concept Terms

Below is a list of vocabulary terms from Topic 1. You should know the definition and facts related to each term.

1. Pure substance
2. Mixture
3. Element
4. Compound
5. Law of definite composition
6. Homogeneous mixture
7. Heterogeneous mixture
8. Aqueous solution
9. Decantation
10. Filtration
11. Distillation
12. Solid
13. Liquid
14. Gas
15. Fusion

16. Freezing
17. Condensation
18. Evaporation
19. Sublimation
20. Deposition
21. Exothermic
22. Endothermic
23. Temperature
24. Kinetic energy
25. Potential energy
26. Ice / liquid equilibrium
27. Water / steam equilibrium
28. Absolute Zero
29. Phase change diagram
30. Heat

31. Joules
32. Specific heat capacity
33. Heat of fusion
34. Heat of vaporization
35. Calorimeter
36. Kinetic molecular theory
37. Ideal gas
38. Avogadro's law
39. Boyle's law
40. Charles law
41. Gay – Lussac's law
42. Combined gas law
43. Physical property
44. Chemical property
45. Physical change
46. Chemical change

Concept Tasks

Below is a list of concept tasks from Topic 1. You should know how to solve problems and answer questions related to each concept task.

1. Recognizing chemical symbol of elements, compounds, and mixtures
2. Recognizing diagram representation of elements, compounds, and mixtures
3. Recognizing symbol representation of substances in different phases
4. Recognizing phase change equations
5. Determining substance with highest and lowest kinetic energy based on temperature
6. Temperature conversion between Kelvin and Celsius units
7. Interpreting phase change diagrams (heating and cooling curves)
8. Determining direction of heat flow based on temperatures of two objects
9. Heat calculation during temperature and phase changes
10. Determining gases that behave most or least like an ideal gas
11. Determining temperature and pressure that a gas behaves most or least like an ideal gas
12. Determining gases that contain equal number of molecules
13. Pressure conversion between atm and kPa units
14. Gas law calculations at constant temperature
15. Gas law calculations at constant pressure
16. Gas law calculation at constant volume
17. Combined gas law calculation
18. Determining physical and chemical properties of a substance
19. Determining physical and chemical changes of a substance

Topic 2 – The Periodic Table

Topic Outline

In this topic, you will learn the following concepts:

. Arrangements of the elements   . Periodic trends

. Types of elements and their properties   . Allotropes

. Groups of elements and their properties

Lesson 1 – Arrangement of the Elements

Introduction:

There are more than 100 known elements. Most of the elements are naturally occurring, while a few are artificially produced. The modern Periodic Table contains all known elements. These elements are arranged on the Periodic Table in order of increasing atomic number.

Important information about an element can be found in the box of the element on the Periodic Table .

In this lesson, you will learn about the arrangement of the elements on the Periodic Table.

1. Properties of the Modern Periodic Table

Concept Facts: Study to remember the followings about the Periodic Table.

. Elements are arranged in order of increasing atomic numbers

. Chemical properties of the elements are periodic function of their atomic numbers

. The elements on the Periodic Table are categorized as metals, nonmetals, or metalloids

. More than two thirds of the elements are metals

. The Periodic Table contains elements that are in all three phases (solid, liquid, and gas) at STP

. The majority of the elements exist as solids at STP

. Only two (mercury and bromine) are liquids at STP

. A few elements are gases at STP

. An element's symbol can be one (O), two (Na), or three (Uub) letters. The first letter must always be capitalized. The second (or third) letter must be lowercase.

The following information can be found in the box of each element.

LOOK on the Periodic Table for these two elements: Oxygen and Gold

NOTE all the information you can get from the box of each element.

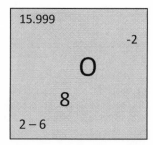

	Atomic Mass	
	Selected oxidation states (charges)	
	Element's symbol	
	Atomic number	
	Electron configuration	

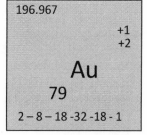

Information listed in the box of each element reveal a lot about atomic structure of the element.

L**OO**KING Ahead ⟹ Topic 3 - The Atomic Structure. You will learn to relate information on the Periodic Table to atomic structures.

Topic 2 - The Periodic Table

2. Groups and Periods

The elements are placed in Groups and Periods. Every element has a Group number and a Period number. For example: Element phosphorus (P) is in Group 15, Period 3.

Groups (families) are the vertical arrangements of the elements.
. Elements in the same group have the same number of valence electrons and similar chemical properties
. There are eighteen (18) groups on the Periodic Table of the Elements

The Group names are listed below.

Group 1 :	Alkali metals
Group 2 :	Alkaline earth metals
Group 3 – 12:	Transition metals
Group 17:	Halogens
Group 18:	Noble gases

Periods (rows) are the horizontal arrangements of the elements.
. Elements in the same Period have the same number of occupied electron shells (energy levels)
. There are seven (7) periods on the Periodic Table of the Elements

The **Periodic Law** states: The properties of the elements are a periodic function of their atomic numbers. In other words, by arranging the elements in the order of increasing atomic numbers, elements with similar properties end up in the same group.

3. Arrangements of the Elements: Practice Problems

Practice 1
Which of the following information cannot be found in the box of an element on the Periodic Table?
1) Oxidation state   3) Atomic number
2) Phase   4) Atomic mass

Practice 2
The Periodic Table of the Elements contains elements that are
1) Solids only   3) Liquids and gases only
2) Solid and liquids only 4) Solid, liquids and gases

Practice 3
The observed regularities in the properties of the elements are periodic functions of their
1) Atomic numbers   3) Atomic mass
2) Oxidation state   4) Reactivity

Practice 4
The similarities in chemical properties of elements within the same group is due to similarity in
1) Number of electron shells   3) Oxidation state
2) Valence electrons   4) Chemical properties

Practice 5
Majority of the elements on the Periodic Table are
1) Metals   3) Metalloids
2) Nonmetals   4) Noble gases

Practice 6
Which of these elements has similar chemical properties as iodine?
1) Xe   2) Te   3) Br   4) Se

Practice 7
Which list contains elements with greatest variation in chemical properties?
1) O, S and Se   3) N, P and As
2) Be, N, O   4) Ba, Sr and Ca

Practice 8
Which two elements have the same number of occupied electron shells?
1) Mg and Be   3) Mg and O
2) Mg and Al   4) Mg and Ca

Practice 9
Element Oxygen and Sulfur can both form a bond with sodium with similar chemical formula. The similarity in their formula is due to
1) Oxygen and Sulfur having the same number of kernel electrons
2) Oxygen and sulfur having the same number of valence electrons
3) Oxygen and sulfur having the same number of protons
4) Oxygen and sulfur having the same molecular structure

Lesson 2 – Types of Elements and their Properties

Introduction

There are three general categories of elements: metal, nonmetals, and metalloids.

Elements in one category have a set of physical and chemical properties that are used to distinguish them from elements in the other categories.

In this lesson, you will learn about the three types of elements, their locations on the Periodic Table, and their properties.

4. Types of Elements

Location of metals, metalloids, and nonmetals

1													13	14	15	16	17	18
H	2	metals			metalloids		nonmetals											He
Li	Be												B	C	N	O	F	Ne
Na	Mg	3	4	5	6	7	8	9	10	11	12		Al	Si	P	S	Cl	Ar
K	Ca	Sc	Ti	V	Cr	Mn	Fe	Co	Ni	Cu	Zn		Ga	Ge	As	Se	Br	Kr
Rb	Sr	Y	Zr	Nb	Mo	Tc	Ru	Rh	Pd	Ag	Cd		In	Sn	Sb	Te	I	Xe
Cs	Ba	La	Hf	Ta	W	Re	Os	Ir	Pt	Au	Hg		Ti	Pb	Bi	Po	At	Rn
Fr	Ra	Ac	Rf	Db	Sg	Bh	Hs	Mt	Ds	Rg	Cn		Uut	Uuq	Uup	Uuh	Uus	Uuo

	La	Ce	Pr	Nd	Pm	Sm	Eu	Gd	Tb	Dy	Ho	Er	Tm	Y b	Lu
	Ac	Th	Pa	U	Np	Pu	Am	Cm	Bk	Cf	Es	Fm	Md	No	Lr

5. Physical Properties of Elements

There are several physical properties that can be used to describe and identify the elements.

The following is a list of these physical properties and their definitions.

Concept Facts: Study and to remember these properties.

Malleable describes a solid that is easily hammered into a thin sheet.

Ductile describes a solid that is easily drawn into thin wire.

Brittle describes a solid that is easily broken or shattered into pieces when struck

Luster describes the shininess of a substance.

Conductivity describes the ability of heat or electricity to flow through a substance.

Electronegativity describes an atom's ability to attract electrons from another atom during bonding.

Ionization energy describes an atom's ability to lose its most loosely bound valence electrons.

Density describes the mass to volume ratio of an element.

Atomic radius describes the size of the atom of an element.

Ionic radius describes the size of the element after it has lost or gained electrons to become an ion

See Table S

Use *Reference Table S* to find and compare electronegativity, ionization energy, atomic radius, and density values of the elements.

6. Metals

Metal elements are located to the left of the Periodic Table.

All elements in Groups 1 – 12 (except hydrogen) are classified as metals.
The rest of the metal elements are located near the top of Groups 13 through 17

The majority (about 75%) of the elements are metals.

Iron (Fe)

Below are some general properties (characteristics) of metals.

Concept Facts: Study to remember these properties.

. Almost all metals are a solid at STP. Exception is mercury (Hg) , which is a liquid metal

. Solid metals are malleable, ductile, and have luster

. Metals tend to have high heat (thermal) and electrical conductivity due to their *mobile valence electrons*

. Metals tend to have low electronegativity values (because they do not attract electrons easily)

. Metals tend to have low ionization energy values (which is why metals lose their electrons easily)

. Metals lose electrons and form positive ions

. Radius (size) of a metal atom decreases as it loses electrons and form a positive ion

. The size of a positive (+) metal ion is always smaller than the size of the neutral metal atom

7. Metalloids

Metalloids (semi-metals) are the seven elements located between the metals and the nonmetals.
Metalloid elements are located on the Periodic Table along the thick zigzag line.

Below are some generally properties (characteristics) of metalloids.

Concept Facts: Study to remember these properties.

. Metalloids tend to have properties of both metals and nonmetals

. Metalloids properties are more like those of metals and less like those of nonmetals

. Metalloids exist only as solids at STP.

Tellurium (Te)

8. Nonmetals

Nonmetal elements are located to the right of the Periodic Table.

All elements in Groups 17 and 18 (except At) are classified as nonmetals. The rest of the nonmetals are located near the bottom of Groups 14, 15, and 16. Hydrogen (in Group 1) is also a nonmetal.

Below are some general properties (characteristics) of nonmetals.

Concept Facts: Study to remember these properties.

. Nonmetals are found in all three phases: solid, liquid, and gas.

. Most nonmetals exist as molecular gases and solids. Bromine is the only liquid nonmetal   **Sulfur (S)**

. Solid nonmetals are generally brittle and dull (lack luster, not shiny)

. Nonmetals have low (poor) electrical and heat conductivity

. Nonmetals tend to have high electronegativity values (because they attract and gain electrons easily)

. Nonmetals tend to have high ionization values (which is why nonmetals don't lose electrons easily)

. Nonmetals gain electrons and form negative ions

. Radius of a nonmetal atom increases as it gains electrons and forms a negative ion

. The size of a negative (-) nonmetal ion is always bigger than its neutral nonmetal atom

9. Types of Elements: Summary of properties of metals, nonmetals, and metalloids

	Phases at STP	Physical properties	Conductivity	Electrone-gativity	Ionization energy	Electrons In bonding	Common ion	Ionic size (radius)
Metals	Solid Liquid	Malleable Luster Ductile	High	Low	Low	Lose electrons	+ (positive)	Smaller than atom
Nonmetals	Solid Liquid Gas	Brittle Dull	Low	High	High	Gain electrons	- (negative)	Bigger than atom
Metalloids	Solid only	Properties of metals and nonmetals	Low	varies	varies	Lose electrons	+ (positive)	Smaller than atom

10. Types of Element: Practice problems

Practice 10
Elements that can be hammered into thin sheets are said to be
1) Ductile   2) Luster   3) Malleable   4) Brittle

Practice 11
The tendency for an atom to give away its electrons during bonding is measured by its
1) Atomic radius value   3) Electronegativity value
2) Density value   4) Ionization energy value

Practice 12
Nonmetal elements on the Periodic Table can be found in which phase or phases at STP?
1) Solid only   3) Solid or liquid only
2) Liquid only   4) Solid, liquid and gas

Practice 13
Which two characteristics are associated with nonmetals?
1) Low first ionization energy and low electronegativity
2) Low first ionization energy and high electronegativity
3) High first ionization energy and low electronegativity
4) High first ionization energy and high electronegativity

Practice 14
Metalloids tend to have properties resembling
1) Nonmetals only
2) Metals only
3) Both metals and nonmetals
4) Neither a metal nor a nonmetal

Practice 15
Which is a property of most metals?
1) They tend to gain electrons easily when bonding.
2) They tend to lose electrons easily when bonding.
3) They are poor conductors of heat.
4) They are poor conductors of electricity.

Practice 16
Which of these elements is a metalloid?
1) Gallium   3) Phosphorus
2) Germanium   4) Tin

Practice 17
Which list consists of a metal, nonmetal, and metalloid respectively?
1) Al, B, Si   3) Ni, Si, P
2) Cr, C, Cl   4) C, Si, Ge

Practice 18
Which element is brittle and a non conducting solid?
1) S   2) Ne   3) Ni   4) Hg

Practice 19
Which of these elements has high thermal and electrical conductivity?
1) Iodine   3) Carbon
2) Phosphorus   4) Iron

Practice 20
Which properties best describes the element mercury?
1) It has luster
2) It is brittle
3) It has a high electronegativity value
4) It a poor electrical conductor

Practice 21
Which is true of element carbon?
1) It is malleable
2) It has Luster
3) It has low electrical conductivity
4) It is a gas at STP

Lesson 3 – Group Properties

Introduction

There are 18 groups (vertical arrangements) on the Periodic Table. Elements within each group share similar chemical characteristics because they have the same number of valence electrons.

In this lesson you will learn more about the groups, and general properties that characterized members of each group.

11. The Periodic Table of the Elements

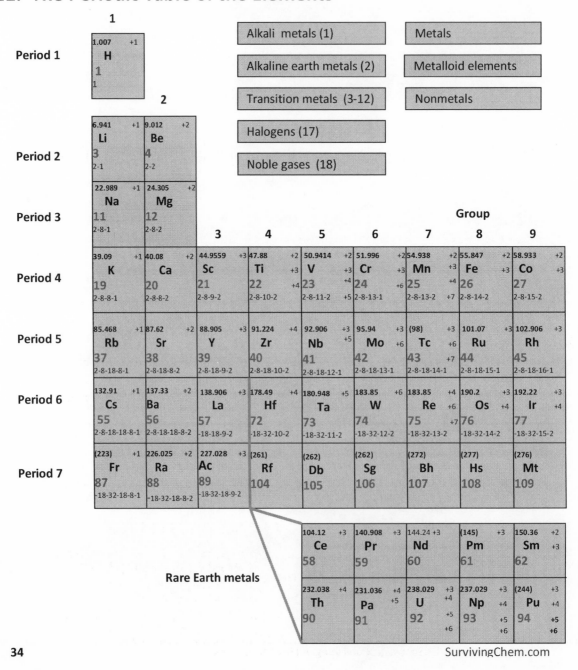

Atomic mass

Element's symbol

Atomic number

Electron configuration

30.973	-3 +3 +5
P	
15	
2 – 8 – 5	

Selected oxidation states

18	Period 1
4.002 0 **He** 2 2	

13	14	15	16	17		
10.81 +3 **B** 5 2-3	12.011 -4 **C** +2 6 +4 2-4	14.006 -3 **N** +2 7 +3 2-5 +4 +5	15.999 -2 **O** 8 2-6	18.998 -1 **F** 9 2-7	20.179 0 **Ne** 10 2-8	Period 2
26.981 +3 **Al** 13 2-8-3	28.085 -4 **Si** +2 14 +4 2-8-4	30.973 -3 **P** +3 15 +5 2-8-5	32.06 -2 **S** +4 16 +6 2-8-6	35.453 -1 **Cl** +1 +3 17 +5 +7 2-8-7	39.948 0 **Ar** 18 2-8-8	Period 3

10	11	12	13	14	15	16	17		
58.69 +2 **Ni** +3 28 2-8-16-2	63.546 +1 **Cu** +2 29 2-8-18-1	65.39 +2 **Zn** 30 2-8-18-2	69.72 +3 **Ga** 31 2-8-18-3	72.59 -4 **Ge** +2 32 +4 2-8-18-4	74.921 -3 **As** +4 33 2-8-18-5	78.96 -2 **Se** +4 34 +6 2-8-18-6	79.904 -1 **Br** +1 35 +5 2-8-18-7	83.80 0 **Kr** +2 36 2-8-18-8	Period 4
106.42 +2 **Pd** +4 46 2-8-18-18	107.868 +1 **Ag** 47 2-8-18-18-1	112.41 +2 **Cd** 48 2-8-18-18-2	114.82 +3 **In** 49 2-8-18-18-3	118.71 +2 **Sn** +4 50 2-8-18-18-4	121.75 -3 **Sb** +3 51 +5 2-8-18-18-5	127.60 -2 **Te** +4 52 +6 2-8-18-18-6	126.905 -1 **I** +1 53 +5 +7 2-8-18-1.	131.29 0 +2 **Xe** +4 +6 54 2-8-18-18-8	Period 5
195.08 +2 **Pt** +4 78 -18-32-17-1	196.967 +1 **Au** +3 79 -18-32-18-1	200.59 +1 **Hg** +2 80 -18-32-18-2	204.383 +3 **Ti** 81 -18-32-18-3	207.2. +2 **Pb** +4 82 -18-32-18-4	208.980 +3 **Bi** +5 83 -18-32-18-5	(209) +2 **Po** +4 84 +5 -18-32-18-6	(210) +2 **At** +4 85 -18-32-18-7	(222) 0 **Rn** 86 -18-32-18-8	Period 6
(281) **Ds** 110	(280) **Rg** 111	(285) **Cn** 112	(284) **Uut** 113	(289) **Uuq** 114	(288) **Uup** 115	(292) **Uuh** 116	(?) **Uus** 117	(294) **Uuo** 118	Period 7

151.96 +2 **Eu** +3 63	157.25 +3 **Gd** 64	158.925 +3 **Tb** 65	162.50 +3 **Dy** 66	164.930 +3 **Ho** 67	167.26 +3 **Er** 68	168.934 +3 **Tm** 69	173.04 +2 **Yb** +3 70	174.967 +3 **Lu** 71	Lanthanoid Series
(243) +3 +4 **Am** +5 +6 95	(247) +3 **Cm** 96	(247) +3 **Bk** 97	(251) +3 **Cf** 98	(252) **Es** 99	(257) **Fm** 100	(258) **Md** 101	(259) **No** 102	(260) **Lr** 103	Actinoid Series

12. Group 1: Alkali Metals

Alkali metals are elements in Group 1 of the Periodic Table.

Members include lithium, sodium, potassium, rubidium, cesium and francium.

Hydrogen is *not* an alkali metal even though it is often placed in Group 1.

H	
1	

Properties (characteristics) of alkali metals are listed below.

Concept Facts: Study to remember these properties.

. One valence (outer shell) electron

. Form positive one (+1) ion from losing one valence electron during bonding

. Very low electronegativity and very low ionization energy values.

. Found in nature as compounds, not as free elements, due to high reactivity

. Are obtained from electrolytic reduction of fused salts (**Na**Cl, **K**Br, etc)

. If **X** represents a **Group 1** atom

    XY is the general formula of a Group 1 atom bonding with a Group 17 halogen (**Y**)

    X₂O is the general formula of a Group 1 atom bonding with **O** (to form an oxide)

. Francium (Fr) is the most reactive metal in Group 1, and of all metals

. Francium is also radioactive.

. All alkali metals exist as solids at STP

Group 1 Alkali	Group 2
Li 3	
Na 11	
K 19	
Rb 37	
Cs 55	
Fr 87	

13. Group 2: Alkaline Earth Metals

Alkaline Earth metals are elements in Group 2 of the Periodic Table.

Members include beryllium, magnesium, calcium, strontium, barium, and radium.

Properties (characteristics) of alkaline earth metals are listed below.

Concept Facts: Study to remember these properties.

. Two valence (outer shell) electrons

. Form positive two (+2) ion from losing all two valence electrons during bonding

. Found in nature as compounds (not as free elements) due to high reactivity

. Are obtained from fused salt compounds ($MgCl_2$, $CaBr_2$, etc)

. If **M** represents a Group 2 atom

    MY₂ is the general formula of a **Group 2** atom bonding with a Group 17 halogen (**Y**)

    MO is the general formula of a **Group 2** atom bonding with **O** (to form an oxide)

. Radium (Ra) is the most reactive metal in this group. Radium is also radioactive.

. All alkaline earth metals exist as solids at STP

Group 1	Group 2 Alkaline Earth
	Be 4
	Mg 12
	Ca 20
	Sr 38
	Ba 56
	Ra 88

14. Groups 3 – 12: Transition Metals

Transition metals are elements in Groups 3 – 12 of the Periodic Table

Properties of these elements vary widely. However, a few unique properties can be observed among them.

Properties (characteristics) of transition metals are listed below.

Concept Facts: Study to remember these properties.

. They tend to form multiple positive oxidation numbers

. They can lose electrons in two or more different sublevels of their atoms

. Their ions usually form colorful compounds

    CuCl$_2$ – is a bluish color compound

    FeCl$_2$ - is an orange color compound

Transition metals

3	4	5	6	7	8	9	10	11	12
Sc	Ti	V	Cr	Mn	**Fe**	Co	Ni	**Cu**	Zn
Y	Zr	Nb	Mo	Tc	Ru	Rh	Pd	Ag	Cd
La	Hf	Ta	W	Re	Os	Ir	Pt	Au	Hg
Ac	Rf	Db	Sg	Bh	Hs	Mt	Uun	Uuu	Uub

15. Group 17: Halogens

Halogens are elements in Group 17 of the Periodic Table.
Members include fluorine, chlorine, bromine, and iodine

Properties (characteristics) of halogens are listed below.

Concept Facts: Study to remember these properties.

. They exist as diatomic (two-atom) elements; (F_2, Cl_2, Br_2)

. Seven (7) valence electrons

. Very high electronegativity and high ionization energy values

. Form negative one (-1) ion from gaining one electron to fill their valence shell

. F and Cl are obtained from their fused salt (Na**F**, Na**Cl**, etc) because of high reactivity

. If **Y** is a Group 17 halogen

    X**Y** is the general formula of a **Group 17** halogen bonding with a Group 1 (**X**) atom

    M**Y**$_2$ is the general formula of a **Group 17** atom bonding with a Group 2 (**M**) atom

. The only group containing elements in all three phases at STP

    Gases (Fluorine and Chlorine)   Liquid (Bromine)   Solid (Iodine)

. Fluorine is the most reactive of the group, and the most reactive nonmetal overall

. Astatine (At) in this group is a metalloid

Group 17 Halogens	Group 18
F 9	
Cl 17	
Br 35	
I 53	
At 85	

16. Group 18 - Noble Gases

Noble gases are elements in **Group 18** of the Periodic Table.

Members include helium, neon, argon, krypton, xenon, and radon

Properties (characteristics) of noble gases are listed below.

Concept Facts: Study to remember these properties.

. They exist as monatomic (one - atom) nonpolar elements (Ne, He, Kr…)

. All are gases are at STP

. They all have full valence shells with eight electrons

   (Exception: Helium is full with only two electrons)

. They neither gain nor lose electrons because their valence shells are full

. They are very stable and non-reactive (do not form too many compounds)

. Argon (Ar) and Xenon (Xe) have been found to produce a few stable compounds with fluorine.

   Example; **Xe**F$_4$ (xenon tetrafluoride)

Group 18
Noble gases

He	2
Ne	10
Ar	18
Kr	36
Xe	54
Rn	86

Group 17

17. Groups and Group Properties: Summary Table

Concept Fasts: Study to learn properties of elements within each Group.

Group number	Group name	Types of elements in the group	Phases (at STP)	Valence electrons (during bonding)	Common oxidation number (charge)	Chemical bonding (general formula)
1	Alkali metals	Metal	Solid (all)	1 (lose)	+1	**XY** with halogens (17) **X$_2$O** with oxygen (16)
2	Alkaline earth	Metal	Solid (all)	2 (lose)	+2	**MY$_2$** with halogens (17) **MO** with oxygen (16))
3-12	Transition metals	Metal	Liquid (Hg) Solid (the rest)	(lose)	Multiple + charges	varies (form colorful compounds)
13	-	Metalloid Metal	Solid (all	3 (lose)	+3	**LY$_3$** with halogens (17) **L$_2$O$_3$** with oxygen (16)
14	-	Nonmetal Metalloid Metal	Solid (all)	4 (some share) (some lose)	vary	varies
15	-	Nonmetal Metalloid Metal	Gas (N) Solid (the rest)	5 (gain or share)	-3	varies
16	Oxygen group	Nonmetal Metalloid	Gas (O) Solid (the rest)	6 (gain or share)	-2	**X$_2$O** with alkali metals (1) **MO** with alkaline earth (2)
17	Halogens (Diatomic)	Nonmetal	Gas (F and Cl) Liquid (Br) Solid (I)	7 (gain or share)	-1	**XY** with alkali metals (1) **MY** with alkaline earths (2)
18	Noble gases (Monatomic)	Nonmetal	Gas (all)	8 (neither gain nor share)	0	Forms very few compounds. **XeF$_4$** is the most common.

18. Groups and Group Properties: Practice problems

Concept Task: Be able to identify an element based on group name	**Concept Task:** Be able to identify and classify an element based on group properties.

Practice 22

Which element is a noble gas?
1) Neon
2) Oxygen
3) Fluorine
4) Nitrogen

Practice 23

Which of these element is an alkaline earth element?
1) Na
2) H
3) K
4) Ra

Practice 24

Iron is best classified as
1) A transition nonmetal
2) A transition metal
3) An alkali metal
4) An alkaline earth metal

Practice 25

The element in Group 17 Period 4 is
1) A transition metal
2) A halogen
3) An alkali metal
4) A noble gas

Practice 26

Which set contains elements that are never found in nature in their atomic state?
1) K and Na
2) K and S
3) Na and Ne
4) Na and C

Practice 27

Element X is a solid that is brittle, lack luster, and has six valence electrons. In which group on the Periodic Table would element X be found?
1) 1
2) 2
3) 15
4) 16

Practice 28

Element Z is in Period 3 of the Periodic Table. Which element is Z if it forms an oxide with a formula of Z_2O_3?
1) Na
2) Al
3) Mg
4) Cl

Practice 29

Which of these oxides will likely form a colored solution when dissolved in water?
1) Na_2O
2) SO_2
3) CaO
4) FeO

Lesson 3. Periodic Trends

Introduction

Periodic trends refer to patterns of properties that exist in a group or period as elements are considered from one end of the table to the other.

Trend in atomic number is a good example (and the most obvious) of a periodic trend found on the Periodic Table.

As the elements are considered one after the other from:

Left to **Right** across a Period: *Atomic number of successive element increases*

Bottom to **Top** up a Group: *Atomic number of successive element decreases*

Many other trends exist on the periodic table even though they are not so obvious.

In this lesson, you will learn of the following trends.

Trends in atomic radius (size).
Trends in metallic and nonmetallic properties.
Trends in electronegativity and ionization energy.

19. Trends in Atomic Size (Atomic Radius)

Atomic radius is defined as half the distance between two nuclei of the same atom when they are joined together. Atomic radius value gives a good approximation of the size of an atom.
The atomic radii of the elements can be found on **Reference Table S.**

General trends in atomic radius found on the Periodic Table are as follow:

Concept Facts: Study to remember the following trends.

Top to **Bottom** down a **Group**: *Atomic radius (size) increases due to an increase in the number of electron shells.*

Left to **Right** across a **Period**: *Atomic radius decreases due to an increase in nuclear charges.*

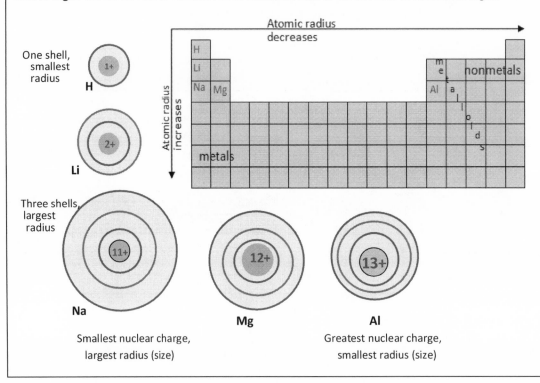

Smallest nuclear charge,
largest radius (size)

Greatest nuclear charge,
smallest radius (size)

20. Trends in Atomic Size: Practice problems

Concept Task: Be able to determine element with the largest or smallest radius (size).   **Use Table S**

Practice 30

Which of the following elements has the largest atomic radius?

1) K   2) Ca   3) Al   4) Na

Practice 31

Which list of elements is arranged in order of increasing atomic radii?
1) Li, Be, B, C   3) Sc, Ti, V, Cr
2) Sr, Ca, Mg, Be   4) F, Cl, Br, I

Practice 32

The atom of which element is bigger than the atom of the element calcium?
1) Sr   2) Sc   3) Mg   4) Be

Practice 33

Which atom has a bigger atomic radius than the atom of Sulfur?
1) Oxygen, because it has more electron shells
2) Oxygen, because it has a smaller nuclear charge
3) Phosphorus, because it more electron shells
4) Phosphorus, because it has a smaller nuclear charge

21. Trends in Metallic and Nonmetallic Properties

Trends in properties and reactivity vary between metals and nonmetals. The bottom left corner contains the most reactive metals. *Francium* is the most reactive of all metals. The top right corner contains the most reactive nonmetals. *Fluorine* is the most reactive of all nonmetals.

Trends in metallic and nonmetallic properties and reactivity are summarized below.

Concept Facts: Study to remember the following trends.

Top to **Bottom** down a **Group**: Metallic properties and reactivity increase.
Nonmetallic properties and reactivity decrease

Left to **Right** across a **Period**: Metallic properties and reactivity decrease.
Nonmetallic properties and reactivity increase

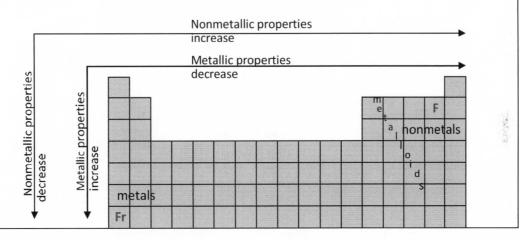

22. Trends in Metallic and Nonmetallic Properties: Practice problems

Concept Task: Be able to determine which element has the most (or least) metallic or nonmetallic properties
Element farthest Left and Lowest down: Strongest metallic / Least nonmetallic

Element farthest right and Highest up: Least metallic / Strongest nonmetallic

Practice 34

Which of the following element has the most pronounced metallic characteristics?

1) C   2) Co   3) Al   4) Rb

Practice 35

Which of these elements has greatest nonmetallic properties?

1) Se   2) Te   3) Br   4) I

Practice 36

Which of these halogens is the least reactive on the Period Table?

1) I   2) Br   3) Cl   4) F

Practice 37

Which of these elements has stronger metallic characteristics than aluminum?

1) He   2) Mg   3) Ga   4) Si

Practice 38

Which of these element has stronger nonmetallic properties than chlorine?

1) Sulfur   3) Fluorine
2) Argon   4) Oxygen

Practice 39

Which part of the Periodic Table contains elements with the strongest nonmetallic properties?

1) Upper right   3) Upper left
2) Lower right   4) Lower left

23. Trends in Electronegativity and Ionization Energy

Electronegativity defines an atom's ability to attract (or gain) electrons from another atom during chemical bonding. The electronegativity value assigned to each element is relative to one another. The higher the electronegativity value, the more likely it is for the atom to attract (or gain) electrons and form a negative ion during bonding.

Fluorine (F) is assigned the highest electronegativity value of 4.0

Francium (Fr) is assigned the lowest electronegativity value of 0.7 .

This means that of all the elements, fluorine has the greatest tendency to attract (or gain) electrons. Francium has the least ability or tendency to attract electrons during bonding.

Ionization energy refers to the amount of energy needed to remove an electron from an atom. The ***first ionization energy*** is the energy to remove the most loosely bound electron from an atom. Ionization energy measures the tendency of (how likely) an atom to lose electrons and form a positive ion. The lower the first ionization energy of an atom, the easier (the more likely) it is for that atom to lose its most loosely bound valence electron and form a positive ion.

Metals lose electrons because of their low ionization energies. The *alkali metals* in Group 1 generally have the lowest ionization energy, which allows them to lose their one valence electron most readily.

Nonmetals have a low tendency to lose electrons because of their high ionization energies. The *noble gases* in group 18 tend to have the highest ionization energy values. Since these elements already have a full valence shell of electrons, a high amount of energy is required to remove any electron from their atoms

Concept Facts: Study to remember the following trends.

Top to **Bottom** down a **Group**:   Electronegativity (tendency to gain or attract electrons) decreases.

Ionization energy (tendency to lose electrons) decreases

Left to **Right** across a **Period**:   Electronegativity increases

Ionization energy increases

NOTE: Electronegativity and ionization energy values for the elements are found on the Reference Table

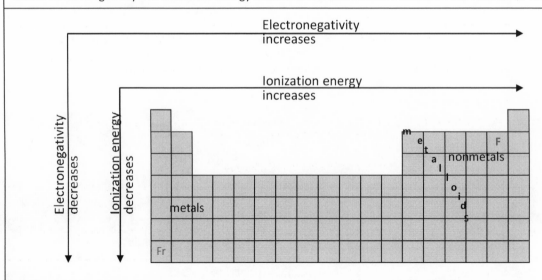

24. Trends in Electronegativity and Ionization Energy: Practice problems

Concept Task: Be able to determine an element that has the greatest or least tendency to attract electrons.

Greatest attraction for electrons (most likely to gain):
   Element with the HIGHEST electronegativity value

Least attraction for electrons (least likely to gain)
   Element with the LOWEST electronegativity value

Concept Task: Be able to determine which element has the greatest or the least tendency to lose electrons.

Greatest tendency to lose electrons
   Element with the LOWEST ionization energy value

Least tendency to lose electrons
   Element with the HIGHEST ionization energy value

Use **Reference Table S** to locate ionization energy values

Practice 40

As the elements of Group 1 on the Periodic Table are considered in order of increasing atomic radius, the ionization energy of each successive element generally

1) decreases
2) increases
3) remains the same

Practice 41

Which of these elements is most likely to attract electrons from another atom during chemical bonding?

1) Fe   2) C   3) Al   4) Fr

Practice 42

Which elements has a greater tendency to attract electron than phosphorus?

1) Silicon   3) Boron
2) Arsenic   4) Sulfur

Practice 43

Which of the following elements has the greatest tendency to lose its valence electrons?

1) Be   2) S   3) Ne   4) Ca

Practice 44

Aluminum will lose its most loosely bound electron less readily than

1) Calcium   3) Indium
2) Nitrogen   4) Scandium

Practice 45

Which sequence of elements is arranged in order of decrease tendency to attract electrons during chemical bonding?

1) Al, Si, P   3) Cs, Na, Li
2) I, Br, Cl   4) C, B, Be

25. Allotropes

Allotropes refer to two or more different molecular forms of the same element in the same state.

Differences in molecular structures give allotropes of the same element different physical properties (color, shape, density, melting point, etc) and different chemical properties (reactivity)

Examples of some common allotropes:

Oxygen allotropes: Oxygen gas (O_2) and Ozone (O_3), both considered oxygen, have different molecular structures and different chemical and physical properties.

Carbon allotropes: Diamond , graphite, and buckminsterfullerene
are different molecular forms of carbon. Each form has different chemical and different physical characteristics.

Phosphorus allotropes: White , Red, and Black are all different forms of element phosphorus.

Topic 2 – The Periodic Table of Elements

Concept Terms

Key vocabulary terms and concepts from Topic 2 are listed below. You should know definition and facts related to each term and concept.

1. Periodic Law
2. Group
3. Period
4. Metal
5. Nonmetal
6. Metalloid
7. Alkali metal
8. Alkaline Earth metal
9. Transition element
10. Halogen
11. Noble gas

12. Malleable
13. Luster
14. Ductile
15. Brittle
16. Density
17. Ionization energy
18. Electronegativity
19. Atomic radius
20. Conductivity
21. Properties of metals
22. Properties of nonmetals
23. Properties of metalloids

24. Properties of Group 1 alkali metals
25. Properties of Group 2 alkaline earth metals
26. Properties of Groups 3 – 12 transition metals
27. Properties of Group 17 halogens
28. Properties of Group 18 noble gases
29. Trends in metallic and nonmetallic properties
30. Trends in atomic size or radius
31. Trends in ionization energy
32. Trends in electronegativity

Concept Task:

Concept tasks from Topic 2 are listed below. You should know how to solve problems and answer questions related to each concept task.

1. Determining elements with the same characteristics

2. Identifying an element as a metal, metalloid, or nonmetal

3. Determining element's name or symbol based on given properties

4. Determining property or properties of a given elements name or symbol

5. Identifying an element based on a given group name

6. Relating elements name or symbol to group properties

7. Determining element with the largest or smallest atomic radius

8. Determining element that has the most or least metallic properties

9. Determining element that has the most or least nonmetallic properties

10. Determining element with greatest or least tendency to attract electrons

11. Determining element with greatest or least tendency to lose electrons

Topic 3 – The Atomic Structure

Topic outline

In this topic, you will learn the following concepts:

- The historical development of the modern atom
- The subatomic particles; protons, electrons, neutrons
- Atomic number, mass number and atomic mass
- Isotopes

- Electron shells and electron configurations
- Ground and excited state of atoms
- Bright-line spectra
- Valence electrons, neutral atoms and ions

Lesson 1 - Historical Development of the Modern Atomic Model

Introduction:

The **atom** is the most basic unit of matter. Since atoms are very small and cannot be seen with the most sophisticated equipment, several scientists for thousands of years have proposed many different models of atoms to help explain the nature and behavior of matter.

In this lesson, you will learn about these historical scientists, their experiments and proposed models of the atom.

1. Historical Scientists

Many scientists over many years have contributed to the development of the modern atomic model.

*The **wave mechanical-model** is the current and most widely accepted model of the atom. According to the wave-mechanical model:

- Each atom has small dense positive nucleus
- Electrons are found outside the nucleus in regions called orbitals

An **Orbital** is the most probable location of finding an electron with certain energy in an atom.

Below is a list of some historical scientists and their proposed models of atom in order from the earliest model to the current model. Descriptions and key features of each model are also given.

Concept Facts: Study to remember order of proposed atomic models.

John Dalton	J.J. Thomson	Ernest Rutherford	Niels Bohr	Many scientists
Hard sphere model (Cannonball model)	**Plum pudding model**	**Empty space model** (Nuclear model)	**Bohr's model** (Planetary model)	**Wave mechanical** (electron cloud)
. No internal structure	. Electrons and positive charges disperse throughout the atom.	. Small dense positive nucleus . Electrons revolve around the nucleus	. Electrons in specific orbits . Orbits have fixed energy . Orbits create electron shells	. Electrons in orbitals **. Orbital** is the area an electron is likely to be found

2. The Cathode Ray Experiment

J.J. Thomson conducted the cathode ray experiment that further supports the existence of negative charge particles in atoms.

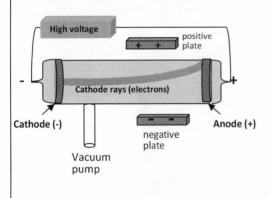

The setup

A tube with a metal disk at each end was set up to trace a beam from an electrical source. The metals were connected to an electrical source.

Anode: The metal disk that is +

Cathode: The metal disk that is –

Results

A beam of light (ray) travels from the cathode end to the anode end of the tube. When electrically charged + and - plates were brought near the tube, the beam (ray) was deflected toward and attracted the positive plate. The beam was repelled by the negative plate.

Conclusions

The beam is composed of negatively charged particles.

The term "electron" was later used to describe the negatively charged particles of an atom.

3. The Gold-Foil Experiment

Ernest Rutherford conducted the gold-foil experiment that led to the proposed empty-space theory of atom.

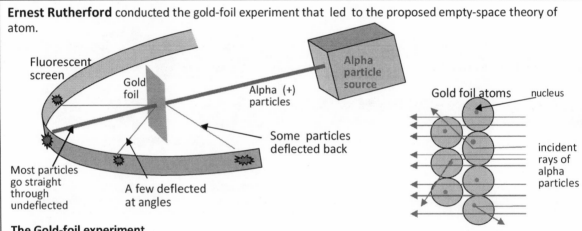

The Gold-foil experiment

The setup

Equipment was set up to fire alpha particles at gold foil.

. Alpha particle area positively charged helium nuclei

A fluorescent screen was set around the foil

. The screen will detect paths of the particles once they had hit the gold foil

Result 1
Most of the alpha particles went straight through the gold foil undeflected.

Conclusions 1
An atom is mostly empty space (Empty Space Theory)

Result 2
A few of the particles were deflected back or hit the screen at angles.

Conclusion 2
The center of the atom is dense , positive, and very small.

Rutherford's atom

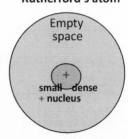

Topic 3 - The Atomic Structure

4. Historical Development of the Modern Atomic Model: Practice problems

Practice 1
The modern model of an atom shows that electrons are
1) Orbiting the nucleus in fixed path
2) Found in regions called orbital
3) Combined with neutrons in the nucleus
4) Located in a solid sphere covering the nucleus

Practice 2
In the wave-mechanical model, the orbital is a region in space of an atom where there is
1) High probability of finding an electron
2) High probability of finding a neutron
3) Circular path in which electrons are found
4) Circular path in which neutrons are found

Practice 3
The modern model of the atom is based on the work of
1) One Scientist over a short period of time
2) One scientist over a long period of time
3) Many Scientists over a short period of time
4) Many scientists over a long period of time

Practice 4
Which conclusion is based on the "gold foil experiment" and the resulting model of the atom?
1) An atom has hardly any empty space, and the nucleus is positive charge
2) An atom has hardly any empty space, and the nucleus is negative charge
3) An atom is mainly empty space, and the nucleus has a positive charge
4) An atom is mainly empty space, and the nucleus has a negative charge

Practice 5
Which group of atomic models is listed in order from the earliest to the most recent?
1) Hard-sphere model, wave-mechanical model, electron-shell model
2) Hard-sphere model, electron-shell model, wave mechanical model
3) Electron-shell model, wave-mechanical model, hard-sphere model
4) Electron-shell model, hard-sphere model, wave-mechanical model

Practice 6
Subatomic particles can usually pass undeflected through an atom because the volume of an atom is composed mainly by
1) Uncharged nucleus
2) Unoccupied space
3) Neutrons only
4) Protons only

Practice 7
Experiment evidence indicates that atoms
1) Have uniform distribution of positive charges
2) Have uniform distribution of negative charges
3) Contains a positively charged , dense center
4) Contains a negatively charged, dense center

Practice 8
Compare to the entire atom, the nucleus of an atom is
1) Smaller and contains most of atom's mass
2) Smaller and contains little of atom's mass
3) Larger and contains most of atom's mass
4) Larger and contains little of atom's mass

Practice 9
Which order of diagrams correctly shows the historical models of the atom from the earliest to the most modern?

1)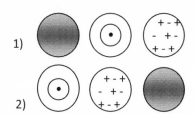

3)

2)

4)

Lesson 2 – Structure of an atom

Introduction

Although the atom is described as the smallest unit of matter, it is also composed of much smaller particles called **subatomic particles**.

The three subatomic particles are: protons, electrons, and neutrons.

In this lesson, you will learn more about the modern atom and the subatomic particles. You will also learn the relationships between the subatomic particles, atomic number, and mass number of an atom.

5. Atom

The **atom** is the basic unit of matter. It is composed of three subatomic particles: Protons, electrons and neutrons. The only atom with no neutron is a hydrogen atom with a mass of 1. (^{1}H)

Concept Facts: Study to remember the followings about the atom.

. An atom is mostly empty space

. An atoms has small dense positive core (nucleus), and negative electron cloud surrounding the nucleus

. Elements are composed of atoms with the same atomic number

. Atoms of the same element are similar

. Atoms of different elements are different

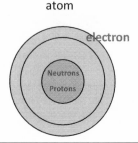

6. Nucleus

The **nucleus** is the center (core) of an atom.

Concept Facts: Study to remember the followings about the nucleus

. The nucleus contains protons (+) and neutrons (no charge)

. Overall charge of the nucleus is positive (+) due to the protons

. The nucleus is very small and very dense relative to the entire atom

. Most of an atom's mass is due to the mass of the nucleus

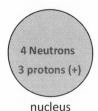

7. Protons

Protons are positively charged subatomic particles that are found in the nucleus of atoms.

Concept Facts: Study to remember the followings about protons

. A proton has a mass of one atomic mass unit (1 amu) and a +1 charge

. A proton is about 1836 times more massive (heavier) than an electron

. Protons are located inside the nucleus

. The number of protons is the same as the atomic number of the element

. All atoms of the same element must have the same number of protons

. The number of protons in the nucleus is also the nuclear charge of the element

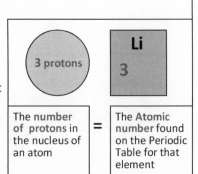

Topic 3 – The Atomic structure

8. Electrons

Electrons are negatively charged subatomic particles that are found in orbitals outside the nucleus of atoms.

Concept Facts: Study to remember the followings about electrons

. An electron has insignificant mass (zero) and a -1 charge.

. An electron has a mass that is $^1/_{1836}{}^{th}$ that of a proton (or neutron)

. Electrons are found in **orbitals** outside the nucleus

. Electron arrangements in an atom determine the chemical properties of the element

. Number of electrons is always equal to the number of protons in a a neutral atom

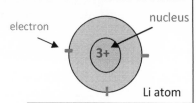

Li atom

In a Li atom, the number of electrons (3 e-) is equal to the number of protons (3+).

In all neutral atoms, there are equal numbers of electrons to protons.

9. Neutrons

Neutrons are neutral (no charge) subatomic particles that are located inside the nucleus of atoms.

Concept Facts: Study to remember the followings about neutrons

. A neutron has a mass of 1 amu and zero charge

. A neutron has the same mass (1 amu) as a proton

. Neutrons are located in the nucleus along with protons

. Atoms of the same element differ in their numbers of neutrons

A Lithium nucleus

A different Lithium nucleus

Nuclei from two different atoms of Lithium have the same number of protons but different numbers of neutrons.

10. The Subatomic Particles: Summary Table

Protons, electrons and neutrons are different in mass, charge, and location in an atom.

The table below summarizes information about all three particles.

NOTE: Some information on this Table can be found on **Reference Table O.**

Subatomic particle	Symbol	Mass	Charge	Location
Proton	$^1_{+1}p$	1 amu	+1	Nucleus
Neutron	^1_0n	1 amu	0	Nucleus
Electron	$^0_{-1}e$	0 amu	-1	Orbital (outside the nucleus)

11. Atomic Number

Atomic number identifies each element.

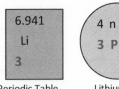

Concept Facts: Study to remember the followings about atomic number

. Atomic number of an element is *equal* to the number of protons

. All atoms of the same element have the same atomic number because they have the same number of protons.

. Atomic number can be found on the Periodic Table

. Elements on the Periodic Table are arranged in order of increasing atomic number

Periodic Table   Lithium Nucleus

Lithium (Li) has *atomic number of 3.*
Nucleus of all Li atoms contains *3 protons.*
No other atoms can have 3 protons.

12. Nucleons

Nucleons are particles (protons and neutrons) in the nucleus of an atom

Concept Facts: Study to remember the followings about nucleons

. Nucleons account for the total mass of an atom

. The total number of nucleons in an atom is equal to the sum of protons *plus* neutrons

| The Total number of nucleons for this Li atom is **7** (3 p + 4 n = 7) | The total number of nucleons of this Li atom is **8** (3 p + 5 n = 8) |

13. Mass Number

Mass number identifies different isotopes of the same element.

Concept Facts: Study to remember the followings about mass number

. Atoms of the same element differ by their mass numbers

. Mass number is equal to the number of protons **plus** neutrons

. The mass number shows the total number of nucleons

Two different nuclei of Li atoms

| The mass number of this Li atom is **7** (3 + 4 = 7 amu) | The mass number of this Li atom is **8** (3 + 5 = 8 amu) |

14. Relating one Particle to another in Neutral Atoms. Practice problems

Concept Task: Be able to determine and compare number of subatomic particles.

Summary of relationships between the atomic particles in neutral atoms

protons = atomic # = nuclear charge = electrons = mass # - neutrons = nucleons - neutrons

electrons = atomic # = nuclear charge = protons = mass # - neutrons = nucleons - neutrons

neutrons = mass # - protons = mass# – atomic number = Mass # - electrons = nucleons – protons

mass # = nucleons = protons + neutrons = nuclear charge + neutrons = atomic # + neutrons

Practice 10
Which particles are found in the nucleus of an atom?
1) Electron, only
2) Neutrons, only
3) Protons and electrons
4) Protons and neutrons

Practice 11
Compare to the entire atom, the nucleus of an atom is
1) Smaller and contains most of atom's mass
2) Larger and contains most of atom's mass
3) Smaller and contains little of atom's mass
4) Larger and contains little of atom's mass

Practice 12
Which is true of protons and neutrons?
1) They have approximately the same mass and the same charge
2) They have approximately the same mass but different charge
3) The have different mass and different charge
4) They have different mass but the same charge

Practice 13
An electron has a charge of
1) -1 and the same mass as a proton
2) -1 and a smaller mass than a proton
3) +1 and the same mass a proton
4) +1 and a smaller mass than a proton

Practice 14
The mass of a proton is approximately
1) 1/2000 times the mass of a neutron and a unit positive charge
2) 1/2000 times the mass of a neutron and a unit negative charge
3) 2000 times the mass of an electron and a unit positive charge
4) 2000 times the mass of an electron and a unit negative charge

Practice 15
The mass number of an element is always equal to the number of
1) Protons plus electron
2) Protons plus positrons
3) Neutrons plus protons
4) Neutrons plus positrons

Practice 16
The number of neutrons in the nucleus of an atom can be determined by
1) Adding the mass number to the atomic number of the atom
2) Adding the mass number to the number of electrons of the atom
3) Subtracting the atomic number from the mass number of the atom
4) Subtracting the mass number from the atomic number of the atom

Practice 17
A neutral atom contains 12 neutrons and 11 electrons. The number of protons in this atom is
1) 1   2) 11   3) 12   4) 23

Practice 18
What is the number of electrons in a neutral atom of Fluorine?
1) 9   2) 19   3) 10   4) 28

Practice 19
The number of neutrons in a neutral atom with a mass number of 86 and 37 electrons is
1) 86   2) 37   3) 123   4) 49

Practice 20
What is the atomic number of a neutral element whose atoms contain 60 neutrons and 47 electrons?
1) 13   2) 47   3) 60   4) 107

Practice 21
What is the mass number of an atom that contains 19 protons, 18 electrons, and 20 neutrons?
1) 19   2) 38   3) 39   4) 58

Practice 22
How many nucleons are there in an atom with a nuclear charge of +20 and 23 neutrons?
1) 58   2) 20   3) 3   4) 43

Practice 23
What is the nuclear charge of an atom with 16 protons, 18 electrons, and 17 neutrons?
1) +16   2) +17   3) +18   4) +33

15. Isotopes

Isotopes are atoms of the same element with the same number of protons but different numbers of neutrons.

*For example, t*here are a few different atoms of the element Lithium. All atoms of lithium contain the same number of protons in their nucleus. The difference between these atoms is the number of neutrons.

Since all Lithium atoms have the same number of protons (3), they all have the same atomic number, 3. Since they have different number of neutrons, they each have a different mass number. These different atoms of lithium are *isotopes* of lithium.

Isotopes of the same element must have:

. *Different* mass numbers (nucleons)

. *Different* number of neutrons

. *Same* atomic number

. *Same* number of protons (nuclear charge)

. *Same* number of electrons

. *Same* chemical reactivity

Symbols showing two isotopes of Lithium

7	mass number	**8**
Li		Li
3	atomic number	**3**

16. Isotope Symbols

Different isotopes of an element have different mass numbers. Therefore, the mass number of an isotope is written next to the element's name (or symbol) to distinguish it from the other isotopes.

Lithium – 7 and Lithium – 8 are names to two of lithium isotopes. The 7 and the 8 are the mass numbers of these two lithium isotopes.

There are other notations that are used to represent isotopes of elements.

When studying the notations below:

. *Pay attention* to how Lithium-**7** and Lithium-**8** are similar, and also how they are different in each notation

. Also pay attention to how each notation of the same isotope is related to the other notations

Element – **mass number** (isotope's name)	*Lithium –* **7**	*Lithium –* **8**
Symbol – **mass number** notation	*Li – 7*	*Li – 8*
Common isotope notation	$^{7}_{3}Li$	$^{8}_{3}Li$
Nuclear diagram notation	4 n 3 p	5 n 3 p

17. Isotope Symbols: Practice problems

Concept Task: Be able recognize symbols that are isotopes of the same element.

Practice 24

Which two notations represent isotopes of the same element?

1) $^{40}_{19}K$ and $^{40}_{20}Ca$

2) $^{20}_{10}Ne$ and $^{22}_{10}Ne$

3) $^{23}_{11}Na$ and $^{24}_{12}Na$

4) $^{16}_{8}O$ and $^{17}_{8}N$

Practice 25

Which pair are isotopes of the same element?

1) $^{226}_{91}X$ and $^{226}_{91}X$

2) $^{227}_{91}X$ and $^{227}_{90}X$

3) $^{226}_{91}X$ and $^{227}_{91}X$

4) $^{226}_{90}X$ and $^{227}_{91}X$

Practice 26

Which symbol could represent an isotope of element iron ?

1) $^{55}_{55}Fe$

2) $^{55}_{26}Fe$

3) $^{26}_{55}Fe$

4) $^{26}_{8}Fe$

Practice 27

Which symbol could be an isotope of calcium ?

1) $^{20}_{20}X$

2) $^{40}_{20}X$

3) $^{20}_{40}X$

4) $^{40}_{40}X$

Practice 28

Which two nucleus diagrams are from atoms of the same element?

1) (10 p, 10 n) (11 p, 11 n)

2) (10 p, 11 n) (10 p, 11 n)

3) (18 p, 20 n) (18 p, 22 n)

4) (18 p, 20 n) (20 p, 10 n)

Practice 29

Which two nuclei are isotopes of phosphorus?

1) (15 P, 16 n) (16 p, 15 n)

2) (15 p, 15 n) (15 p, 16 n)

3) (15 p, 15 n) (16 p, 16n)

4) (31 p, 15 n) (15 p, 31 n)

Concept Task: Be able to interpret isotope symbols

Practice 30

The isotope symbol $^{27}_{13}Al$ can also be represented as

1) Aluminum–13

2) Aluminum–14

3) Aluminum–27

4) Aluminum-40

Practice 31

Which nuclide name is correct for the symbol $^{223}_{85}X$

1) Fr – 85

2) Fr – 138

3) Fr – 223

4) Fr – 308

Practice 32

Chlorine – 37 can also be represented as

1) $^{35}_{17}Cl$

2) $^{17}_{35}Cl$

3) $^{37}_{17}Cl$

4) $^{17}_{37}Cl$

Practice 33

Which isotope notation is correct for magnesium -26 ?

1) $^{26}_{26}Mg$

2) $^{12}_{26}Mg$

3) $^{26}_{12}Mg$

4) $^{12}_{12}Mg$

Practice 34

Which diagram correctly represents the nucleus for the isotope symbol $^{59}_{28}X$?

1) (59 p, 28 n)

2) (31 p, 28 n)

3) (28 p, 59 n)

4) (28 p, 31 n)

Practice 35

The nucleus of an atom is shown below:

(45 n, 35 p)

Which isotope symbol correctly represents this atom?

1) $^{35}_{45}Rh$

2) $^{80}_{45}Rh$

3) $^{80}_{35}Br$

4) $^{45}_{35}Br$

18. Determining and Comparing Particles in Isotope Symbols

In any given isotope notations, you should be able to determine and compare the following information.
. Mass number, number of nucleons, and the sum of protons and neutrons
. Atomic number, number of protons, nuclear charge, and number of electrons
. Number of neutrons

Two isotope symbols are given below. Note the differences and similarities in the number of particles between them.

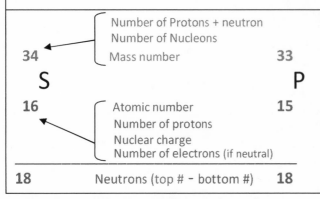

Number of Protons + neutron	
Number of Nucleons	
34 ← Mass number	**33**
S	**P**
16 Atomic number	**15**
Number of protons	
Nuclear charge	
Number of electrons (if neutral)	
18 Neutrons (top # – bottom #)	**18**

The following comparisons can be made of the two isotope symbols to the left:

^{34}S has **more nucleons** than ^{33}P

$^{33}_{15}$P has one **fewer proton** than $^{34}_{16}$S

$^{34}_{16}$S has a **greater nuclear charge** than $^{33}_{15}$P

P-**33** has the **same** number of **neutrons** as S-**34**

19. Determining and Comparing Particles in Isotope Symbols: Practice problems

Concept Tasks: Be able to determine and compare the number of subatomic particles from given isotope notations. *Be sure to utilize the Periodic Table.*

Practice 36
What is the total number of protons and neutrons in the nuclide $^{127}_{53}$I

1) 53   2) 127   3) 74   4) 180

Practice 37
The nucleus of the atom $^{107}_{47}$Ag contains

1) 60 neutrons, and has a nuclear charge of +47
2) 60 electrons, and has a nuclear charge of +47
3) 47 neutrons, and has a nuclear charge of +107
4) 47 electrons, and has a nuclear charge of +107

Practice 38
What is the structure of of krypton - 85?

1) 49 electrons, 49 protons, and 85 neutrons
2) 49 electrons, 49 protons, and 49 neutrons
3) 36 electrons, 36 protons, and 85 neutrons
4) 36 electrons, 36 protons, and 49 neutrons

Practice 39
The nucleus of chlorine – 35 has
1) 17 protons, and the atom has a mass number of 35
2) 17 electrons, and the atom has a mass number of 35
3) 35 protons, and the atom has a mass number of 17
4) 35 electrons, and the atom has a mass number of 17

Practice 40
An atom of K- 37 and an atom of K – 42 differ in their total number of
1) Electrons   3) Neutrons
2) Protons   4) Positron

Practice 41
Compare to the atom of $^{40}_{20}$Ca, the atom of $^{38}_{18}$Ar has

1) a greater nuclear charge
2) the same number of nuclear charge
3) greater number of neutrons
4) the same number of neutrons

Practice 42
Which nuclide contains the greatest number of neutrons?
1) ^{207}Pb   2) ^{203}Hg   3) ^{207}Ti   4) ^{208}Bi

Practice 43
Which symbol has the smallest nuclear charge?
1) Cu – 65   3) Zn – 64
2) Ga – 69   4) Ge - 72

Practice 44
In which nucleus is the ratio of protons to neutrons 1 : 1?
1) B – 12   3) C – 13
2) N – 14   4) O – 15

20. Atomic Mass Unit

Atomic mass unit (amu): unit for measuring mass of atoms relative to the mass of carbon – 12.

$$1 \text{ amu} = \frac{1}{12}^{th} \text{ the mass of } {}^{12}C$$

Interpretations:

Hydrogen – **1** (${}^{1}H$) has a mass that is $1/12^{th}$ the mass of ${}^{12}C$

Lithium – **6** (${}^{6}Li$) has a mass that is $6/12^{th}$ or half the mass of ${}^{12}C$

Magnesium – **24** (${}^{24}Mg$) has a mass that is $24/12^{th}$ or 2 times the mass of ${}^{12}C$

Practice 45

Which could have an atom with a mass that is approximately three times that is of C-12 ?

1) O   3) Li

2) Cl   4) Kr

21. Atomic Mass

Atomic mass of an element is the average mass of all its naturally occurring stable isotopes.

Atomic mass is based on the masses of the stable isotopes and their percent abundance in a sample.

To get a better understanding of what this means, read the explanation below.

A natural sample of an element consists of a mix of two or more isotopes (different atoms). Usually there is a lot of one isotope and very little of the others.

For an example: A natural sample of chlorine consists mainly of two chlorine isotopes: Chlorine atoms with a mass of 35 **(Cl-35)** and chlorine atoms with a mass of 37 **(Cl-37)**. The relative percentages (abundances) of these isotopes are approximately 75% of Cl-35 and 25% of Cl-37. That means three of every four chlorine atoms in a natural sample of chlorine will have a mass of 35 amu.

The atomic mass of chlorine given on the Periodic Table is the average mass of these two isotopes.

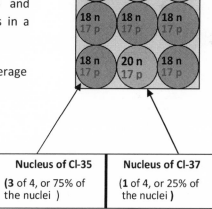

Atomic mass $\longrightarrow$

35.453

Cl

17

Nucleus of Cl-35	Nucleus of Cl-37
(**3** of 4, or 75% of the nuclei)	(**1** of 4, or 25% of the nuclei)

Although atomic mass of the elements can be found on the Periodic Table you may be asked to calculate the atomic mass of an element given percentages and mass numbers of its isotopes.

On the next page you will see an example of how to calculate the average atomic mass of an element.

22. Average Atomic Mass Calculations: Example and practice problems

Concept Task: Be able to calculate the average atomic mass of an element given the mass numbers and percent abundances of its isotopes .

Study the steps below.

Example

A natural sample of chlorine contains 75% of ^{35}Cl and 25% of ^{37}Cl. Calculate the atomic mass of chlorine?

	Step 1 (Change % to decimal)	**Step 2** (multiply by mass #)	*product*	**step 3** (add all products to get **mass**)
75% of ^{35}Cl	.75	x 35	= 26.25	
25% of ^{37}Cl	.25	x 37	= 9.25	= **35.5 amu**

The above numerical setup (*steps 1 – 3*) can also be written as:

$$(.75 \times 35) + (.25 \times 37) = 35.5 \, amu$$

Practice 46

Which statement best explains why most atomic masses on the Periodic Table are decimal numbers?

1) Atomic masses are determined relative to an H–1 standard.
2) Atomic masses are determined relative to an O–16 standard.
3) Atomic masses are a weighted average of the naturally occurring isotopes.
4) Atomic masses are an estimated average of the artificially produced isotopes.

Practice 47

Two isotopes of elements X have average atomic mass of 54 amu. What are the relative percentages of these two isotopes of element X?

1) 80% of ^{50}X and 20% of ^{55}X
2) 20 % of ^{50}X and 80% of ^{55}X
3) 50% of ^{50}X and 50% of ^{55}X
4) 75 % of ^{50}X and 25 % of ^{55}X

Practice 48

A 100.00-gram sample of naturally occurring boron contains 19.78 grams of boron-10 (atomic mass = 10.01 amu) and 80.22 grams of boron-11 (atomic mass = 11.01 amu). Which numerical setup can be used to determine the atomic mass of naturally occurring boron?

1) $(0.1978)(10.01) + (0.8022)(11.01)$

2) $\dfrac{(0.1978)\,(10.01)}{(0.8022)\,(11.01)}$

3) $(0.8022)(10.01) + (0.1978)(11.01)$

4) $\dfrac{(0.8022)\,(10.01)}{(0.1978)\,(11.01)}$

Practice 49

Element X has two naturally occurring isotopes. If 72% of the atoms have a mass of 85 amu and 28% of the atoms have a mass of 87 amu, what is the atomic mass of element X. Show numerical setup and the calculated result.

Practice 50

Show the numerical setup and the calculated atomic mass of silicon given the following three natural isotopes.

92.23% ^{28}Si

4.67% ^{29}Si

3.10% ^{30}Si

23. Isotopes of Hydrogen:

Element hydrogen has three main isotopes: protium, deuterium, and tritium

As with all isotopes, these three isotopes of hydrogen differ in their numbers of neutrons.

Names, symbol notations and nuclear diagrams of these isotopes are shown below.

	Isotopes of hydrogen		
	Protium	*Deuterium*	*Tritium*
Nuclide name	Hydrogen-**1** (H-**1**)	Hydrogen-**2** (H-**2**)	Hydrogen-**3** (H-**3**)
Isotope symbol	^1_1H	^2_1H	^3_1H
Mass number	**1**	**2**	**3**
Protons (atomic number)	1	1	1
Neutrons	0	1	2
Nuclear diagram	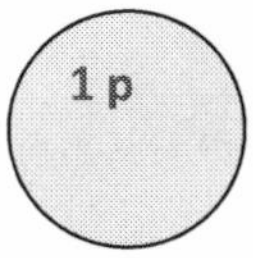 1 p	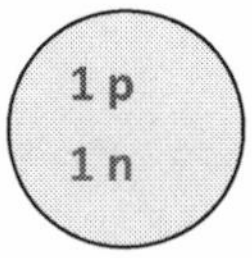 1 p 1 n	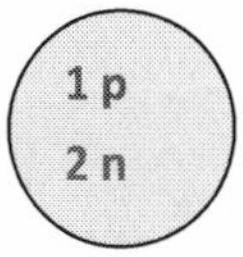 1 p 2 n

Protium
Hydrogen-1 atom has the most basic atomic structure of all atoms. It is composed of 1 proton and 1 electron. It is the only atom without a neutron in its nucleus. When H-1 loses its only electron, the hydrogen ion (H+) that forms is just a proton.

A sample of hydrogen is composed almost entirely (about 99.9%) of protium (H-1). Only traces of deuterium (H-2) and tritium (H-3) would be found in a natural sample of hydrogen.

The H-1 is the main hydrogen isotope found in water (^1H_2O).

Deuterium.
In a sample of water, there will be traces of ^2H_2O *molecules*. This is called *heavy water* because the molecule is composed of the heavier hydrogen atom, deuterium. Heavy water is commonly used in nuclear power plants to cool down the reactors.

Tritium
Tritium's main application is also in nuclear reactions. It is the most commonly used reactant in nuclear fusion. A tritium atom can fuse (join) with another hydrogen isotope to form a helium atom, and a release of a tremendous amount of nuclear energy.

   L**OO**KING Ahead ⟹   Topic 12-Nuclear chemistry: You will learn about nuclear fusion.

Lesson 3 – Location and Arrangements of Electrons

Introduction

Introduction

According to the wave-mechanical model of atoms, electrons are found in orbitals outside the nucleus. **Orbitals** describe the area (or region) outside the nucleus where an electron is likely to be found.

The orbital an electron occupies depends on the energy of the electron. While one electron of an atom may have enough energy to occupy an orbital far from the nucleus, another electron of that same atom may have just enough energy to occupy a region closer to the nucleus. The result is the formation of energy levels (or electron shells) around the nucleus of the atom.

The arrangement of electrons in atoms is complex. In this lesson, you will learn the basic and simplified arrangement of electrons in electron shells. You will also learn of electron transition (movement) from one level to another, and the production of a spectrum of colors (spectral lines).

24. Electron Shells and Electron Configurations

Electron shells refer to the energy levels the electrons of an atom occupy.

Concept Facts: Study to remember the followings about electron shells
. An atom may have one or more electron shells
. The electron shell (1st) closest to the nucleus always contains electrons with the least amount of energy
. The electron shell farthest from the nucleus contains electrons with the most amount of energy
. On the Periodic Table, the period (horizontal row) number indicates the total number of electron shells in the atoms of the elements

Electron configurations show the arrangement of electrons in an atom.
Electron configurations can be found in the box of each element on the Periodic Table.

Bohr's (shell) diagram can be drawn to show electrons in the electron shells of an atom.
Below, Bohr's atomic models for three atoms are drawn using information from the Periodic Table.

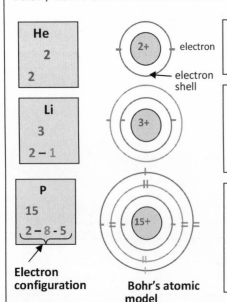

Electron configuration

Bohr's atomic model

According to the electron configuration, a helium atom has all its electrons in **ONE** electron shell:

1st shell: **2** electrons

According to the electron configuration, a lithium atom has all its electrons in **TWO** electron shells:

1st shell: **2** electrons (electrons with lowest energy)

2nd shell : **1** electron (electron with greatest energy)

According to the electron configuration, a phosphorus atom has all its electrons in **THREE** electron shells:

1st shell: **2** electrons (electrons with least energy)

2nd shell : **8** electrons (electrons with a little more energy)

3rd shell : **5** electrons (electrons with greatest energy)

25. Electron Configurations

Concept Task: Be able to interpret electron configurations

Study the electron configuration below.

$$2 - 8 - 8 - 1$$

1st   2nd   3rd   4th

ELECTRON   SHELLS

The configuration shows:

4 electron shells (the atom is of a **4th** Period element)

1st shell is the shell containing electrons with lowest energy

4th shell is the shell containing electrons with greatest energy

4th shell is the valence (outermost) shell

1 is the number of valence electrons

19 is the total number of electrons (2 + 8 + 8 + 1 = 19)

Practice 51
How many electron shells containing electrons are found in an atom of strontium?
1) 2   2) 5   3) 18   4) 38

Practice 52
The total number of electron shells in the configuration 2 – 8 – 1 is
1) 1   2) 2   3) 3   4) 11

Practice 53
In which electron shell would an electron with the most energy be found in an atom of astatine?
1) 2   2) 6   3) 7   4) 18

Practice 54
Which electron configuration is of an atom with three electron shells?
1) 2 – 1   3) 2 – 8 - 8
2) 2 - 3   4) 2 – 8 – 18 – 3

Practice 55
Which of these atoms in the ground state has the most number of electron shells containing electrons?
1) Cs-132   3) Xe - 134
2) I - 127   4) Na - 23

Practice 56
In the electron configuration below,
    2 – 8 – 3 – 1
Which shell contains electrons with the greatest energy?
1) 1st   2) 2nd   3) 3rd   4) 4th

Practice 57
In a bromine atom in the ground state, the electrons that has the least amount of energy are located in the
1) First electron shell   3) Third electron shell
2) Second electron shell   4) Fourth electron shell

Practice 58
How do the energy and the most probable location of an electron in the third shell of an atom compare to the energy and the most probable location of an electron in the first shell of the same atom?

1) In the third shell, an electron has more energy and is closer to the nucleus.
2) In the third shell, an electron has more energy and is farther from the nucleus.
3) In the third shell, an electron has less energy and is closer to the nucleus.
4) In the third shell, an electron has less energy and is farther from the nucleus.

Practice 59
How many electrons are in the 4th electron shell of a neutral zirconium atom ?
1) 2   2) 5   3) 8   4) 10

Practice 60
The total number of electrons in the configuration 2 – 8 – 17 – 2 is
1) 4   2) 2   3) 29   4) 11

Practice 61
What is the total number of valence electrons in a germanium atom in the ground state?
1) 8   2) 2   3) 14   4) 4

Practice 62
Which element has a total of 5 valence electrons present in the fifth shell?
1) Sb   2) Bi   3) I   4) Br

Practice 63
Which set of symbols represents atoms with valence electrons in the same electron shell?
1) Ba, Br, Bi   3) O, S, Te
2) Sr, Sn, I   4) Mn, Hg, Cu

---

26. Maximum Number of Electrons In Electron Shells : Practice problems

Each electron shell has the maximum number of electrons that can occupy that shell.
If **n** represents the electron shell in question: For example: n = 1 means the 1st shell, n= 3 means 3rd shell .

Maximum number of electrons in a shell = 2(n)^2   Square the electron shell in question, then multiply by 2

Concept Task: Be able to determine maximum number of electrons in any given electron shell

Example

What is the maximum number of electrons that can occupy the third shell of an atom?

For third shell: n = 3
Maximum e- = 2(n)^2 = 2(3)^2 = 2(9) = 18 electrons in 3rd

Practice 64
What is the maximum number of electrons that can occupy the second energy level of an atom?
1) 2   2) 8   3) 7   4) 17

Practice 65
What is the most number of electrons that can be found in the 4th energy level of an atom?
1) 2   2) 8   3) 18   4) 32

Practice 66
Which electron shell of an atom can hold a maximum of 72 electrons?
1) 7th shell   3) 5th shell
2) 6th shell   4) 4th shell

27. Completely and Partially Filled Shells: Example and practice problems

An electron shell (n) is completely filled if it has the maximum number of electrons according to the equation 2(n)^2. A partially or an incompletely filled shell, therefore, has less than the maximum number of electrons that can occupy that shell.

Concept Task: Be able to determine an atom with a completely or partially filled electron shell

Example
Which of these elements has a completely filled third electron shell?
1) Al   2) Ca   3) Ar   4) Kr

Note their electron configurations (use Periodic Table)

Al	Ca	Ar	Kr
2 – 8 – 3	2 – 8 – 8 – 2	2 – 8 – 8	2 – 8 – **18** – 8

Note:
18 is the maximum number of electron in the third shell. (see example above)

An atom with a completely filled third shell must have 18 in the third spot of its configuration.

Choice 4: Of the the four choices, only Kr has 18 electrons in the third shell.

Practice 67
Which of these ground state electron configurations is of an atom with two partially filled electron shells?
1) 2 – 8 – 8 – 1   3) 2 – 8 – 18 – 2
2) 2 – 8 – 18 – 7   4) 2 – 8 – 2

Practice 68
Which element has an incomplete 4th electron shell?
1) Hg   2) Rn   3) Cs   4) W

Practice 69
An atom of which element in the ground state has a partially filled second electron shell ?
1) Hydrogen   3) Lithium
2) Potassium   4) Sodium

Practice 70
Which Period 5 atom in the ground state has a half-filled fourth shell?
1) Rh   2) Tc   3) Y   4) Rb

28. Ground State, Excited State, and Spectral Lines

An atom is most stable when its electrons occupy the lowest available electron shells. When this is the case, the atom is said to be in the **ground state.** When one or more electrons of an atom occupy a higher energy level than they should, the atom is said to be in the **excited state**. The electron configurations given for all the elements on the Periodic Table are of atoms in the ground state. This means that each configuration on the Periodic Table shows electrons of the atoms filling from the lowest to the highest electron shells.

Below are definitions and facts related to ground and excited state atoms and spectral lines

Concept Facts: Study to remember the followings

Ground state

When an atom is in the ground state:

. The electron configuration is the same as given on the Periodic Table

. Electrons are filled in order from lowest to highest energy shells

. The energy of the atom is at its lowest, and the atom is stable

. An electron in a ground state atom must absorb energy to go from a lower level to a higher level

. As an electron of a ground state atom absorbs energy and moves to the excited state, the energy of the electron and of the atom increases

Ground state configuration for Nitrogen.

Same as on the Periodic Table

Excited state:

When an atom is in the excited state:

. The electron configuration is different from that of the Periodic Table

. The energy of the atom is at its highest , and the atom is unstable

. An electron in the excited state atom must release energy to return from a higher level to a lower level

. As an electron in the excited state atom releases energy to return to the ground state, the energy of the electron and of the atom decreases.

. *Spectra of colors* are produced when excited electrons release energy and return to the ground state

Quanta are discrete (specific) amounts of energy absorbed or released by an electron to go from one level to another.

Two possible excited state configurations for Nitrogen.

NOTE:

Configurations are different from that of the Periodic Table for Nitrogen

BUT

the total number of electrons in each excited state configuration is still **7**

Spectral lines:

Spectral lines are bands of colors produced when the energy released by excited electrons is viewed through a spectroscope.

. Spectral lines are produced from energy released by excited electrons as they return to the ground state

. Spectral lines are called "fingerprints' of the elements because each element has its own unique pattern of colors at specific wavelengths.

Spectral lines (bright-line spectra)

29. Excited and Ground State: Examples and practice problems

Concept Task: Be able to determine which electron configuration is of an atom in the ground or excited state. Be sure to utilize the Periodic Table.

Examples:
2 – 8 – 5 is the **ground state** configuration for P   2 – 7 – 6 is an e**xcited state** configuration for P

Practice 71
Which is the ground state configuration for a chlorine atom?
1) 2 – 8 – 7 – 1   3) 2 – 8 – 8 – 7
2) 2 – 8 – 8 – 1   4) 2 – 8 – 6 – 1

Practice 72
What is the ground state electron configuration of a neutral atom with 27 protons?
1) 2 – 8 – 14 – 3   3) 2 – 8 – 15 – 2
2) 2 – 8 – 8 – 8 – 1   4) 2 – 8 – 17

Practice 73
Which electron configuration is possible for a strontium atom in the excited state?
1) 2 – 8 – 18 – 10   3) 2 – 8 – 18 – 8 – 1
2) 2 – 8 – 18 – 7 – 3   4) 2 – 8 – 18 – 8 – 2

Practice 74
Which is an excited state electron configuration for a neutral atom with 16 protons and 18 neutrons?
1) 2 – 8 – 5 – 1   3) 2 – 8 – 6 – 2
2) 2 – 8 – 8   4) 2 – 8 – 6

Practice 75
The electron configuration 2 – 8 – 2 is of a
1) Sodium atom in the ground state
2) Magnesium atom in the ground state
3) Sodium atom in the excited state
4) Magnesium atom in the excited state

Practice 76
The electron configuration 2–8–18–5–1 could be of
1) an arsenic atom in the ground state
2) an arsenic atom in the excited state
3) a selenium atom in the ground state
4) a selenium atom in the excited state

Practice 77
The electron configuration 2 – 8 – 18 – 2 – 1 is of
1) Ga atom in the excited state
2) Al atom in the excited state
3) Ga atom in the ground state
4) Al atom in the ground state

30. Spectral Lines: Example and practice problems

Concept Task: Be able to determine which electron transition will produce spectral lines.

Note:

Electron transition from:
        Low   to   **higher** shell
  Ex: 5th shell to 6th shell
     . Energy is absorbed (gained) by the electron
     . Energy of the atom increases

        High   to   **Lower** shell
  Ex: 6th shell to 5th shell
    . Energy is released (emitted) by the electron
    . Produces bright-line spectrum (spectra) of colors
    . Energy of the atom decreases

NOTE:
The greater the difference between the two electron shells, the more energy is absorbed or released.

Practice 78
As an electron moves from 3rd electron shell to the 4th electron shell, the energy of the atom
1) Increases as the electron absorbs energy
2) Increases as the electron releases energy
3) Decreases as the electron absorbs energy
4) Decreases as the electron releases energy

Practice 79
Electron transition between which two electron shells will produce bright-line spectrum of colors?
1) 2nd to 3rd 3) 1st to 4th
2) 3rd to 4th 4) 2nd to 1st

Practice 80
As an electron in an atom moves between electron shells, which transition would cause the electron to absorb the most energy?
1) 1st to 2nd 3) 2nd to 4th
2) 2nd to 1st 4) 4th to 2nd

31. Flame Test and Spectral Chart

A **flame test** is a lab procedure in which compounds of metallic ions are heated to produce different flame colors.

. Flame colors produced are due to the energy released by excited electrons in the metal atoms as they return from high (excited) state to low (ground) state

. Flame colors produced can be used to identify the metal ions present in the substances. However, since two or more metallic ions can produce flame colors that are similar, flame test results are not very reliable for identification.

Spectroscope is equipment that is used to separate a light into color patterns (spectrum of colors) at different wavelengths. Color flames produced during flame tests can be viewed through a spectroscope. The bright-line spectra of each color flame will be unique to each metallic ion, and will provide a more reliable result for identification.

A chart showing bright-line spectra for hydrogen, lithium, sodium and potassium is shown below.

Bright-line spectra of an unknown mixture was compared to those of H, Li, Na and K. Substances in the unknown can be identified by matching the lines in the unknown to the lines for H, Li, Na and K.

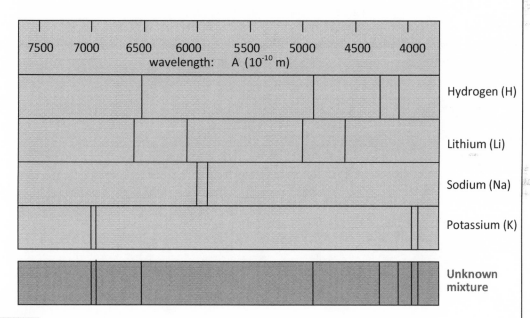

Concept Task: Be able to interpret spectral lines chart

Practice 81

Which elements are in the unknown substance?

1) H and Na   2) K and Li   3) H and K   4) K and Na

Practice 82

Which element produces bright line spectra with the following wavelengths:

6600×10^{-10} A, 6100×10^{-10} A, 5000×10^{-10} A and 4600×10^{-10} A

1) H   2) Li   3) Na   4) K

Lesson 4 – Valence Electrons and Ions

Introduction:

Most atoms (with the exception of the noble gases) are unstable because they have incomplete valence (outermost) electron shells. For this reason, most atoms need to lose, gain or share electrons to fill their valence shell so they can become stable. When an atom loses or gains electrons, it forms an ion.

In this lesson, you will learn about valence electrons, neutral atoms and ions.

LKING Ahead ⟹ Topic 4: Chemical Bonding. You will learn more about the role of valence electrons in chemical bonding.

32. Valence Electrons

Valence electrons are electrons in the outermost electron shell of an atom. Valence shell of an atom is the last (outermost) shell that contains electrons.

Recall: Elements in the same Group (vertical column) of the Periodic Table have the same number of valence electrons, and similar chemical reactivity.

Concept Task: Be able to determine the number of valence for any atom or a given configuration.

In any electron configuration, the last number is always the number of valence electrons.

P
15
2 – 8 – 5

LOOK on the Periodic Table for Phosphorus:
The configuration for phosphorus is : 2 – 8 – **5**
The last number is **5**.
Phosphorus has **5** valence electrons in its valence (third) shell.

33. Ions (charged atom) and Neutral Atoms

For most atoms, a completely filled valence shell must have eight (8) electrons.
NOTE: H and He need only two (2) to fill their valence shell.
A neutral atom may lose its entire valence electrons to form a new valence shell that is completely filled.
A neutral atom may also gain electron(s) to fill its valence shell.
An Ion is formed when a neutral atom loses or gains electrons.
Below, definitions and facts related to neutral atoms and ions

Concept Facts: Study to remember these facts.

	Symbols of neutral atoms and ions

Neutral atom
. A neutral atom has equal numbers of protons and electrons
. The electron configurations given on the Periodic Table are for neutral atoms of the elements in the ground state

Na — a neutral sodium atom

S — a neutral sulfur atom

Ion
. An ion is a charged atom with unequal numbers of protons and electrons
. An ion is formed when an atom loses or gains electrons

Positive ion
. A positive ion is a charged atom containing *fewer* electrons (-) than protons (+)
. A positive ion is formed when a neutral atom loses one or more electrons
. Metals and metalloids tend to lose electrons and form positive ions

Na^+ — a positive sodium ion

Negative ion
. A negative ion is a charged atom containing *more* electrons (-) than protons (+)
. A negative ion is formed when a neutral atom gains one or more electrons
. Nonmetals tend to gain electrons and form negative ions

S^{2-} — a negative sulfide ion

34. Ions vs. Neutral Atoms

When electrons are lost or gained by a neutral atom, the ion formed will be different in many ways from the neutral atom. Number of electrons, electron configuration, size, as well as properties of the ion will all be different from that of the neutral atom.

The following note summarizes the comparisons between positive and negative ions to their parent neutral atoms.

Concept Facts: Study to learn these comparisons.

Comparing a positive ion to its neutral (metallic) atom.
When a neutral atom (usually a metal or metalloid) loses its valence electron(s):

. The positive ion has *fewer* electrons than the parent neutral atom
. The positive ion electron configuration has one fewer electron shell than the neutral atom

. As the neutral atom loses electrons, its size (atomic radius) decreases

. Ionic radius (size) of a positive ion is always smaller than the atomic radius of the neutral atom

. The positive ion has a different chemical reactivity than the neutral atom

Below, Bohr's diagrams showing size comparison of a neutral Na atom to Na$^+$ ion.

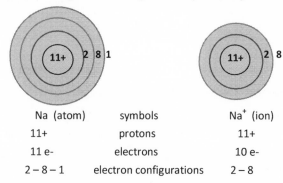

Na (atom)	symbols	Na$^+$ (ion)
11+	protons	11+
11 e-	electrons	10 e-
2 – 8 – 1	electron configurations	2 – 8

Comparing a negative ion to its neutral (nonmetallic) atom.
When a neutral atom (usually a nonmetal) gains electrons to fill its valence shell:

. The negative ion has *more* electrons than its parent neutral atom
. The negative ion electron configuration has the same number of electron shell as the neutral atom

. As the neutral atom gains electrons, its size (atomic radius) increases

. Ionic radius (size) of a negative ion is always larger than the atomic radius of the neutral atom

. The negative ion has a different chemical reactivity than the neutral atom

Below, Bohr's diagrams showing size comparison of a neutral S atom to S^{2-} ion

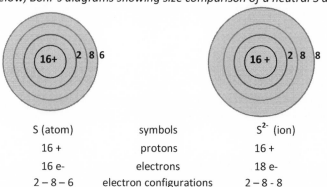

S (atom)	symbols	S^{2-} (ion)
16 +	protons	16 +
16 e-	electrons	18 e-
2 – 8 – 6	electron configurations	2 – 8 - 8

NOTE: Electron configuration of an ion is similar to that of the nearest Group 18 Noble gas element.

Sulfur is Atomic # 16

Argon, atomic # 18, is the closest noble gas to Sulfur.

The configuration of a sulfur ion (2 – 8 – 8) is the same as that of Argon. (Look on the Periodic Table to confirm)

35. Ions: Examples and practice problems

Concept Task: Be able to determine number of electrons and electron configuration of ions.	**Concept Task:** Be able to recognize the correct comparisons between ion and atom.
Number of electrons in ion = Atomic # - Charge = Protons - Charge **Charge of an ion** = protons - electrons **Electron configuration of an ion is** similar to that of the nearest noble gas atom.	**Examples:** Na^+ ion has 1 **FEWER** electron than Na atom S atom is **SMALLER** than S^{2-} ion.

Practice 83
The total number of electrons in a Br^- ion is
1) 36   2) 35   3) 34   4) 54

Practice 84
How many electrons are in a N^{2-} ion?
1) 7   2) 9   3) 10   4) 5

Practice 85
What is the total number of electrons in a Cr^{3+} ion?
1) 3   2) 21   3) 24   4) 27

Practice 86
How many electrons will be found in a particle with a nuclear charge of +41 and a +5 charge?
1) 41   2) 46   3) 205   4) 36

Practice 87
An atom has a nuclear charge of +50 and 46 electrons. The net ionic charge of this atom is
1) +46   2) -46   3) -4   4) +4

Practice 88
An atom has a nuclear charge of +7, 10 electrons, and 8 neutrons. What is the ionic charge of this atom?
1) +7   2) -1   3) -3   4) +3

Practice 89
Which electron configuration is correct for B^{3+} ion?
1) 2 – 2 – 1   2) 2 – 2 – 1   3) 2 – 3   4) 2

Practice 90
Which is the correct electron configuration for Ca^{2+}?
1) 2 – 8 – 2   3) 2 – 8 – 8
2) 2 – 8   4) 2 – 6 – 1 – 1

Practice 91
The electron configuration for As^{3-} is
1) 2 – 8 – 18 – 5   3) 2 – 8 – 17 – 6
2) 2 – 8 – 18 – 8   4) 2 – 8 – 18 – 5 – 3

Practice 92
The electron configuration 2 – 8 – 18 – 8 could represent which particle?
1) Ca^{2+} 2) Ge^{4+} 3) Cl^- 4) Br^{5+}

Practice 93
Which changes occur as an atom becomes a positively charge ion?
1) The atom gains electrons, and the number of protons increases
2) The atom gains electrons, and the number of protons remains the same
3) The atom loses electrons, and the number of protons decreases
4) The atom loses electrons, and the number of protons remains the same

Practice 94
Compared to a phosphorus atom, a P^{3-} ion has
1) More electrons and a larger radius
2) More electrons and a smaller radius
3) Fewer electrons and a larger radius
4) Fewer electrons and a smaller radius

Practice 95
A neutral oxygen atom (O) differs from an ion of oxygen (O^{2-}) in that the atom has
1) More protons   3) Fewer protons
2) More electrons   4) Fewer electrons

Practice 96
Which changes occur as a cadmium atom, Cd, becomes a cadmium ion, Cd^{2+}?
1) The Cd atom gains two electrons and its radius decreases.
2) The Cd atom gains two electrons and its radius increases.
3) The Cd atom loses two electrons and its radius decreases.
4) The Cd atom loses two electrons and its radius increases.

Practice 97
How does the size of N^{3-} ion compares to N atom?
1) N^{3-} is bigger than N because the N^{3-} has 3 more electrons
2) N^{3-} is bigger than N because the N^{3-} has 3 fewer electrons
3) N^{3-} is smaller than N because the N^{3-} has 3 more electrons
4) N^{3-} is smaller than N because the N^{3-} has 3 fewer electrons

Topic 3 – The Atomic Structure

Concept Terms

Key vocabulary terms and concepts from Topic 3 are listed below. You should know definition and facts related to each term and concept.

1. Atom
2. Hard sphere model
3. Plum-pudding model
4. Empty space model
5. Bohr's atomic model
6. Wave mechanical model
7. Gold foil experiment
8. Cathode ray experiment
9. Orbital
10. Nucleus
11. Neutron
12. Proton
13. Electron
14. Nucleon
15. Nuclear charge
16. Atomic number
17. Mass number
18. Atomic mass
19. Atomic mass unit
20. Isotope
21. Electron shell
22. Electron configuration
23. Ground state
24. Excited state
25. Flame test
26. Spectral lines (bright line spectrum)
27. Balmer series
28. Valence electron
29. neutral atom
30. Ion
31. Positive ion
32. Negative ion
33. Ionic configuration
34. Ionic radius

Concept Tasks

Concept tasks from Topic 3 are listed below. You should know how to solve problems and answer questions related to each concept task.

1. Determining and comparing number of one subatomic particle to another
2. Determining or recognizing which two symbols are of isotopes of the same element
3. Determine number of subatomic particles from a given isotope notation
4. Comparing number of subatomic particles of two given isotope symbols
5. Calculating average atomic mass from mass numbers and percentages of isotopes
6. Drawing Bohr's atomic model from electron configuration
7. Determine number of electron shells in an atom or a configuration
8. Determining the electron shell containing electrons with highest or lowest energy.
9. Determining number (or total number) of electrons in any electron shell of an atom or configuration
10. Determining electron transition between electron shells that will produce spectral lines
11. Interpreting electron transition between electron shells
12. Determining and interpreting electron configuration in ground or excited state.
13. Interpreting spectral lines chart
14. Determining and comparing number particles between an ion and the neutral atom.
15. Determining number of electrons and/or protons of an ion.
16. Determining the correct charge of an atom from number of protons and electrons
17. Determining and interpreting ionic configuration

Topic 4 – Chemical Bonding

Topic outline

In this topic, you will learn the following concepts:

. Chemical bonds and stability of atoms   . Molecular substances and molecular polarity

. Chemical bonding and energy   . Intermolecular forces

.Types of chemical bonds between atoms   . Types of substances and their properties

Lesson 1: Chemical Bonding and Stability of atoms

Introduction

Chemical bonding is the simultaneous attraction of positive nuclei to negative electrons.

Chemical bonding is said to be the "glue" that holds particles (atoms, ions, molecules) together in matter.

When atoms bond they become much more stable than when they are in their free states. Since most atoms do not have a full valence shell, they are unstable. For these atoms to attain a full valence shell and be stable, they bond with other atoms.

1. Chemical Bonding and Stability

Atoms bond so they can attain full valence shells and become stable.
The **octet rule** states that a stable valence shell configuration must have eight electrons.

 NOTE: Not every atom needs eight valence electrons to be stable.

An atom can get a full and stable valence shell configuration by:
 Transferring or accepting electrons (during ionic bonding) or *sharing* electrons (during covalent bonding)

Recall that all noble gas atoms have full valence shell of electrons , which make them very stable.
. The ground state electron configuration of a bonded atom is the same as that of the nearest noble gas (Group 18) atom

2. Chemical Bonding and Atom Stability : Practice problems

Concept Task: Be able to determine which noble gas elements that atoms in a bond resemble.

Note
Most atoms in a bond has the same number of electrons and similar electron configuration as the nearest noble gas (Group 18) atom.

Example
In a bond between sodium and chlorine in the formula NaCl: Na resembles Ne. Cl resembles Ar.

Na (atomic # 11): The closest noble gas is Ne (atomic #10).
 In **NaCl**, **Na** is **Na$^+$** ion (10 electrons) . Its configuration is 2–8 , which is the same as that of Ne (2–8).

Cl (atomic # 17): The closest noble gas is Ar (atomic # 18).
 In Na**Cl**, Cl is **Cl$^-$** ion (18 electrons). Its configuration is 2–8–8 , which is the same as that of Ar (2–8–8).

Practice 1
When a sulfur atom bonds with sodium atoms to form the compound Na_2O, the configuration of oxygen in the compound is similar to
1) Na   2) O   3) Ne   4) Ar

Practice 2
The electron configuration of Sr and H ions in the formula SrH_2 are similar to those of elements
1) Kr and He   3) Ar and Ne
2) Rb and He   4) Ca and Li

Practice 3
Atom X and atom Y bond to form a compound. The electron configuration of X in the bond is 2 – 8 – 8. The electron configuration of Y in the compound is 2 – 8. Which two atoms could be X and Y ?
1) X could be magnesium and Y could be sulfur
2) X could be calcium and Y could be sulfur
3) X could be magnesium and Y could be nitrogen
4) X could be calcium and Y could be nitrogen

Topic 4 – Chemical Bonding

Lesson 2 – Chemical Bonding and Energy

Introduction

All chemical substances contain certain amounts of potential energy.

Potential energy is stored in the bonds holding particles of substances together.

The amount of potential energy of a substance depends on *composition and structure* of the substance.

In this lesson, you will learn the relationship between bonding and energy.

3. Bond and Energy

Bond formation between two atoms is exothermic.
Exothermic processes releases heat energy. When two atoms come together to form a bond, heat energy is always released. Since energy is released, the energy of the atoms decreases. The atoms are more stable when they are bonded than when they were not.

$$H + Cl \ \text{------>} \ H - Cl \ + \ \textbf{Energy}$$

A **chemical bond formed** between H and Cl atoms. The bonded H and Cl atoms are more stable than the free H and Cl atoms on the left.

Summary of bond formation and energy

Concept Facts: Study to remember these facts

. Bond formation is exothermic (heat energy released)

. As energy is released during bond formation
  - Potential energy of the atoms decreases
  - Stability of the atoms increases
  - Stability of the chemical system increases

Bond breaking is endothermic .
Endothermic processes absorb heat energy.
When a bond between atoms of a substance is to be broken, energy is always absorbed. Since energy is absorbed, the energy of the atoms increases. The atoms, separated, are now less stable than when they were bonded together.

$$H - Cl \ + \ \textbf{Energy} \ \text{------>} \ H + Cl$$

A **chemical bond** to be broken

Summary of bond breaking and energy.

Concept Facts: Study to remember these facts

. Bond formation is endothermic (heat energy absorbed)

. As energy is absorbed during bond breaking
  - Potential energy of the atoms increases
  - Stability of the atoms decreases
  - Stability of the chemical system decreases

Concept Task: Be able to relate energy to bonding

Practice 4
When two atoms form a bond to produce a chemical substance, the stability of the chemical system
1) Decreases as energy is absorbed
2) Increases as energy is absorbed
3) Decreases as energy is released
4) Increases as energy is released

Practice 5
Given the balanced equation:

$$I_2 \ ^+ \ energy \ \text{------------>} \ I \ + \ I$$

Which statement describes the process represented by this equation?

1) A bond is formed, and energy is absorbed
2) A bond is formed, and energy is released
3) A bond is broken, and energy is absorbed
4) A bond is broken, and energy is released

Practice 6
Given the equation

$$H_2 \ + \ O_2 \ \text{-------->} \ H_2O$$

Which statement best describes the process taking place as bonds are broken and formed?

1) The breaking of O–O bond releases energy
2) The breaking of H–H bond releases energy
3) The forming of H–O bond absorbs energy
4) The forming of H–O bond releases energy

Practice 7
When two fluorine atoms combined to form a molecule of fluorine, energy is
1) Always absorbed
2) Always released
3) Sometimes absorbed
4) Sometimes released

Topic 4 – Chemical Bonding

Lesson 3 – Types of Bonding between Atoms

Introduction:

Intramolecular forces describe forces that hold atoms together to create molecules and compounds.

Bonding between atoms is a result of the atoms competing for electrons to get full valence shells. Bonding between atoms can occur by atoms sharing electrons to form a covalent bond, or by atoms transferring and accepting electrons to form an ionic bond.

In this lesson, you will learn about the different types of bonding between atoms.

4. Ionic Bond

Ionic bonds are the forces holding charged particles together in ionic compounds.

Facts related to ionic bonding are summarized below.

Concept Facts: Study to remember these facts

. Ionic bonds are formed by the *transfer of electron(s)* from a metal to a nonmetal
. The metal atom always loses (or transfers) its electron to become a positive ion
. The nonmetal atom always gains (or accepts) electrons to become a negative ion
. Ionic bonds are formed by the electrostatic attraction between the positive metal ion and the negative nonmetal ion
. Electronegativity difference between the nonmetal atom and the metal atom in ionic bonding is generally 1.7 or greater

Examples of substances containing ionic bonds:

NaCl	CaF$_2$	Fe$_2$O$_3$
sodium chloride	calcium fluoride	iron oxide

NOTE: Each formula above consists of a metal atom and a nonmetal atom.

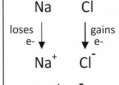

An ionic bond is the electrostatic attraction between oppositely (+ and -) charged ions.

5. Covalent Bond

Covalent bonds are the forces holding atoms of nonmetals together in covalent and molecular substances.

Facts related to covalent bonding are summarized below.

Concept Facts: Study to remember these facts

. Covalent bonding occurs between two nonmetal atoms that are sharing electrons
. Electronegativity difference between the two nonmetals in a covalent bond is usually less than 1.7
. Polar, nonpolar, network solid and coordinate, are types of covalent bonding

Example formulas of substances containing covalent bonds.

H$_2$O HCl	H$_2$ O$_2$	SiC C	NH$_4$$^+$ H$_3$O$^+$
polar bonding	nonpolar bonding	network solid	coordinate

NOTE: Each formula consists only of nonmetal atoms.

A **covalent bond** between H and Cl atoms.

A (−) between two nonmetal atoms represents two (a pair of) shared electrons of a single covalent bond.

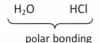

6. Polar Covalent Bond

Polar covalent bonds are formed by *unequal sharing* of electrons between two different nonmetal atoms.

Facts related to polar covalent bonding are summarized below.

Concept Facts: Study to remember these facts

. Sharing of electrons in polar covalent bonding is unequal

. Electronegativity difference between the two nonmetal atoms is generally greater than 0 but less than 1.7

. Polar covalent bonds are the most common bond between atoms of molecular substances

Examples of substances containing Polar Covalent bond

H_2O	HCl	NH_3
water	hydrogen chloride	ammonia

NOTE : Each formula consists of two different nonmetal elements

Unequal sharing of electrons in a polar covalent bonding between two different nonmetals.

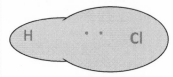

A molecule of HCl

The electrons (**. .**) shared by H and Cl are located closer to the Cl atom. This represents unequal sharing of electrons.

The electrons are closer to Cl because Cl has a greater electronegativy value than H.

7. Nonpolar Covalent Bond

Nonpolar covalent bonds are formed by equal sharing of electrons between two of the same nonmetal atoms.

Facts related to nonpolar covalent bond is summarized below.

Concept Facts: Study to remember these facts

. Sharing of electrons in nonpolar covalent bonding is equal

. Electronegativity difference is zero

. Nonpolar bonds are commonly found in *diatomic* (two-atom) molecules

Example of substances containing nonpolar covalent bond

H_2	N_2
Hydrogen	Nitrogen

NOTE: Each formula consists of the same nonmetal element

Equal sharing of electrons in a nonpolar covalent bonding between two identical nonmetals.

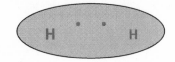

A molecule of H_2

The electrons (**. .**) shared by both H atoms are equal distance from both atoms. This represents equal sharing.

The electrons are shared equally because identical atoms have the same electronegativity value.

8. Network Solid Covalent Bond

A **network covalent bond** is formed between nonmetal atoms in network solid compounds.

Compounds formed by network solid bonding cannot exist as discrete individual molecules.

Examples of network solid compounds.

These are the *only three* you need to know: Study and remember them

C	SiO_2	SiC
(Diamond)	(Silicon dioxide)	(Silicon carbide)

Diamond

9. Coordinate Covalent Bond

A **coordinate covalent bond** is formed when both shared electrons are provided by *only one* of the atoms. This bond is formed when H^+ (hydrogen ion or proton), which does not have an electron, bonds with a molecule such as NH_3 (ammonia) or H_2O (water).

Two formulas containing coordinate covalent bonds are NH_4^+ H_3O^+

NH_4^+ (ammonium ion) *forms from a coordinate covalent bond between NH_3* (ammonia) and H^+ (hydrogen ion)

H_3O^+ (hydronium ion) *forms from a coordinate covalent bond is between H_2O* (water) and H^+ (hydrogen ion)

NH_3 and H_2O molecules have lone pairs (two unbonded) electrons that they share with an H^+ (a proton), which has no electron.

10. Metallic Bond

A **metallic bond** is a force that holds metal atoms together in metallic substances.

Concept Facts: Study to remember these facts about metallic bonding.

. Metallic bonding is described as positive ions *"immersed in a sea of mobile valence electrons"*
. The high electrical conductivity of metals is due to their mobile (free moving) valence electrons

Examples of formulas containing metallic bonds

Ca (calcium)   Au (Gold)   Fe (iron)

Note: These substances are metallic elements

11. Bond Types: Summary Table

Bond Type	Type of elements involve in bonding	Bond description	Electronegativity difference	Type of substances containing bond	Example formula containing bond
Metallic	metal atoms of the same element	positive ions in sea of electrons	--------------	metallic substances	Ag K
Ionic	metal - nonmetal	transfer (losing & gaining) of electrons	1.7 or greater	ionic substances	NaCl K_2O
Covalent	nonmetals only	sharing of electrons	less than 1.7	molecular substances	HCl
Polar covalent	two different nonmetals	unequal sharing	greater than 0 but less than 1.7	polar and nonpolar substances	H_2O CH_4
Nonpolar covalent	nonmetal atoms with the same electronegativity	equal sharing of electrons	zero (0)	diatomic nonpolar substances	H_2 O_2
Coordinate Covalent	two different nonmetals	One atom provides both shared electrons	------------------	polyatomic ions	NH_4^+ H_3O^+
Network solid covalent	nonmetals only	No discrete particles	------------------	network solids	C , SiC, SiO_2

Topic 4 – Chemical Bonding

12. Types of Bonding: Practice problems

Concept Task: Be able to recall facts relating to bond types.

Practice 8
Which type of bond is formed when electrons are shared between two atoms?
1) Covalent
2) Metallic
3) Ionic
4) Hydrogen

Practice 9
The transfer of electrons from a metal to a nonmetal will result in the formation of
1) Hydrogen bond
2) Covalent bond
3) Ionic bond
4) Metallic bond

Practice 10
Two atoms share electrons equally, the bond formed is mostly
1) Polar and covalent
2) Ionic and covalent
3) Metallic and covalent
4) Nonpolar and covalent

Practice 11
Two atoms with an electronegativity difference of 0.4 form a bond that is
1) Ionic, because electrons are shared
2) Ionic, because electrons are transferred
3) Covalent, because electrons are shared
4) Covalent, because electrons are transferred

Practice 12
When one atom loses one or more electrons to another, the bond formed between the two atoms is best described as
1) Ionic with electronegativity difference greater than 1.7
2) Ionic with electronegativity difference of less than 1.7
3) Covalent with electronegativity difference greater than 1.7
4) Covalent with electronegativity difference of less than 1.7

Practice 13
Atom X bonds with another atom X to form X_2 molecule. The bond in this molecule is
1) Polar because electrons are shared equally
2) Nonpolar because electrons are shared equally
3) Polar because electrons are shared unequally
4) Nonpolar because electrons are shared unequally

Practice 14
The ability to conduct electricity in the solid state is a characteristic of metallic substances. This characteristics is best explained by the presence of
1) High ionization energy
2) High electronegativity
3) Mobile protons
4) Mobile electrons

Practice 15
When a nonmetal atom forms ionic bond with a metal, the nonmetal becomes a
1) Positive ion, because it had gained electrons
2) Positive ion, because it had gained protons
3) Negative ion, because it had gained electrons.
4) Negative ion, because it had gained protons.

Concept Task: Be able to relate formulas to bond types.

Practice 16
Which formula contains ionic bonds?
1) ClO_2 2) SO_2 3) Li_2O 4) HI

Practice 17
In which compound would the atoms form a bond by sharing their electrons?
1) CS_2 2) CaS   3) AgI   4) Hg

Practice 18
Which two atoms are held together by a polar covalent bond?
1) H – H
2) H – O
3) Al – H
4) Al – O

Practice 19
In which substance do the atoms share electrons equally to form a bond?
1) SiC   2) Ag   3) NH_3 4) Br_2

Practice 20
Metallic bonding will form between the atoms of which substance?
1) Nickel
2) Sodium chloride
3) Carbon
4) Hydrogen

Practice 21
Which compound contains both ionic and covalent bonds?
1) Mg_3N_2
2) $NaClO_3$
3) H_2O_2
4) O_2

Practice 22
Element X combines with rubidium to form an ionic bond. In which Group of the Periodic Table could element X be found?
1) Group 1
2) Group 13
3) Group 2
4) Group 16

Practice 23
Which element would most likely form a covalent bond with a chlorine atom?
1) Iron
2) Beryllium
3) Phosphorus
4) Potassium

Practice 24
Which pair of electrons configurations belong to atoms that will share electrons when they bond with each other?
1) $2 - 8 - 2$ and $2 - 8 - 1$
2) $2 - 8 - 6$ and $2 - 8 - 18 - 7$
3) $2 - 8 - 18 - 8$ and $2 - 8 - 13 - 1$
4) $2 - 8 - 5$ and $2 - 8 - 18 - 8 - 1$

Topic 4 – Chemical Bonding

Lesson 4 – Types of Substances and their Properties

Introduction

In the last lesson, you learned about the different types of bonds found between atoms of substances. For the most part, the bond name and the type of substances containing that bond are usually the same.

For examples:

. Ionic substances contain atoms held together by ionic bonds

. Metallic substances contain atoms held together by metallic bonds

. Network solid substances contain atoms held together by network solid bonds

. Molecular (covalent) substances contain atoms held together by covalent bond

. Polar molecular substances contain atoms held together by polar covalent bonds.

Nonpolar molecular substances are the only substances which this is not always the case.

Only a few nonpolar substances contain atoms held together by nonpolar bonds.

Most nonpolar substances actually contain atoms held together by polar covalent bonds.

This exception will be explained later in this lesson.

In this lesson, you will first learn of the four types of substances and their properties.

Later, you will learn the relationship between bond polarity, molecular symmetry, molecular shape, and molecular polarity.

13. Types of Substance and their Properties: Summary Table

Type of substance	Phase at room temperature	Physical Properties (characteristics)		
		Melting point	Conductivity	Solubility (in water)
Metallic	solid (*except Hg - liquid*)	Very High	Good (High) *as solids and liquids*	No (insoluble)
Ionic	solid only	High	Good (High) *as liquid and aqueous*	Yes (soluble)
Molecular	solid, liquid, gas	Low	Poor (low) *in all phases*	Yes (slightly soluble)
Network solid	Solid only	Extremely high	Very poor *in all phases*	No (Insoluble)
More information about each type of substance are discussed in the next few page.				

14. Four Types of Substances and their Melting Points

Below are solid forms of the four types of substances mentioned in the above table are given.

Note the differences in temperature at which each solid will melt at STP.

Type of substance	Molecular substance	Ionic substance	Metallic substance	Network solid
Example solid	Ice (H_2O)	Salt (NaCl)	Gold (Au)	Diamond (C)
Melting point	0°C	801°C	1065°C	3550°C

Topic 4 – Chemical Bonding

15. Metallic Substances and their Properties

Metallic substances are metallic elements.
. Metallic substances contain atoms held together by metallic bonding
. Metallic substances normally exist as solid at room temperature
. Mercury (Hg) is the only liquid metallic element

Examples of some metallic substances:
Ca (calcium)   Ni (nickel)

Properties of metallic substances

. High melting points (because they are highly stable)
. Hard solid
. Insoluble in water
. High (good) conductor of heat and electricity (as solids and liquids)
   Electrical conductivity is due to mobile valence electrons

Gold (Au)

Practice 25
Which is a metallic substance?
1) C   2) H_2 3) Sn   4) F

Practice 26
Which substance at STP conducts electricity because the substance contains mobile electrons?
1) NaCl   2) S   3) Mg   4)K_2O

16. Ionic Substances and their Properties

Ionic substances are crystalline compounds formed by repeated patterns of positive and negative ions. Electrostatic attraction holds the oppositely charged ions together.
The positive ion in ionic compounds is usually that of a metallic element. Exceptions are ionic compounds formed by NH_4^+ (ammonium ion).

The negative ion in ionic compounds is usually that of a nonmetal element or polyatomic ion. *Reference Table E* lists some common polyatomic ions.

Two categories of ionic substances are given below

Binary ionic compounds containing *only* ionic bonds
   Formulas of compounds from this category usually contain two different elements (a positive metal ion and a negative nonmetal ion)
   Examples: NaCl (sodium chloride) Al_2O_3 (aluminum oxide)

Ionic compounds containing *both* ionic and covalent bonds
   These compounds usually have three or more different atoms because they typically contain a polyatomic ion. Polyatomic ions are ions containing two or more nonmetal atoms with an excess charge. Bonding within all polyatomic ions is covalent. A compound of this category is generally formed by the electrostatic attraction (ionic bond) between a positive metal (or ammonium) ion and a negative polyatomic ion.
   Examples: $MgSO_4$ (magnesium sulfate) NH_4Cl (ammonium chloride)

Properties of ionic substances.
. High melting points (stable, and require high heat to decompose)
. Most are hard solids
. Soluble or slightly soluble in water
. High or good electrical conductivity as liquids and aqueous

*Ionic compounds are good **electrolytes** because they produce ions when melted or dissolved in water to make a solution. Electrical conductivity of ionic compounds is due to these mobile ions .*

salt

Practice 27
Which is binary ionic compound?
1) CaS   3) CO_2
2) $CaSO_4$ 4) CH_4

Practice 28
Which compound contains both ionic and covalent bonds?

1) $AlCl_3$ 3) C_2H_6
2) NO_3 4) KNO_3

Practice 29
A solid substance was tested in the laboratory. The test results are listed below.
. Dissolves in water
. Is an electrolyte
. Melts at a high temperature
Based on these results, the solid substance could be
1) Cu   3) $CuBr_2$
2) C   4) $C_6H_{12}O_6$

Topic 4 – Chemical Bonding

17. Molecular Substances and their Properties

Molecular substances are substances that contain molecules. A **molecule** is the smallest discrete unit of a molecular substance that can exist on its own. A molecule is usually a group of nonmetal atoms covalently bonded. Molecular substances are found in all three phases: solid, liquid, and gas. A molecular substance can be polar or nonpolar depending on the charge distribution within its molecule. (*see next page for explanations.*)

Examples of some common molecular substances.

H_2O (water)   Ne (neon) CO_2 (carbon dioxide) H_2 (Hydrogen)

Properties of molecular substances

. Lower melting points (when compared to metallic or ionic substance)
. Low (poor) electrical conductivity in all phases
. Solids are usually soft and brittle
. Most are slightly soluble in water

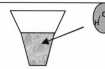

Water (H_2O) is a molecular substance because it is composed of individual water molecules.

Practice 30
Which is a molecular compound?
1) K_2O 3) Li_2SO_4
2) CH_4 4) Hg

Practice 31
Which two substances are covalent compounds?
1) $C_6H_{12}O_6$(s) and KI (s)
2) $C_6H_{12}O_6$(s) and HCl(g)
3) KI(s) and NaCl(s)
4) NaCl(s)   and HCl(g)

18. Properties of Substances: Practice Problems

Practice 32

The table below contains properties of compounds A, B, C, and D.

Compound	Melting point	Conductivity	Solubility in water
A	High	Excellent (liquid	soluble
B	High	Very poor (solid)	Insoluble
C	Low	Poor (solid)	Slightly soluble
D	High	Excellent (solid)	Insoluble

Which list identifies the type of solid each compound represents?
1) A – ionic, B – network ,   C – metallic, D-molecular
2) A – network,   B – ionic, C – molecular, D – metallic
3) A – metallic, B – molecular, C – network, D – ionic
4) A – ionic, B – network, C – molecular, D – metallic

Practice 33
Which set of properties best describes I_2 (iodine) solid?
1) High conductivity and high melting point
2) High conductivity and low melting point
3) Low conductivity and high melting point
4) Low conductivity and low melting point

Practice 34
Which set of properties best describes NH_4Cl(s)?
1) It is a good electrolyte with high melting point
2) It is a poor electrolyte with high melting point
3) It is a good electrolyte with low melting point
4) It is a poor electrolyte with low melting point

Practice 35
The compound $C_{12}H_{22}O_{11}$ is best described as
1) A molecular solid with low melting point and low electrical conductivity as aqueous
2) A molecular solid with high melting point and high electrical conductivity as aqueous
3) An ionic solid with low melting point and low electrical conductivity as aqueous
4) An ionic solid with high melting point and high electrical conductivity as aqueous

19. Bonds, Molecular Polarities, Symmetry and Shapes

A molecular substance can be classified as nonpolar or polar based on the symmetry of its molecules.

Nonpolar substances have symmetrical molecules.

Most nonpolar molecules are formed by polar covalently bonded atoms that are symmetrically arranged. Below are two examples.

CH_4 (Methane) CO_2 (Carbon dioxide)

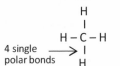

4 single polar bonds

$O = C = O$

2 double polar bonds

A few nonpolar molecules are formed by nonpolar covalently bonded atoms that are symmetrically arranged. This category of nonpolar substances includes all the diatomic elements. Below are two examples

Cl_2 (Chlorine) N_2 (Nitrogen)

Cl – Cl   N ≡ N

The noble gas (monatomic) elements in Group 18 of the Periodic Table are also considered nonpolar substances.

Polar substances have asymmetrical molecules .

All polar (dipole) molecules are formed by polar covalently bonded atoms that are asymmetrically arranged. Examples are shown below.

HCl (hydrogen chloride) H_2O (water)

H – Cl

In a polar molecule, due to the uneven electron sharing, the higher electronegativity atom (Cl and O in the above examples) will have a partial negative (-) charge. This is because the higher electronegativity atom always gets a greater share of the shared electrons. The lower electronegativity atom (H in the above examples) will have a partial positive (+) because it gets the smaller share of the shared electrons.

The diagrams below show the + and – ends on HCl and H_2O molecules.

Polar substances are sometimes called **di**pole because of the **two** poles (+ and –) on their molecules.

Concept Task: Be able to recognize a substance as polar or nonpolar.

Practice 36

The structure of which molecule is nonpolar with polar covalent bonds?

1) H – S
           |
           H

2) O = O

3) Cl–C– Cl   with Cl above and Cl below

4) Na – F

Practice 37

Which substance is nonpolar with nonpolar covalent bonds?

1) Br_2 3) $NaNO_3$

2) SO_2 4) CF_4

Practice 38

Which structural formula represents a polar molecule?

1) H – H   3) Na – H

2) H – Br   4) Cl – Cl

Practice 39

Which type of molecule is CF_4?

1) Polar, with a symmetrical distribution of charge

2) Polar, with an asymmetrical distribution of charge

3) Nonpolar, with a symmetrical distribution of charge

4) Nonpolar, with an asymmetrical distribution of charge

Molecular shapes

When nonmetal atoms bond, the shape of the molecule depends on factors such as types of nonmetal atoms, as well as the number of shared and unshared electrons. Below are examples of molecular shapes.

Linear	Tetrahedral	Angular (bent)	Pyramidal	*molecular shape*
O = O	H H – C – H H	O H H	H – N – H H	*molecular structure*
O_2	CH_4	H_2O	NH_3	*molecular formula*
oxygen	methane	water	ammonia	*substance name*

20. Degree of Bond and Molecular Polarity

Bond polarity refers to the extent of the electrical (positive and negative) charges on the bonded atoms. Bond polarity depends largely on the electronegativity difference (ED) between the two bonded atoms. The bigger the difference in electronegativity, the greater the ionic and polar characteristics of the bond. The smaller the difference in electronegativity values, the greater the nonpolar characteristics of the bond.

Molecular polarity refers to the extent of the overall positive and negative charges on a molecule. Molecular polarity of a substance depends largely on the electronegativity difference between the bonded atoms, as well as the symmetry of its structure.

Recall that electronegativity measures an atom's ability to attract (pull) electrons from another atom during chemical bonding. Electronegativity values for the elements can be found on Reference Table S.

To calculate electronegativity difference between two atoms in a bond:

Step 1 : Use Table S to get electronegativity values for both elements in the formula

Step 2: Electronegativity difference (ED) = High electronegativity – Low electronegativity

To determine which formula is most or least ionic or polar: Consider the scale below.

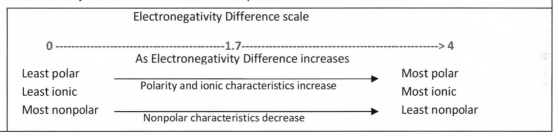

Electronegativity Difference scale

0 --1.7--> 4

As Electronegativity Difference increases

Least polar	Polarity and ionic characteristics increase →	Most polar
Least ionic		Most ionic
Most nonpolar	Nonpolar characteristics decrease →	Least nonpolar

21. Degree of Bond and Molecular Polarities. Example and practice questions

Concept Task: Be able to determine which formula is most or least ionic, covalent or polar.

Example:
Which substance has the most ionic characteristics?
1) LiCl   2) NaCl   3) KCl   4) FrCl

Determine and compare electronegativity difference (ED)

LiCl	NaCl	KCl	FrCl
Cl = 3.2	Cl = 3.2	Cl = 3.2	Cl = 3.2
Li = 1.0	Na = 0.9	K = 0.8	Fr = 0.7
ED = 2.2	2.3	2.4	2.5
(Smallest difference)			*(Highest difference)*

LiCl : Least ionic
    Least polar
    Most nonpolar

FrCl : Most ionic
    Most polar
    Least nonpolar

Choice 4 because the electronegativity difference in FrCl is the highest of the four formulas.

Practice 40
Which bond is the least ionic?
1) Al – O   3) Li – O
2) N – O   4) S – O

Practice 41
The bonding in which compound has the greatest degree of ionic character?
1) KBr   3) HF
2) BeO   4) PCl_3

Practice 42
Which chemical bond has the least degree of covalent characteristics?
1) C – O   3) H – O
2) F – O   4) N – O

Practice 43
Which molecule is the most polar?
1) H – Br   3) H – Cl
2) H – F   4) H – I

22. Bond Polarity, Molecular Polarity, Molecular Symmetry, Molecular Shapes: **Summary Table**

Below is a table summarizing bond and molecular polarity, as well as symmetry and molecular shapes.

Concepts	Explanations	Depends on	Types	Descriptions	Examples
Bond polarity	Describes polarity (+ and − charges) of a covalent bond between two atoms	Depends largely on the type of atoms or their electronegativity difference	Polar bond	A bond that produces + and - ends on bonded atoms. Found between two different nonmetals	$C-H$ $\quad$ $P-Cl$
			Nonpolar bond	A bond that does not produce + and − ends on the bonded atoms. Found between two of the same nonmetal atoms	$H-H$ $\quad$ $O=O$
Molecular polarity	Describes the overall polarity (+ and − charges) of a molecule	Depends largely on the symmetry and charge distributions on a molecule	Polar molecule	Asymmetrical structure Uneven + and − charge distributions	HF $\quad$ H_2O $H-F$
			Nonpolar molecule	Symmetrical structure Even + and − charge distributions	Cl_2 $\quad$ CH_4 $Cl-Cl$ $\quad$ H-C-H
Molecular symmetry	Describes the overall arrangement of atoms in molecules	Depends largely on the nature, type, and the number of each atom of the molecule	Symmetrical molecules	Arrangement of atoms is evenly distributed	$Br-Br$ $\quad$ H-C-H
			Asymmetrical molecules	Arrangement of atoms is unevenly distributed	H- Cl $\quad$ H-N-H
Molecular shapes	Describes structural shapes of molecules due to arrangements of its atoms	Depends on several factors including types of and number of atoms, as well as number of shared and unshared electrons	Linear		H-Cl $\quad$ O=C=O
			Tetrahedral		Cl-C-Cl with Cl
			Angular (bent)		S, H H
			Pyramidal		H-N-H

Lesson 5 – Lewis Electron-dot Symbols and Bonding

Introduction

Valence electrons are electrons in the outermost electron shell of an atom. Valence electrons are directly involve in all chemical bonding. During ionic bonding, valence electrons are lost by a metal to form a positive ion, and are gained by a nonmetal to form a negative ion. During covalent bonding, nonmetal atoms share their valence electrons.

In this lesson, you will learn how to show different bond types using Lewis electron-dot diagrams.

23. Lewis Electron –dot Diagrams for Neutral Atoms and Ions

A **Lewis electron- dot diagram** is a notation that shows the symbol of an atom and dots to represents valence electrons of the atom. Lewis electron-dot diagrams can be drawn for neutral atoms, ions and compounds.

Neutral atoms

A Lewis electron-dot diagram for a neutral atom is the symbol of the atom and dots equal to the number of its valence electrons.

	e- configuration	valence electrons	dot diagram
Sodium atom (Na)	2 – 8 – **1**	**1**	Na ·
Phosphorus atom (P)	2 – 8 – **5**	**5**	· P :

Positive ions

A Lewis dot-diagram for a positive ion is just the symbol of the positive ion, which can be determined from the Periodic Table.

	e- configuration	valence electrons	dot diagram
Sodium ion (Na$^+$)	2 – 8	8	Na$^+$
Beryllium ion (Be^{2+})	2	2	Be^{2+}

Negative ions

A Lewis electron-dot diagram for a negative ion is the symbol of the ion and 8 dots around it.
A negative hydrogen ion (H$^-$) is the only exception with just 2 dots .
Hydrogen has only one occupied electron shell (the 1st), which has enough orbitals for just two electrons.

	e- configuration	valence electrons	dot diagram
Phosphide ion (P^{3-})	2 – 8 – 8	8	$\left[: P :\right]^{3-}$
Hydride ion (H$^-$)	2	2	$\left[H: \right]^-$

Note: Use the Periodic Table to get the correct charge of an ion

---

Concept Task: Be able to draw Lewis electron-dot diagrams

Practice 44

Draw the Lewis electron-dot diagrams for the following atoms.

Magnesium

Silicon

Argon

Practice 45

Draw the Lewis electron-dot diagrams for the following ions

Calcium ion

Potassium ion

Oxide ion

Bromide ion

---

24. Lewis Electron-dot for Ionic Compounds

Recall that ionic compounds are composed of positive (+) and negative (-) ions.

Also recall that the positive ion is formed by a metal transferring (losing) its valence electrons to a nonmetal.
The nonmetal accepts (gains) the electrons to become a negative ion.

Lewis electron-dot diagrams for ionic formulas must show the Lewis electron-dot symbols for both the positive and negative ions of the ionic compound.

A *correct* Lewis electron-dot diagram for a given ionic formula must show the following:

The *correct* symbol and charge of the positive ion in the formula.

The *correct* symbol and charge of the negative ion in the formula.

The *correct* number of each ion in the formula.

The *correct* number of dots around the negative ion of the formula.
A bracket should surround the dot diagram of the negative ion.

If any of these is incorrect,
the Lewis dot diagram for
the ionic formula will also be
incorrect.

Below, Lewis electron-dot diagrams for three ionic compounds are given.

	Lewis dot diagrams of the ions	*Correct Lewis dot-diagram (must include the **correct** number of each ion)*	**Concept Task:** Be able to draw Lewis electron-dot diagrams for ionic compounds.
Sodium chloride	Na^+ $\left(\overset{\cdot\cdot}{\underset{\cdot\cdot}{\times}} Cl \overset{\cdot\cdot}{} \right)-$	$Na^+ \left[\overset{\cdot\cdot}{\underset{\cdot\cdot}{\times}} Cl : \right]-$	**Practice 46** Draw the Lewis electron-dot diagrams for the following ionic compounds.
Calcium bromide	Ca^{2+} $\left(\overset{\cdot\cdot}{\underset{\cdot\cdot}{\times}} Br : \right)-$	$Ca^{2+}\ 2\ [\overset{\cdot\cdot}{\underset{\cdot\cdot}{\times}} Br :] -$ or $- [: \overset{\cdot\cdot}{\underset{\cdot\cdot}{Br}} \overset{x}{.}]\ Ca^{2+}\ [\overset{x}{.} \underset{\cdot\cdot}{Br} :] -$	Lithium Iodide Magnesium chloride Potassium hydride
Potassium oxide	$K^+ [\overset{\cdot\cdot}{\underset{\cdot\cdot}{\times}} O :]^{2-}$	$2\ K^+ [\overset{\cdot\cdot}{\underset{\cdot\cdot}{\times}} O :]^{2-}$ or $K^+ [\overset{\cdot\cdot}{.} O \overset{x}{.} .]^{2-}\ K^+$	Aluminum fluoride Aluminum oxide Strontium oxide Barium sulfide Calcium hydride

Note: **x** represents the valence electrons
transferred from the metal atom.

Note the importance of having the correct number of each ion.

Compounds are neutral, so the sum of charges in compound
formulas must equal zero .

In calcium bromide, 2 bromides (each a -1 ion) are needed to
equalize the charge of 1 calcium ion (a +2 ion).

In potassium oxide, 2 potassium ions (each a +1 ion) are needed to
equalize the charge of 1 oxide ion (a -2 ion).

25. Lewis electron-dot Diagrams for Molecular Substances

Recall that covalent bonding and covalent molecules are formed from the sharing of valence electrons by nonmetal atoms. Each pair of electrons (2 electrons) shared between two atoms forms a single covalent bond.

Lewis electron-dot diagrams for covalently bonded atoms and molecules must show the sharing of electrons by the nonmetal atoms.

A *correct* Lewis electron-dot diagram for a molecular formula must show the following:

The *correct* symbol and number of each nonmetal atom.

The *correct* number of shared (bonding) electrons between the atoms.

The *correct* number of valence electrons around each atom.

} If any of these is incorrect, the Lewis diagram for the covalent formula will also be incorrect.

In the examples below, Lewis electron-dot diagrams are drawn for some common polar and nonpolar substances. Note that for each substance two different but correct Lewis structures are drawn.

Polar substances (note how these diagrams have asymmetrical shapes)

Molecular name	Molecular formula	Lewis electron-dot diagram
Hydrogen chloride	HCl	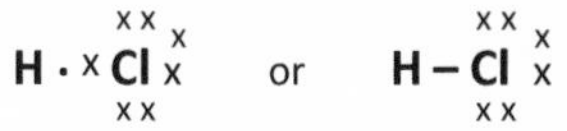 H · ×Cl × ×× or H – Cl × ××
Water	H_2O	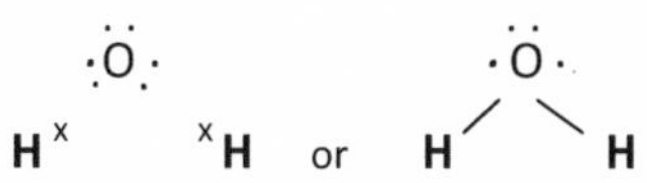 ·O· H× ×H or H O H
Ammonia	NH_3	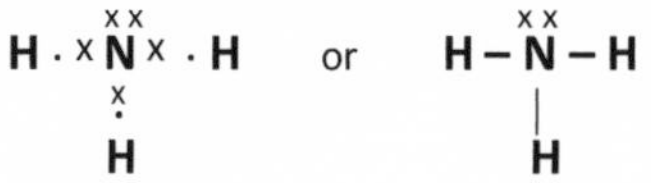 H · ×N× · H H or H – N – H H

Nonpolar substances (note how these diagrams have symmetrical shapes)

Molecular name	Molecular formula	Lewis electron-dot diagrams
Chlorine	Cl_2	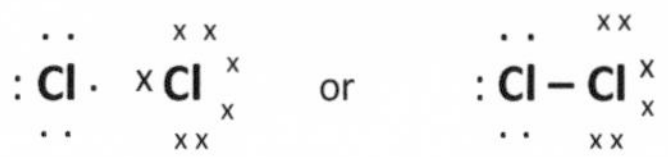 :Cl· ×Cl × × or :Cl – Cl × ×
Carbon dioxide	CO_2	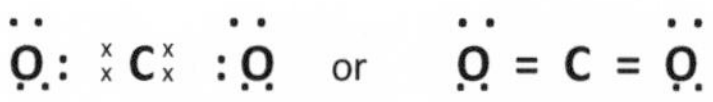 O: ×C× :O or O = C = O
Methane	CH_4	 H · ×C× · H H or H – C – H H
Carbon tetrachloride	CCl_4	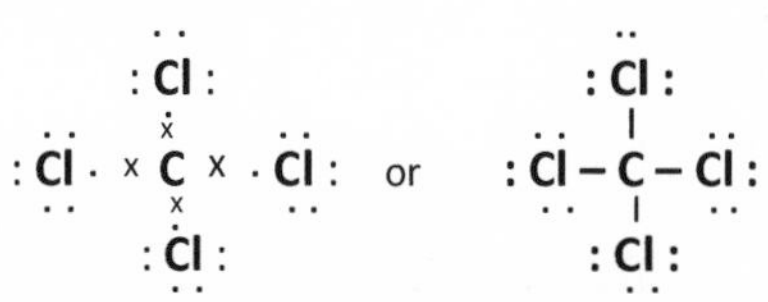 :Cl: :Cl· × C × ·Cl: :Cl: or :Cl: :Cl – C – Cl: :Cl:

Concept Task: Be able to draw Lewis electron-dot diagrams for molecular compounds

Practice 47

Draw the Lewis electron-dot diagrams for the following molecular compounds.

Hydrogen fluoride

Hydrogen sulfide

Hydrogen

Bromine

Carbon tetrafluoride

26. Lewis Electron-dot Diagrams: Practice problems

Concept Task: Be able to recognize the correct Lewis electron-dot diagram for neutral atoms, ions, and compounds.

Practice 48

Which Lewis electron-dot notation is correct for a calcium atom?

1) Ca: 2) :Ca: 3) :Ca: $^{2+}$ 4) [Ca]$^{2+}$

Practice 49

Which is a correct electron-dot symbol for a Strontium ion?

1) [Sr:]$^{2+}$ 2) [:Sr:]$^{2+}$ 3) [:Sr:]$^{2+}$ 4) Sr^{2+}

Practice 50

Which electron-dot diagram is correct for a fluoride ion, F$^-$?

1) [:F:]$^-$ 2) [:F:]$^-$ 3) [F ·]-   4) [F]-

Practice 51

Which is the correct Lewis electron-dot diagram for strontium bromide?

1) Sr$^+$:Br:-   2) :Sr:$^{2+}$ Br-   3) Sr^{2+} [:Br:]$^-$ 4) Sr^{2+} 2[:Br:]$^-$

Practice 52

Which Lewis diagram is correct for a molecule of fluorine , F$_2$?

1) :F::F: 2) :F:F: 3) · F:F ·   4)   F : F

Practice 53

Which Lewis electron-dot diagram represents a compound that contains both ionic and covalent bonds?

1) 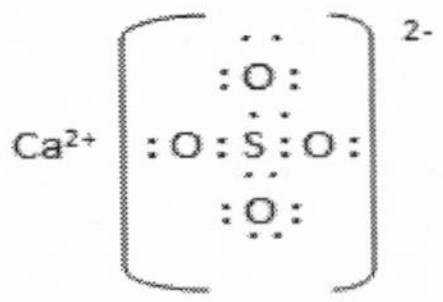 Ca^{2+} [:O:\n:O:S:O:\n:O:]$^{2-}$ 2) K$^+$ [:Br:] -   3) H :S:\nH   4) :Br:Br:

Practice 54

In the Lewis electron-dot diagram   H : Cl : , the dots represent

1) Valence electrons of H atom only   3) Valence electron for both H and Cl atom

2) Valence electrons of Cl atom only   4) All the electrons found in H and Cl atoms

Topic 4 – Chemical Bonding

Lesson 6 – Intermolecular Forces

Introduction:

Intermolecular forces are forces that exist between molecules in molecular substances. Intermolecular forces hold molecules of molecular substances together in liquid and solid states. These forces exist in molecular substances because of the unequal charge distribution within molecules. Intermolecular forces are generally weaker than the intramolecular forces (bonding between atoms) of the substance.

In this lesson, you will learn the relationship between intermolecular forces and certain physical properties of molecular substances.

27. Properties of Molecular Substances and Intermolecular Forces

Certain physical properties of molecular substances depend on the strength of the intermolecular forces holding the molecules together.

These properties include:

Melting point, boiling point and vapor pressure.

The stronger the strength of intermolecular forces:

The higher the melting and boiling points of the substance.

The lower the vapor pressure of the substance.

Strength of intermolecular forces holding molecules together depends on the following three factors:

The polarity of the molecules

The phase of the substance (or distance between molecules)

The size of the molecules

28. Bonding in Water

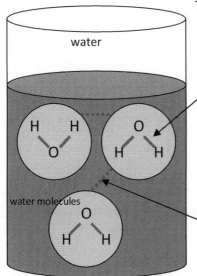

water

water molecules

Two types of bonding exist in water and in all molecular substances:

Intramolecular and intermolecular bonding.

Intramolecular (polar covalent bonding)

. Holds O and H atoms together to make water molecules

. Chemical properties (or reactions) of water require the breaking of this bond

. A stronger bond than the intermolecular force

Intermolecular (hydrogen bonding)

. Holds water molecules together in the solid and liquid states

. Physical properties (such as vapor pressure, boiling and melting points) depend on the strength of this bond

. A weaker force than the intramolecular bond

29. Molecular Polarity and Intermolecular Forces

The strength of intermolecular forces in molecular substances varies depending on the polarity of the molecules. In general, intermolecular forces are stronger in polar substances than in nonpolar substances. In other words, molecules in polar substances are held more strongly and tightly to each other than molecules in nonpolar substances. For this reason, polar substances generally have higher melting and boiling points, and a lower vapor pressure in comparison to nonpolar substances.

Below is a comparison of boiling points between two substances.

Molecular substance	Relative strength of intermolecular force	Relative boiling point
CH_4 (nonpolar)	Weaker	Lower ($-161^{\circ}C$)
H_2O (polar)	Stronger	Higher ($100^{\circ}C$)

Concept Task: Be able to determine which molecular substance (by formula) has the highest or lowest Boiling Point (BP).

For Lowest BP:
Look for a formula of a nonpolar substance

For Highest BP :
Look for a formula of a polar substance

30. Phases of Substances and Intermolecular Forces

The strength of intermolecular forces of a substance vary depending on the phase of the substance.

In general, intermolecular forces are stronger between molecules of a substance in the solid phase. The force is weaker when the substance is in the gas phase. In other words, molecules of a substances in a solid phase are held more tightly together than molecules of the substance in a gas phase. For this reason, substances with high intermolecular forces may exist as a solid, while similar substances with weaker intermolecular forces, under the same conditions, will exist as a liquid or gas. This relationship between strength of intermolecular and phase is best seen among the halogens (group 17 elements).

Below is a comparison among the halogens .

Note the relationship between the phase of each halogen relative to the strength of intermolecular forces.

Halogen	Phase at STP	Relative Strength of intermolecular forces
F_2 and Cl_2	Gas	Weaker
Br_2	Liquid	A little stronger
I_2	Solid	Strongest

At STP, Iodine is a solid, and fluorine and chlorine are gases because iodine has stronger intermolecular forces when compared to fluorine or chlorine.

31. Size of molecule and Intermolecular Forces

The strength of intermolecular forces vary among similar nonpolar substances depending on the size of their molecules. In general, intermolecular forces are stronger in a nonpolar substance with large molecular mass than in a similar substance with a smaller molecular mass. In other words, molecules of a nonpolar substance with a large molecular mass are held more strongly and tighter together when compared to molecules of a similar substance with a smaller molecular mass. For this reason, the boiling and melting points of a nonpolar substance with a large molecular mass are generally higher than those of a similar substance with a smaller molecular mass.

Concept Task: Be able to determine which nonpolar substance has the highest or lowest boiling point (BP)

For Lowest BP: Determine and choose a substance with the smallest mass.

For Highest BP: Determine and choose a substance with the biggest mass.

Below, three groups of nonpolar substances are given. Note the relationship between the size of the molecules in each group to their strength of intermolecular forces (IMF) and boiling points.

Halogens	Noble gases	Hydrocarbons	Relative Size of molecule	Relative Strength of IMF	Relative Boiling point
F_2	He	CH_4	Smallest	Weakest	Lowest
Cl_2	Ne	C_2H_6			
Br_2	Ar	C_3H_8	Biggest	Strongest	Highest

Note: As the size of the molecules increases among similar nonpolar substances, the strength of intermolecular forces, as well as boiling and melting points also increase.

32. Hydrogen Bonding

Hydrogen bonding is a type of intermolecular force that exists in highly polar substances.

Among similar polar substances, the degree of polarity varies. This is to say that when similar polar substances are compared, one is always going to be more polar than the other. Because of the differences in polarity, the strength of intermolecular forces also varies among similar polar substances.

Hydrogen bonding is a strong intermolecular force that exists in **H_2O** (water) , **NH_3** (ammonia) and **HF** (hydrogen fluoride), but not in similar substances.

When H_2O is compared to a similar substance (such as H_2S), H_2O has a stronger intermolecular force (hydrogen bonding) than H_2S, which has a weaker dipole-dipole attraction. As a result, the *boiling point* and *melting point of H_2O is higher than those of H_2S.*

The same can be said of NH_3 and HF when they are compared to similar substances (PH_3 and HCl respectively).

Hydrogen bonding exists in these three substances (H_2O, NH_3 and HF) but not in similar substances because the hydrogen atom in each formula is bonded to an atom (O, N, or F) which has a *small radius* and *high electronegativity.* The combination of small radius and high electronegativity allow molecules of H_2O, NH_3 and HF to be highly polar (more polar) in comparison to similar substances.

Topic 4 – Chemical Bonding

33. Intermolecular Forces: Practice questions

Concept Task: Be able to answer questions relating to intermolecular forces

Practice 55
Which set of properties are due to the strength of intermolecular forces between molecules?
1) Vapor pressure and boiling point
2) Boiling point and Molar density
3) Molar mass and vapor pressure
4) Vapor pressure and Molar density

Practice 56
Hydrogen bonding is formed between molecules when the molecules contain a hydrogen atom that is covalently bonded to an atom that has
1) Small atomic radius and low electronegativity
2) Large atomic radius and low electronegativity
3) Small atomic radius and high electronegativity
4) Large atomic radius and low electronegativity

Practice 57
Oxygen, Nitrogen, and Fluorine bond with hydrogen to form molecules. These molecules are attracted to each other by
1) Ionic bonds
2) Hydrogen bonds
3) Electrovalent bonds
4) Coordinate covalent bonds

Practice 58
Which kind of bonds are found in a sample of H_2O (l) ?
1) Covalent bonds, only
2) Hydrogen bonds, only
3) Both covalent and hydrogen bonds
4) Both ionic and hydrogen bonds

Practice 59
In which substance would the force of attraction between the molecules be considered hydrogen bonding?
1) O_2 (g)   2) NH_3(l)   3) NaCl (s)   4) CO_2 (g)

Practice 60
Which of the following compounds has the highest normal boiling point?
1) H_2O(l)   2) H_2S(l)   3) H_2Se(l)   4) H_2Te (l)

Practice 61
Which of these compounds would have the highest boiling point?
1) HI   2) HBr   3) HCl   4) HF

Practice 62
Which of these nonpolar substances at STP likely has the highest boiling point?
1) I_2 2) Br_2 3) Cl_2 4) F_2

Practice 63
Which of the followings has the lowest boiling point?
1) He   2) Xe   3) Ne   4) Kr

Practice 64
Which of the following substance has the lowest normal boiling point?
1) C_5H_{10} 2) C_4H_8 3) C_3H_6 4) C_2H_4

Practice 65
The abnormally high boiling point of HF as compared to HCl is primarily due to intermolecular forces of attraction called
1) Network bonds
2) Van der Waals forces
3) Electrovalent forces
4) Hydrogen bonding

Practice 66
At 298 K, the vapor pressure of H_2O is less than the vapor pressure of CH_3OH because H_2O has
1) Larger molecules
2) Smaller molecules
3) Stronger intermolecular forces
4) Weaker intermolecular forces

Concept Terms

Key vocabulary terms and concepts from Topic 4 are listed below. You should know definition and facts related to each term and concept.

1. Chemical bonding
2. Octet of electrons
3. Potential energy
4. Exothermic
5. Endothermic
6. Intramolecular forces
7. Electronegativity
8. Electronegativity difference an bonding
9. Ionic bond
10. Covalent bond
11. Polar covalent bond
12. Nonpolar covalent bond
13. Network solid covalent bond
14. Coordinate covalent bond
15. Metallic bond
16. Ionic substance
17. Molecular (covalent) substance
18. Metallic substance
19. Properties of metallic substance
20. Properties of ionic substances
21. Properties of molecular substances
22. Properties of network solids
23. Bond polarity
24. Molecular polarity
25. Molecular symmetry
26. Molecular shapes
27. Polar molecule
28. Nonpolar molecule
29. Lewis electron-dot diagram
30. Intermolecular forces
31. Hydrogen bonding

Concept Tasks

Concept tasks from Topic 4 are listed below. You should know how to solve problems and answer questions related to each concept task.

1. Determining which noble gas element an atom (or atoms) in a bond resembles
2. Recognizing and interpreting bond formation or exothermic reaction equation
3. Recognizing and interpreting bond breaking or endothermic reaction equation
4. Determining which formula contains a given bond type
5. Recognizing and determining formulas and names of metallic substances
6. Recognizing and determining formulas and names of ionic substances
7. Recognizing and determining formulas or names of binary compounds
8. Recognizing formulas or names of substances containing both ionic and covalent bond
9. Recognizing and determining formulas and names of molecular substances
10. Determining formula or name of a substance with a given set of properties
11. Determining properties given of formula or name of a substance
12. Determining molecular symmetry of a formula or structure
13. Recognizing molecular shapes of a formula
14. Determining formula or name of nonpolar substance (or molecule)
15. Determining formula or name of polar substance (or molecule)
16. Determining which formula is most or least ionic, covalent or polar
17. Drawing and recognizing Lewis electron-dot diagrams for neutral atom
18. Drawing and recognizing Lewis electron-dot diagrams for positive ions
19. Drawing and recognizing Lewis electron-dot diagrams for negative ions
20. Drawing and recognizing Lewis electron-dot diagrams for ionic compounds
21. Drawing and recognizing Lewis electron-dot diagrams for diatomic molecules
22. Drawing and recognizing Lewis electron-dot diagrams molecular substances
23. Determining which molecular substance (by formula) has the highest or lowest Boiling Point (BP)
24. Determining which nonpolar substances has the highest or lowest Boiling Point (BP).
25. Determining and recognizing formulas and names of substances with hydrogen bonding

Topic 5 – Chemical Formulas and Equations

Topic outline

In this topic, you will learn the following concepts:

. Interpretation of chemical formulas

. Types of chemical formulas

. Chemical nomenclature

. Interpretation of chemical equations

. Types of chemical equations

. Balancing chemical equations

Lesson 1 – Counting Atoms in Chemical Formulas

Introduction

Chemical formulas are used to represent the composition of elements and compounds (pure substances).

A chemical formula expresses the *qualitative* and *quantitative* compositions of a substance.

Qualitative information of a formula shows the types of atoms (or ions) that make up the substance.
Quantitative information of a formula shows how many of each atom (or ion) is in the formula.
The number of each atom in a formula is usually shown with a subscript.
A **subscript** in a chemical formula is the whole number written on the bottom right of each atom in a formula.

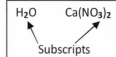

H_2O $Ca(NO_3)_2$

Subscripts

Examples of chemical formulas

NaCl (sodium chloride)   **CO$_2$** (carbon dioxide)   **H$_2$O** (water)   **H$_2$** (hydrogen)

Each of these formulas shows both qualitative and quantitative composition of the substance.

In this topic, you will learn how to interpret chemical formulas by determining their qualitative and quantitative compositions.

1. Number of Atoms in Formulas

One way to express the qualitative and quantitative compositions of a substance is to determine the number of each element in the formula.

This can be done by counting how many of each element (or atom) is shown in the formula.

Three types of compound formulas that you will often see are listed below.
For each type, example formula, number of each atom and the total number of atoms in the formula are given. Study these examples to learn how to count atoms in similar formulas.

Concept Task: Be able to count atoms in different types of formulas.

Types of formulas	Example formula	Number of each atom	Total number of atoms
Simple formula	H_2SO_4	2 **H** atoms 1 **S** atom 4 **O** atoms	**Three** different atoms. **7** total atoms
Formula with parentheses	$(NH_4)_2O$	2 **N** atoms (1 x 2) 8 **H** atoms (4 x 2) 1 **O** atom	**Three** different atoms. 11 total atoms
Formula of a hydrate	$CuSO_4 \cdot 5H_2O$	1 **Cu** atom 1 **S** atom 9 **O** atoms (4 + 5) 10 **H** atoms (5 x 2)	**Four** different atoms. 21 total atoms

91

Topic 5 – Chemical Formulas and Equations

2. Ratio of Ions in Formulas

Another way of expressing the qualitative and quantitative compositions of a substance is to determine the ratio of ions in the formula. Ionic compounds are composed of positive and negative ions. Qualitative and quantitative composition of ionic compounds can also be expressed by the number of each ion in a formula.

Three types of ionic compound formulas that you will often see are listed on the table below.
For each type, example formula, ions in the formula, and ratio of these ions are given.

Type of formulas	Example formula	Ions in formula	Ratio of ions in formula
Binary ionic formula	$CaCl_2$ calcium chloride	Ca^{2+} Cl^{-} calcium ion chloride ion	**1** Ca^{2+} : **2** Cl^{-}
Polyatomic ion formula (with parentheses)	$Al_2(SO_4)_3$ aluminum sulfate	Al^{3+} SO_4^{2-} aluminum ion sulfate ion	**2** Al^{3+} : **3** SO_4^{2-}
Polyatomic ion formula (without parentheses)	KNO_3 potassium nitrate	K^{+} NO_3^{-} potassium ion nitrate ion	**1** K^{+} : **1** NO_3^{-}

Use Reference *Table E* to confirm symbol and name of a polyatomic ion.
Use the *Periodic Table* to confirm charge and symbol of an element.

3. Qualitative and Quantitative Composition: Practice problems

Concept Task: Be able to determine number of atoms or total number of atoms in formulas

Practice 1
What is the total number of moles of sulfur atoms in 1 mole of $Fe_2(SO_4)_3$?
1) 1   2) 12   3) 3   4) 4

Practice 2
How many hydrogen atoms are found in the hydrate $(NH_4)_3PO_4 \cdot 5H_2O$?
1) 12   2) 19   3) 22   4) 14

Practice 3
What is the total number of atoms in the formula $Ca(ClO_3)_2$?
1) 3   2) 7   3) 2   4) 9

Practice 4
What is the total number of atoms in one formula unit of $MgSO_4 \cdot 7H_2O$?
1) 27   2) 13   3) 16   4) 20

Practice 5
How many different kinds of atoms are present in NH_4NO_3 ?
1) 7   2) 9   3) 3   4) 4

Concept Task: Be able to determine ratio of ions in formulas

Practice 6
In the compound Al_2S_3, the mole ratio of aluminum ion to sulfur ion is
1) 2 : 3   2) 3 : 2   3) 13 : 16   4) 27 : 16

Practice 7
What is the ratio of sodium ion to phosphate ion in the formula Na_3PO_4 ?
1) 4 : 3   2) 3 : 4   3) 1 : 3   4) 3 : 1

Practice 8
In a sample of solid $Ba(NO_3)_2$, the ratio of barium ions to nitrate ions is
1) 1 : 1   2) 1 : 2   3) 1 : 3   4) 1 : 6

Practice 9
What is the ratio of ammonium ion to sulfate ion in the formula $(NH_4)_2SO_4$?
1) 2 : 1   2) 1 : 2   3) 8 : 4   4) 4 : 1

Topic 5 – Chemical Formulas and Equations

Lesson 2 – Types of Chemical Formulas

Introduction:

There are three types of chemical formulas that are used to show compositions of substances.

In this lesson, you will learn about molecular formulas, empirical formulas, and structural formulas.

4. Types of Formulas

A **molecular formula** is a formula showing the true composition of a known substance.

A **structural formula** is a formula showing how atoms of a substance are bonded together.

An **empirical formula** is a formula in which the elements are in the smallest whole-number ratio.

Examples of the three formulas are shown below:

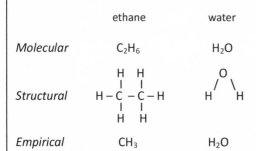

	ethane	water
Molecular	C_2H_6	H_2O
Structural		
Empirical	CH_3	H_2O

C_2H_6 is reduced to CH_3 by dividing each subscript of the formula by **2** (The Greatest Common Factor)

$C_6H_{12}O_6$ can be reduced to CH_2O by dividing each subscript of the formula by **6** (The Greatest Common Factor)

Concept Task: Be able to recognize empirical formulas

Practice 10

Which is an empirical formula?

1) C_2H_4 3) Ca_3P_2
2) $C_6H_{12}O_6$ 4) C_4H_6

Practice 11

Which compound has the same empirical and molecular formula?

1) C_2H_6 3) $C_6H_{12}O_6$
2) H_2O_2 4) N_2O

Practice 12

An example of an empirical formula is

1) C_4H_{10} 3) $C_6H_{12}O_6$
2) $HC_2H_3O_2$ 4) CH_2O

Concept Task: Be able to reduce a molecular formula to empirical form

Practice 13

Which is the empirical formula for C_6H_{10}?

1) C_5H_3 3) CH_2
2) C_3H_5 4) C_3H_6

Practice 14

Which molecular formula is correctly paired with its empirical formula?

1) C_2H_2 and C_2H_4 3) HO and H_2O
2) CH_2 and C_3H_8 4) NO_2 and N_2O_4

Practice 15

What is the empirical formula for a compound with the molecular formula of $C_6H_{12}Cl_2O_2$?

1) C_3H_6ClO 3) CHClO
2) CH_2ClO 4) $C_6H_{12}Cl_2O_2$

Practice 16

What is the empirical formula for the structure shown below?

```
    H  H  H  H  H  H
    |  |  |  |  |  |
H – C – C – C – C –C – C – H
    |  |  |  |  |  |
    H  F  F  F  F  H
```

1) $C_6H_{10}F_4$ 3) $C_3H_2F_2$
2) $C_3H_5H_2$ 4) CHF

Topic 5 – Chemical Formulas and Equations

Lesson 3 – Chemical Nomenclature

Introduction

There are millions of known chemical substances, with many being discovered.

Chemical nomenclature refers to the systematic rules for naming and writing formulas of chemical substances. The International Union of Pure and Applied Chemistry (**IUPAC**) is an organization that makes recommendations as to how chemical substances are named.

In this lesson, you will learn how to apply IUPAC rules to writing formulas and names for compounds in different classes of *inorganic* compounds.

LOOKing Ahead ⟹ Topic 10-Organic Chemistry: You will learn IUPAC names for *organic* compounds.

Formula Writing

A chemical formula is correctly written for a known substance when both the qualitative and quantitative information of the formula are both correct. This to say that:
. The element (or ion) symbols in the formula must all be correct for the substance it represents
. The subscripts of the elements (or ions) must also be correctly represented in the formula

A compound formula must be neutral: This is to say that:
 . The sum of positive and negative charges in the formula must be equal to Zero. (equalization of charges
Correct subscripts in a formula allow charges to balance out and produce a formula that is neutral.

Steps to writing correct formulas to substances are discussed in the next few sets.

5. Writing Formulas for Ionic Compounds

When the IUPAC name for an ionic compound is given, use the steps below to write its correct formula.

Step 1: **Write** the correct ion symbols for the chemical name.
   Use the Periodic Table to get the correct ion symbol for an element.
   Use Table E to get the correct polyatomic ion symbol.
    Always put parentheses around polyatomic atoms. Ex. $(SO_4)^{2-}$

Step 2: **Criss-cross** charge values so one becomes the subscript for the other.

Step 3: **Clean up** formula after criss-crossing by:
   Reducing subscripts that are reducible to empirical form.

   For polyatomic ion compounds:
   Do not change subscripts of the polyatomic ion

   Remove parentheses if subscript outside parentheses is a 1

   Keep parentheses if subscript outside parentheses is greater than a 1

Steps shown above and on the next pages are to ensure that your final (correct) formula has the correct element symbols and correct subscripts for the compound name that is given. If you can write correct formulas without going through all these steps, you should do so.

Topic 5 – Chemical Formulas and Equations

6. Writing Formulas Ionic Compounds

Binary ionic compounds have formulas that are composed of two different elements: A metal and a nonmetal. IUPAC names of binary compounds always end with –*ide*.
Examples: Calcium brom*ide*, Aluminum sulf*ide*, and Zinc ox*ide*

Concept Task: Be able to write correct chemical formulas to binary ionic compounds.

Examples
Steps listed on the previous page are used to write correct formulas to the three binary ionic compounds below.

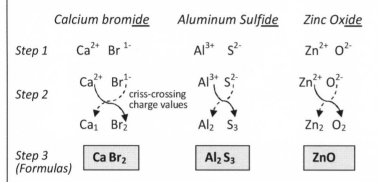

	Calcium bromide	*Aluminum Sulfide*	*Zinc Oxide*
Step 1	Ca^{2+} Br^{1-}	Al^{3+} S^{2-}	Zn^{2+} O^{2-}

Step 3 (Formulas)   **Ca Br$_2$**   **Al$_2$S$_3$**   **ZnO**

Ionic compounds containing a polyatomic ion

Polyatomic ions are composed of two or more atoms with an excess charge. Most polyatomic ions have negative charges. *Reference Table E lists some common polyatomic ions .* A polyatomic ion can combine with element or another polyatomic ion of opposite charge to form various compounds. IUPAC names of polyatomic ions typically end with -*ate* or –*ite*. Examples of compounds containing a polyatomic ion are: sodium *nitrate*, calcium *sulfite*, and *ammonium* oxide.

Concept Task: Be able to write correct chemical formulas to ionic compounds containing a polyatomic ion.

Examples
Steps listed on the previous page are used to write correct formulas to three ionic compounds containing a polyatomic ion.

	Sodium Nitrate	*Calcium Sulfite*	*Ammonium Oxide*
Step 1	$Na^{+1}(NO_3)^{1-}$	$Ca^{2+}(SO_3)^{2-}$	$(NH_4)^{1+}$ O^{2-}
Step 2	$Na_1(NO_3)_1$	$Ca_2(SO_3)_2$	$(NH_4)_2O_1$

Step 3 (formulas)   **NaNO$_3$**   **CaSO$_3$**   **(NH$_4$)$_2$O**

Practice 17
What is the correct chemical formula for cesium oxide?
1) CsO_2 3) Cs_2O_3
2) CsO 4) Cs_2O

Practice 18
Which formula is correct for magnesium sulfide?
1) MgS 3) Mg_2S_2
2) MnS 4) Mn_2S_2

Practice 19
Which is the formula for calcium nitride?
1) CaN 3) Ca_2N_3
2) Ca_3N_3 4) Ca_3N_2

Practice 20

Write the correct formulas for:

Aluminum nitride

Strontium fluoride

Silver iodide

Practice 21
Which formula is correct for magnesium phosphate?
1) Mg_2PO_7 3) $MgPO_4$
2) $Mg_2(PO_4)_3$ 4) $Mg_3(PO_4)_2$

Practice 22
Which is the correct formula for ammonium sulfate?
1) NH_4SO_4 3) $NH_4(SO_4)_2$
2) $(NH_4)_2(SO_4)_2$ 4) $(NH_4)_2SO_4$

Practice 23
Which is the correct formula for zinc carbonate?
1) $ZnCO_3$ 3) $Zn_2(CO_3)_2$
2) $ZnCO_6$ 4) $ZnCO$

Practice 24
Write the correct formulas for:

Lithium hydrogen carbonate

Cadmium nitrite

Calcium thiosulfate

Topic 5 – Chemical Formulas and Equations

7. Writing Formulas for Compounds Containing Element with Multiple + Charges

The **stock system** nomenclature uses Roman numerals in parentheses to distinguish names of compounds produced by different positive oxidation states of an atom. For an elements with multiple positive (+) oxidation numbers, a compound made with one oxidation charge of the element has a different formula, as well as properties, from a compound made with another oxidation charge of that same element. Examples of stock system names and the interpretation of the Roman numerals are given below.

Iron (**II**) chloride   (**II**) indicates that iron with a charge of **+2** formed this compound with chlorine.

Iron (**III**) chloride   (**III**) indicates that iron with a charge of **+3** formed this compound with chlorine.

Nitrogen (**IV**) oxide   (**IV**) indicates that nitrogen with a charge of **+4** formed this compound with oxygen

Concept Task: Be able to write correct chemical formulas to compounds with Stock System nomenclature.

Examples

Iron (**II**) chloride	Iron (**III**) chloride	Nitrogen (**IV**) oxide
↓	↓	↓
Fe^{2+} Cl^{1-}	Fe^{3+} Cl^{1-}	N^{4+} O^{2-}
FeCl₂	**FeCl₃**	N_2O_4
		NO₂

Practice 25
The formula for lead (II) oxide is
1) PbO 3) PbO_2
2) Pb_2O 4) Pb_2O_3

Practice 26
The correct formula for manganese (IV) sulfide is
1) Mn_4S 3) MnS_2
2) Mn_4S_2 4) Mn_4S_4

Practice 27
Which formula is correct for copper (II) chlorate?
1) Cu_2Cl 3) $CuCl_2$
2) Cu_2ClO_3 4) $Cu(ClO_3)_2$

Practice 28
Which formula correctly represents lead (IV) thiosulfate?
1) $Pb_2S_2O_3$ 3) $Pb(S_2O_3)_2$
2) PbS_2O_3 4) $PbSO_3$

Practice 29.

Write the chemical formulas for:

Chromium (III) oxide

Titanium (IV) sulfate

Iron (II) dichromate

Phosphorus (V) sulfide

Naming Formulas

8. Naming Ionic Formulas

The IUPAC name is correctly written for a given formula when all of the following are represented correctly.
. Atoms and/or ions in the formula are named correctly
. Name ending , if necessary, is applied correctly
. Roman numeral, if necessary, is correctly used

When a chemical formula of an ionic compound is given, use the following steps to determine its correct IUPAC name.

Step 1: ***Write*** names of elements and/or polyatomic ions in the formula

Step 2: ***Change*** ending of a nonmetal element to –*ide*

       Do not make any change to name of a metal or polyatomic ion.

Step 3: For a metal with multiple positive (+) oxidation numbers, determine its charge value and use it in parentheses to name the compound

Topic 5 – Chemical Formulas and Equations

9. Naming Ionic Compounds

Binary ionic compounds contain just two elements: a metal and a nonmetal. *Examples* are $ZnCl_2$, CaO and Al_2N_3. Nomenclature of binary compounds involves changing the nonmetal ending to -*ide*

Concept Task: Be able to name binary ionic compound formulas.

Examples
Steps listed on the previous page are used to write correct the name to each of the three formulas below.

$ZnCl_2$	CaO	Al_2N_3
Zinc Chlor*ine*	Calcium Ox*ygen*	Aluminum Nitr*ogen*
Zinc Chlor*ide*	**Calcium ox*ide***	**Aluminum nitr*ide***

Compounds containing a polyatomic ion generally contain three or more elements. Examples are $Mg_2(PO_4)_3$, NH_4NO_3 and NH_4Cl. When naming compounds containing a polyatomic ion, no change should be made to the name of the polyatomic ion or to the name of the metal. Polyatomic ions are listed on *Reference Table E*.

Concept Task: Be able to name ionic compounds containing a polyatomic ion

$Mg_2(PO_4)_3$	NH_4NO_3	NH_4Cl
Magnesium phosphate	**Ammonium nitrate**	**Ammonium chlor*ide***

Compounds containing an element with multiple oxidation numbers must be named using the Stock System. In each of the three formulas below, the first element has multiple + oxidation numbers (See the Periodic Table to confirm). A Roman numeral (in parentheses) is used in naming to identify which positive charge of the element formed the compound.

SnF_4	N_2O	$Fe_3(PO_4)_2$
Tin (IV) fluor*ide*	**Nitrogen (I) ox*ide***	**Iron (II) phosphate**

In some formulas (like the three above) the *subscript* of the second symbol in each formula is used as the Roman Numeral (or the +charge) value in the ( ). In some formulas (like the two below), the *+ charge value* of the metal is determined mathematically by following steps given in the box to left.

Assign –charge value.

Multiply – charge by *subscript* to get total – in formula .

Determine **total +** needed to make charges = 0

Use **+ charge** as **Roman numeral** in ( ) to name the formula.

CrN_2	$MnSO_4$
$Cr\ N_2^{3-}$	$Mn\ (SO_4)^{2-}$
$2 \times 3- = -6$	$1 \times 2- = -2$
+6	**+2**
Chromium (VI) nitr*ide*	**Manganese (II) sulfate**

Practice 30
What is the correct IUPAC name for the formula Na_2S?
1) Sodium (III) sulfide
2) Sodium sulfide
3) Sodium (III) sulfate
4) Sodium sulfate

Practice 31
Write the correct names for:

FrO

Ag_2S

ZrI_4

Practice 32
What is the correct name for the compound with the formula $AlPO_4$
1) Aluminum (IV) phosphate
2) Aluminum (III) phosphite
3) Aluminum phosphate
4) Aluminum phosphite

Practice 33
Write the correct names for:

$Ca(MnO_4)_2$

$Al_2(SO_3)_3$

Practice 34
What is the correct name for the compound $CrPO_4$?
1) Chromium (II) phosphate
2) Chromium (II) phosphide
3) Chromium (III) phosphate
4) Chromium (III) phosphide

Practice 35
The correct IUPAC name for PbO_2 is
1) Lead (I) oxide
2) Lead (II) oxide
3) Lead (III) oxide
4) Lead (IV) oxide

Practice 36
Write the correct IUPAC names for the following compounds:

VBr_2

$Co(HSO_4)_3$

$Mn(CrO_4)_2$

10. Writing and Naming Covalent (Molecular) Substances

Molecular (covalent) compounds are composed only of nonmetal atoms. **Binary molecular** compounds, which contain two different nonmetals, are commonly named with IUPAC recommended prefixes. A **prefix** in a chemical name indicates how many of the nonmetal atom is in the given compound.

The table below lists prefixes for naming covalent compounds.

Number of atom	Prefix	Number of atom	Prefix
1	mono-	6	hexa-
2	di-	7	hepta-
3	tri-	8	octa-
4	tetra-	9	nona-
5	penta-	10	deca-

Concept Task: Be able to write a formula to a given molecular name.

Examples

Three common molecular substances are given below. Their formulas are written by following a few simple rules that are listed below.

. The prefix next to a nonmetal name is used as subscript for that element.

. Absence of a prefix indicate that there is just one of that atom.

. No criss-crossing or reducing of formula into empirical form.

Molecular name	Carbon **di**oxide	Carbon **mono**xide	**di**nitrogen **mono**xide
Interpretation	1 C **2** O	**1** C **1** O	**2** N 1 O
Formula	CO_2	CO	N_2O

Concept Task: Be able to name a molecular substance from a given formula.

Examples

Formulas to three molecular substances are given below. Their IUPAC names are determined by following a few simple rules that are listed below.

. Subscripts are used as prefixes in naming.

. No prefix is used when there is just one of the first nonmetal atom (see PCl_3).

. The "a" or "o" of a prefix is dropped if the addition of the prefix resulted in a name having two vowels next to each other (see N_2O_5).
In N_2O_5, the *a* in pent**ao**xide is dropped, and the formula is correctly named *pentoxide*.

. Name ending for the second nonmetal atom must be changed to *-ide*

PCl_3	N_2O_5	H_2S
1 Phosphorus **3** Chlorine	**2** nitrogen **5** oxygen	**2** hydrogen **1** sulfur
Phosphorus **trichloride**	**di**nitrogen **pent**oxide	**di**hydrogen **mono**sulfide

Practice 37

Write the correct chemical formulas for the following compounds:

Dibismuth trichloride

Silicon tetrafluoride

Ditatanium trioxide

Tetraphosphorus hexoxide

Carbon disulfide

Boron triiodide

Practice 38

Write the correct IUPAC name for each of the following formulas:

H_2S

OF_2

Hg_2Cl_2

XeF_6

V_2H

PF_5

Topic 5 – Chemical Formulas and Equations

Lesson 4 – Chemical Equations

Introduction

Equations show changes that are taking place in a substance. There are three major types of changes. Each can be represented with an equation.

Chemicals equations show changes in chemical compositions of one or more substances to other substances.

Example $2H_2(g) + O_2(g) ---> 2H_2O(l)$

Physical equations show a change of a substance from one phase to a different phase without changing its chemical compositions.

Example $H_2O(s) -------> H_2O(l)$

Nuclear equations show changes in the nucleus contents of one or more atoms to that of other atoms.

Example $^{220}Fr ---------> {}^4He + {}^{216}At$

In this lesson of Topic 5, only chemical changes and equations will be discussed.

⇐L👀KING Back : Topic 1 – Matter and energy : Phase (physical) changes and equations were discussed.

L👀KING Ahead ⇒ Topic 12 – Nuclear chemistry: Nuclear changes and equations will be discussed.

11. Chemical Equations

A **chemical equation** uses symbols to show changes in chemical compositions of substances during a chemical change. A **chemical reaction** is a means by which chemical changes occur.

Reactants are the starting substances that will go through the chemical change.
Reactants are shown to the *left* of the arrow in equations.

Products are the substances that remained after a change has occurred.
Products are shown to the *right* of the arrow in equations.

An **arrow** separates reactants from products, and can be read as "yields" or "produces."

A **coefficient** is a whole number in front of the substances to show the number of moles of each substance taking part in the reaction. In all balanced equations the relative number of moles of substances can be determined. Moles is a unit of quantity used to express the amount of substances present a sample matter.

L👀KING AHEAD ⇒Topic 6: Moles will be discussed in more details.

An example of a chemical equation is shown below.

Reactants	yields or produces	Products

$Zn(s) + \mathbf{2}HCl(aq)$ ------------------------> $ZnCl_2(aq) + H_2(g)$

Coefficient of 2 : (indicates that there are 2 moles of HCl)

Coefficient of 2 or more is always written in front of the substance in equations.

Coefficient of 1: Indicates that there is 1 mole of $ZnCl_2$.

A coefficient of 1 is never written in front of the substance.

(s) , (l) , (g) , (aq) are sometimes written to show phases of the substances taking part in the reaction.

Topic 5 – Chemical Formulas and Equations

12. Types of Reactions

Four types of chemical reactions are defined below. To the right of each type of reaction are example diagram and equation to represent the reaction..

Synthesis reactions always involve two or more substances as reactants. During a synthesis reaction, the reactants combine to form one product.

Decomposition reactions always involve a single substance as a reactant. During a decomposition reaction, the reactant breaks down (or decomposes) into two or more products.

Single replacement reactions likely involve a compound and a free element as reactants. During a single replacement reaction, the free element replaces one of the elements in the compound to form a different compound and a different free element. This reaction occurs spontaneously only when the free element reactant is more reactive than the similar element in the compound it is replacing.

Double replacement (**metathesis**) reactions usually involve two compounds in aqueous phase. During a double replacement reaction, the ions of the compounds switch with each other. The result is a formation of products with two different compound formulas.

Combustion reactions typically involve the burning of an organic substance in the presence of oxygen. Water and carbon dioxide are usually the products in most combustion reactions. You will learn more about combustion reactions in Topic 10.

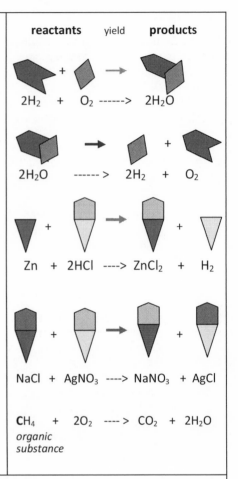

reactants   yield   **products**

$2H_2$ + O_2 ------> $2H_2O$

$2H_2O$ ------ > $2H_2$ + O_2

Zn + $2HCl$ ----> $ZnCl_2$ + H_2

$NaCl$ + $AgNO_3$ ----> $NaNO_3$ + $AgCl$

CH_4 + $2O_2$ ---- > CO_2 + $2H_2O$
organic substance

Concept Task: Be able to identify reaction types.

Practice 39

Which equation represents a single replacement reaction?
1) H^+ + OH^- -------- > H_2O
2) $2Cu$ + O_2 --------- > $2CuO$
3) $CuCO_3$ -------------- > CuO + CO_2
4) Ag + $2CuNO_3$ ----- > $Ag(NO_3)_2$ + $2Cu$

Practice 40

Which of the following equations is showing a decomposition reaction?
1) $(NH_4)_2CO_3$ ---------> $2NH_3$ + CO_2 + H_2O
2) $4NH_3$ + $5O_2$ ------ > $4NO$ + $6H_2O$
3) NH_3 + H_2O ------- > NH_4OH
4) N_2 + $3H_2$ ------ > $2NH_3$

Practice 41

The reaction
$$3CaO + P_2O_5 \ -----> Ca_3(PO_4)_2$$
is best described as

1) Synthesis
2) Decomposition
3) Single replacement
4) Double replacement

Practice 42

Given the equation:
$$CuSO_4 + Pb(NO_3)_2 \ ---> PbSO_4 + Cu(NO_3)_2$$
What type of reaction is represented by the equation?

1) Decomposition
2) Single replacement
3) Synthesis
4) Double replacement

13. Balanced Equations (Conservation of Atoms)

Law of Conservation states that during a chemical reaction neither atoms, mass, charges nor energy are created or destroyed. This means that during a chemical reaction, atoms, mass, charges, and energy are conserved so that their amounts are the same before and after the reaction.

A **Balanced chemical** equation is a way of showing conservation in chemical reactions.

In the balanced equation below, atoms on the reactant and product sides are counted to show conservation.

$$N_2 \quad + \quad 3H_2 \quad \text{-----------} \rightarrow \quad 2NH_3$$

2 N	2 N
6 H	6 H
atoms of reactants =	**atoms of product**
(before reaction)	(after reaction)

The equation above is balanced because the correct combination of the *whole-number coefficients* allows the number of atoms on both sides of the equation to be equal. In other words, the substances in the reaction are represented in the correct proportion.

Note: When counting atoms in an equation, always multiply the coefficient by the subscript.

Example: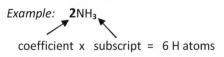

coefficient x subscript = 6 H atoms

Concept Task: Be able to recognize a balanced equation.

Practice 43
Which of the following equations is correctly balanced?

1) $CO \quad + \quad O_2 \quad \text{-------} > \quad 2CO_2$
2) $2SO_2 \quad + \quad O_2 \quad \text{--------} > \quad SO_3$
3) $CO \quad + \quad 2O_2 \quad \text{-------} > \quad CO_2$
4) $2SO_2 \quad + \quad O_2 \quad \text{---------} > \quad 2SO_3$

Practice 44
Which of these equations shows conservation of atoms?

1) $2KBr \quad \text{-------} > \quad 2K \quad + \quad Br_2$
2) $CuCO_3 \quad \text{-------} > \quad CuO \quad + \quad CO_2$
3) $2KClO_3 \quad \text{----} > \quad 2KCl \quad + \quad 2O_2$
4) $CaCO_3 \quad \text{-------} > \quad CO_2 \quad + \quad 2CaO$

Practice 45
If equation is balanced properly, both sides of the equation must have the same number of

1) atoms
2) molecules
3) coefficients
4) moles of molecules

14. How to Balance Equations

An equation is balanced when it contains the correct combination of *smallest whole-number coefficients*. The coefficients allow the number of each atom on both sides of the equation to be the same (conserved).

Rules to balancing equations:
. Change only the coefficients of substances. Don't ever change the subscripts of a formula
. Coefficients in the balanced equation must be in the smallest whole-number ratio

Suggestions to balancing equations
. Make a table to keep track of the number of atoms as coefficients are changed
. Try balancing one atom at a time
. Every time a coefficient is changed, RECOUNT and note the number of
 each atom affected by the change (be sure to count atoms correctly)
. Always change coefficients of free elements (ex. Na, Cl_2) last
. Always put parentheses around polyatomic ions and count them as one unit
. Be sure that your final coefficients are in smallest whole-number ratios

Topic 5 – Chemical Formulas and Equations

15. Balancing Equations

When a balancing equation problem is given as a multiple choice question, you are likely to be asked one of the following questions.

What is the coefficient in front of one of the substances in the equation?

What is the sum of all coefficients?

What is the mole ratio of the substances?

To correctly answer any of these questions you must first balance the given equation correctly. Keep in mind that if your equation is not correctly balanced, you are likely to choose the wrong choice as your answer. If the equation is balanced correctly, any of the above questions is easy to answer correctly.

Concept Task: Be able to balance equation and answer questions relating to the equation.

Example 1
Given the equation

$$NH_3 + O_2 \longrightarrow HNO_3 + H_2O$$

What is the smallest whole-number coefficient of O_2 when the equation is correctly balanced?
1) 1   2) 2   3) 3   4) 4

First: Balance the equation
Note: When counted correctly, the number of N and H are equal on both sides of the unbalanced equation. O atom is not equal on both sides. There are 4 O atoms on the right and only 2 O atoms on the left. A change in coefficient of O_2 from 1 to 2 will equalize the O atom.

$$NH_3 + \mathbf{2}O_2 \longrightarrow HNO_3 + H_2O \text{ is balanced}$$

Second: Answer question

Choose: Choice 2

Example 2
Given the unbalanced equation below:

$$\_C_3H_4 + \_O_2 \longrightarrow \_CO_2 + \_H_2O$$

What is the sum of all coefficients when the equation is correctly balanced with the smallest whole-number coefficients?

1) 20   2) 9   3) 10   4) 15

First: Balance the equation

$$\_C_3H_4 + \mathbf{\underline{4}}O_2 \longrightarrow \mathbf{\underline{3}}CO_2 + \mathbf{\underline{2}}H_2O$$

Note and add all
coefficients: **1   +   4   +   3   +   2 = 10**

Second: **Choose Choice 3**

Note: When determining sum of all coefficient, be sure to add all coefficients of 1 (as in C_3H_4). A coefficient of 1 is often not written down. Failure to add the 1 in the above problem will give choice 2 as the answer, which is wrong.

Practice 46
When the equation   _____Na + _____H_2O ----> ____H_2 + _____NaOH
is correctly balanced using the smallest whole number coefficients, what is the coefficient of H_2O ?
1) 1   2) 2   3) 3   4) 4

Practice 47
When the equation   ___C_3H_4 + ____O_2 --------> ____ CO_2 + ___H_2O
is correctly balanced using the smallest whole-number, what is the coefficient of O_2 ?
1) 1   2) 2   3) 3   4) 4

Practice 48
Given the unbalanced equation   _____H_2O_2 ---------> _____H_2O + _____O_2
What is the sum of all coefficients when the equation is balanced using the smallest whole- number coefficients?
1) 5   2) 9   3) 3   4) 4

Practice 49
Given the unbalanced equation: __$Ca(OH)_2$ + __ $(NH_4)_2SO_4$ -----> ___$CaSO_4$ + ___NH_3 + __H_2O
What is the sum of all coefficients when the equation is correctly balanced using the smallest whole-number coefficients?
1) 5   2) 7   3) 9   4) 11

Topic 5 – Chemical Formulas and Equations

16. Completing Equations

Some balancing equation problems involve determining substances that are missing in the equation. The missing substance you determined must result in a balanced equation (conservation of atoms).

Concept Task: Be able to predict a missing substance in equations.

Example 1
Given the incomplete equation below:
$$X \text{ --------> } MgCl_2 + 3O_2$$
Substance X is
1) $MgClO$ 2) $Mg(ClO)_2$ 3) $Mg(ClO_2)_2$ 4) $Mg(ClO_3)_2$

First: Count atoms on the product side:
            1 Mg   2 Cl   6 O

Note: Substance X (correct choice) must have exact same atoms

Choose: Choice 4 $Mg(ClO_3)_2$ because it contains
            1 Mg   2 Cl   6 O

Check: $Mg(ClO_3)_2$ ----> $MgCl_2 + 3O_2$ is balanced

Example 2
Given the incomplete equation:
$$4Fe + 3O_2 \text{ ----------> } 2X$$
Which compound is represented by X ?
1) FeO 2) Fe_2O_3 3) Fe_3O_2 4) Fe_3O_4

First: Count atoms on the reactant side:
            4 Fe   6 O

Note: Coefficient of X is 2. Substance X (correct choice) must have half the atoms counted above.

Choose : Choice 2 Fe_2O_3 because it contains 2 Fe and 3 O

Check: $4Fe + 3O_2 \text{ ----------> } 2Fe_2O_3$ is balanced

Practice 50
Given the balanced equation:
$$2Na + 2H_2O \text{ ----------> } 2X + H_2$$
What is the correct formula for the product represented by the letter X?
1) NaO 3) Na_2O
2) $NaOH$ 4) Na_2OH

Practice 51
Given the incomplete equation:
$$2N_2O_5 \text{ ----------------> }$$
Which set of products completes and balances the incomplete equation?
1) $2N_2 + 3O_2$ 3) $2N_2 + 2O_2$
2) $4NO_2 + O_2$ 4) $2NO + 2O_2$

Practice 52
Given the incomplete equation below:
$$3Ca(OH)_2 + 2H_3PO_4 \text{ ---> } Ca_3(PO_4)_2 + X$$
Which correctly represents X?
1) $3H_2$ 3) $3H_2O$
2) $6H_2$ 4) $6H_2O$

Practice 53
In the equation
$$X + 7O_2 \text{ -----> } 4CO_2 + 6H_2O$$
Which correctly represents X?
1) $2C_4H_6$ 3) $2C_2H_6$
2) C_2H_6 4) C_4H_6

17. Conservation of Mass in Reactions

During a chemical reaction, mass of substances before and after the reaction is conserved (stay the same), as shown below.

$$3Fe + 2O_2 \text{ ----> } Fe_3O_4$$
$$20.9 \text{ g} + 8.0 \text{ g} \qquad\qquad 28.9 \text{ g}$$

Total mass before reaction = *Total mass after reaction*
            (28.9 g)   *(28.9 g)*

Practice 54
Given the balanced equation representing a reaction:
$$2H_2 + O_2 \text{ ------> } 2H_2O$$
What is the total mass of oxygen that must react with 8 grams of hydrogen to form 72 grams of water?
1) 8 g   3) 64 g
2) 36 g   4) 80 g

Topic 5 – Chemical Formulas and Equations

Concept Terms

Below is a list of vocabulary terms from Topic 5. You should know definition and facts related to each term.

1. Chemical formula
2. Qualitative
3. Quantitative
4. Subscript
5. Molecular formula
6. Empirical formula
7. Structural formula
8. Binary compound
9. Polyatomic ion
10. Molecular compound

11. Chemical equation
12. Reactant
13. Product
14. Coefficient
15. Balanced equation
16. Law of conservation

Concept Tasks

Concept tasks from Topic 5 are listed below. You should know how to solve problems and answer questions related to each concept task .

1. Determining number of each atom and total number of atoms in simple formulas
2. Determining number of an atom and total number of atoms in formulas with parentheses
3. Recognizing empirical formulas
4. Determining empirical formula of a given molecular formula
5. Writing and recognizing appropriate chemical formulas from binary compound names
6. Writing and recognizing appropriate chemical formulas from name containing polyatomic ions
7. Writing and recognizing appropriate chemical formulas from names containing Roman numeral
8. Writing and recognizing appropriate chemical formula from names containing prefixes
9. Naming and recognizing formulas of binary ionic compounds
10. Naming and recognizing formulas of compounds containing polyatomic ions
11. Naming and recognizing formulas of compounds containing an element with multiple + charges
12. Naming and recognizing formulas of compounds containing prefixes
13. Determining reactants and products of a chemical equation
14. Determining coefficient (number of mole) of a substance in an equation
15. Determining sum of all coefficient (total number of moles) in an equation
16. Determining mole ratio of substances from equations
17. Determining types of reactions from equations
18. Determining and recognizing equation of a given type of reaction
19. Determining which equation is balanced or demonstrates conservation of mass
20. Balancing equations
21. Completing equation by determining the missing substance

Topic 6 – Stoichiometry: Mole Interpretations and Calculations

Topic outline

In this topic, you will learn the following concepts:

. Moles and Calculations in Formulas

. Gram formula mass calculation

. Mole - mass calculation

. Percent composition

. Molecular formulas

. Moles and Calculations in Equations

. Mole ratio in balanced equations

. Mole – mole problems

. Volume – volume problems

. Mass – mass calculations

Lesson 1 – Mole Calculations in Formulas

Introduction

A **mole** is a unit that describes a quantity of 6.02×10^{23}. A mole is, therefore, a unit of quantity in the same sense that a dozen refers to the quantity of 12.

The following are all units of quantities:

> **1 dozen** eggs   = **12** eggs

> **1 gross** of apples = **144** apples.

> **1 mole** of atoms = **602000000000000000000000** atoms.

A mole is a very large unit of quantity that is only used to represent the amount of particles (atoms, molecules, ions, or electrons, etc) in chemical substances.

The number, **602000000000000000000000**, is called **Avogadro's number**. It is always written in its scientific notation form: 6.02×10^{23} .

Stoichiometry is the study and calculations of relative quantities of substances in chemical formulas (composition stoichiometry) and in chemical equations (reaction stoichiometry).

In this lesson, you will learn to interpret and calculate molar quantities in formulas.

$$1 \text{ mole } = 6.02 \times 10^{23}$$

1. Mole Interpretations in Chemistry Questions

The term "mole" shows up often in chemistry questions that involve formulas and equations. How you interpret "mole" in a question depends on the context in which it is being used in that question.

Below are example questions in which the term "mole" is being used.

How many **moles** of hydrogen are in **1 mole** of the formula H_3PO_4?

What is the mass of **one mole** of H_3PO_4?

What is the **mole ratio** of H_2 to O_2 in the equation: $2H_2$ + O_2 ------ > $2H_2O$

The mole terminology is used in slightly different ways in each question. Your ability to answer the above questions correctly depends on your understanding of mole concepts and its many interpretations.

2. Moles of Atoms in Formulas

The number of moles of atoms in a given formula can be determined by counting how many atoms there are in the formula. However, when there are more (or fewer) than one mole of a formula, determining the number of moles of atoms becomes a bit more involve than just counting the atoms.

⇐ LⓞⓞKing Back: Topic 5: Chemical formulas. You learned how to count atoms in formulas.

Concept Task: Be able to determine the number of moles of an atom in a given mole of a formula

moles of atom = Given moles x number of the atom in formula

Given the formula $Al_2(SO_4)_3$

Example 1

How many moles of sulfur atoms are in 1 mole of $Al_2(SO_4)_3$?

moles of S = 1 mole x 3 S atoms = **3 moles S atom**

Example 2 (two different setups to solve)

How many moles of sulfur atoms are in 2 moles of $Al_2(SO_4)_3$?

Setup and solve using above equation

moles of S = 2 moles x 3 S atoms = **6 moles S atom**

Setup and solve using mole ratio (factor labeling) method

$$2 \text{ moles } Al_2(SO_4)_3 \quad x \quad \frac{3 \text{ moles S atom}}{1 \text{ mole } Al_2(SO_4)_3} = 6 \text{ moles S atom}$$

Given the hydrate $CaCO_3 \cdot 2H_2O$

Example 3

How many moles of oxygen atoms are in 1 mole of $CaCO_3 \cdot 2H_2O$?

moles of O = 1 mole x 5 O atoms = **5 moles O atom**

Example 4 (two different setups to solve)

How many moles of oxygen atoms are in 0.5 moles of $CaCO_3 \cdot 2H_2O$?

Setup and solve using above equation

moles of O = 0.5 moles x 5 O atoms = **2.5 moles O atom**

Setup and solve using mole ratio (factor labeling) method

$$0.5 \text{ moles } CaCO_3 \cdot 2H_2O \quad x \quad \frac{5 \text{ moles O}}{1 \text{ mole } CaCO_3 \cdot 2H_2O} = 2.5 \text{ moles O atom}$$

Practice 1
What is the total number of moles of hydrogen in 1 mole of $(NH_4)_2HPO_4$?

1) 5   2) 7   3) 8   4) 9

Practice 2
How many moles of oxygen atoms are present in one mole of $CaSO_4 \cdot 3H_2O$?

1) 7   2) 4   3) 3   4) 5

Practice 3
What is the total number of atoms in one mole of $Mg(ClO_4)_2$?

1) 13   2) 11   3) 8   4) 3

Practice 4
The total number of atoms in one mole of $BaCl_2 \cdot 2H_2O$ is

1) 6   2) 7   3) 8   4) 9

Practice 5
What is the total number of moles of hydrogen atoms in 2 mole of $(NH_4)_2SO_4$?

1) 8   2) 4   3) 16   4) 2

Practice 6
The total number of oxygen atoms in 0.5 mole of $CaCO_3 \cdot 7H_2O$ is

1) 10   2) 2   3) 5   4) 4

Practice 7
What is the total number of moles of atoms in 2 moles of H_2SO_4?

1) 14   2) 7   3) 12   4) 6

Practice 8
How many moles of water are in 2.5 moles of $(NH_4)_2CO_3 \cdot 5H_2O$?

1) 5   2) 2.5   3) 12.5   4) 18

Topic 6 – Stoichiometry: Mole Interpretations and Calculations

3. Molar Mass

The **molar mass** of a substance is the mass, in grams, of 1 mole of that substance. *Recall* that one mole of a substance contains 6.02×10^{23} particles (atoms, molecules, or ions) found in that substance.

For example, water is composed of water molecules:
One mole of water contains 6.02×10^{23} (602000000000000000000000) molecules of water.

The molar mass of water, which is known to be 18 g, is the mass of 6.02×10^{23} molecules of water.

Below are the different variations of molar mass.

Atomic mass specifically refers to the average mass of 1 mole of an element.
Formula mass is commonly used when referring to the mass of 1 mole of an ionic substance.
Molecular mass is commonly used when referring to the mass of 1 mole of a molecular substance.

Regardless of the formula, the mass of one mole of a substance is the sum of the masses of all the atoms in the formula. You are shown how to determine or calculate the molar mass in the set below.

4. Molar Mass Calculations

Gram-atomic mass is the mass, in grams, of 1 mole of an element.
Gram-atomic mass can be found on the Periodic Table of the Elements.

Atomic mass ──▶ 83.80
Kr
36

Concept Task: Be able to determine the gram-atomic mass of an element.

Gram-atomic mass = mass of 1 mole of atoms = **Atomic mass** of the element on the Periodic Table

Gram-formula (or molecular) mass is the mass of 1 mole of a substance.
Gram-formula mass is the sum of all the atomic masses in a formula.

Concept Task: Be able to setup and calculate formula mass of a substance.

Gram-formula mass = Mass of 1 mole of a substance = The sum of the atomic masses in formula

There a few different methods you can use to setup and calculate the formula mass of a given substance. Regardless of the method, the following three steps will be involved.

Step 1: Determine how many of each element is in the formula (*Be sure to count correctly*)

Step 2: Multiply the number of each element by the rounded atomic mass from Periodic Table

Step 3: Add up the total mass of all the elements in the formula to get the formula mass.

Error in any of these steps may result in incorrect formula mass.

Example 1

What is the formula mass of $Al(OH)_3$?

Step 1: 1 Al   3 O   3 H

Step 2: 1(27) + 3 (16) + 3(1)   *setup*

Step 3: 27   +   48   +   3

Formula mass = | 78 g/mole | *calculated result*

Example 2

What is the gram-formula mass of $NaNO_3 \cdot 4H_2O$?

Atoms	Atomic Mass ✗	How Many	= Total Mass
Na	23	1	23 g
N	14	1	14 g
H	1	8	8 g
O	16	7	112 g

You can also setup with a table like this   **Formula mass** = | 157 g/mol |

5. Molar Mass Calculations: Practice Questions

Practice 9
What is the gram-atomic mass of gold?
1) 11 g/mol   2) 79 g/mol   3) 197 g/mol   4) 80 g/mol

Practice 10
What is the mass in grams of 1 mole of Co?
1) 27   2) 28   3) 12   4) 59

Practice 11
Which of these elements has the greatest gram-atomic mass?
1) Br   2) Ge   3) Fe   4) Ca

Practice 12
What is the mass of 1 mole of H_3PO_4?
1) 82   2) 98   3) 24   4) 30

Practice 13
The gram formula mass of $(NH_4)_3PO_4$ is
1) 149 g   2) 120 g   3) 404 g   4) 300 g

Practice 14
What is the molecular mass of $C_3H_5(OH)_3$?
1) 48 g/mole   2) 58 g /mole   3) 74 g/mole   4) 92 g/mole

Practice 15
What is the gram formula mass of $CuSO_4 \cdot 3H_2O$?
1) 214 g   2) 250 g   3) 294 g   4) 178 g

Practice 16
Which of these substances has the smallest gram-molecular mass?
1) CO_2 2) HNO_3 3) HCl 4) H_2O_2

Practice 17
Calculate the formula mass of $Al_2(SO_4)_3$. Show setup and the calculated result.

Practice 18
Calculate the molecular mass of $CH_3(CH_2)_2COOH$. Show setup and the calculated result.

Practice 19
Calculate the molar mass of the hydrate $Ba(OH)_2 \cdot 8H_2O$. Show setup and the calculated result.

6. Mole – Mass relationship

The mass of one mole of a substance is the gram-formula mass of that substance. In other words, 6.02×10^{23} particles (one mole) of a given substance has a mass equal to the calculated gram-formula mass. What if there is more than one mole (more than 6.02×10^{23} particles of that substance)? It makes sense to think that a sample containing more than one mole of a substance (more than 6.02×10^{23} particles) will have a mass that is greater than the calculated gram-formula mass. Likewise, a sample containing less than one mole (fewer than 6.02×10^{23} particles) will have a mass that is less than the calculated gram-formula mass. The equation and examples below show how to calculate the mass of a substance if the number of moles of the substance is given.

7. Mass Calculations from Moles

Concept Task: Be able to setup and calculate mass of substance from a given number of moles.

Calculations of mass from moles can be setup and solve using equation below, or by using mass-mole conversion (factor label) method.

$$\boxed{\textbf{Mass} = \text{Given moles} \quad x \quad \text{Formula mass}}$$

Example 1

What is the mass of 0.25 moles of O_2?

Setup and solve using equation above

Mass = mole x Formula mass of O_2

Mass = 0.25 x 32   *setup*

Mass = **8.0 g O_2**   *calculated result*

Example 2

What is the mass of 2.0 moles of $Mg(C_2H_3O_2)_2$?

Setup and solve using factor-label (conversion) method

Mass = Given moles x mass/mole ratio

Mass = 2.0 moles x $\dfrac{142 \text{ g } Mg(C_2H_3O_2)_2}{1 \text{ mole}}$ *setup*

Mass = **284 g $Mg(C_2H_3O_2)_2$**   *calculated result*

Note: 142 g is the gram-formula mass of $Mg(C_2H_3O_2)_2$.

1 Mg 4 C 6 H 4 O = 1(24) + 4 (12) + 6(1) + 4(16) = 142 g

Practice 20
What is the total mass of 2 moles of Ar?
1) 18 g   3) 40 g
2) 36 g   4) 80 g

Practice 21
The total mass of 0.25 mole of H_2 gas?
1) 2 g   3) 8 g
2) 0.5 g   4) 4 g

Practice 22
What is the total mass in grams of 3 moles of $Al_2(CrO_4)_3$?
1) 134   3) 1206
2) 402   4) 1530

Practice 23
Which set up is correct for calculating the mass of 0.6 mole of $Ca(OH)_2$?

1) $\dfrac{74}{0.6}$ 3) $\dfrac{58}{0.6}$

2) 0.6 x 74   4) 0.3 x 58

Practice 24
Calculate the mass of grams of 0.1 mole of $C_6H_{12}O_6$? Show setup and the calculated result.

Practice 25
What is the mass of 2.3 moles of $CuSO_4 \cdot 5H_2O$? Show setup and the calculated result.

8. Mass – Mole Relationship

Recall that the gram-formula mass of a substance is the mass of one mole (6.02×10^{23} particles) of the substance. Therefore, a sample of a substance that weighs more than the calculated gram-formula mass is more than one mole (contains more than 6.02×10^{23} particles) of the substance. Likewise, a sample that weighs less than the calculated gram-formula mass is less than one mole (contains fewer than 6.02×10^{23} particles) of the substance. The equation and examples below show how to calculate the number of moles of a substance if the mass of the substance is given.

9. Mole Calculations from Mass

Concept Task: Be able to setup and calculate the number of moles of any given mass of a substance

Calculation of moles from mass can be setup and solve using the Reference Table T equation below, or by using factor-label (conversion) method.

Reference Table T equation:

$$\text{Moles} = \frac{\text{Given Mass}}{\text{Formula mass}}$$

Example 1
What is the number of moles of zinc in a 130.8-gram sample?

Setup and solve using equation above

$$\text{Moles} = \frac{130.8 \text{ g Zn}}{65.4 \text{ g/mol}} \quad setup$$

Moles = **2.0 moles Zn**   *calculated result*

Example 2
What is the total number of moles represented by 77.5 grams of $Ca_3(PO_4)_2$?

Setup and solve using factor-label (conversion) method

Moles =   Given mass   x   mole/mass ratio

$$\text{Moles} = 77.5 \text{ g } Ca_3(PO_4)_2 \text{ x } \frac{1 \text{ mole } Ca_3(PO_4)_2}{310 \text{ g } Ca_3(PO_4)_2} \quad setup$$

Moles = **0.25 moles $Ca_3(PO_4)_2$**   *calculated result*

Note: 310g is the gram-formula mass of $Ca_3(PO_4)_2$:

3Ca 2P 8O = 3(40) + 2(31) + 8(16) = *310g g*

Practice 26
What is the total number of moles represented by 46 grams of Na?
1) 23 moles   3) 2.0 moles
2) 0.5 moles   4) 1.0 moles

Practice 27
A student measured 56 grams of Fe_2O_3 for a laboratory experiment. How many moles of Fe_2O_3 is this mass represents?
1) 1.00   3) 0.50
2) 0.35   4) 2.00

Practice 28
Which setup is correct for calculating the number of moles in 576 g of $Al(ClO_3)_3 \cdot 6H_2O$?
1) 576 x 384   3) 6 x 576

2) $\frac{576}{384}$ 4) $\frac{384}{576}$

Practice 29

Calculate the number of moles in 184g of $C_3H_5(OH)_3$. Show setup and the calculated result.

Practice 30

What is the number of moles represented in 100 grams of $Na_2CO_3 \cdot 10H_2O$? Setup and calculate.

10. Molar Volume: Mole – Volume Calculations

Molar volume describes the volume of a one mole (6.02 x 10^{23} particle) of a gas at STP. Molar volume of any gas at STP is 22.4 liters.

$$\boxed{1 \text{ mole } = 22.4 \text{ L}}$$
at STP

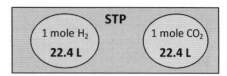

If there are more than one mole (more than 6.02 x 10^{23} particles) of a gas at STP, it makes sense to think that the volume of the gas will be greater than 22.4 liters. Likewise, a gas sample that occupies a smaller volume than 22.4 liters at STP is less than one mole (contains fewer than 6.02 x 10^{23} particles) of the gas. The mathematical relationships between moles and volume are given in the equations below.

Volume = Given moles x 22.4 L	or	**Moles** $= \dfrac{\text{Given volume}}{22.4 \text{ L}}$

Concept Task: Be able to setup and calculate problems that involve moles and volume.

Example 1
How much volume is occupied by 5 moles of O_2 gas at STP?

1) 2 L   2) 4.5 L   3) 10 L   *4) 112 L*

Setup and calculate using equation above

Volume   =   5   x   22.4   *setup*

Volume = 112 L   *calculated result*
          Choice 4

Example 2
At STP, a sample of H_2 gas has a volume of 15 liters. How many moles of H_2 is in the sample?

Setup and calculate using factor-label (conversion)

Given volume   x   mole/liters ratio

$$15 \text{ liters } O_2 \quad x \quad \frac{1 \text{ mole } O_2}{22.4 \text{ liters } O_2} \quad setup$$

0.67 moles O_2   *calculated result*

Practice 31
What is the volume of 1.50 moles of an ideal gas at STP?
1) 11.2 L   3) 33.6 L
2) 22.4 L   4) 14.9 L

Practice 32
What is the volume of 0.1 mole of O_2 gas at STP?
1) 2.24 L   3) 44.8 L
2) 4.48 L   4) 224 L

Practice 33
Which substance will occupy a volume of 67.2 L at STP?
1) 1.0 mole of He
2) 3.0 mole of H_2
3) 67.2 mole of Ne
4) 1509 mole of N_2

Practice 34
A closed cylinder at STP contains 3.5 moles of CO_2. Calculate the volume of the gas.
Show setup and the calculated result.

Practice 35
Helium gas occupies a volume of 10 L .Calculate the number of moles of the gas at STP?
Show setup and the calculated result.

11. Mole – Avogadro's Number Calculations

Avogadro's number describes the amount of particles in one mole of a substance. One mole of any substance contains 6.02×10^{23} particles (atoms, molecules, ions, formula unit..etc) of that substance. 6.02×10^{23} is called the Avogadro's number, named after the Italian scientist Amedeo Avogadro, who first proposed this number.

$$1 \text{ mole } = 6.02 \times 10^{23}$$
at STP

1 mole Na	STP	1 mole CO_2
6.02×10^{23} atoms of Na		6.02×10^{23} molecules of CO_2

If there are more than one mole of a substance, it makes sense to think that there will be more than 6.02×10^{23} particles of that substance. It could be also be said that a substance containing fewer than 6.02×10^{23} particles is less than one mole. The mathematical relationships between moles and Avogadro's number are given in the equations below.

Number of Particles $= \text{Given moles} \times (6.02 \times 10^{23})$ or **Moles** $= \dfrac{\text{Given number of particles}}{6.02 \times 10^{23}}$

Concept Task: Be able to setup and calculate problems involving moles and Avogadro's number

Example 1
How many molecules of F_2 are in 2.5 moles of the substance?

1) 5.0   3) 2.41×10^{23}
2) 90   4) 1.51×10^{24}

Setup and calculate using equation above

Number of molecules $= 2.5 \times 6.02 \times 10^{23}$ *setup*

Number of molecules $= \mathbf{1.51 \times 10^{24}}$ *calculated result*
                Choice 4

Example 2
A sample of sodium contains 4.5×10^{23} atoms. How many moles does this represents?

Setup and calculate using factor-label method

Given molecules   x   mole/particle ratio

4.5×10^{23} Na atoms x $\dfrac{1 \text{ mole Na}}{6.02 \times 10^{23} \text{ Na atoms}}$ *setup*

0.75 moles Na   *calculated result*

Practice 36
What is the total number of molecules in 0.25 mole of NO_2?
1) 2.5×10^{23} 3) 24.08
2) 4.515×10^{23} 4) 1.5×10^{23}

Practice 37
What is the total number of atoms in 2.31 moles of sodium?
1) 1.39×10^{24} 3) 2.31×10^{24}
2) 2.606   4) 1.39×10^{23}

Practice 38
Which gas sample contains 9.03×10^{23} molecules of the gas?
1) 0.5 mole of N_2 3) 1.5 moles of NH_3
2) 1 mole of He   4) 2 moles of CH_4

Practice 39
A 5.0 moles of gold is used to electroplate a jewelry piece. Calculate the number of gold atoms that coated the jewelry piece.
Show setup and the calculated result.

Practice 40
A helium balloon is filled with 8.12×10^{25} molecules of helium. Calculate the number of moles of the gas in the balloon.
Show setup and the calculated result.

12. Mixed Problems

The **mole map** below may be useful in solving mole problems involving mixed quantities. *Note:* The dot (•) end of an arrow indicates what's given, and the pointy(▲) end of an arrow points to what needs to be calculated. The conversion factor for the quantities (mass, volume..etc) are given between the arrows.

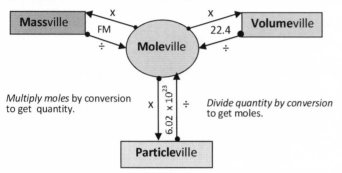

Multiply moles by conversion to get quantity.

Divide quantity by conversion to get moles.

Example 1

What is the number of liters in 50 grams of O_2 at STP?

1) 22.4 L   2) 44.8 L   3) 35.0 L   4) 1120 L

Solve in steps using the mole map

Step 1: Find moles   = Given mass ÷ Formula mass (O_2)

  moles   =   50 g ÷ 32 g/mol = 1.6 mol

Step 2: Find Volume =   Moles x 22.4 L

  Volume =   1.6 x 22.4 = 35.0 L *Choice 3*

Example 2

How many grams of carbon dioxide, CO_2, are in a 100 L sample of the gas at STP ?

Setup and solve using factor- label (conversion) method

$$100 \text{ L } CO_2 \quad \text{x} \quad \frac{1 \text{ mole } CO_2}{22.4 \text{ L } CO_2} \quad \text{x} \quad \frac{44 \text{ g } CO_2}{1 \text{ mole } CO_2} \quad setup$$

196.4 g CO_2   *calculated result*

Example 3

How many particles of NaCl are in a 10-gram sample of the salt?

Setup and solve using factor- label (conversion) method.

$$10 \text{ g NaCl} \quad \text{x} \quad \frac{1 \text{ mole NaCl}}{58 \text{ g NaCl}} \quad \text{x} \quad \frac{6.02 \text{ x } 10^{23} \text{ NaCl}}{1 \text{ mole NaCl}} \quad setup$$

1.04 x 10^{23} NaCl particles   *calculated result*

Practice 41

What is the total volume occupied by 132 g of CO_2 (g) at STP?

1) 22.4 L   3) 44.8 L
2) 33.6 L   4) 67.2 L

Practice 42

How many molecules are contained in 127 g of iodine (I_2) ?

1) 1.50 x 10^{23} 3) 9.03 x 10^{23}
2) 3.01 x 10^{23} 4) 12.4 x 10^{23}

Practice 43

1.0 x 10^{24} molecules of water , H_2O, has a mass of

1) 18 g   3) 30 g
2) 1.67 g   4) 60 g

Practice 44

A closed cylinder contains 576 grams of SO_2 gas at STP. Calculate the volume of the gas? *Show setup and the calculated result.*

Practice 45

A 2-gram sample of sodium, Na, reacted with water. How many atoms of sodium was in the sample?

Show setup and the calculated result.

Practice 46

Calculate the mass of a 72.5 L sample of ammonia gas, NH_3, at STP. *Show setup and the calculated result.*

13. Percent Composition

Percent composition by mass indicates the portion of a mass of a substance that is due to the mass of an individual element in the substance.

Concept Task: Be able to calculate percent compositions of elements in a formula

Use *Reference Table T* equation below to calculate percent composition.

Reference Table T equation

Percent Composition =	$\dfrac{\text{Mass of element in a formula \quad (part)}}{\text{Formula mass of the given formula (whole)}}$ x 100

To determine percent composition of any element in a formula

Step 1: *Determine* the total mass of each element in the formula

Step 2: *Add up* all masses to get the formula mass

Step 3: *Divide* the mass of the element in question by the formula mass, then multiply by 100

Example 1

What is the percent composition of each element in $Mg(ClO_3)_2$?

Step 1: *Determine mass of each element in* $Mg(ClO_3)_2$

$$1\ Mg \quad = \quad 1(24\ g) \quad = \quad 24\ g\ Mg$$
$$2\ Cl \quad = \quad 2(35\ g) \quad = \quad 70\ g\ Cl$$
$$6\ O \quad = \quad 6(16\ g) \quad = \quad 96\ g\ O$$
$$\overline{}$$

Step 2: Formula mass $MgCl_2$ = 190 g $Mg(ClO_3)_2$

Step 3: *Calculate percent composition of each element*

$$\%\ Mg \quad = \quad \frac{24\ g}{190\ g} \quad x \quad 100 \qquad setup$$

% Mg = 12.6 %   *calculated result*

$$\%\ Cl \quad = \quad \frac{70\ g}{190\ g} \quad x \quad 100 \qquad setup$$

% Cl = 36.8 %   *calculated result*

$$\%\ O \quad = \quad \frac{96\ g}{190\ g} \quad x \quad 100 \qquad setup$$

% O = 50.5 %   *calculated result*

Practice 47

In the formula $Mg(CN)_2$, what is the approximate percent by mass of carbon?

1) 16 %   3) 32 %
2) 24 %   4) 48 %

Practice 48

What is the approximate percent composition of $CaBr_2$?

1) 20 % calcium and 80 % bromine
2) 25 % calcium and 75 % bromine
3) 30 % calcium and 70 % bromine
4) 35 % calcium and 65 % bromine

Practice 49

Which compound has the greatest composition of sulfur by mass?

1) $Fe_2(SO_4)_3$ 3) $FeSO_4$
2) $Fe_2(SO_3)_3$ 4) $FeSO_3$

Practice 50

Which compound of gold will produce the least mass of gold?

1) Gold (I) oxide   3) Gold (I) sulfide
2) Gold (III) oxide   4) Gold (III) sulfide

Practice 51

Calculate the percent by mass of hydrogen in the formula $C_3H_5(OH)_3$?

Show setup and the calculated result.

---

14. Percent Composition in Hydrates

Hydrates are ionic compounds that contain water within their crystalline structures.

Names and formulas of three common hydrates are given below:

Water molecules

$CaCl_2 \cdot 2H_2O$ Calcium chloride dihydrate   (**di**hydrate means **2**H_2O)

$MgSO_4 \cdot 7H_2O$ Magnesium sulfate heptahydrate   (**hepta**hydrate means **7**H_2O)

$CuSO_4 \cdot 5H_2O$ Copper(II) sulfate pentahydrate   (**penta**hydrate means **5**H_2O)

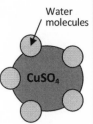

Gram-formula mass (mass of 1 mole) of a hydrate is due in part to the mass of the water. **Percent composition** of water in a hydrate can be calculated using the equation below.

A particle of $CuSO_4 \cdot 5H_2O$

Concept Task: Be able to calculate percent by mass of water in a hydrate

$$\textbf{Percent } H_2O \textbf{ in a hydrate } = \frac{\text{Total mass of } H_2O \quad (\text{part})}{\text{Formula mass of hydrate} \quad (\text{whole})} \times 100$$

To determine percent of water in a hydrate:

Step 1: Determine total mass of water in the hydrate

Step 2: Determine the formula mass of the hydrate.

Step 3: Divide the mass of water by the formula mass of the hydrate, then multiply by 100.

Example 1

What is the percent composition of water in the hydrate $MgSO_4 \cdot 7H_2O$

Step 1: Mass of water, $7H_2O$

$14 H = 14(1) = 14 g$

$7 O = 7(16) = 112 g$

Mass of $7H_2O$ = $126 g$ H_2O

Step 2: Formula Mass of hydrate $MgSO_4 \cdot 7H_2O$

$1 Mg = 1(24) = 24 g$

$1 S = 1(32) = 32 g$

$14 H = 14(1) = 14 g$

$11 O = 11(16) = 176 g$

Formula mass of hydrate = $246 g$ $MgSO_4 \cdot 7H_2O$

Step 3: Calculate % H_2O *in the hydrate using equation*

$$\% H_2O = \frac{126 g}{246 g} \times 100 \quad setup$$

$\mathbf{\% H_2O} = \textbf{51.2 \%}$ *calculated result*

Practice 52

The percent composition of water in the hydrate $CoCl_2 \cdot 6 H_2O$ is

1) 45.6%   3) 7.6%

2) 60.0%   4) 2.5%

Practice 53

The percent by mass of water in $BaCl_2 \cdot 2H_2O$ (formula mass = 243) is equal to

1) $\dfrac{18}{243} \times 100$ 3) $\dfrac{36}{243} \times 100$

2) $\dfrac{243}{18} \times 100$ 4) $\dfrac{243}{36} \times 100$

Practice 54

Which hydrate contains the greatest percent of water by mass?

1) $LiCl \cdot H_2O$ 3) $CuSO_4 \cdot 5H_2O$

2) $CaCl_2 \cdot 2H_2O$ 4) $FeBr_3 \cdot 6H_2O$

Practice 55

Calculate the percent composition of water in $Ca(NO_3)_2 \cdot 3H_2O$ (calcium nitrate trihydrate)

Show setup and the calculated result.

15. Percent Composition of Hydrates from Experiment Data

A **hydrate** can be heated to remove its water (by evaporation) in a laboratory experiment.

An **anhydrous** solid remains after a hydrate is heated and the water is removed. If the mass of a hydrate and of the anhydrous solid are known, the mass of water that was in the hydrate can be determined. From this mass, percent of water in the hydrate can be calculated.

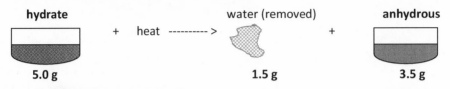

hydrate	water (removed)	**anhydrous**
5.0 g	1.5 g	3.5 g

$$\textbf{% Water} = \frac{\text{Mass of water}}{\text{Mass of hydrate}} \times 100$$

$$\text{% water} = \frac{1.5\,\text{g}}{5.0\,\text{g}} \times 100 = \textbf{30%}$$

Concept Task: Be able to setup and calculate percent composition of water in a hydrate from lab data.

To determine percent of water in a hydrate from experiment.

Step 1: If necessary, *determine* mass of anhydrous and mass of hydrate from the experiment information

Step 2: Determine mass of water = Mass of hydrate - Mass of anhydrous

Step 3: Divide mass of water by mass of hydrate, then multiply by 100

Example 1

A 2.8-gram sample of a hydrate is heated until all the water of hydration is driven off. The substance remaining in the evaporation dish has a mass of 2.1 grams. What is the percent of water in the hydrate?

Mass of water = hydrate - anhydrous
Mass of water = 2.8 g - 2.1 g = 0.7 g

$$\text{% water} = \frac{0.7\,\text{g}}{2.8\,\text{g}} \times 100 \qquad setup$$

% water = **25 %**   *calculated result*

Example 2

During a laboratory experiment to determine percent of water in a hydrate, a student collected the following data.

     Mass of evaporated dish .... 32.5 g
     Mass of hydrate + dish .... 36.5 g
     Mass of anhydrous + dish .... 35.8 g

What is the percent of water in the hydrate?

Step 1: Mass of hydrate = 37.5 g – 32.1 g = 5.4 g
     Mass of anhydrous = 35.8 g – 32.5 g = 3.3 g

Step 2: Mass of water = 5.4 g – 3.3 g = 2.1 g

Step 3: Percent of water

$$\text{% water} = \frac{2.1\,\text{g}}{5.0\,\text{g}} \times 100 \qquad setup$$

% water = **38.9 %**   *calculated result*

Practice 56

A student heated a 9.10-gram sample of an unknown hydrated salt to a constant mass of 5.41 grams. What percent by mass of water did the salt contain?

1) 3.69 %   3) 40.5 %
2) 16.8 %   4) 59.5 %

Practice 57

A 4.10 grams of a hydrate was heated to a constant mass. The anhydrous that remained has a mass of 3.70 g. What is the percent by mass of water in this crystal?

1) 9.8 %   3) 11%
2) 90 %   4) 0.40 %

Practice 58

A hydrated salt was heated in a crucible until the anhydrous compound that remained has a constant mass. The following data were recorded.

Mass of crucible	17.2 g
Mass of hydrate + crucible	22.0 g
Mass of anhydrous + crucible	20.4 g

Calculate the percent composition of water in the hydrated compound?

Show setup and the calculated result.

---

16. Molecular Formula from Empirical Formula and Mass

A **molecular formula** of a substance shows the true compositions of a substance. For example, water has a molecular formula of H_2O. This formula shows the true composition of water. The Molecular mass (mass of 1 mole) of water (18 grams) is the mass calculated from this formula.

The **empirical formula** of a substance shows atoms in a formula in their lowest ratio.

If the empirical formula and molecular mass of a substance are known, the molecular formula of the substance can be determined by following the steps below.

Concept Task: Be able to determine a molecular formula of a substance from molecular mass and empirical formula

To determine molecular formula

Step 1: Determine the mass of the empirical formula

Step 2: Determine how many units of the empirical formula there are by dividing the given molecular mass by the calculated empirical mass from step 1

Step 3: Determine molecular formula by multiplying each subscript of the empirical formula by step 2 answer.

Example 1

A substance has a molecular mass of 116 g and an empirical formula of C_2H_5. What is the molecular formula of this substance?

Step 1: Mass of C_2H_5 = 2 C + 5 H = 2(12) + 5(1) = 29 g

Step 2: $\dfrac{\text{molecular mass}}{\text{Empirical mass}} = \dfrac{116 \text{ g}}{29 \text{ g}} = 4$

Step 3: Molecular formula = 4 (C_2H_5) = $\boxed{C_8H_{20}}$

Practice 59

What is the molecular formula of a substance with a molecular mass 54 g and an empirical formula of C_2H_3?

1) C_2H_3 3) C_6H_9

2) C_4H_6 4) C_3H_2

Practice 60

A compound has a molecular mass of 284g and an empirical formula of P_2O_5. What is the molecular formula of this compound?

1) P_4O_{10} 3) P_5O_2

2) P_2O_5 4) $P_{10}O_4$

Practice 61

A compound has an empirical formula of HCO_2 and a mass of 180 g/mole. What is the molecular formula of this compound?

1) HCO_2 3) $H_4C_4O_8$

2) $H_2C_2O_4$ 4) $H_6C_6O_{12}$

17. Empirical Formula from Percent Composition

Empirical formula of a substance can be determined if the percent composition of the substance are known.

Concept Task: Be able to determine empirical formula of a substance from percent composition.

To determine the empirical formula:

Step 1: Change percent to mass by assuming a 100-g sample.

Step 2: Determine mole *of each* element by dividing mass by the atomic mass of the element

Step 3: Find mole ratio (subscripts) by diving each mole (step 2) by the smallest of the moles

Step 4: Write empirical formula using smallest whole-number ratio

Example 1

A compound was found to consist of 85.6% carbon and 14.4% hydrogen. What is its empirical formula?

	Step 1	Step 2	Step 3	Step 4
85.6 % C	85.6 g	85.6/12 = 7.1	$\dfrac{7.1}{7.1}$ = 1 C	
14.4% H	14.4 g	14.4/1 = 14.4	$\dfrac{14.4}{7.1}$ = 2 H	$\boxed{CH_2}$

Practice 62

What is the empirical formula of a compound that contains 30.4% nitrogen and 69.6% oxygen by mass?

1) NO   3) N_2O_3

2) NO_2 4) N_2O_5

Practice 63

A compound contains 40% calcium, 12% Carbon, and 48% oxygen by mass. What is the empirical formula of this compound?

1) $CaCO_3$ 3) CaC_2O_4

2) CaC_3O_6 4) $CaCO_2$

Lesson 2– Mole Calculations in Equations

Introduction:

⬅️ L👀KING Back: Topic 5 : Chemical equation. You learned about chemical equations.

A chemical equation shows changes that are taking place in a chemical reaction. A balanced chemical equation is a recipe for changing one or more chemical substances to different substances.

Consider the balanced equation: N_2 + $3 H_2$ -------- > $2 NH_3$

This balanced equation reads as a recipe in the following way:

1 mole of nitrogen (N_2) is combined (or reacted) with **3** moles of hydrogen (**3H$_2$**)
to yield (to produce) **2** moles of ammonia (**2** NH_3).

A balanced chemical equation shows substances that are reacting and are being produced, as well as mole proportions (or mole ratios) of the substances in the reaction. Since mole ratios of substances in a given reaction is fixed, knowing the mole ratio of the reactants will allow you to make any amounts of the products by combining more or less of the reactants in the same ratio as given in the balanced equation.

In this lesson, you will learn how to solve problems that involve mole proportions in chemical equations.

---

18. Mole Ratio in Equations

Recall that coefficients in front of substances in a balanced equation indicate the numbers of moles of the substances.

Concept Task: Be able to determine mole ratio of substances in balanced equations.

To determine mole ratio of substances in an equation:

Step 1: Indicate the coefficients of the substances

Step 2: If the coefficients you indicated are reducible, be sure to reduce them by the Common Greatest Factor (CGF).

Example 1

In the equation:

  $4NH_3$ + $5O_2$ ---- > $4NO$ + $6H_2O$

Mole ratios (proportions) of substances in the equation are listed below .

Mole ratio of NH_3 to O_2 is **4 : 5**

Mole ratio of NH_3 to NO is **1 : 1**
            (reduced from 4 : 4 by GCF of 4)

Mole ratio of NO to H_2O is **2 : 3**
            (reduced from 4 : 6 by GCF of 2)

Practice 64

In the balanced equation below:

   $2KClO_3$ --------- > $2KCl$ + $3O_2$

What is the mole ratio of $KClO_3$ decomposed to O_2 produced?

1) 2 : 2   3) 2 : 3

2) 1 : 3   4) 1 : 1

Practice 65

Given the balanced equation

   $2C_2H_6$ + $7O_2$ ----> $4CO_2$ + $6H_2O$

What is the mole ratio of C_2H_6 combusted to that of H_2O produced in the reaction?

1) 4 : 6   3) 3 : 1

2) 1 : 3   4) 1 : 1

Practice 66

Given the reaction:

$3Cu$ + $8HNO_3$ ---> $3Cu(NO_3)_2$ + $2NO$ + $4H_2O$

The number of moles of NO produced to that of HNO_3 reacted is

1) 1 : 4   3) 8 : 2

2) 4 : 1   4) 2 : 8

---

19. Mole – Mole problems in Equations

In mole to mole problems, you will be given:
. A balanced chemical equation (a recipe for making the chemical substances)
. A follow up question that gives a different number of moles of one of the substances in the equation.
. You'll be asked to determine the relative number of moles of another substance in the equation.

Concept Task: Be able to setup and solve mole to mole problems in balanced chemical equations.

The two example problems below show you two methods of setting up and solving mole to mole problems.

Example 1

Given the balanced equation below:

$$2\,C + 3H_2 \text{----------} > C_2H_6$$

How many moles of C are needed to react with 12 moles of H_2 ?

1) 2 moles   3) 24 moles
2) 6 moles   4) 8 moles

Setup and solve using mole proportion

2 C + **3**H_2 -------> C_2H_6	*Re-write equation*	
X 12	*Write moles from question*	

$$\frac{2}{X} = \frac{3}{12} \qquad \text{\textit{Setup by writing proportion}}$$

$$3X = 24 \qquad \text{\textit{Cross multiply}}$$

X = 8 moles of C   *Solve for X (calculated result)*
       Choice 4

Example 2

Given the balanced equation below:

$$4NH_3 + 5O_2 \text{----} > 4NO + 6H_2O$$

What is the total number of moles of oxygen that will be consumed to produce 10 moles of water?

Setup and solve using factor-label method

Given moles of H_2O x   Mole ratio of O_2/H_2O
in question   *in equation*

10 *moles* H_2O x $\dfrac{5 \text{ moles } O_2}{6 \text{ moles } H_2O}$ *setup*

8.33 moles O_2   *calculated result*

Practice 67

Given the reaction below:

$$Mg + 2H_2O \text{----} > Mg(OH)_2 + H_2$$

The number of moles of water needed to react with 3 moles of magnesium is

1) 6 moles   3) 3 moles
2) 0.50 moles   4) 4 moles

Practice 68

Given the reaction

$$C_3H_8 + 5O_2 \text{----------} > 3CO_2 + 2H_2O$$

What is the total number of moles of CO_2 produced from reacting 0.25 mole of C_3H_8?

1) 0.75   3) 5.0
2) 0.80   4) 11

Practice 69

Given the reaction:

$$6CO_2 + 6H_2O \text{-------} > C_6H_{12}O_6 + 6O_2$$

Calculate the number of moles of CO_2 that will react to produce 1.75 moles of $C_6H_{12}O_6$.
Show setup and the calculated result

Practice 70

Given a balanced chemical equation below:

$$3Cu(s) + 2H_3PO_4\,(aq) \text{---} > Cu_3(PO_4)_2\,(s) + 3H_2(g)$$

Calculate the number of moles of copper needed to react with 0.15 moles of phosphoric acid. *Show setup and the calculated result.*

---

20. Volume – Volume problems in Equations

In volume to volume problems, you'll be given:
. A balanced chemical equation (a recipe for making the chemical substances)
. A follow up question that gives a volume of a substance in the equation.
. You'll be asked to determine the volume of another substance in the equation.

Concept Task: Be able to setup and solve volume to volume problems in balanced equations.

The two example problems below show you two methods of setting up and solving volume to volume problems.

Example 1

Given the balanced equation below:

$$C_3H_8 \ + \ 5O_2 \ ------> \ 3CO_2 \ + \ 4H_2O$$

How much volume of oxygen, O_2, will react to produce 10 liters of carbon dioxide, CO_2, at STP?

1) 50 liters   3) 16.7 liters
2) 22.4 liters   4) 1.7 liters

Setup and solve using mole-volume proportion

$$C_3H_8 \ + \ 5O_2 \ --> \ 3CO_2 \ + \ 4H_2O \quad \textit{Re-write equation}$$

$$ X 10 \qquad \textit{Write volumes from question}$$

$$\frac{5}{X} \ = \ \frac{3}{10} \qquad \textit{Setup by writing proportion}$$

$$3X \ = \ 50 \qquad \textit{Cross multiply}$$

$$\mathbf{X} \ = \ \mathbf{16.7 \ moles \ of \ O_2} \qquad \textit{Solve for X}$$

$$\textit{Choice 3}$$

Example 2

Given the balanced equation

$$N_2 \ (g) \ + \ 3H_2 \ (g) \ --------> \ 2 \ NH_{3 \ (g)}$$

Calculate the number of liters of ammonia, NH_3, produced from reacting 8.0 liters of hydrogen, H_2, at STP?

Setup and solve using factor-labeling method

Liters of H_2 x   Mole ratio of NH_3/H_2
in question   *in equation*

$$8.0 \ \textbf{liters} \ H_2 \quad \text{x} \quad \frac{2 \ moles \ \textbf{NH}_3}{3 \ moles \ H_2} \qquad \textit{setup}$$

5.33 Liters of NH₃   *calculated result*

Practice 71

According to the reaction below:

$$2SO_2 \ (g) \ + \ O_2(g) \ --------> \ 2 \ SO_3(g)$$

What is the total number of liters of $O_2(g)$ that will react completely with 89.6 liters of SO_2 at STP?

1) 1.0 L   3) 0.500 L
2) 22.4 L   4) 44.8 L

Practice 72

Given the reaction:

$$C_2H_4 \ + \ 3O_2 \ ------------> \ 2CO_2 \ + \ 2H_2O$$

At STP, how many liters of CO_2 are produced when 15 liters of O_2 are consumed?

1) 10 L   3) 15 L
2) 30 L   4) 45 L

Practice 73

Given the reaction:

$$2C_2H_6(g) \ + \ 7O_2(g) \ -----> \ 4CO_2(g) \ + \ 6H_2O(g)$$

Calculate the total number of liters of $CO_2(g)$ produced by the complete combustion of 35 liters of $C_2H_6(g)$ at STP.

Show setup and the calculated result.

Practice 74

Given the balanced combustion reaction below

$$C_3H_8 \ + \ 5O_2 \ --------------> \ 3CO_2 \ + \ 2H_2O$$

Calculate the volume of propane, C_3H_8, that will completely react with 22.4 L liters of oxygen, O_2, at STP. *Show setup and the calculated result.*

21. Mass – Mass problems in Equations

In mass to mass problems, you'll be given:
. A balanced chemical equation (a recipe for making the chemical substances)
. A follow up question that gives the mass of one of the substances in the equation.
. You'll be asked to determine the mass of another substance in the equation.

In the previous problem (volume – volume), proportions were setup with a mix of two units (mole/volume). This was done because at STP, the volume of one mole of all gases is the same. In mass to mass problems, mole/mass proportion cannot be used to setup and solve the problems because the mass of one mole of substances are different. Mass to mass problems must be set up with mass/mass proportion only.

Concept Task: Be able to setup and solve mass-mass problems in balanced chemical equations.

The two example problems below show you two methods of setting up and solving mass-mass problems.

Example 1

Given the balanced equation below:

$2KClO_3$ ----------> $2KCl$ + $3O_2$

How many grams of KCl is produced by decomposing 100 g of $KClO_3$?

1) 122 g   2) 244 g   3) 50 g   4) 61 g

Solve using mass-mass proportion

$2KClO_3$ --------> $2KCl$ + $3O_2$ *Re-write equation*

100 g   X g   *Write masses from questions*

$$\frac{Mass\ of\ 2KClO_3}{100\ g} = \frac{Mass\ of\ 2KCl}{X\ g}$$

$$\frac{244\ g}{100\ g} = \frac{148\ g}{X\ g}$$ *setup mass-mass proportion*

244 X   =   14800   *Cross multiply*

X   =   **60.65 g** KCl   *solve for X (calculated result)*

Choice 4

Example 2

Given the reaction:
$4Al(s) + 3O_2(g)$ ------------ > $2Al_2O_3(s)$

What is the minimum number of grams of O_2 gas required to produce 51 grams of Al_2O_3?

Setup and solve using factor-label method

51 g Al_2O_3 x $\dfrac{1\ mole\ Al_2O_3}{102\ g\ Al_2O_3}$ x $\dfrac{3\ moles\ O_2}{2\ moles\ Al_2O_3}$ x $\dfrac{32\ g\ O_2}{1\ mole\ O_2}$ *setup*

24 g O_2   *calculated result*

Practice 75

Given the reaction:

Mg + $2HCl$ -----> $MgCl_2$ + H_2

What is the total number of grams of Mg consumed when 1 g of H_2 is produced?

1) 6.0 g   3) 3.0 g
2) 12 g   4) 24 g

Practice 76

Given the balanced equation below:

$3Cu$ + $8HNO_3$ ----> $3Cu(NO_3)_2$ + $2NO$ + $4H_2O$

The total number of grams of Cu needed to produce 188 grams of $Cu(NO_3)_2$

1) 64   3) 32
2) 128   4) 124

Practice 77

According to the reaction:

$2C_2H_2$ + $5O_2$ ------ > $4CO_2$ + $2H_2O$

Calculate grams of CO_2 produced from combusting 80 grams of C_2H_2?

Show setup and the calculated result.

Practice 78

Given the reaction:

$4Fe$ + $3O_2$ ----------- > $2Fe_2O_3$

Calculate the mass of Fe_2O_3, iron (III) oxide, that will be produced from 20 grams of Fe?

Show work and the calculated result.

Topic 6 – Stoichiometry: Mole Interpretations and Calculations

Concept Terms

Key vocabulary terms and concepts from Topic 6 are listed below. You should know definition and facts related to each term and concept.

1. Mole
2. Avogadro's number
3. Molar mass
4. Gram-atomic mass
5. Gram-formula mass
6. Gram-molecular mass
7. Molar volume
8. Percent composition
9. Hydrate
10. Anhydrous
11. Percent composition of hydrate

Concept Tasks

Concept tasks from Topic 6 are listed below. You should know how to solve problems and answer questions related to each concept task.

1. Determining the number of moles of each atom in a given mole of formula
2. Determining the total number of moles of atoms in a given formula
3. Determining the gram-atomic mass (molar mass) of an element.
4. Calculating the gram-formula mass (gram-molecular mass, molar mass) of a compound
5. Calculating the mass of any given mole of a substance
6. Calculating number of moles of any given mass of a substance
7. Calculating percent composition by mass of an element in a formula
8. Calculating percent of composition of water in a hydrate
9. Calculating percent composition of water in a hydrate from lab information
10. Determining molecular formula from molecular mass and empirical formula
11. Determining empirical formula from percent composition and mass
11. Determining mole ratio of substance in a balanced equation
12. Solving mole to mole problem in a balanced chemical equation
13. Solving volume to volume problem in a balanced chemical equation
14. Solving mass to mass problem in a balanced chemical equation

Topic 7 - Solutions

Topic outline

In this topic, you will learn the following concepts:

. Properties of aqueous solutions
. Descriptions of solutions
. Solubility factors
. Soluble and insoluble substances
. Types of solutions

. Expression of concentration of solutions
. Molarity and parts per million calculations
. Vapor pressure
. Effects of a solute on physical properties of water

Lesson 1 - Properties of Aqueous Solutions

Introduction

Solutions are homogeneous mixtures. A homogeneous mixture is a type of mixture in which all of the components are evenly and uniformly mixed throughout the mixture. One good example of a solution is salt-water. Milk is also a homogeneous mixture (or solution). Although there are many different kinds of solutions, the discussion of solutions in this topic will focus on aqueous solutions only.

Aqueous solutions are solutions in which one of the substances in the mixture is water (solvent).
In this lesson, you will learn about properties of aqueous solutions.

1. Components of Aqueous Solutions

All aqueous solutions consist of two main components:

Below are definitions and facts related to these components.

Concept Facts: Study to remember the following solution related information

Solute

A solute is the substance that is being dissolved in a solution.
A solute is always present in a smaller amount than the solvent.
Solute can be a solid, liquid or gas. Dissolving of a solute is a physical change.

Solvent (Water)

A solvent is the substance in which the solute is dispersed.
A solvent is always present in a greater amount relative to the solute .
In aqueous solutions the solvent is always water. In all solutions the solvent is usually a liquid.

Aqueous Solution

An aqueous solution is a mixture of a solvent (water) and solute.

The equation below shows the dissolving of a salt (solute) in water.

$LiCl_{(s)}$ + $H_2O_{(l)}$ ----------------> $LiCl_{(aq)}$
Solute   **solvent**   **mixture**

(s) solid   **(l)** liquid   **(aq)** aqueous

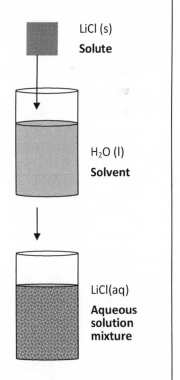

LiCl (s)
Solute

H_2O (l)
Solvent

LiCl(aq)
**Aqueous
solution
mixture**

2. Hydration of Ions in Solution

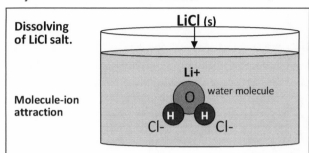

Dissolving of LiCl salt.

Molecule-ion attraction

When a salt (**LiCl**) is placed in water, the salt crystals interact with the water molecules, H_2O, to dissolve.

In LiCl solution : LiCl $_{(aq)}$

Li+ (the positive ion of the salt) attracts
O   (the negative end of a water molecule)

Cl- (the negative ion of the salt) attracts
H   (the positive ends of a water molecule)

Recall: Opposites attract

3. Examples of Solutions

A chemical formula can only be used to represent pure substances such as elements and compounds. Aqueous solutions are represented by symbols, not chemical formulas.   A symbol for an aqueous solution is not a chemical formula of that solution.

Below are examples of five aqueous solutions

Solution name	Solution (mixture) symbol	Solute formula	Solvent formula
Sodium chloride solution	NaCl (aq)	NaCl (s) or Na$^+$Cl$^-$	H_2O (l)
Potassium nitrate solution	KNO$_3$ (aq)	KNO$_3$ (s) or K$^+$NO$_3^-$	H_2O (l)
Sugar solution	$C_6H_{12}O_6$ (aq)	$C_6H_{12}O_6$ (s)	H_2O (l)
Carbon dioxide solution	CO$_2$ (aq)	CO$_2$ (g)	H_2O (l)
Ethanol (alcohol) solution	C_2H_5OH (aq)	$C_2H_5(OH)$(l)	H_2O (l)

NOTE: The aqueous symbol (aq) next to a formula of a substance always indicates that the substance is dissolved in water.

4. Properties of Solutions

A properly made solution will have the following characteristics.

Concept Facts: Study to remember these characteristics of solutions

. Solutions are homogenous mixtures.

. Solutions are generally clear.

. Solutions that are colorful likely contain an ion of a transition element.

. Solutions are transparent and do not disperse light.

. Particles in a solution will not settle to the bottom of the container or separate into layers.

. Solute and solvent can be separated by boiling, evaporation or distillation processes.

Crystallization is a process of recovering a salt (solute) from a mixture by evaporating (or boiling) off the water. When a solution is boiled, particles of water will evaporate out of the mixture, leaving behind ions of the solute to re-crystallize.

Filtration *CANNOT* be used to separate the solute from the solvent of a mixture. Both the solute and solvent particles are generally smaller than holes of a filter paper. As a result, both solute and solvent will filter through during a filtration process

5. Properties of Solutions: Practice Problems

Practice 1
All aqueous mixtures must contain
1) Water   2) Sodium chloride   3) Oxygen   4) Sand

Practice 2
The process of recovering a salt from a solution by evaporating the solvent is known as
1) Decomposition   2) Crystallization   3) Reduction   4) Filtration

Practice 3
In a true solution, the dissolved particles
1) Are visible to the eyes   3) Are always solids
2) Will settle out on standing   4) Cannot be removed by filtration

Practice 4
Aqueous solutions are best described as a
1) Homogenous compounds   3) Heterogeneous compounds
2) Homogeneous mixtures   4) Heterogeneous mixtures

Practice 5
When sample X is passed through a filter paper and a white residue, Y, remains on the paper and a clear liquid, Z, passes through. When Z is vaporized, another white residue remains. Sample X is best classified as
1) An element   3) A heterogeneous mixture
2) A compound   4) A homogeneous mixture

Practice 6
An aqueous solution of copper sulfate is poured into a filter paper cone. What passes through the filter paper?
1) Only the solvent   3) Both solvent and solute
2) Only the solute   4) Neither the solvent nor solute

Practice 7
In an aqueous solution of potassium fluoride, the solute is
1) K^+ only   2) F^- only   3) K^+F^- 4) H_2O

Practice 8
A small of $LiNO_3$ is dissolved in H_2O to make a solution. In this solution
1) $LiNO_3$ is the solute   3) H_2O is the solute
2) $LiNO_3$ is the solvent   4) H_2O is the precipitate

Practice 9
What happens when KI(s) is dissolved in water?
1) I^- ions are attracted to the oxygen atoms of water
2) K^+ ions are attracted to the oxygen atoms of water
3) K^+ ions are attracted to the hydrogen atoms of water
4) No attractions are involved, the crystal just falls apart

Practice 10
Which diagram best illustrates the molecule-ions attractions that occur when NaBr(s) is added to water?

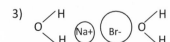

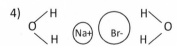

Lesson 2 – Solubility Factors

Introduction:

Not every substance that is put in water will dissolve. Some substances dissolve very well, others very little, and some not at all. In addition, how well a given substance dissolves in water is affected by conditions such as temperature and/or pressure.

In this lesson, you'll learn about factors that affect how well substances dissolve in water. You will also learn how to determine which substance will dissolve and which will not dissolve in water.

6. Solubility

Solubility describes the extent to which a substance will dissolve in water at specific conditions.

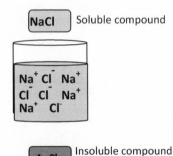

Soluble means that a substance has HIGH solubility.
Soluble salts dissolve very well in water to produce a solution with high ion concentration.
Ex. NaCl (sodium chloride salt) is soluble in water.

Insoluble means that a substance has LOW solubility.
Insoluble salts dissolve very little in water to produce a solution with low ion concentration.
Ex. AgCl (silver chloride salt) is insoluble in water.

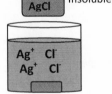

Miscibility describes the extent to which two liquids will mix.

Miscible refers to two liquids with HIGH miscibility.
Two miscible liquids will mix evenly, and will not form layers.
Ex. Ethanol and water are miscible liquids.

miscible liquids

Immiscible refers to two liquids with LOW miscibility.
Two immiscible liquids will not mix evenly, and may separate into layers.
Ex. Oil and water are immiscible liquids.

immiscible liquids

Topic 7 - Solutions

7. Solubility Factors

The extent to which a solute dissolves in water depends largely on the following three factors:
Temperature, pressure, and the nature of the solute.
In the notes below, you will learn how these three factors affect how well a solute dissolves in water.

Concept Facts: Study to remember these factors that affect solubility

Temperature
The effect of temperature on solubility of a solute varies depending if the solute is a solid or a gas.

Solid solutes: Examples. $NaNO_3(s)$, $KCl(s)$, and Sugar.
Solubility of most solids increases as the water temperature increases. $NaNO_3(s)$, $KCl(s)$ or sugar dissolves better at a high water temperature than at a lower water temperature.

Gaseous solutes: Examples. $O_2(g)$ and $CO_2(g)$
Solubility of all gases increases as the water temperature decreases. $O_2(g)$ or $CO_2(g)$ dissolves better at a lower water temperature than at a higher water temperature.

Pressure
For a given gaseous solute, the solubility of the gas changes with a change in pressure.

Gaseous solutes: Solubility of all gases increases as the pressure increases. $O_2(g)$ or $CO_2(g)$ will dissolve better in a high pressure system than in a low pressure system.

Solid solutes: Pressure has no effect on solubility of solids in water. The amount of $NaNO_3(s)$, $KCl(s)$ or sugar that will dissolve in water will not be affected by a change in pressure.

Nature of solutes
"Like dissolves like" is a saying that emphasizes the fact that polar solutes and ionic solutes dissolve better in polar solvents (like water).

Ionic solutes (such as NaCl) dissolve well in water because they are alike in terms of polarity.
. Water is a polar substance with + and – ends
. Ionic substances are composed of + and – ions

Nonpolar solutes (such as I_2) have no + and no – ends. As a result, nonpolar solutes dissolve very little in water, but will dissolve better in nonpolar solvents such as CCl_4.

Temperature

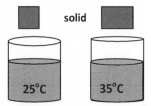

At a higher water temp of $35^{\circ}C$, a greater amount of the solid can be dissolved in water.

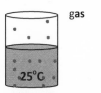

At a lower temperature of $25^{\circ}C$, the water contains more dissolved gas particles.

Pressure

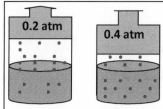

At a higher pressure of 0.4 atm, more gas particles are pushed into the water, and the water will contain more dissolved gas particles .

Nature of solutes

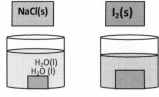

NaCl dissolves well in water, while I_2 dissolves very little in water.

8. Solubility Factors: Practice Problems

Practice 11
The solubility of a salt in a given volume of water depends largely on the
1) Surface area of the salt crystals
2) Pressure on the surface of the water
3) Rate at which the salt and water are stirred
4) Temperature of the water

Practice 12
Which change will have the least effect on the solubility of a solid?
1) Increase in temperature
2) Increase in surface area
3) Decrease in temperature
4) Decrease in pressure

Practice 13
A change in pressure has the greatest effect on the solubility of a solution that contains a
1) Solid in a liquid
2) Gas in a liquid
3) Liquid in a liquid
4) Liquid in a solid

Practice 14
Which change will increase the solubility of a gas in water?
1) Increase in pressure and increase in temperature
2) Increase in pressure and decrease in temperature
3) Decrease in pressure and increase in temperature
4) Decrease in pressure and decrease in temperature

9. Solubility Factors: Practice Problems

Concept Task: Be able to relate solubility of a substance to temperature and pressure

Recall:

↑**Temperature:** ↑ Solubility of solids ↓Solubility of gases

↓**Temperature:** ↓Solubility of solids ↑Solubility of gases

↑**Pressure:** ↑Solubility of gases, no affect on solids

↓**Pressure :** ↓Solubility of gases , no effect on solids

Practice 15
The solubility of which substance will not be affected by an increase in pressure?
1) N_2 2) SO_3 3) CO_2 4) LiCl

Practice 16
As temperature of water increases, which substance will show a decrease in solubility?
1) $CaBr_2$ 2) KNO_3 3) CO   4) KBr

Practice 17
As the pressure of a system is changed from 1 atm to 2 atm, the solubility of which substance will be most affected by this change?
1) HCl (l)   2) HCl(g)   3) LiCl (s)   4) LiCl (l)

Practice 18
At standard pressure, water at which temperature will contain the most dissolved NH_4Cl particles?
1) $5^{\circ}C$ 3) $15^{\circ}C$
2) $10^{\circ}C$ 4) $20^{\circ}C$

Practice 19
At which temperature would 100 g $H_2O(l)$ contain the most dissolved oxygen?
1) $10^{\circ}C$ 3) $30^{\circ}C$
2) $20^{\circ}C$ 4) $40^{\circ}C$

Practice 20
At which temperature would water contain the least amount of dissolved $NaNO_3$ at 1 atm?
1) $70^{\circ}C$ 3) 320 K
2) $80^{\circ}C$ 4) 330 K

Practice 21
Under which conditions would carbon dioxide be most soluble in water?
1) $10^{\circ}C$ and 1 atm   3) $20^{\circ}C$ and 1 atm
2) $10^{\circ}C$ and 2 atm   4) $20^{\circ}C$ and 2 atm

Practice 22
Under which two conditions would water contain the least number of dissolved $NH_3(g)$ molecules?
1) 101.3 KPa and 273 K
2) 101.3 kPa and 546 K
3) 60 KPa and 273 K
4) 60 KPa and 546 K

Topic 7 - Solutions

10. Soluble and Insoluble Salts: Using Solubility Guideline Table F.

As mentioned earlier, not every substance will dissolve in water. Soluble substances dissolve well to produce high dissolved ion concentration. Insoluble substances dissolve very little to produce low dissolved ion concentration. Solubility of an ionic solute depends on the nature of the ions it contains. The *Solubility Guideline (Table F)* shown below lists ions that form soluble and insoluble compounds. Table F is used for determining if an ionic solute is soluble or insoluble.

NOTE that this table is composed of two different tables.

Table F Solubility Guidelines for Aqueous Solution

Soluble ions

Ions That Form *Soluble* Compounds	Exceptions
Group 1 ions (Li^+, Na^+, etc.)	
ammonium (NH_4^+)	
nitrate (NO_3^-)	
acetate ($C_2H_3O_2^-$ or CH_3COO^-)	
hydrogen carbonate (HCO_3^-)	
chlorate (ClO_3^-)	
halides (Cl^-, Br^-, I^-)	when combined with Ag^+, Pb^{2+}, or Hg_2^{2+}
sulfates (SO_4^{2-})	when combined with Ag^+, Ca^{2+}, Sr^{2+}, Ba^{2+}, or Pb^{2+}

Insoluble ions

Ions That Form *Insoluble* Compounds*	Exceptions
carbonate (CO_3^{2-})	when combined with Group 1 ions or ammonium (NH_4^+)
chromate (CrO_4^{2-})	when combined with Group 1 ions, Ca^{2+}, Mg^{2+}, or ammonium (NH_4^+)
phosphate (PO_4^{3-})	when combined with Group 1 ions or ammonium (NH_4^+)
sulfide (S^{2-})	when combined with Group 1 ions or ammonium (NH_4^+)
hydroxide (OH^-)	when combined with Group 1 ions, Ca^{2+}, Ba^{2+}, Sr^{2+}, or ammonium (NH_4^+)

*compounds having very low solubility in H_2O

Concept Task: Be able to determine if a given ionic solute is soluble or insoluble.

Table F is used in explaining why compounds below are soluble or insoluble.

LiCl   *Soluble*
Li^+ ion (and all Group 1 ions) is listed on the soluble side.
Cl- ion, a halide ion, is also listed on the soluble side.
Neither ion is listed as an exception for the other.
Therefore, LiCl is a soluble compound.

AgSO₄   *Insoluble*
SO_4^{2-} (sulfate ion) is listed on the soluble side with exceptions.
Ag^+ (silver ion) is listed as one of the exceptions for sulfate.
Therefore, AgSO₄ is an insoluble compound.

Barium hydroxide   *Soluble*
Hydroxide ion (OH^-) is listed on the insoluble side with exceptions.
Barium (Ba^{2+}) is listed as one of the exceptions for OH^- ion.
Therefore barium hydroxide is a soluble compound

Magnesium sulfide   *Insoluble*
Sulfide ion (S^{2-}) is listed on the insoluble side with exceptions.
Magnesium ion (Mg^{2+}) is not listed as an exception for S^{2-} ion.
Therefore, magnesium sulfide is an insoluble compound.

Practice 23
Based on Reference Table F, which substance is most soluble?
1) AgI   3) $CaSO_4$
2) $PbCl_2$ 4) $(NH_4)_3PO_4$

Practice 24
Which of these saturated solutions has the lowest concentration of dissolved ions?
1) NaCl(aq)   3) $NiCl_2$(aq)
2) $MgCl_2$(aq)   4) AgCl(aq)

Practice25
Which ion, when combined with chloride ions, Br–, forms an insoluble substance in water?
1) Fe^{2+} 3) Pb^{2+}
2) Mg^{2+} 4) Zn^{2+}

Practice 26
According to Table F, which chromate salt is soluble?
1) Calcium chromate
2) Zinc chromate
3) Cobalt (II) chromate
4) Iron (II) chromate

Copyright © 2012 E3 Scholastic Publishing. All Rights Reserved.   **129**

Topic 7 - Solutions

Lesson 3 - Descriptions of Solution and the Solubility Curves.

Introduction

A solution can be described as saturated, unsaturated, supersaturated, dilute, or concentrated depending on four factors of the solution:

Type of solute, amount of the solute, amount and temperature of water.

Since it is difficult to classify a solution just by looking at it, a Solubility Curve Table is often used to determine and describe types of solutions.

In this lesson, you will learn terms that are used to describe solutions. You will also learn how to use the Solubility Curve (Table G) to answer questions about a solution.

11. Solubility Curves Table G

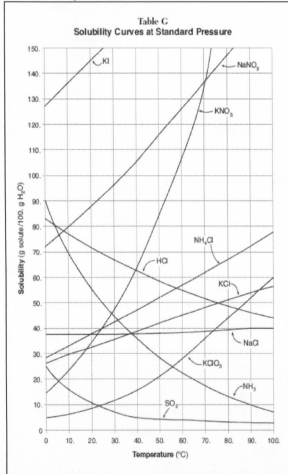

The curves on Table G show changes in solubility of a few selected solid and gaseous solutes in 100 grams of water at different temperatures.

Note the following about the curves.

. *Solid solutes (ex. KCl)* have curves with positive slopes because the solubility of a solid increases as water temperature increases.

. *Gaseous solutes (ex. NH₃)* have curves with negative slopes because the solubility of a gas decreases as water temperature increases.

Table G can be used to answer the following questions about a solution at a specified temperature.

. How many grams of a solute is needed to form a saturated solution?

. Is a solution saturated, unsaturated, or supersaturated?

. Which solute is most or least soluble?
  Which solute is most or least dilute?
  Which solute is most or least concentrated?

12. Descriptions of Solutions

Saturated solution
A solution containing the maximum amount of the solute that can be dissolved at a given water temperature. In a saturated solution, equilibrium exists between dissolved and undissolved particles. If additional solute is added, it will settle to the bottom as crystals.

Unsaturated solution
A solution containing less than the maximum amount of the solute that can be dissolved at the given water temperature. An unsaturated solution can dissolve more solute.

Supersaturated solution
An unstable solution containing more than the maximum amount of the solute that can be dissolved at the given water temperature. A supersaturated solution is made by heating a saturated solution, adding more solute (which will dissolve at the new temperature) and then cooling down the solution.

Dilute solution
A solution containing a smaller amount of dissolved solute relative to the amount of water (solvent)

Concentrated solution
A solution containing a larger amount of dissolved solute relative to the amount of water (solvent)

To determine type of solution from Table G

Step 1: Locate temp of the solution, Go up the temp line

Step 2: Stop when you've gone up as high as the solute amount in the solution

> ### *Very important before using Table G*
> If 100 g H_2O: Make no change to grams of solute
>
> If 50 g H_2O: Double grams of solute first
>
> If 200g H_2O: Halve grams of solute first

Step 3: Note where you've stopped relative to the curve.

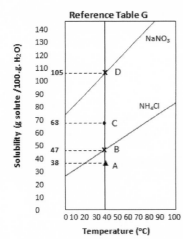

Reference Table G

If you stop

Above the Curve (C):
Solution is supersaturated

On the Curve (B & D):
Solution is saturated

Below Curve (A):
Solution is unsaturated

Solution A is dilute:
It contains small amount of solute (38 g) in large amount of water (100 g).

Solutions C and D are concentrated:
They contain large amounts of solutes relative to amount of water (100g)

Practice 27
A solution containing 75 grams of KNO_3 in 100 grams of water at $50^{\circ}C$ is considered to be
1) Unsaturated   2) Supersaturated   3) Saturated

Practice 28
A solution containing 15 grams of NH_3 in 100 grams of water $90^{\circ}C$ is best classified as
1) Unsaturated   2) Supersaturated   3) Saturated

Practice 29
A solution of KCl contains 90 grams of the solute in 200g of water at $60^{\circ}C$. This solution can be best classified as
1) Unsaturated   2) Supersaturated   3) Saturated

Practice 30
If 70 grams of KI is dissolved in 50 g of H_2O at $10^{\circ}C$, what will be the best description of this solution?
1) Unsaturated   2) Supersaturated   3) Saturated

Practice 31
Based on Reference Table G, a solution of SO_2 that contains 15 grams of the solute dissolved in 100 g of H_2O at $10^{\circ}C$ is best described as
1) Saturated and dilute
2) Unsaturated and concentrated
3) Saturated and concentrated
4) Supersaturated and concentrated

Practice 32
A solution containing 100 grams of $NaNO_3$ in 100 g at $40^{\circ}C$ is best described as
1) Unsaturated and dilute
2) Unsaturated and concentrated
3) Saturated and concentrated
4) Supersaturated and concentrated

Practice 33
Based on Reference Table G, which of these substances is most soluble at $50^{\circ}C$?
1) $KClO_3$ 2) NaCl   3) NH_3 4) $NaNO_3$

Practice 34
Which of these saturated solution is the most dilute at $20^{\circ}C$?
1) $NH_4Cl(aq)$ 2) KCl(aq)   3) $KClO_3(aq)$ 4) $NaNO_3(aq)$

Practice 35
According to Reference Table G, which solution at equilibrium contains 50 grams of solute per 100 grams of H_2O at $75^{\circ}C$?
1) An unsaturated solution of KCl
2) An unsaturated solution of $KClO_3$
3) A saturated solution of KCl
4) A saturated solution of $KClO_3$

Practice 36
A solution contains 100 grams of a nitrate salt dissolved in 100 grams of water at $50^{\circ}C$. The solution could be a
1) Supersaturated solution of $NaNO_3$
2) Supersaturated solution of KNO_3
3) Saturated solution of $NaNO_3$
4) Saturated solution of KNO_3.

Topic 7 - Solutions

13. Amount of Solute to Saturated a Solution

Recall that a *saturated solution* contains the maximum amount of the solute that can be dissolved in the given amount of water at a specified temperature.

Concept Task: Be able to determine grams of solute to form a saturated solution using Table G.

Step 1: Locate the given temperature on the x axis

Step 2: Go up from the temperature point to intersect the curve for the given substance

Step 3: Go left (from where you intersect) to the y axis and read the grams of solute

Note that the grams of solute you determined on Table G is for 100 grams of H_2O.

You can adjust the ***grams of solute to saturate*** if the amount of water in question is different from 100 g.

If amount of water is 100 grams: The amount you determined in step 3 is the saturated amount.
72 g NH_4Cl

If amount of water is 200 grams: Double the amount you determined in step 3 **144 g NH_4Cl**

If amount of water is 50 grams: Halve the amount you determined in step 3 . **36 g NH_4Cl**

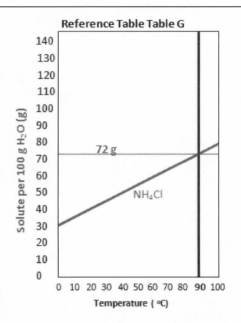

Reference Table Table G

Solute per 100 g H_2O (g) vs Temperature (°C)

72 g — NH_4Cl

Practice 37
How many grams of KCl must be dissolved in 100 g of H_2O at 60°C to make a saturated ?

1) 30 g   2) 45 g   3) 56 g   4) 90 g

Practice 38
What is the approximate amount of $NaNO_3$ needed to saturate 50 grams of water that is at 10°C?

1) 80 g   2) 100 g   3) 40 g   4) 50 g

Practice 39
What is the maximum grams of ammonia that must be dissolved in 200 g of H_2O at 20°C to form a saturated ammonia solution ?

1) 400 g   2) 110 g   3) 27.5 g   4) 55 g

Practice 40
According to Reference Table G, what is the approximate amount of potassium chlorate needed to form a saturated solution in 100 g of water at 10°C?

1) 10 g   2) 30 g   3) 15 g   4) 6 g

Practice 41
According to Reference Table G, which solution is a saturated solution at 30°C?

1) 12 grams of $KClO_3$ in 100 grams of water
2) 12 grams of $KClO_3$ in 200 grams of water
3) 30 grams of NaCl in 100 grams of water
4) 30 grams of NaCl in 200 grams of water

Practice 42
Which is a saturated solution?

1) 40 g NH_4Cl in 100 g of water at 50°C
2) 2 g SO_2 in 100 g water at 10°C
3) 52 g KCl in 100 g of water at 80°C
4) 120 g KI in 100 g water at 20°C

Practice 43
A solution contains 130 grams of KNO_3 dissolved in 100 grams of water. When 3 more grams of KNO_3 is added, none of it dissolves, nor do any additional crystals appear. Based on Reference Table G, the temperature of the solution is closest to

1) 65°C   2) 68°C   3) 70°C   4) 72°C

Topic 7 - Solutions

14. Adding Solute to an Unsaturated Solution.

Recall that an *unsaturated solution* contains less solute than can be dissolved. A solution that is unsaturated can be made saturated by adding more of the solute. The amount of solute to add is the difference between the grams of solute to saturate at the given temperature, and the grams of solute that is in the unsaturated solution.

Grams to add = Grams to saturated − Grams in solution
           (use Table G)   *(given in question)*

Concept Task: Be able to determine amount of solute that can be added to a solution to make it a saturated solution.

Example

A solution of NH_4Cl contains 60 g of the solute in 100 g of water at 90°C. How many more grams of NH_4Cl must be added to make it a saturated solution at that temperature.

1) 90 g   2) 72 g   3) 40 g   4) 12 g

Grams to add = Grams to saturated − Grams in solution
              (use Table G)   *(given in question)*
Grams to add =   72 g   −   60 g   = **12 g**

Choice 4

Practice 44
A solution contains 14 grams of KCl in 100 grams of water at 40°C. What is the maximum amount of KCl that must be added to make this a saturated solution?
1) 14 g   2) 20 g   3) 25 g   4) 54 g

Practice 45
An unsaturated solution of $NaNO_3$ contains 70 grams of $NaNO_3$ dissolved in 100 g of water at 20°C. How many more grams of $NaNO_3$ are needed to make this a saturated solution?
1) 70 g   2) 95 g   3) 30 g   4) 18 g

Practice 46
How many more grams of HCl are needed in a solution containing 100 g of the solute in 200 grams of water at 20°C to make the solution saturated?
1) 44 g   2) 72 g   3) 144 g   4) 100 g

Practice 47
A student dissolved only 40 grams of NaCl in 80 grams of water that is at 90°C. To make this a saturated solution, the student must add to the solution
1) 10 g of NaCl   3) 10 g of H_2O
2) 20 g of NaCl   4) 20 g of H_2O

15. Re-crystallizing Salt (Precipitate)

When a salt solution that is saturated at one temperature is cooled to a lower temperature, a smaller amount of the solute will be soluble. As a result, the ions of the solute will re-crystallize and precipitate (settle out) from solution.

  cooled to 60°C

A saturated solution
of NH_4Cl at 90°C

Undissolved NH_4Cl precipitated at the lower temperature of 60°C.

A **precipitate** is a solid that forms out of a solution. The amount of solute that precipitated (settled out) at the lower temperature can be determined by taking the difference between the saturated amounts of the solute at the two temperatures.

Example

According to Table G, how many grams of NH_4Cl will precipitate when a saturated solution made with 100 grams of water at 90°C is cooled to 60°C?

Grams precipitated = Saturated amount − Saturated amount
                    at the higher Temp   *at the lower temp*

Grams precipitated =   72 g   −   57 g   = **15 g**
                                                        of NH_4Cl

Practice 48
A saturated solution of KNO_3 is prepared with 100 grams of water at 70°C. What amount of KNO_3 will precipitate if the solution is cooled to 50°C ?
1) 215 g   3) 135 g
2) 50 g   4) 20 g

Practice 49
When a saturated solution of $KClO_3$ that is made with 100 g of H_2O is cooled from 25°C to 10°C, some salt crystals reformed at the bottom of the beaker. How many grams of the $KClO_3$ salt is at the bottom of the beaker?
1) 5 g   3) 15 g
2) 10 g   4) 20 g

Practice 50
A test tube contains a saturated solution of KNO_3 that was prepared with 100 grams of H_2O at 60°C. If the test tube is cooled to 30°C, what will be found at the bottom of the test tube?
1) 30 g of KNO_3 3) 30 g of H_2O
2) 57 g of KNO_3 4) 57 g of H_2O

Topic 7 - Solutions

Lesson 4 – Expressions of Solution Concentration

Introduction

Concentration of a solution indicates how much dissolved solute is in a given amount of the solution (or the solvent). Most questions dealing with concentration involve calculations. Two equations for calculating concentrations can be found on Reference Table T.

In this lesson, you will learn about the two concentration expressions: Molarity and parts per million.

16. Molarity Calculations

Molarity expresses the concentration of a solution in number of moles of solute per liter of the solution.

Molarity of a solution can be calculated using *Table T* equation :

$$\text{Molarity (M)} = \frac{\text{moles of solute (mol)}}{\text{volume of solution (L)}}$$

Molarity interpretation: a 0.5 M solution contains 0.5 moles of the solute in 1 liter of the solution.

Concept Task: Be able to use Molarity equation in calculations

Example 1: *Calculating Molarity*

What is the concentration of a solution that contains 1.4 moles of solute in 2.0 L of the solution?

$$\text{Molarity} = \frac{1.4 \text{ moles}}{2.0 \text{ L}} \qquad \textit{numerical setup}$$

Molarity = **0.7 M** or **0.7** $\frac{\text{moles}}{\text{L}}$ *calculated result*

Example 2: *Calculating Molarity from mass of solute*
A solution contains 80 grams of NaOH in 1000 mL of solution. What is the concentration of this solution? (formula mass of NaOH = 40 g)

$$\text{Molarity} = \frac{\text{Given mass}}{\text{Formula mass x Volume}} = \frac{80}{40 \text{ x } 1} \qquad \textit{setup}$$

Molarity = 2.0 M   *calculated result*

Example 3: *Calculating moles*
How many moles of a solute are there in 0.6 L of a 1.5 molar solution?

moles = Molarity x Volume
moles =   1.5   x   0.6   *numerical setup*

moles =   0.9 moles   *calculated result*

Example 4: *Calculating volume*
How much volume of a 3 M H_2SO_4 solution will contain 2 moles of the solute?

$$\text{Volume} = \frac{\text{moles}}{\text{Molarity}} = \frac{2}{3} = \textbf{0.67 L}$$

      setup   *calculated result*

Practice 51
A 0.25 liter of potassium chloride solution contains 0.75 mole of KCl. What is the concentration of this solution?
1) 0.33 M   3) 3.0 M
2) 0.75 M   4) 6.0 M

Practice 52
What is the concentration of a solution of KNO_3 (molecular mass = 101 g/mole) that contains 50.5 g of KNO_3 in 2.00 liters of solution?
1) 25.25 M   3) 2.00 M
2) 0.500 M   4) 0.25 M

Practice 53
What is the total number of moles of solute in 2230 mL of 3.0 M NaOH solution
1) 1.5 moles   3) 3.0 moles
2) 6.7 moles   4) 0.743 moles

Practice 54
What is the total number of grams of KCl in .250 liter of .200 molar solution?
1) 3.7 g   3) 7.46 g
2) 14.9 g   4) 37 g

Practice 55
How many milliliters of a .1 M KNO_3 solution would contain .02 moles of the solute?
1) 2000 mL   3) 5000 mL
2) 200 mL   4) 500 mL

Practice 56
What is the total number of moles in 500 mL of a 3.0 M solution of KI solution?
Show setup and the calculated result.

Practice 57
What is the total volume of a 2.0 molar HCl solution that contains 45 grams of HCl? Show setup and the calculated result.

17. Parts Per Million Calculation

Parts per million expresses the concentration of a solution in number of grams of solute that is in every one million parts of the solution.

Parts per million (ppm) concentrations can be calculated using *Reference Table T* equation below:

Parts per million (ppm) = $\dfrac{\text{mass of solute}}{\text{mass of Solution}}$ x 1 000 000

Parts per million interpretation: In a 0.3 ppm solution, every one million parts of the solution contains 0.3 part solute.

Concept Task: Be able to use parts per million equation to solve concentration problems.

Example 1
A solution of carbon dioxide contains 0.5 grams of the solute in 500 grams of the solution. What is the concentration in parts per million?

ppm = $\dfrac{0.5\text{ g}}{500\text{ g}}$ x 1000000   *setup*

ppm = **1000 ppm**   *calculated result*

Example 2
A solution of sodium nitrate contains 50 grams of the solute in 1000 grams of water. What is the concentration of the solution in parts per million?

ppm = $\dfrac{\text{Mass of solute}}{\text{Mass of solute + Mass of water}}$ x 1000000

ppm = $\dfrac{50\text{ g}}{50\text{ g + 1000 g}}$ x 1000000   *setup*

ppm = **0.045 ppm**   *calculated result*

Note: In example 2, mass of solute (50 g) is high relative to mass of water (1000 g). The two masses must be added together to get the mass of solution.

Example 3
How many grams of NH_4Cl is dissolved in 2000 grams solution to produce a concentration of 150 ppm?

Grams of solute = $\dfrac{\text{ppm} \times \text{Grams of solution}}{1000000}$

Grams of solute = $\dfrac{150 \times 2000}{1000000}$ *setup*

Grams of solute = **0.3 g NH_4Cl**   *calculated result*

Practice 58
What is the concentration of $O_2(g)$, in parts per million, in a solution that contains 0.008 grams of $O_2(g)$ dissolved in 1000 grams of $H_2O(l)$?
1) 0.8 ppm   3) 8 ppm
2) 80 ppm   4) 800 ppm

Practice 59
What is the concentration in parts per million of a solution containing 20 grams of $C_6H_{12}O_6$ in 80.0 grams of H_2O?
1) 2.50 x 10^5 ppm   3) 4.00 x 10^6 ppm
2) 2.00 x 10^5 ppm   4) 5.00 x 10^6 ppm

Practice 60
What is the concentration in parts per million of a solution containing 333 grams of $NaNO_3$ in 700 grams of H_2O?
1) 2.10 x 10^6 ppm   3) 4.75 x 10^5 ppm
2) 3.10 x 10^6 ppm   4) 3.22 x 10^5 ppm

Practice 61
How many grams of NaCl are needed to be dissolved in water to make 2000 grams of a 100 ppm solution?
1) 2 g   3) 0.2 g
2) 0.05 g   4) 0.5 g

Practice 62
A 500 gram $C_6H_{12}O_6$ solution has a concentration of 300 ppm. How many grams of $C_6H_{12}O_6$ (s)) is in this solution?
1) 1.5 x 10^1 g   3) 4.5 x 10^1 g
2) 1.5 x 10^{-1} g   4) 4.5 x 10^{-1} g

Practice 63
A 3000 grams solution contains 1.5 grams of dissolved NaCl salt. What is the concentration of this solution in ppm? Show setup and the calculated result.

Practice 64
How many grams of KNO_3 are needed to be dissolved in water to make 100 grams of a 250 ppm? Show setup and the calculated result.

Topic 7 - Solutions

Lesson 5 : Boiling Point and Vapor pressure

18. Boiling and Vapor Pressure

A **vapor** is a gas form of a substance that is normally a liquid. For example, water is normally a liquid. Water vapor is the evaporated molecules of water in the gas phase. **Vapor pressure** is the pressure exerted by the evaporated particles (vapor) of a liquid on the surface of the liquid. Vapor pressure of a liquid is dependent upon the temperature of the liquid. The relationship between vapor pressure and temperature is shown on *Reference Table H* (see next page)

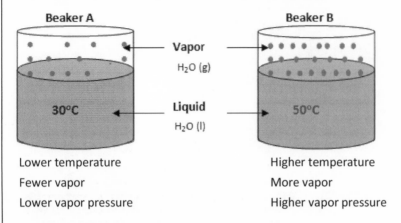

Beaker A	Beaker B
Lower temperature	Higher temperature
Fewer vapor	More vapor
Lower vapor pressure	Higher vapor pressure

Boiling is a rapid phase change of a liquid to the vapor phase. Boiling occurs when the vapor pressure of a liquid is equal to the atmospheric pressure. **Atmospheric pressure** is the pressure exerted on the surface of an object by the weight of the air above that object.

Normal atmospheric pressure = Standard Pressure = 101.3 KPa or 1 atm (Reference Table A)

The **boiling point** of a liquid is the temperature at which the vapor pressure of the liquid equals the atmospheric pressure.

For example: Water boils at 100°C at normal atmospheric pressure (101.3 KPa or 1 atm) because 100°C is the temperature of water that will produce a vapor pressure of 101.3 Kpa or 1 atm. At different atmospheric pressures (higher or lower elevation), water boils at different temperatures. Different substances have different boiling points because the strength of intermolecular forces varies among substances. Intermolecular forces are forces holding molecules of a substance together in solid and liquid phases. Intermolecular forces must be broken for molecules of a liquid to vaporize. The stronger the intermolecular forces, the higher the temperature needed to break these forces. As a result, substances with strong intermolecular forces have higher points than substances with weaker intermolecular forces.

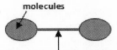

Weak intermolecular forces:
Low temperature (or heat) to break.
Low boiling point of the liquid.

Strong intermolecular force:
High temperature (or heat) to break.
High boiling point of the liquid.

Concept Facts: Study to remember these facts relating to vapor pressure and boiling

. Vapor pressure varies depending on the temperature of a liquid

. The higher the temperature of a liquid, the higher its vapor pressure

. Different substances have different vapor pressure at a given temperature

. Substance with strong intermolecular forces have low vapor pressures and high boiling points

. Substances with weak intermolecular forces have high vapor pressures and low boiling points

Topic 7 - Solutions

19. Reference Table H: Temperature vs. Vapor pressure table

Table H below shows the relationship between temperature and vapor pressure of four liquids: propanone, ethanol, water, and ethanoic acids.

Table H can be used to determine the boiling point of any of the liquids at any atmospheric pressure.

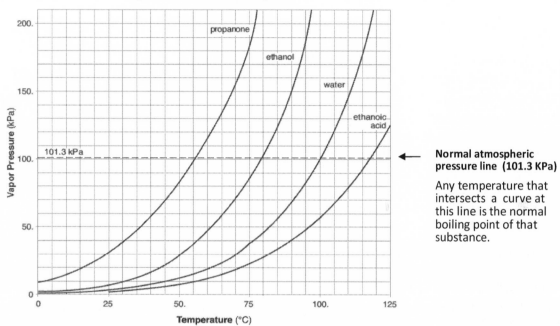

Table H
Vapor Pressure of Four Liquids

Normal atmospheric pressure line (101.3 KPa)

Any temperature that intersects a curve at this line is the normal boiling point of that substance.

Practice 65

 As water in a sealed container is cooled from 20°C to 10°C, its vapor pressure
1) Decreases   2) Increases   3) Remains the same

Practice 66

When the vapor pressure of a liquid is equal to the atmospheric pressure, the liquid will
1) Freeze   3) Melt
2) Boil   4) Condense

Practice 67

What is the vapor pressure of propanone at 45°C?
1) 70 KPa   3) 120 KPa
2) 101.3 KPa   4) 45 KPa

Practice 68

Which sample of water has the lowest vapor pressure?
1) 100 mL at 50°C   3) 300 mL at 40°C
2) 200 mL at 30°C   4) 400 mL at 20°C

Practice 69

What is the boiling point of ethanol at normal atmospheric pressure?

1) 80°C   2) 100°C   3) 200°C   4) 90°C

Practice 70

A liquid has a vapor pressure of 90 kPa at 75°C and a vapor pressure of 120 kPa at 90°C. At standard atmospheric pressure, the liquid will boil
1) At 75°C   3) Above 75°C but below 90°C
2) At 90°C   4) Above 90°C but below 100°C

Practice 71

Which liquid has the highest normal boiling point?
1) Propanone   3) Ethanol
2) Water   4) Ethanoic acid

Practice 72

Using your knowledge of chemistry and the information in Reference Table H, which statement concerning propanone and water at 50°C is true?

1) Propanone has a higher vapor pressure and stronger intermolecular forces than water.

2) Propanone has a higher vapor pressure and weaker intermolecular forces than water.

3) Propanone has a lower vapor pressure and stronger intermolecular forces than water.

4) Propanone has a lower vapor pressure and weaker intermolecular forces than water.

Topic 7 - Solutions

Lesson 6 : Changes in Physical Properties of Solutions

Introduction:

When a solute dissolves in water to make a solution, physical properties of the solution will be different from those of water.

In this lesson, you will learn about changes in physical properties of water when a solute is added to water to make a solution. You will also learn how to determine which solute and which concentration of a solution will have the greatest or least effect on the properties of water.

20. Effect of Solute on Physical Properties of Water

Pure water has the following physical properties :

No dissolved particles.

Boiling point at 100°C (at normal pressure)

Freezing point at 0°C (at normal pressure)

Vapor pressure of 101.3 KPa (at 100°C)

No electrical conductivity

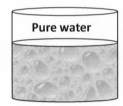

Pure water

No dissolved particles

When a solute is dissolved in water to make a solution, these physical properties of water will change. These changes are listed below.

Number of dissolved particles is increased. And as a result:

Boiling point is increased or elevated.
(The solution will boil at a temperature higher than 100°C)

Freezing point is decreased or depressed.
(The solution will freeze at a temperature lower than 100°C)

Vapor pressure is decreased or lowered.
(The solution will have a vapor pressure lower than that of pure water at any given temperature)

Electrical Conductivity is increased.
(The solution will conduct electrical current better than pure water)

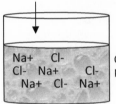

NaCl solute added

Contains dissolved particles.

NaCl solution

How much higher or lower the boiling and freezing points of a solution compared to that of pure water depends on the following factors.

. Concentration of particles in the solution

. Number of dissolved particles the solute produces in the water

These factors are discussed on the next page.

Practice 73
What occurs as a salt dissolves in water?
1) The number of ions in the solution increases, and the conductivity decreases
2) The number of ions in the solution increases, and the conductivity increases
3) The number of ions in the solution decreases, and the conductivity decreases
4) The number of ions in the solution decreases, and the conductivity increases

Practice 74
How do the boiling point and freezing point of a solution of water and calcium chloride at standard pressure compare to the boiling point and freezing point of water at standard pressure?
1) Both the freezing point and boiling point of the solution are higher.
2) Both the freezing point and boiling point of the solution are lower.
3) The freezing point of the solution is higher and the boiling point of the solution is lower.
4) The freezing point of the solution is lower and the boiling point of the solution is higher.

1. Effects of Concentration on Physical Properties

Effects of concentration

Consider the following diagrams of three solutions. The solutions contain the same solute (**KCl**) , but their Molarity concentrations are different.

Lowest concentration

Lowest boiling point

Highest freezing point

Highest concentration

Highest boiling point

Lowest freezing point

A solution of a higher concentration will produce a lower freezing point and a higher boiling point than a solution of a lower concentration.

Effects of number of dissolved particles

Consider the following diagrams of three solutions. The solutions have different solutes (each producing different number of dissolved particles), but their Molarity concentrations are the same (1 M)

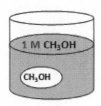

Molecular solute (CH_3OH)

1 dissolved particle

Lowest boiling point

Highest freezing point

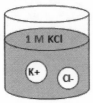

Ionic solute (KCl)

2 dissolved particles

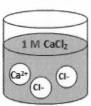

Ionic solute ($CaCl_2$)

3 dissolved particles

Highest boiling point

Lowest freezing point

The effects of a solute on boiling and freezing points depend on the number of particles the solute produces when dissolved.

Ionic solutes will always produce more dissolved particles than molecular (covalent) solutes because ionic substances are composed of two or more ions, and will ionize into those ions in water.

Molecular solutes only disperse in water, and do not ionize.

Practice 75
Which concentration of NaOH has the lowest freezing and highest boiling temperatures?

1) 2.0 M   3) 1.5 M
2) 1.0 M   4) 0.1 M

Practice 76
Which 1 M solution will produce the greatest increase in boiling point of water?

1) CH_3OH (aq)   3) $CuCl_2$ (aq)
2) $C_2H_4(OH)_2$(aq)   4) $C_6H_{12}O_6$ (aq)

Practice 77
Which 1 M solution has the lowest boiling point?

1) KNO_3 (aq)   3) $Ca(OH)_2$ (aq)
2) K_2SO_4 (aq)   4) $C_6H_{12}O_6$ (aq)

Practice 78
Which solution will boil at the lowest temperature?

1) 0.1 M $C_6O_{12}O_6$ 3) 0.1 M LiBr
2) 0.2 M $C_6H_{12}O_6$ 4) 0.2 M LiBr

Practice 79
Which of the preparation of solutions will have the lowest freezing point?

1) 0.2 M KOH   3) 0.2 M $Mg(OH)_2$
2) 0.2 M NaOH   4) 0.2 M $CH_2(OH)_2$

Practice 80
Of the following solutions, the one that will boil at the highest temperature contains 1 mole of NaCl dissolved in

1) 250 g of H_2O 3) 750 g of H_2O
2) 500 g of H_2O 4) 1000 g of H_2O

Practice 81
A 1000 grams sample of water will have the lowest freezing point when it contains

1) 1×10^{17} dissolved particles
2) 1×10^{19} dissolved particles
3) 1×10^{21} dissolved particles
4) 1×10^{23} dissolved particles

Practice 82
Which solute, when added to 1000 grams of water, will produce a solution with the highest boiling point?

1) 29 g of NaCl
2) 58 g of NaCl
3) 31 g of $C_2H_6O_2$
4) 62 g of $C_2H_6O_2$

Topic 7 – Solutions

Concept Terms

Key vocabulary terms and concepts from Topic 7 are listed below. You should know definition and facts related to each term and concept.

1. Aqueous solution
2. Homogeneous mixture
3. Solution
4. Properties of solutions
5. Solute
6. Solvent
7. Hydration of ion
9. Solubility
9. Soluble
10. Miscibility
11. Miscible
12. Immiscible
13. Solubility factors

14. Saturated
15. Unsaturated
16. Supersaturated
17. Dilute
18. Concentrated
19. Molarity
20. Parts per million
21. Vapor
22. Vapor pressure
23. Boiling Point
24. Physical properties of water
24. Effect of solute on properties of water

Concept Tasks

Concept tasks from Topic 7 are listed below. You should know how to solve problems and answer questions related to each concept task.

1. Determining solute and solvent of a solution.

2. Determining a substance whose solubility changes with increase or decrease in temperature (or pressure).

3. Determining temperature and pressure that a solute is most or least soluble.

4. Determining and recognizing which substance is soluble or insoluble Using Table F

5. Determining grams of solute to form a saturated solution using Solubility Curve Table G.

6. Determining grams of solute to add to a solution to make it saturated

7. determining grams of solute that precipitated when a solution is cooled to a lower temperature

7. Determining if solution is saturated, supersaturated or unsaturated

9. Determining if a solution is concentrated or dilute using Table G

10. Determining which saturated solution is most or least soluble, dilute, or concentrated from Table G

11. Interpreting Molarity concentration value (M) of a solution.

12. Calculations using Molarity equation

13. Interpreting part per million (ppm) concentration of a solution

14. Calculations using parts per million equation

15. Determining vapor pressure of any liquid at a given temperature using Reference Table H

16. Determining normal boiling point of the four liquids using Table H

17. Determining boiling point of any of the liquids at a given atmospheric pressure

18. Determining concentration of a solution that will affect water properties the most (or least)

19. Determining solute of a solution that will affect water properties the most (or least)

Topic 8 – Acids, Bases and Salts

Topic outline:

In this topic, you will learn about the following concepts:
- General properties of acids and bases
- Definitions of acids and bases
- Arrhenius theory
- Alternate theory
- Relative ions concentration
- pH values
- Changes on indicators
- Relating H+ to pH
- Reactions of acids and bases
- Titration
- Salts
- Electrolytes

1. Properties of Acids and Bases: Summary of general characteristics

Acids and bases have sets of properties that are used to identify them. Below is a summary of these properties. In the next few sets, you will learn more about these properties of acids and bases.

Concept Facts: Study to remember the following properties of acids and bases.

Note the similarities and differences between them.

Acids   Bases

Similarities

Acids	Bases
1) Are electrolytes	1) Are electrolytes
2) Change color of indicators	2) Change color of indicators
3) React with bases (in neutralization reactions) to produce water and a salt	3) React with acids (in neutralization reaction) to produce water and a salt

Differences

Acids	Bases
4) Produce H^+ as only positive ion in solutions	4) Produce OH^- as the only negative ion in solutions
5) Contain more H^+ than OH^- in solutions	5) Contain more OH^- than H^+ in solutions
6) When added to water, increase H^+ concentration of the water	6) When added to water, decrease H^+ ion concentration of the water
7) When added to water, decrease OH^- concentration of the water	7) When added to water, increase OH^- ion concentration of the water
8) When added to water, decrease pH	8) When added to water, increase pH
9) Have pH less than 7	9) Have pH greater than 7
10) Turn litmus red	10) Turn litmus blue
11) Have no effect on phenolphthalein (stays colorless)	11) Turn colorless phenolphthalein to pink
12) Taste sour	12) Taste bitter and feel slippery
13) React with certain metals to produce salt and hydrogen gas	

Neutral substances

1) Have pH of 7

2) Have equal amount of H^+ and OH^- ions

Lesson 1: Defining Acids and Bases

Introductions

What is an acid? What is a base? These questions cannot be answered with one simple definition. Acids and bases can be defined by many different characteristics.

In this topic, you will learn how acids and bases are defined by theories and other characteristics . As you study this lesson, pay attention to the similarities and differences between acids and bases.

2. Arrhenius Theory of Acids and Bases

Arrhenius theory defines acids and bases by the ion each can produce in solutions.

Arrhenius Acids

Arrhenius acids are substances that produce H^+ (hydrogen ion, proton) in solutions .

. The H^+ produced by acids is the only the positive ion in acidic solutions

. Properties of acids (listed in the summary table) are related to properties of H+ ions they produce

. The H^+ ions produced by acids usually combine with H_2O to form H_3O^+ (hydronium ion)

$$H^+ \quad + \quad H_2O \quad \text{---------->} \quad H_3O^+$$

hydrogen ion   *water*   *hydronium ion*

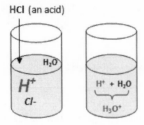

. Common Arrhenius acids are listed on Reference Table K (page 322)

Arrhenius Bases

Arrhenius bases are substances that produce OH- (hydroxide ion) in solutions.

. The OH^- produced by bases is the only negative ion in basic solutions

. Properties of bases (listed in the summary table) are related to properties of OH^- ions they produced

. Most bases are ionic compounds

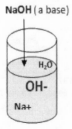

. Common bases are listed on Reference Table L (page 322)

Practice 1

According to Arrhenius theory, which list of compounds includes only acids?
1) HNO_3, H_2SO_4, and $C_6H_{12}O_6$
2) H_2PO_4, HCO_3, and NH_4Cl
3) $LiOH$, HNO_3, and CH_3OH
4) HF, H_2CO_3, and HNO_3

Practice 2

According to Arrhenius theory, which list of compounds includes only bases?
1) KOH, $Ca(OH)_2$, and CH_3OH
2) $LiOH$, $Ca(OH)_2$, and $C_2H_4(OH)_2$
3) $Mg(OH)_2$, $NaOH$, and $LiOH$
4) $NaOH$, $Ca(OH)_2$, and CH_3COOH

Practice 3

Aqueous solution of which of these substances contains hydroxide ions as the only negative ion?

1) C_2H_5OH 3) Na_2SO_4

2) $Ba(OH)_2$ 4) H_2SO_4

Practice 4

Which substance will dissolve in water to produce H_3O^+ (hydronium ion) as the only positive ion in solutions?

1) HF   3) NaOH

2) NH_4OH 4) KCl

Topic 8 – Acids, Bases and Salts

3. Alternate Theory of Acids and Bases

Brönsted-Lowry Theory is an alternate theory that defines acids and bases by their ability to donate or accept a proton (H$^+$ or hydrogen ion) in certain reactions.

Brönsted-Lowry acids are substances that can **donate a proton** (H$^+$ or hydrogen ion) during a reaction.

Brönsted-Lowry bases are substances that can **accept a proton** (H$^+$ or hydrogen ion) during a reaction.

$$H_2O \quad + \quad NH_3 \quad <\text{-------}> \quad NH_4^+ \quad + \quad OH^-$$

acid   *base*   *conjugate acid*   *conjugate base*

H$_2$O is an acid because it gives up an H$^+$ and becomes **OH- (a base)**
NH$_3$ is a base because it accepts the H$^+$ and becomes **NH$_4^+$ (an acid)**

When Brönsted-Lowry acids and bases react:

    Two conjugate **acid** - **base** pairs can be determined:

conjugate pair 1: H$_2$O and OH$^-$

conjugate pair 2 NH$_4^+$ and NH$_3$

Note: Each conjugate acid-base pair contains similar species that differ only by one H atom. The acid in each pair contains one more H than the base.

Practice 5
In the reaction:
$$HBr + H_2O <\text{------}> H_3O^+ + Br\text{-}$$
Which two species are Bronzed-Lowry acids?
1) HBr and H$_2$O   3) H$_2$O and Br-
2) HBr and H$_3$O$^+$ 4) H$_3$O$^+$ and Br-

Practice 6
Given the reaction:
$$H_2SO_4 + HPO_4^{2-} \text{----}> HSO_4^- + H_2PO_4^-$$
Which pair represents an acid and its conjugate base?
1) H$_2$SO$_4$ and HSO$_4^-$ 3) HSO$_4^-$ and H$_2$PO$_4$–
2) H$_2$SO$_4$ and HPO$_4^{2-}$ 4) HSO$_4^-$ and HPO$_4^{2-}$

4. pH Values of Acids and Bases

pH is a measure of the hydrogen ion (H$^+$) or hydronium ion (H$_3$O$^+$) concentration of a solution. A pH scale ranges in value from 0 - 14. Acids and bases can be defined by their pH values.

Acids are substances with pH values *less* than 7.

Neutral substances have pH *equal* to 7.

Bases are substances with pH values *greater* than 7.

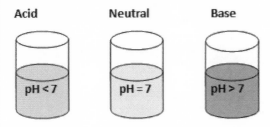

Acid   Neutral   Base

pH < 7   pH = 7   pH > 7

The strength of an acid or a base can be determined by its pH value:
Strong acids have very low pH values.
Strong bases have very high pH values

A typical **pH scale** is shown below. Some common substances are indicated below the scale to show where their pH values would likely be.

	Acid	Neutral	Base	
Strong	Weak	Weak	Strong
1-------------------------------7----------------------------14
		H$_2$O		
HCl	Acetic acid	NH$_3$	NaOH

Practice 7
Which of these pH numbers indicates the highest level of acidity?
1) 7   2) 5   3) 10   4) 8

Practice 8
Which pH indicates a basic solution?
1) 1   2) 5   3) 7   4) 12

Practice 9
A compound whose water solution conducts electricity and have a pH of 9 could be
1) HCl   3) LiCl
2) NH$_3$ 4) C$_2$H$_5$OH

Practice 10
Which aqueous solution would have a pH of 3?
1) H$_2$O(l)   3) KOH (aq)
2) CH$_3$OH(aq)   4) HNO$_3$(aq)

Practice 11
Which solution could have a pH of 10 ?
1) NH$_4$OH   3) NaCl
2) NaNO$_3$ 4) Na$_2$SO$_4$

Practice 12
Substance X is dissolved in water to produce a solution with a pH of 2. Substance X is most likely
1) Lithium hydroxide   3) Ammonia
2) Methanol   4) Sulfuric acid

5. Acid-Base Indicators

Acid–Base indicators are substances that change color in the presence of an acid or a base.

Acids and bases can be defined by changes they cause on indicators. Two common acid-base indicators are litmus paper and phenolphthalein .

Phenolphthalein is substance that dissolves in water to produce a colorless indicator solution.

Acids are substances that have *no effect* on phenolphthalein . Phenolphthalein stays colorless in the presence of an acid.

Bases are substances that change colorless phenolphthalein to *pink*. . Phenolphthalein is a good indicator to test for presence of a base

Phenolphthalein

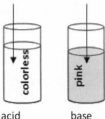

acid   base

Litmus paper comes in a variety of colors. When wet with an acidic or a basic solution, a litmus will change its color.

Acids are substances that will change litmus to *red*.

Bases are substances that will change litmus to *blue*.

Litmus papers

acid   base

Other common indicators are listed on Reference Table M below.

Table M
Common Acid–Base Indicators

Indicator	Approximate pH Range for Color Change	Color Change
methyl orange	3.1–4.4	red to yellow
bromthymol blue	6.0–7.6	yellow to blue
phenolphthalein	8–9	colorless to pink
litmus	4.5–8.3	red to blue
bromcresol green	3.8–5.4	yellow to blue
thymol blue	8.0–9.6	yellow to blue

Reading Table M:

Methyl orange will be :

Red in pH below 3.1

Yellow in pH above 4.4

Thymol blue will be:

Yellow in pH below 8.0

Blue in pH above 9.6

Practice 13
An indicator is used to test a water solution with a pH of 12. Which indicator color could be observed?
1) Colorless with litmus
2) Red with litmus
3) Colorless with phenolphthalein
4) Pink with phenolphthalein

Practice 14
In aqueous HNO_3 solution, phenolphthalein will be
1) pink, and litmus will be blue
2) pink, and litmus will be red
3) colorless, and litmus will be blue
4) colorless, and litmus will be red

Practice 15
Which substance would likely change bromcresol green from yellow to blue?
1) CH_3COOH 3) CH_3OH
2) NaOH   4) NaCl

Practice 16
In which solution will thymol blue indicator
appear blue?
1) 0.1 M CH_3COOH 3) 0.1 M HCl
2) 0.1 M KOH   4) 0.1 M H_2SO_4

Practice17
The following results were obtained when a solution is tested with methyl orange and litmus.

Methyl orange......yellow
Litmus.................. Red

What is the pH of the solution?
1) 1   2) 3   3) 5   4) 10

Practice 18
Which indicator, when added to a solution, changes color from yellow to blue as the pH of the solution is changed from 5.5 to 8.0?
1) bromcresol green
2) bromthymol blue
3) methyl
4) litmus orange

Practice 19
Which indicator would best distinguish between a solution with a pH of 3.5 and a solution with a pH of 5.5?
1) thymol blue
2) litmus
3) bromthymol blue
4) bromcresol green

6. Relative Ion Concentrations of Acids and Bases

Any solution made with water contains both H^+ and OH^- ions. A solution can be defined as acidic or basic depending on the relative amount of H^+ and OH^- in the solution.

Acidic solutions contain *more* (higher concentration of) H^+ ions than OH^- ions.

The stronger the acid, the greater the H^+ ion concentration in comparison to OH^- ion concentration.

Example: HCl(aq) (hydrochloric acid solution) contains more H^+ ions than OH^- ions.

Neutral solutions and pure water contain *equal* amounts of H^+ and OH^-.

Example: NaCl (a neutral salt solution) contain equal concentrations
of H^+ and OH^- ions

Basic solutions contain *more* (higher concentration of) OH^- ion than H^+ ion.

The stronger the base, the greater the OH^- ion concentration in comparison to H^+ ion concentration.

Examples: NaOH(aq) (sodium hydroxide solution) contains more OH^- ions than H^+.

The mathematical relationships between H^+, OH^-, and pH are discussed on the next page.

Practice 20
The aqueous solution of CH_3COOH contains
1) Equal molar of hydroxide and hydronium ions
2) More of hydroxide than hydronium ions
3) More hydronium than hydroxide ion
4) Neither hydronium nor hydroxide ion

Practice 21

Which are true of aqueous solution of $Mg(OH)_2$?

1) It contains more OH^- ion than H^+ ion, and is a nonelectrolyte
2) It contains more OH^- ion that H^+ ion, and is an electrolyte
3) It contains more H^+ than OH^-, and is a nonelectrolyte
4) It contains more H^+ than OH^-, and is an electrolyte

Practice 22
A solution with a pH of 7 contains
1) More H^+ than OH^-
2) More OH^- than H^+
3) Equal number of H^+ and OH^-
4) Neither H^+ nor OH^-

Practice 23

Which of these solutions contains higher concentrations of OH^- ions than H_3O^+ ion than OH^- ions?

1) HCl(aq)   3) $C_6H_{12}O_6$(aq)
2) KCl(aq)   4) $Ca(OH)_2$ (aq)

Practice 24

Which substance will produce a solution with a higher concentration of hydrogen ions than hydroxide ions?

1) NH_3 3) KCl
2) H_2SO_4 4) CH_3COH

Practice 25
When tested, a solution turns red litmus to blue. This indicates that the solution contains more
1) H_3O^+ than OH^- ions, and has a pH above 7
2) H_3O^+ than OH^- ions, and has a pH below 7
3) OH^- than H_3O^+ ions, and has a pH above 7
4) OH^- than H_3O^+ ions, and has a pH below 7

Topic 8 – Acids, Bases and Salts

7. Relating pH to H⁺ Ion Concentration

Mathematically, **pH** is defined as the –log of H⁺ ion concentration of a solution.

$$pH = -\log [H^+] \quad or \quad [H^+] = 10^{-pH}$$

pH is, therefore, a measure of how much (concentration of) **H⁺** or H_3O^+ ion are in a solution.

A calculator is not required to calculate pH if the H⁺ concentration is given as 1×10^{-x} M . The **x** being a value (between 1 to 14) of a negative exponent.

When the [H⁺] or [H_3O^+] of a solution is given in the form of 1×10^{-x} M, the **pH** value of the solution = **x**

Examples are given below.

[H_3O^+]	pH value	Type of solution
1.0×10^{-2} M	2	Acidic
1.0×10^{-8} M	8	Basic

If H⁺ concentration is not given as 1×10^{-x} , a scientific calculator will be needed to calculate the pH.

For example, if a solution has [H⁺] = 5.4×10^{-8} M

$$pH = -\log (5.4 \times 10^{-8}) = \textbf{7.3}$$

Practice 26

What is the pH of a solution with H_3O+ concentration of 1.0×10^{-6} M?

1) 1   2) 10   3) 6   4) 8

Practice 27

What is the pH of a solution with H+ concentration of 4.5×10^{-8} M?

1) 4.5   2) 8.0   3) 10.8   4) 7.3

Practice 28

A solution of which H⁺ concentration would have a pH of 2?

1) 1×10^{-12} M   3) 1×10^{-2} M

2) 1×10^{-10} M   4) 1×10^{-14} M

Practice 29

What is the hydronium ion concentration of a solution with a pH of 5.8

1) 1.0×10^{-5} M   3) 6.3×10^{-5} M

2) 1.6×10^{-6} M   4) 5.0×10^{-8} M

8. Relative H⁺ Concentrations of Solution

As you know a solution with a pH of 3 is more acidic than a solution with pH of 4. Since it is the concentration of H⁺ ions in a solution determines its pH, a solution with a pH of 3 has a greater concentration of H⁺ ions than a solution with a pH of 4.

. The lower the pH, the more H⁺ ions there are in a solution
. As [H⁺] in a solution increases, pH of the solution decreases

How much more (or fewer) H⁺ is in one solution in comparison to another solution can be determined if the pH values of the two solutions are known. Because of the mathematical relationship between H⁺ concentration and pH (shown above):

Difference in H⁺ of two solutions = 10 (difference in pH)

That means:

1 value difference in pH = 10 times (fold) difference in [H⁺]

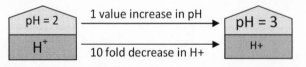

Example

If a solution with a pH of 2 is changed to a pH of 3.

Difference in [H⁺] = $10^{(3-2)} = 10^1 = 10$ fold

As the solution changes from pH of 2 to pH of 3, there will be a 10 fold decrease in H⁺ concentration.

Practice 30

Compared to a solution with a pH of 5, a solution with a pH of 2 has

1) 1000 times more H⁺, and is more acidic
2) 1000 times more H+, and is more basic
3) 3 fold more H+, and is more acidic
4) 3 fold more H+, and is more basic

Practice 31

Liquid A has a neutral pH and liquid B has a pH of 9. The H⁺ ion in B is

1) 1/10th as great as that of A
2) 1/100th as great as that of A
3) 10 fold as great as that of A
4) 100 fold as great as that of A

Practice 32

What is the pH of a solution that has a hydronium ion concentration 100 times greater than a solution with a pH of 6?

1) 4   3) 5

2) 3   4) 7

Lesson 2: Reactions of acids and bases

Introduction:

Acids and bases undergo chemical reactions with other substances and with each other.

In this lesson, you will learn about reactions of acids with reactive metals, and reactions of acids and bases with each other.

9. Reactions Acids with Metals

Acids react with certain metals to produce hydrogen gas and a salt. The reaction between an acid and a metal is a single replacement reaction. General equation and two example equations showing this reaction are given below:

	Reactants			*products*		
General equation:	Metal	+	Acid ------------- >	Salt	+	Hydrogen gas
Example equation 1:	Zn	+	$2HCl$ --------------- >	$ZnCl_2$	+	H_2
Example equation 2:	Mg	+	$2HNO_3$ ------------ >	$Mg(NO_3)_2$	+	H_2

Not all metals react with acids to produce hydrogen gas and a salt. **Reference Table J** shows the activity series of metals. This table can be used to determine which metals will react with acids to produce hydrogen gas and a salt.

Table J
Activity Series

Most Active	Metals	Nonmetals	Most Active
	Li	F_2	
	Rb	Cl_2	
	K	Br_2	
	Cs	I_2	
	Ba		
	Sr		
	Ca		
	Na		
	Mg		
	Al		
	Ti		
	Mn		
	Zn		
	Cr		
	Fe		
	Co		
	Ni		
	Sn		
	Pb		
	H_2		
	Cu		
	Ag		
Least Active	Au		Least Active

**Activity Series is based on the hydrogen standard. H_2 is not a metal.

NOTE the following facts about the table.

The most active metals are located toward the top.

The least active metals are located toward the bottom.

H_2 separates metals that will react with acids from those that will not react with acids .

Metals above H_2 will react spontaneously with acids to produce H_2 gas.

Metals below H_2 *will not* react spontaneously with acids.

Practice 33

Which of the following metals is likely to react with nitric acid to produce hydrogen gas?

1) Silver   3) Chromium
2) Gold   4) Copper

Practice 34

Which reaction will not occur under standard conditions?

1) $Ag + H_2SO_4 ------ > Ag_2SO_4 + H_2$

2) $Pb + H_2SO_4 ---- > PbSO_4 + H_2$

3) $Zn + HCl ------ > ZnCl_2 + H_2$

4) $Li + HCl ------ > LiCl + H_2$

Practice 35

Which equation is showing a reaction that is likely to occur under STP?

1) $Au(s) + 2HBr(aq) \rightarrow H_2(g) + AuBr_2(aq)$
2) $Cu(s) + 2HBr(aq) \rightarrow H_2(g) + CuBr_2(aq)$
3) $Ag(s) + 2HBr(aq) \rightarrow H_2(g) + AgBr_2(aq)$
4) $Sn(s) + 2HBr(aq) \rightarrow H_2(g) + SnBr_2(aq)$

10. Neutralization Reactions

Neutralization is a reaction between an acid and a base to produce *water* and a *salt*.
During neutralization reactions:
  . Equal moles of H^+ (of the acid) and OH^- (of the base) combine to neutralize each other
  . Water and salt are produced
  . The salt formed depends on the acid and the base that reacted

Below, general equation, example equation, and net ionic equation showing neutralization reaction are given:

	Reactants			*Products*	
General equation:	Acid +	Base	------- >	Water +	Salt

Example reaction equation: HCl + $NaOH$ ------- > H_2O + $NaCl$
                            (hydrochloric acid)   (Sodium hydroxide)   (water)   (sodium chloride)

Formation of water in neutralization H^+ + OH^- ---------> H_2O

Neutralization reactions are double replacement type reactions.
The water (H_2O) is formed from the H^+ ion of the acid and the OH^- of the base.
The salt (NaCl) is formed from the metal of the base (Na) and the non-hydrogen part of the acid (Cl)

11. Neutralization Reactions: Practice problems

Concept Task: Be able to determine which equations represent neutralization reactions.

Practice 36
Which reaction represents a neutralization reaction?

1) Pb + $AgNO_3$ -------- > Ag + $PbNO_3$
2) LiOH + $HC_2H_3O_2$ ---- ---- > H_2O + $LiC_2H_3O_2$
3) NH_4Cl + $AgNO_3$ --------- > NH_4NO_3 + AgCl
4) CH_4 + $2O_2$ -------- > CO_2 + $2H_2O$

Practice 37
Which equation represents a neutralization reaction?
1) $Ca(OH)_2$ --------> Ca^{2+} + $2OH^-$
2) $CaCl_2$ ---------> Ca^{2+} + $2Cl^-$
3) H^+ + OH^- ------------> HOH
4) H^+ + F^- ------------> HF

Practice 38
A neutralization reaction would likely occur between which two substances?

1) H_2S (aq) and $Ca(ClO_4)_2$ (s)
2) H_2SO_3 (aq) and $Ca(NO_3)_2$ (aq)
3) H_2SO_4 (aq) and $Sr(OH)_2$(aq)
4) SO_2 (g) and CaO (s)

Concept Task: Be able to complete neutralization reactions.

water
HNO_3 + KOH --------> H_2O + KNO_3
salt (be sure that the salt formula is correctly written)

⇐LOOKing Back: Topic 5-Formulas and Equations: You learned how to complete equations.

Practice 39
In the neutralization equation
$Ca(OH)_2$ + H_3PO_4 ---------> X + H_2O,
X is
1) $CaPO_4$ 3)CaH
2) $Ca_3(PO_4)_2$ 4) CaO

Practice 40
In the neutralization reaction:
  HF + NH_4OH ------> X + H_2O ,
 substance X is
1) NH_3 3) $(NH_4)_2O$
2) H_2 4) NH_4F

Practice 41
Complete the two neutralization reactions below.

2KOH + H_2SO_3 -----> _____ + ____

$2HC_2H_3O_2$ + $Mg(OH)_2$ ----> _____ + ___

12. Titration

Titration is a lab process used for determining the concentration of an unknown solution by reacting it with a solution of known concentration.

A titration process usually involves an acid and a base (acid – base titration). During an acid – base titration lab, a base (usually from a buret) is slowly added to an acid (usually in the flask). When moles of H+ and OH- are equal, neutralization has occurred, and the **endpoint** of the titration is reached. Phenolphthalein (a base indicator) is usually added to the acid beaker to indicate the endpoint. Titration is stopped when the solution in the beaker has a faint pink color. This indicates that all the acid in the beaker has been neutralized, and the solution in the beaker is slightly basic.

If any three of the following information about a titration process are known:
. Volume of the acid (V_A) or base (V_B)
. Concentration of the acid (M_A) or the base (M_B)
You can calculate for the unknown in the titration process using the *Reference Table T* titration equation below.

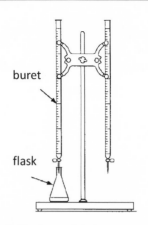

buret

flask

Acid – base titration set up

M_A x V_A = M_B x V_B	Use this equation if the mole ratio of H^+ (of acid) to OH^- (of base) is 1 : 1. *For example:* A titration involving HCl and NaOH has **1**H^+ : **1**OH^- ratio.

#H^+ x M_A x V_A = #OH^- x M_B x V_B	Use this equation if the mole ratio of H^+ to OH^- *is not* 1: 1. *For examples:* A titration involving H_2SO_4 and NaOH has **2**H^+ : **1**OH^- ratio. A titration involving HCl and Ca(OH)$_2$ has **1**H^+ : **2**OH^- ratio.

13. Titration Calculations: **Practice problems**

Concept Task: Be able to solve for an unknown in a neutralization problem using titration equation.

Example 1
30 mL of 0.6 M HCl solution is neutralized with 90 mL NaOH solution. What is the concentration of the base?

M_A x V_A = M_B x V_B

0.6 x 30 = M_B x 90

$\dfrac{0.6 \ x \ 30}{90}$ = M_B *numerical setup*

0.2 M = M_B *calculated result*

Example 2
How many milliliters of 1.5 M H_2SO_4 are needed to exactly neutralize 20 milliliters of 1.5 M NaOH solution.

#OH^- x M_B x V_B = #H^+ x M_A x V_A

1 x 20 x 1.5 = 2 x 1.5 x V_A

$\dfrac{1 \ x \ 20 \ x \ 1.5}{2 \ x \ 1.5}$ = V_A *setup*

10 mL = V_A *calculated result*

Practice 42
If 100 mL of a 0.75 M HNO_3 is required to exactly neutralize 50 mL of NaOH, what is the concentration of the base?
1) 0.25 M   2) 0.75 M   3) 1.0 M   4) 1. 5 M

Practice 43
How many milliliters of a 2.5 M LiOH solution are needed to completely neutralize 25 mL of a 1.0 M H_2SO_4 solution?
1) 10 mL   2) 50 mL   3) 20 mL   4) 8 mL

Practice 44
How many mL of a 0.4 M nitric acid solution are required to neutralize 200 mL of a 0.16 M potassium hydroxide? Show setup and result.

Practice 45
20 mL of a 3.0 M HCl solution is titrated to the endpoint with 60 mL of Mg(OH)$_2$. What is the concentration of the base? Show setup and result.

Lesson 3 – Salts and Electrolytes

Introduction

One property that acids, bases and salts share is their ability to conduct electricity in aqueous solutions. Acids, bases and salts are considered electrolytes.

In this lesson, you will learn about substances that are electrolytes and how electrolytes conduct electricity.

14. Salts

Salts are ionic compounds composed of a positive ion (other than H^+) and a negative ion (other than OH^-).

. Salt is one of the products of acid-base neutralization reactions

. Salts are electrolytes (conduct electricity when dissolved in water)

. Soluble salts are better electrolytes than insoluble salts

Recall that Table F can be used to determine soluble and insoluble salts.

Examples of salt formulas and names are given below.

NaBr	$CaSO_4$	NH_4Cl
sodium bromide	*calcium sulfate*	*ammonium chloride*
metal -nonmetal	*metal - polyatomic ion*	*NH_4 - nonmetal*

Practice 46
Which compound is a salt?
1) $Ba(OH)_2$ 3) H_2SO_4
2) $BaCl_2$ 4) CH_3OH

Practice 47
Which list of compounds includes only salts?
1) HNO_3, $NaNO_3$, and $Ca(NO_3)_2$
2) C_2H_5OH, CH_3COOH, and $CaCl_2$
3) CH_3OH, $NaOH$, and $NaCl$
4) $Ca(NO_3)_2$, Na_2SO_4, and $MgCl_2$

15. Electrolytes

Electrolytes are substances that can conduct electricity when dissolved in water.

. Electrolytes dissolve in water to produce a solution with positive (+) and negative (-) ions.

. Electrolytes conduct electricity because of mobile ions in the solution.

. Acids (Table K), bases (Table L) and salts are electrolytes.

Nonelectrolytes are substances that do not produce ions when dissolved, therefore, do not conduct electricity in solutions. Organic substances (other than organic acids) are typically nonelectrolytes. Organic substances are discussed in Topic 10.

Practice 48
Which 0.1 M solution contains electrolytes?
1) $C_6H_{12}O_6$ (aq)   3) CH_3COOH (aq)
2) CH_3OH (aq)   4) CH_3OCH_3 (aq)

Practice 49
Which two substances are electrolytes?
1) KCl and CH_3OH 3) C_2H_6 and $C_6H_{12}O_6$
2) $CaCl_2$ and LiOH   4) HCl and CH_3OH

Practice 50
An example of a nonelectrolyte is
1) C_2H_5CHO (aq)   3) K_2SO_4 (aq)
2) NH_4NO (aq)   4) HF (aq)

Practice 51
Which compound is a nonelectrolyte?
1) NH_3 3) CH_4
2) KBr   4) $CuCl_2$

Practice 52
Which salt will form a saturated solution with the highest electrical conductivity?

1) Potassium nitrate
2) Lead sulfate
3) Silver bromide
4) Potassium carbonate

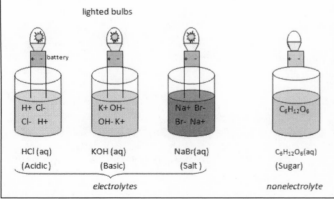

Topic 8 – Acids, Bases and Salts

Lesson 4 – Acid Formulas and Names

Introduction

An acid can be classified as organic or inorganic. Inorganic acids can further be classified as binary or ternary acids. In this lesson you will learn about different types of acids and how they are named.

L**OO**KING Ahead: ⟹ Topic 10 : Organic Compounds. You will learn more about organic acids

Chemical Formulas of Acids

Inorganic acids	Practice 53
Chemical formulas of inorganic acids usually start with H, follow by a nonmetal or a negative polyatomic ion.	Write formulas for the following acids
Binary acid formulas are composed of just two nonmetal atoms: hydrogen atom and another nonmetal atom.	a) hydroiodic acid
Examples HCl hydrochloric acid	
H_2S hydrosulfuric acid	b) chlorus acid
Ternary acid formulas are composed of three atoms: hydrogen atom and a polyatomic ion (Table E)	
Examples HNO_3 nitric acid	
H_2SO_3 sulfurous acid	c) carbonic acid
Organic acids	
Chemical formulas of organic acids usually end with –COOH.	
Examples: CH_3COOH ethanoic (acetic) acid	
$HCOOH$ methanoic acid	

Chemical Names of Inorganic Acids

Chemical names of acids vary depending on if an acid is a binary, ternary, or an organic acid.	Practice 54
	Name the following acids
Binary acids have names that begin with **hydro-** and end with **–ic.**	
Names of binary acids are formed by dropping the –gen of hydrogen and modifying the name ending of the nonmetal element to –ic.	a) HClO
Examples HCl H_2S	
Compound name: Hydro*gen* chlor*ide* Hydro*gen* sulf*ide*	b) $HClO_4$
Acid name: Hydrochlor*ic* acid Hydrosulfur*ic* acid	
Ternary acids have names that reflect only the name of the polyatomic ion (See Table E).	c) H_2Te
If an acid formula contains a polyatomic ion ending with **–ate**, the name ending of the acid is **–ic.**	
If an acid formula contains a polyatomic ion ending with **–ite**, the name ending of the acid is **–ous.**	d) $H_2C_2O_4$
Examples $H_2 SO_4$ $H_2 SO_3$	
Ion name: sulf**ate** sulf**ite**	
Acid name : sulfur**ic acid** sulfur**ous acid**	

Concept Terms

Key vocabulary terms and concepts from Topic 8 are listed below. You should know definition and facts related to each term and concept.

1. Arrhenius acid
2. Arrhenius base
3. Alternate acid theory
4. Alternate base theory
5. Hydrogen ion
6. Hydronium ion
7. Hydroxide ion
8. Acidity
9. Alkalinity
10. Relative ions concentration of acids and bases
11. pH
12. Indicator
13. Neutralization
14. Titration
15. Endpoint
16. Salt
17. Electrolyte
18. Properties of acids
19. Properties of bases
20. Properties of neutral substances

Concept Tasks

Concept tasks from Topic 8 are listed below. You should know how to solve problems and answer questions related to each concept task.

1. Determining and recognizing formulas of Arrhenius acids
2. Determining and recognizing formulas of Arrhenius bases
3. Determining and recognizing formulas of a substance based on relative ion concentration
4. Determining pH of a based on formula or name of the substance
5. Determining and recognizing name of a substance based on pH value
6. Determining and choosing a property of a substance based on other given properties
7. Determining a metal that will react with an acid to produce H_2 gas and salt.
8. Determining correct salt formulas from metal - acid reactions.
9. Determining and recognizing neutralization reaction equation
10. Determining correct salt formula from acid – base neutralization reaction
11. Solving for unknown in a neutralization problem using the titration equation
12. Determining pH of a solution from H^+ or H_3O^+ concentration
13. Determining H^+ or H_3O^+ concentration of a solution from pH
14. Comparing the level of H+ (or acidity) of two solutions with different pH values
15. Determining formula or name of a salt.
16. Determining formulas or names of substances that are electrolytes (or are nonelectrolytes)

Topic 9 - Kinetics and Equilibrium

Topic outline:

In this topic, you will learn the following concepts:

. Kinetics
. Rate of reactions
. Factors that affect rate of reactions
. Energy and chemical reactions
. Exothermic and endothermic reactions
. Potential energy diagrams

. Equilibrium
. Physical equilibrium
. Chemical equilibrium
. Le Chatelier's principle
. Entropy
. Spontaneous reactions

Lesson 1 : Kinetics

Introduction

Kinetics is the study of rates and mechanisms of chemical reactions.

A **rate** is the speed at which a reaction is taking place.

A **mechanism** is a series of reactions that lead to stable products of a reaction.

In this lesson, you will learn mostly about the rate of chemical reactions and factors that affect rate. You will also learn the relationship between chemical reactions and energy.

1. Rate of Reactions

*The **rate of a reaction*** is the speed at which a chemical or physical change occurs. Rate of a reaction can be measured in different ways.

For examples, rate can be measured by:
.The number of moles of a reactant consumed (used up) per unit time
.The number of moles of a product produced per unit time

Chemical and physical changes occur at different rates. Many factors affect the speed in which a reaction occurs.

Below are a list of factors that affect how fast a reaction will occur.

. Nature (or type) of the reactants

. Concentration (or amount) of the reactants

. Temperature (or heat) of the reactions

. Pressure (or volume) of gaseous reactants

. Adding of catalysts

Equal amount of solid **X** and **Y** are placed in water at the same time.

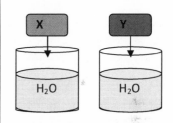

X and Y react with water, and are consumed as they react.

After 5 minutes, **less of Y** remained. **Y** reacts with (or is consumed in) water at a faster rate than **X.**

It is important to note that *not all* of these factors will affect how fast a reaction occurs. In one reaction, the nature of reactants may be the key factor in determining the rate of the reaction. In a different reaction involving different substances, pressure may determine how fast the reaction will occur.

To understand how the above factors affect rate, it is important to learn about effective collisions, activation energy, and catalysts. On the next page you will learn what each terms means. You will also learn the relationship between these terms and rate of chemical reactions.

2. Effective Collision

Collision theory states: For a chemical reaction to occur between reactants, there must be *effective collisions* between the reacting particles.

Effective collisions occur when reacting particles collide with *sufficient (right amount of) kinetic energy* and at a *proper orientation (angle)*.

. Rate of a reaction depends on frequency of (how often) effective collisions occur between particles.

. Any factor that can change frequency of effective collisions between reacting particles will change the rate of that reaction.

The diagrams below show the difference between effective and ineffective collisions.

Reacting particles   Particles colliding   Result of collision

Bad angle   Insufficient energy

Ineffective collisions   **No Product is formed**

Proper angle and sufficient energy

Effective collision   **Product is formed**

3. Activation Energy and Catalysts

Activation energy is the energy needed to start a chemical reaction.
. All chemical reactions, both endothermic and exothermic, require some amount of activation energy.
. Chemical reactions that require low activation energy are faster than those that require high activation energy.

. Any factor that can change the amount of activation energy needed for a reaction will change the rate of that reaction

. Any substance that can lower the activation energy for a reaction will increase (speed up) the rate for that reaction.

A **catalyst** is any substance that can increase the speed (rate) of a reaction by lowering the activation energy

. A catalyst in a reaction provides an alternate (lower activation energy) pathway for a reaction to occur faster.

Mg strip and **O₂** react (burn) to produce MgO as shown in equation below.

$$2Mg + O_2 \text{ ------} > 2MgO$$

However, Mg strip must be lit with Bunsen burner or matches flame before it can burn and combine with O_2.

The flame provides the activation energy needed to start the reaction.

4. Concentration and Reaction Rate

A change in concentration (amount) of one or more reactants will affect the rate (speed) of certain chemical reactions.

Consider the reaction of Mg (a metal) with HNO_3 (an acid) that is represented below:

$Mg(s)$ + $2HNO_3(aq)$ ------> $Mg(NO_3)_2(aq)$ + $H_2(g)$

The rate (or speed) that H_2 gas is produced depends on the concentration of the acid.

The diagram to the right shows a comparison of this reaction in a 2 M HNO_3 and in a 4 M HNO_3 solutions.

The relationship between concentration and the rate of a reaction is summarized below.

. Increasing concentration increases rate of a reaction because there will be more particles to collide, and the frequency of effective collisions will increase

. Decreasing concentration decreases the rate of a reaction because there will be fewer particles to collide, and the frequency of effective collisions will decrease

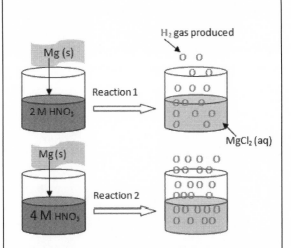

More H_2 gas is produced when magnesium (Mg) is placed in acidic solution of a higher concentration (4 M) than in acidic solution of a lower concentration (2 M) .

Rate of reaction is faster in 4 M HNO_3 than in 2 M HNO_3

5. Temperature and Reaction Rate

A change in temperature of one or more reactants will affect the speed (rate) of certain chemical reactions and physical changes.

Consider a reaction in which solutions A and B will be combined and allow to react.

$A + B$ ------> AB

The rate that AB is formed depends on the temperature of the solutions.

The diagram to the right shows how to test the rate of a this reaction by reacting the solutions at different temperatures.

The relationship between temperature and the rate of a reaction is summarized below.

. Increasing temperature of reacting solutions increases rate because kinetic energy of the particles will increase, resulting in an increase in frequency of effective collisions

. Decreasing temperature of reacting solutions decreases rate because kinetic energy of the particles will decrease, resulting in a decrease in frequency of effective collisions

Solutions A and B are placed in water baths of different temperatures.

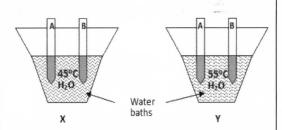

When solutions A and B are combined from each water bath, the reaction of A and B from Y will be faster. This is because solutions A and B from Y were raised to a higher temperature (55°C) than the solutions in X (45°C).

6. Pressure and Reaction Rate

A change in pressure will affect rate of a reaction when one or more reactants is a gas. A change in pressure of a reaction typically involve changing the volume (space) in which the reaction is occurring.

Consider a reaction below between hydrogen and iodine.

$$H_2(g) \ + \ I_2(g) \ \text{-------} > 2HI(g)$$

The rate that HI is produced depends on the pressure on the gases.

The diagram to the right shows the effect of two different pressures on the concentration of the reacting particles.

The relationship between pressure and the rate of a reaction is summarized below.

. Increasing pressure on a reaction that involves gases increases the reaction rate because concentrations of the reactants will increase due to a decrease in the volume of the system

. Decreasing pressure on a reaction that involves gases decreases the reaction rate because concentrations of the reactants will decrease due to an increase in the volume of the system

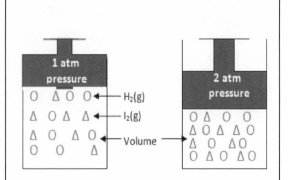

At a higher pressure of 2 atm, the volume of the reaction is decreased, resulting in a greater concentration of reactants $H_2(g)$ and $I_2(g)$. The reaction at the higher pressure will, therefore, be faster.

7. Surface area and Reaction Rate

Surface area is the amount of exposed area of a set mass of a solid substance.

A change in the surface area of a reacting solid will affect the rate of the reaction.
Consider the reaction below between Zn and HCl.

$$Zn(s) \ + \ 2HCl \,(aq) \ \text{-------} > \ ZnCl_2(aq) \ + \ H_2(g)$$

The rate that (how fast) zinc reacts with the acid will depend on the amount of exposed areas of the zinc.

The diagram to the right shows the differences in surface area (exposed area) of three different forms of zinc that will react with the acid.

The relationship between surface area and the rate of a reaction is summarized below.
. Increasing surface area of a solid increases reaction rate because there will be more exposed areas for effective collisions to occur

. Decreasing surface area of a solid decreases reaction rate because there will be fewer exposed areas for effective collisions to occur

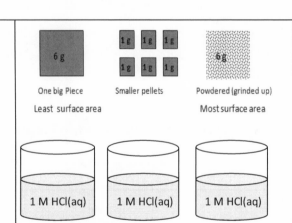

If the Zn forms are each reacted in separate beakers of 1 M HCl solution, the powdered zinc will react most vigorously (fastest rate) with the acid to produce hydrogen gas.

8. Factors that Affect Rate of Reactions: Summary table

The list of factors that will increase rate of reactions is summarized below.

Concept Facts: Study to remember these factors and how the increase reaction rates.

NOTE the followings as you study the factors below:

Left column lists *factors* that will *increase reaction rate.*

Right column explains how each factor leads to an increase in reaction rate.

Factors that will increase reaction rate	*Reasons why rate increases*
1. *Increasing* **concentration** of reactants	Increases number of reacting particles. Increases frequency of effective collisions between reacting particles.
2. *Increasing* **temperature** of reactants	Increases kinetic energy of reacting particles. Increases frequency of effective collisions.
3. *Increasing pressure* on the reaction	Decreases volume of gaseous reactants. Increases concentration of gaseous reactants. Increases frequency of effective collisions.
4. *Increasing surface area* of reacting solids	Exposes more area for reactions to occur. Increases frequency of effective collisions.
5. *Addition of a catalyst* to a reaction	Provides a lower activation energy (alternate) pathway for a reaction to occur.

6. **Nature of reactants:**

   Reactions of ionic solutions are very fast (almost instantaneous) because no bond breaking is required.

   Reactions of molecular substances are slow because reactions require breaking of strong covalent bonds. High activation energy is usually required for reactions involving molecular substances.

   Some metals, because of their nature, react faster than others in solutions.
   Sodium reacts more vigorously in water than lithium because of the nature of sodium.

Topic 9 - Kinetics and Equilibrium

9. Reaction Rate: Practice problems

Practice 1
Which conditions will increase the rate of a chemical reaction?
1) Decreased temperature and decreased concentration
2) Decreased temperature and increased concentration
3) Increased temperature and decreased concentration
4) Increased temperature and increased concentration

Practice 2
Given the reaction,

$A_2(g)$ + $B_2(g)$ -----------------> $2AB(g)$ + heat

An increase in concentration of $A_2(g)$ increases the rate of the reaction because of
1) A decrease in activation energy
2) An increase in activation energy
3) A decrease in frequency of collision
4) An Increase in frequency of collision

Practice 3
Given the reaction

$A(s)$ + $B(s)$ ------------------> $C(aq)$ + $D(aq)$

Which change would increase the rate of this reaction?
1) A decrease in temperature
2) An increase in temperature
3) A decrease in pressure
4) An increase in pressure

Practice 4
Given the reaction

$Mg(s)$ + $2HNO_3(aq)$ ------> $Mg(NO_3)_2(aq)$ + $H_2(g)$

At which temperature will the reaction occurs at the greatest rate?
1) 10^oC 2) 30^oC 3) 50^oC 4) 70^oC

Practice 5
At 20.°C, a 1.2-gram sample of Mg ribbon reacts rapidly with 10.0 milliliters of 1.0 M HCl(aq). Which change in conditions would have caused the reaction to proceed more slowly?
1) increasing the initial temperature to 25°C
2) decreasing the concentration of HCl(aq) to 0.1 M
3) using 1.2 g of powdered Mg
4) using 2.4 g of Mg ribbon

Practice 6
A 1-g piece of copper will react the slowest in

1) 1 M $HNO_3(aq)$ because there will be more effective collisions
2) 1 M $HNO_3(aq)$ because there will be fewer effective collisions
3) 2 M $HNO_3(aq)$ because there will be more effective collision
4) 2 M $HNO_3(aq)$ because there will be fewer effective collisions

Practice 7
Four aluminum samples are each reacted with separate 1 M copper sulfate solution under the same conditions of temperature and pressure. Which aluminum sample would react most rapidly?
1) 1 gram of Al block
2) 1 gram of Al ribbon
3) 1 gram of Al Powder
4) 1 gram of Al pellet

Practice 8
When a catalyst is added to a reaction, the speed of the reaction will increase because the catalyst provides
1) Alternate higher activation energy pathway for the reaction
2) Alternate lower activation energy pathway for the reaction
3) Alternate higher pressure environment for the reaction to occur
4) Alternate lower pressure environment for the reaction to occur

Lesson 2 - Energy and chemical reactions

Introduction

Every chemical substance contains some amount of energy that is stored within the bonds of the substance. During chemical and physical changes , substances absorb and release energy as bonds are formed and broken.

In this lesson, you will learn the relationship between energy and chemical (or physical) changes.

10. Energy and Reactions

Potential energy is stored energy in chemical substances. The amount of potential energy in a substance depends on its *structure* and *composition.*

Potential Energy of reactants is the amount of energy stored in the bonds of the reactants.
Recall that reactants are substances that are present at the start of a chemical reaction.

Potential Energy of products is the amount of energy stored in the bonds of the products.
Recall that products are substances that remain at the end of a chemical reaction.

Heat of reaction (ΔH) is the overall energy absorbed or released during a reaction.

ΔH of a reaction is the difference between the potential energy of the products and of the reactants.

$$\Delta H \quad = \quad \text{Energy of products} \quad - \quad \text{Energy of reactants}$$

Heat of reaction (ΔH) can be negative or positive.

Negative heat of reaction (-ΔH) means that:
. The products of a reaction have *less energy* than the reactants
. The reaction is exothermic (releases heat)

Positive heat of reaction (+ΔH) means that:
. The products of a reaction *have more* energy than the reactants
. The reaction is endothermic (absorbs heat)

11. Exothermic and Endothermic Reactions

Some chemical reactions absorb energy, while others release energy. Reactions that release energy are exothermic. Reactions that absorb energy are endothermic. Since most chemical processes occur in some form of a liquid (water or aqueous) environment, measuring temperature of the liquid before and after a reaction is usually one way to tell if a reaction is exothermic or endothermic.
If heat was released during a reaction, the temperature of the liquid will be higher after the reaction.
If heat was absorbed during a reaction, the temperature of the liquid will be lower after the reaction.

In the next set of notes, you will learn more about exothermic and endothermic reactions, and how each relates to heat of reactions (ΔH).

12. Exothermic Reactions and Energy

Exothermic reactions occur when products formed from a reaction contain less energy than the reactants. Since the products have less energy than the reactants, the reactants lost (or released) energy during the chemical change. When heat energy is released to the surrounding area where the reaction is occurring, the temperature of the surroundings will go up (or increase). *SEE DIAGRAM TO THE RIGHT.*

Heat of reaction, ΔH, is always negative (-ΔH) for all exothermic reactions.

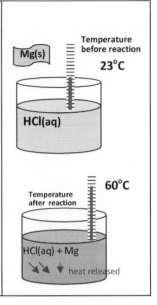

Concept Facts: Study and remember these facts about exothermic reactions.

In exothermic reactions:
. Products have less potential energy than the reactants
. Energy is released or lost, and the temperature of the surrounding increases
. Heat of reaction, ΔH ,is always negative (-ΔH)
. Equations of exothermic reactions always have energy released to the *right* of the arrow

Example equation of an exothermic reaction:

$$Mg + 2HCl \text{-----} > MgCl_2 + H_2 + \textbf{Energy}$$

13. Endothermic Reactions and Energy

Endothermic reactions occur when products formed from the reaction contain more energy than the reactants. Since the products have more energy than the reactants, the reactants gained (or absorbed) energy during the chemical change. When heat energy is absorbed from the surrounding area where the reaction is occurring, the temperature of the surroundings will go down (or decrease). *SEE DIAGRAM TO THE RIGHT.*

Heat of reaction, ΔH, is always positive (+ΔH) for all endothermic reactions.

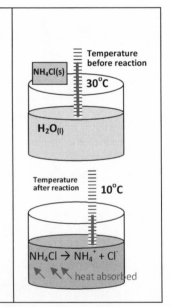

Concept Facts: Study to remember these facts about endothermic reactions.

In endothermic reactions:
. Products have more potential energy than the reactants
. Energy is absorbed, and the temperature of the surrounding area decreases
. Heat of reaction, ΔH, is always positive (+ΔH)
. Equations of endothermic reactions always have energy absorbed to the *left* of the arrow

Example equation of an endothermic reaction:

$$NH_4Cl(s) + \textbf{Energy} \text{-----} > NH_4^+(aq) + Cl^-(aq)$$

Below is a summary of exothermic an endothermic reactions. Use this table for a quick study, and comparisons of the two reactions.

Process	Potential Energy of reactants	Potential Energy of products	Energy change	Temperature of surrounding	Heat of reaction (ΔH)
Exothermic	Higher	Lower	Released	Increases	Negative (- ΔH)
Endothermic	Lower	Higher	Absorbed	Decreases	Positive (+ΔH)

14. Exothermic and Endothermic Reactions: Practice problems

Concept Task: Be able to determine certain information about energy of a reaction from the given temperature before and after the reaction.

Practice 9
Solid X and solid Y were dissolved in separate 100 mL beakers of water. The water temperatures were recorded as shown in the table below.

	Salt X	Salt Y
Initial water temperature	40.3°C	40.3°C
Final water temperature	34.5°C	46.1°C

Which statement is the best conclusion from the above information?
1) The dissolving of only Salt X was exothermic
2) The dissolving of only Salt Y was endothermic
3) The dissolving of both Salt X and Salt Y was exothermic
4) The dissolving of Salt X was endothermic and the dissolving of Salt Y was exothermic

Practice 10
A thermometer is in a beaker of water. Which statement best explains why the thermometer reading initially increases when LiBr (s) is dissolved in the water?
1) The dissolving of the LiBr(s) is endothermic, so energy is gained by the water
2) The dissolving of the LiBr(s) is exothermic, so energy is is gained by the water
3) The dissolving of the LiBr(s) is endothermic, so energy is lost by the water
4) The dissolving of the LiBr(s) is exothermic, so energy is is lost by the water

Concept Task: Be able to determine information about energy of a reaction from a given equation

Practice 11
Given the reaction   XW + energy ------ > W

Which is true of this reaction?

1) The reaction is exothermic with − ΔH
2) The reaction is exothermic with +ΔH
3) The reaction is endothermic with −Δ H
4) The reaction is endothermic with +ΔH

Practice 12

Given the reaction below   A ------ > B + energy

Which statement is true of the reaction below?

1) A has more energy than B, and ΔH is positive
2) B has more energy than A, and ΔH is positive
3) A has more energy than B, and ΔH is negative
4) B has more energy than A, and ΔH is negative

Practice 13
Given the reaction $H_2 + Br_2$ ----- > 2HBr + 73 KJ

The heat of reaction, ΔH, is

1) +73, because energy is released
2) +73, because energy is absorbed.
3) -73, because energy is released.
4) -73, because energy is absorbed.

Practice 14
Given the reaction $H_2O(l)$ + 286 KJ <==== > $H_2(g)$ + ½ $O_2(g)$

Which statement describes the forward reaction?

1) It is endothermic and releases 286 KJ
2) It is endothermic and absorbs 286 KJ
3) It is exothermic and releases 286 KJ
4) It is exothermic and absorbs 286 KJ

15. Reference Table I - Heat of Reaction

Reference Table I (below) lists equations for selected physical and chemical changes and their ΔH (heat of reaction) values. Some equations have -ΔH, and some have +ΔH.

Everything you had learned about exothermic reactions in the previous pages applies to all reactions on this table with − ΔH.

Everything you had learned about endothermic reactions in the previous pages applies to all reactions on this table with +ΔH.

Table I
Heats of Reaction at 101.3 kPa and 298 K

Reaction	ΔH (kJ)*
$CH_4(g) + 2O_2(g) \longrightarrow CO_2(g) + 2H_2O(\ell)$	–890.4
$C_3H_8(g) + 5O_2(g) \longrightarrow 3CO_2(g) + 4H_2O(\ell)$	–2219.2
$2C_8H_{18}(\ell) + 25O_2(g) \longrightarrow 16CO_2(g) + 18H_2O(\ell)$	–10943
$2CH_3OH(\ell) + 3O_2(g) \longrightarrow 2CO_2(g) + 4H_2O(\ell)$	–1452
$C_2H_5OH(\ell) + 3O_2(g) \longrightarrow 2CO_2(g) + 3H_2O(\ell)$	–1367
$C_6H_{12}O_6(s) + 6O_2(g) \longrightarrow 6CO_2(g) + 6H_2O(\ell)$	–2804
$2CO(g) + O_2(g) \longrightarrow 2CO_2(g)$	–566.0
$C(s) + O_2(g) \longrightarrow CO_2(g)$	–393.5
$4Al(s) + 3O_2(g) \longrightarrow 2Al_2O_3(s)$	–3351
$N_2(g) + O_2(g) \longrightarrow 2NO(g)$	+182.6
$N_2(g) + 2O_2(g) \longrightarrow 2NO_2(g)$	+66.4
$2H_2(g) + O_2(g) \longrightarrow 2H_2O(g)$	–483.6
$2H_2(g) + O_2(g) \longrightarrow 2H_2O(\ell)$	–571.6
$N_2(g) + 3H_2(g) \longrightarrow 2NH_3(g)$	–91.8
$2C(s) + 3H_2(g) \longrightarrow C_2H_6(g)$	–84.0
$2C(s) + 2H_2(g) \longrightarrow C_2H_4(g)$	+52.4
$2C(s) + H_2(g) \longrightarrow C_2H_2(g)$	+227.4
$H_2(g) + I_2(g) \longrightarrow 2HI(g)$	+53.0
$KNO_3(s) \xrightarrow{H_2O} K^+(aq) + NO_3^-(aq)$	+34.89
$NaOH(s) \xrightarrow{H_2O} Na^+(aq) + OH^-(aq)$	–44.51
$NH_4Cl(s) \xrightarrow{H_2O} NH_4^+(aq) + Cl^-(aq)$	+14.78
$NH_4NO_3(s) \xrightarrow{H_2O} NH_4^+(aq) + NO_3^-(aq)$	+25.69
$NaCl(s) \xrightarrow{H_2O} Na^+(aq) + Cl^-(aq)$	+3.88
$LiBr(s) \xrightarrow{H_2O} Li^+(aq) + Br^-(aq)$	–48.83
$H^+(aq) + OH^-(aq) \longrightarrow H_2O(\ell)$	–55.8

*The ΔH values are based on molar quantities represented in the equations. A minus sign indicates an exothermic reaction.

Concept Task: Be able to determine which reaction (or which substance) is formed with energy absorbed or released.

Practice 15
which substance is formed through endothermic reaction?
1) HI(g) 2) $H_2O(l)$ 3) $NH_3(g)$ 4) $H_2O(g)$

Practice 16
Based on Reference Table I, the formation of I mole of which substance releases the greatest amount of heat energy?
1) C_2H_2 2) NO 3) C_2H_6 4) NH_3

Practice 17
In which reaction, according to Reference Table I, do the products have lower energy content than the reactants?

1) $C(s) + O_2(g) \longrightarrow CO_2(g)$
2) $2C(s) + H_2(g) \longrightarrow C_2H_2(g)$
3) $N_2(g) + O_2(g) \longrightarrow 2NO(g)$
4) $N_2(g) + 2O_2(g) \longrightarrow 2NO_2(g)$

Concept Task: Be able to interpret a reaction based on its ΔH value.

Practice 18
Given the reaction: $CH_4(g) + 2O_2(g) \longrightarrow 2H_2O(g) + CO_2(g)$

What is the overall result when $CH_4(g)$ burns according to this reaction?

1) Energy is absorbed and ΔH is negative.
2) Energy is absorbed and ΔH is positive.
3) Energy is released and ΔH is negative.
4) Energy is released and ΔH is positive.

Practice 19
Which is true for formation of 1 mole of NH_3 from its elements?
1) It releases 91.8 KJ of energy   3) It releases 45.9 KJ of energy
2) it absorbs 91.8 KJ of energy   4) It absorbs 45.9 KJ of energy

Practice 20
When 2 moles of $KNO_3(s)$ is dissolved in water, the water temperature
1) increases as 34.89 KJ of energy is released.
2) increases as 69.78 KJ of energy is released.
3) decreases as 34.89 KJ of energy is absorbed.
4) decreases as 69.78 KJ of energy is absorbed

Practice 21
According to Reference Table I, what is the heat of reaction for the formation of 2 moles of $H_2O(l)$ from hydrogen gas and oxygen gas at 1 atmosphere and 298 K?

1) -571.6 KJ 2) -483.6 KJ 3) -285.8 KJ 4) -241.8 KJ

Practice 22
Given the balanced equation:

$4Fe(s) + 3O_2(g) \longrightarrow 2Fe_2O_3(s) + 1640 kJ$

Which phrase best describes this reaction?
1) endothermic with ΔH = +1640 kJ
2) endothermic with ΔH = −1640 kJ
3) exothermic with ΔH = +1640 kJ
4) exothermic with ΔH = −1640 kJ

Topic 9 - Kinetics and Equilibrium

16. Potential Energy Diagrams

Potential energy diagrams show changes in heat energy of substances over a course of a reaction. To understand potential energy diagrams, it is important to review components of a chemical reaction. These components are represented on all potential energy diagrams.

Consider this equation:

A + B₂ -----> ABB -------> AB + B

Reactants   *Activated complex*   *Products*

Note the following three substances about the equation:

Reactants (A and B₂) are substances that are present at the beginning of the reaction.

Products (AB and B) are substances formed at the end of the reaction.

An **activated complex** (ABB) is a high energy intermediate substance that is formed during the reaction. Because of its high energy, an activated complex is very unstable and will always break down or rearrange to form more stable *products.* An activated complex is not usually shown in a reaction equation. However, for a potential energy diagram to be accurately drawn for any reaction, an activated complex must be represented on the diagram.

Exothermic Reaction Potential Energy Diagram
(drawn for the reaction above)

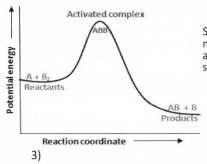

Since this is exothermic, note how the products are at a lower energy state than the reactants.

3)

Endothermic Reaction Potential Energy Diagram
(drawn for the reverse of the reaction above)

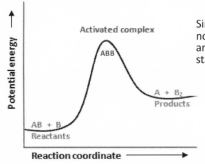

Since this is endothermic, note how the products are at a higher energy state than the reactants.

Practice 23

Which potential energy diagram best represents a reaction that has a positive heat of reaction ?

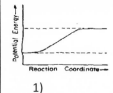
1)

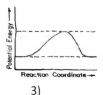
3)

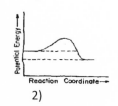
2)

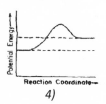
4)

Practice 24
Given the reaction

A + B ----------> C + 50 KJ

Which diagram below best represents the Potential energy change for this reaction?

1)

3)

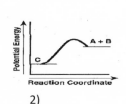
2)

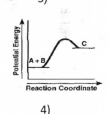
4)

Practice 25
The potential energy diagram below was drawn for a reaction that forms 2 moles of a substance.

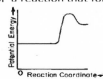

According to reference Table I, which substance was formed from the reaction?

1) 2Al₂O₃(s)   3) 2H₂O(l)

2) 2HI(g)   4) 2NH₃(g)

17. Potential Energy Diagram Measurements

The potential energy diagrams below show the important energy measurements . The left diagram shows measurements for a reaction that is uncatalyzed. The right diagram shows energy measurements for the same reaction with a catalyst added. Recall that a catalyst speeds up a reaction by lowering the activation energy. Note how certain energy measurements for the reaction are changed (lowered) with a catalyst.

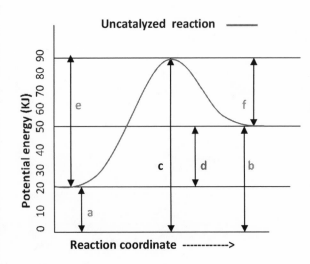
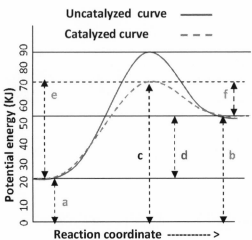

NOTE the following about each diagram:

The y axis is potential energy.

The x axis is the reaction coordinate (or progress of reaction).

Each curve shows the potential energy of substances that are present at different times over the course of a reaction (starting with reactants, ending with products).

Potential energy measurements of three substances are shown with arrows a, b and c.
These arrows are always drawn from the bottom of the diagram:

   (a) Potential energy of the reactants   (no change with catalyst)

   (b) Potential energy of the products   (no change with catalyst)

   (c) Potential energy of the activated complex   (lower with catalyst)

Differences of two potential energies are shown with arrows d, e and f.
These arrows are always drawn between two energies of the diagram.

   (d) Heat of reaction, ΔH (b − a)   (no change with catalyst)

   (e) Activation energy for forward reaction (c − a)   (lower with catalyst)

   (f) Activation energy for reverse reaction (c − b)   (lower with catalyst)

18. Potential Energy Diagram Measurements: Practice problems

Answers practice questions **26 through 28** based on the potential energy diagram below.

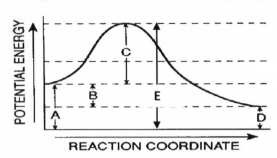

Practice 26
Which potential energy measurements will change if a catalyst is added to the reaction?
1) A and B only   2) C and E only   3) B, C, and E   4) A, B, and D

Practice 27
Which arrow represents the difference between the potential energy of the products and that of the reactants?
1) A   2) B   3) D   4) E

Practice 28
 Potential energy of reactants for the forward reaction can be determined by the length of arrow
1) A   2) B   3) C   4) E

Base your answers to questions 29 and 32 on the potential energy diagram below

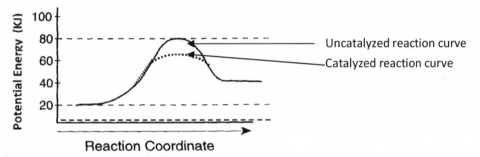

Practice 29
 Which statement correctly describes the potential energy changes that occur in the forward uncatalyzed reaction?
1) The activation energy is 40 KJ and a ΔH of +20 KJ
2) The activation energy is 40 KJ and a ΔH of -20 kJ
3) The activation energy is 60 KJ and a ΔH of +20 KJ
4) The activation energy is 60 KJ and a ΔH of -20 KJ

Practice 30
 Which reaction requires the lowest amount activation energy?
1) Forward uncatalyzed reaction
2) Forward catalyzed reaction
3) Reverse uncatalyzed reaction
4) Reverse catalyzed reaction

Practice 31
What is the heat of reaction (ΔH)
 for the reverse catalyzed reaction?

1) + 20 KJ
2) − 20 KJ
3) + 40 KJ
4) − 40 KJ

Practice 32
What is the energy of the activated complex for the uncatalyzed reaction?

1) 20 KJ
2) 40 KJ
3) 60 KJ
4) 80 KJ

Topic 9 - Kinetics and Equilibrium

Lesson 3: Entropy

19. Entropy

During chemical and physical changes, particles of a substance may rearrange from one phase to another. Particles can become more or less organized depending on the type of change the substance has gone through.

Entropy is a measure of randomness or disorder of a system. In chemistry, a system refers to any chemical or physical process that is taking place.

Entropy of chemical and physical systems is relative., meaning that randomness or disorder of one system can only be described when compared to another system.

. Entropy increases from solid to liquid to gas
. Entropy decreases from gas to liquid to solid
. As temperature increases, so does the entropy of the system
. As pressure increases, entropy of the system decreases
. Entropy of free elements is higher than entropy of compounds

Change in entropy diagrams

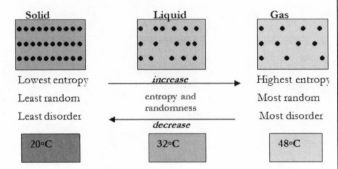

Solid	Liquid	Gas
Lowest entropy	*increase*	Highest entropy
Least random	entropy and randomness	Most random
Least disorder	*decrease*	Most disorder
20◦C	32◦C	48◦C

A physical or chemical change tends to occur by itself (spontaneously) if the change leads to a greater entropy and lower enthalpy (energy) state.

In physical changes, entropy increases as a substance changes from:

   solid to liquid to aqueous to gas

Ex: NaCl₂(**s**) ----increase entropy----> NaCl(**aq**)

In chemical changes, entropy increases if the reactants are changed in any of the orders listed below.

 solid to liquid to aqueous to gas

  Ex. C(**s**) + O₂(g) --------------------> CO₂(**g**)
                          increase entropy

smaller moles of reactants to greater moles of products.

  Ex **2**H₂O(g) -----------------> **2**H₂(g) + **1**O₂(g)
                   increase entropy

 a compound reactant is changed to free elements
   Ex   2AB -----------------------> A₂ + B₂
                    increase entropy

Entropy decreases if any of the above changes is reversed.

Practice 33
Under the same temperature and pressure, which sample of carbon dioxide contains particles with the highest entropy?
1) CO₂(g)   3) CO₂(l)
2) CO₂(s)   4) CO₂(aq)

Practice 34
Which substance will have the lowest entropy?
1) O₂(g) at 35°C   3) O₂(g) at 320 K
2) CO(g) at 50°C   4) CO(g) at 280 K

Practice 35
Which 10-milliliter sample of water has the greatest degree of disorder?
1) H₂O(g) at 120°C   3) H₂O(l) at 20°C
2) H₂O(l) at 80°C   4) H₂O(l) at 0°C

Practice 36
Which temperature change of ethanol will lead to a decrease in randomness of its molecules?
1) 5°C to -10°C   3) 0°C to 5°C
2) -10°C to 5°C   4) -5°C to 0°C

Practice 37
Which change is accompanied by an increase in entropy of the substance?
1) Hg(l) ------ > Hg(s)
2) N₂(l) ------- > N₂(g)
3) I₂(g) --------- > I₂(s)
4) H₂O(g) ------ > H₂O(g)

Practice 38
Which of these changes produces the greatest increase in entropy?
1) CaCO₃(s) ----- > CaO(s) + CO₂(g)
2) 2Mg(s) + O₂(g) ----- >   2MgO(s)
3) H₂O(g) --------- > H₂O(l)
4) CO₂(g) --------- > CO₂(s)

Practice 39
Even though the process is endothermic, snow can sublime. Which tendency in nature accounts
for this phase change?
1) a tendency toward greater entropy
2) a tendency toward greater energy
3) a tendency toward less entropy
4) a tendency toward less energy

Lesson 4: Equilibrium

Introduction:

Equilibrium refers to a state of balance between two opposing processes taking place at the same time and at equal rates. One example of two opposing processes would be the freezing of water to ice and the melting of the ice back to water. Another example would be a reaction in which two elements are joining together (synthesizing) to make a compound, and the compound that is being made breaking up (decomposing) into the elements.

In this lesson, you will learn about physical and chemical equilibrium. You will also learn about Le Chatelier's Principle, which describes changes in equilibrium reactions when a stress is applied to reactions.

20. Equilibrium

Equilibrium is a state of balance between two opposing (opposite) processes occurring at the same time (simultaneously).

When equilibrium is reached in a system:

. *Rate* of the forward process is *equal* to rate of the reverse process

. *Concentrations* (or amounts) of substances remain *constant*

Equilibrium can only occur in a closed system in which changes that are taking place are *reversible*. A closed system is a system in which nothing is allowed in or out. For an example, if a soda can is left closed, carbon dioxide gas will not be able to get inside the can from the outside, or allowed to escape out of the can to the outside. Inside the can, carbon dioxide will move in and out of the liquid of the soda can. If left undisturbed, equilibrium will be reached when the movements of carbon dioxide gas into the liquid (*dissolving*) and out of the liquid (*undissolving*) is occurring at the same rate. (see next page).

Equations showing a reversible process at equilibrium always contain a double ended arrow. (< ------- > or < ======= >)

$$CO_2(g) \;\xrightarrow[\text{Reverse}]{\text{Forward}}\; CO_2\,(aq)$$

Both physical and chemical changes can reach a state of equilibrium.

Closed can
Equilibrium process will occur in this can.

Open soda can
Equilibrium process CANNOT occur in this can.

21. Physical Equilibrium

Physical equilibrium occurs in reversible physical changes. Recall that during a physical change, compositions of a substance do not change. Physical equilibrium, therefore, occurs in processes that do not change one substance to another.

Examples of physical equilibrium are:

Phase equilibrium
Solution equilibrium

Examples and descriptions of these equilibrium systems are discussed on the next page.

22. Physical Equilibrium – Phase equilibrium

A **phase equilibrium** occurs in a *closed system* in which phase changes are occurring. Recall that temperature is important to phase changes. At a specific temperature of a substance, a state of balance (equilibrium) can be reached between two opposing phase changes of the substance. The temperature at which a particular phase equilibrium is reached is different for different substances.
Phase change equilibrium in water are described below.

Ice / water equilibrium: at 0°C or 273 K (melting and freezing points of water at normal pressure)

. Equilibrium exists between ice melting and liquid freezing
. *Rates* of melting and freezing are *equal*
. *Amounts* of ice and liquid water remain *constant*

$$H_2O(s) \quad < \underset{\text{freezing}}{\overset{\text{melting}}{=========}} > H_2O(l) \qquad \text{Ice/liquid water equilibrium equation}$$

Water /steam (vapor) equilibrium: at 100°C or 373 K (boiling point of water at normal pressure)

. Equilibrium exists between liquid evaporating and gas condensing

. *Rates* of evaporation and condensation are *equal*

. *Amounts* of liquid and gas remain *constant*

$$H_2O(l) \quad < \underset{\text{condensation}}{\overset{\text{evaporation}}{=========}} > H_2O(g) \qquad \text{water/steam equilibrium equation}$$

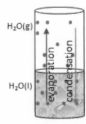

23. Physical Equilibrium – Solution equilibrium:

Solution equilibrium occurs in a closed system in which a substance is dissolving in a liquid.

Two examples of solution equilibriums are described below.

Solid in liquid equilibrium: In a saturated solution

. Equilibrium exists between dissolved particles and undissolved particles
. *Rates* of dissolving of solid and crystallization of ions are equal
. *Amounts* of solid and ions remain *constant* in the solution

$$NaCl(s) \quad < \underset{\text{crystallizing}}{\overset{\text{dissolving}}{=========}} > \ Na^+(aq) \ + \ Cl^-(aq)$$

Gas in liquid equilibrium in a closed soda can.

Gas in liquid equilibrium: In a gaseous solution

. Equilibrium exists between dissolved gas in the liquid
  and undissolved gas above the liquid

. *Rates* of dissolving and undissolving of gas are *equal*

. *Amounts* of undissolved gas (above liquid) and dissolved
  gas (in liquid) remain *constant*

$$CO_2(g) \quad < \underset{\text{undissolving}}{\overset{\text{dissolving}}{=========}} > CO_2(aq)$$

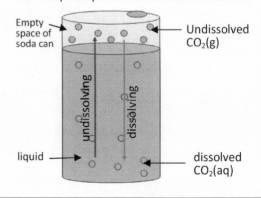

24. Physical Equilibrium: Practice problems

Practice 40
Which changes can reach equilibrium?
1) Chemical changes, only
2) Physical changes, only
3) Both physical and chemical changes
4) Neither physical nor chemical changes

Practice 41
Given the phase change equation $H_2O(g)$ <========> $H_2O(l)$

At 1 atm, at what temperature would equilibrium be reached?
1) 273 K   2) 0 K   3) 373 K   4) 298 K

Practice 42
Solution equilibrium always exists in a solution that is
1) Unsaturated   2) Saturated   3) Concentrated   4) Dilute

Practice 43
A sample of water in a sealed flask at 298 K is in equilibrium with its vapor. This is an example of
1) Chemical equilibrium
2) Phase equilibrium
3) Solution equilibrium
4) Energy equilibrium

Practice 44
Which of the followings is NOT an example of a physical equilibrium?
1) The equilibrium process for the synthesis and the decomposition of ammonia
2) The equilibrium process dissolving and crystallization of salt in a saturated solution
3) The equilibrium process for the evaporation and condensation of water at 373 K and 1 atm
4) The equilibrium process for the freezing and melting of water at 273 K and 1 atm

Practice 45
Which description applies to a system in a sealed flask that is half full of water?
1) Only evaporation occurs, but it eventually stops
2) Only condensation occurs, but it eventually stops
3) Neither evaporation nor condensation occurs
4) Both evaporation and condensation occur

Practice 46
A solution equilibrium is reached in a saturated solution when
1) Dissolving stops occurring
2) Crystallization stops occurring
3) Both dissolving and crystallization stop occurring
4) Dissolving occurs at the same rate as crystallization is occurring

Practice 47
In the reaction $Pb(NO_3)_2(s)$ <========> $Pb^{2+}(aq)$ + $NO_3^{-}(aq)$

Equilibrium is reached when
1) The rate of dissolving of salt and the rate of crystallization of ions is constant
2) The concentration of $Pb(NO_3)_2$ (aq) , Pb^{2+}(aq), and NO_3^{-}(aq) are constant
3) The rate of dissolving of salt is slower than the rate of crystallization of ions
4) The concentration of Pb^{2+} is the same as the concentration of $Pb(NO_3)_2(s)$

Practice 48
The diagram to the right represents a sealed flask.

Which equation represents a system that will reach
equilibrium in the flask?

1) NaCl (s) <----> NaCl (l)
2) NaCl (s) <----> H_2O (l)
3) H_2O (g) <----> NaCl (aq)
4) H_2O (g) <----> H_2O (l)

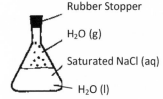

Rubber Stopper

H_2O (g)

Saturated NaCl (aq)

H_2O (l)

25. Chemical Equilibrium

Chemical equilibrium occurs in chemical changes that are reversible. *Recall* that chemical changes lead to changes in composition of substances. Chemical equilibrium, therefore, occurs in changes in which one or more substances are changing to other substances.

$$N_2\,(g) \quad + \quad 3H_2(g) \qquad \xrightarrow[\text{Reverse reaction}]{\text{Forward reaction}} \qquad 2NH_3(g)$$

Consider the *Haber process* reaction above:
At the start of the of the reaction, the reactants N_2 and H_2 will combine to produce NH_3 in the forward reaction. As NH_3 is being produced, the reverse reaction, in which NH_3 is decomposing to produce N_2 and H_2 will start. The speed (or rate) of this reverse reaction will be slow at first. As more and more NH_3 are being produced, the forward reaction will slow down, while the reverse reaction will speed up. Eventually, the forward and reverse reactions will be occurring at the same rate (equal speed). This means that if at a given time period 10 molecules of NH_3 are being produced, there will be 10 other molecules of NH_3 breaking up to produce N_2 and H_2. When the rates of the reactions (forward and reverse) are equal, the reaction is said to have reach a state of equilibrium.

At equilibrium:
. *Rate* of forward is *equal* to the rate of reverse.
. *Concentrations* of N_2, H_2, and NH_3 will be *constant* (unchanged).

A **stress** is any change in concentration, temperature, or pressure to an equilibrium reaction. Questions on chemical equilibrium often involve determining a result of a stress to an equilibrium reaction, or determining which stress will cause a particular change to a reaction.

Le Chatelier's Principle states that when a stress is introduced into a reaction at equilibrium, the reaction will change by speeding up in one direction and slowing down in the other direction to bring back or re-establish the reaction to a new equilibrium point. The concentrations of the substances at the new equilibrium point will be different from those at the old equilibrium point. There will be an increase in concentration of some substances, and a decrease in others.

On the next few sets, you will learn how to determine changes in rates, concentrations, and shift of equilibrium reactions from different types of stresses.

26. Notes on Le Chatelier's Principle

When studying notes on equilibrium on the next few pages, note the followings:

. A stress is given

. General changes to rate, concentration, and shift are listed as *a* through *e*.

. Example equation is given to the right of the stress

. Stress is indicated with a solid arrow up or down

. Results of stress (or changes) to the given reaction are indicated with dotted arrows.

    An "upward" dotted arrow indicates an increase in concentration

    A "downward" dotted arrow indicates a decrease in concentration

    A "longer" dotted arrow indicates an increase in rate in that direction

    A "shorter" dotted arrow indicates a decrease in rate in that direction

27. Change in Concentration (adding or removing substance)

A change in concentration of a substance in equilibrium reaction will change the reaction to compensate for the added (or the removed) substance.

Increasing concentration (by adding a substance).

. *Shifts* (speeds) the reaction *away* from the side of the increased

In general, when a concentration is increased:

a) *Rate* increases away from the side of the stress
b) *Rate* decreases toward the side of the stress
c) *Concentration* of other substances on the side of the stress decreases
d) *Concentration* of all substances on the opposite side of the stress increases
e) Reaction *shifts (speeds up) away* from the side of the stress

Decreasing concentration (by removing a substance).

. *Shifts* (speeds) the reaction *toward* the side of the decreased

In general, when a concentration is decreased:

a) *Rate* increases toward the side of the stress
b) *Rate* decreases away from the side of the stress
c) *Concentration* of other substances on the same side of the stress increases
d) *Concentration* of all substances on the opposite side of the change decreases
e) Reaction *shifts (speeds up) toward* the side of the stress

Concept Task: Be able to determine changes to equilibrium reactions when concentration of a substance is changed.

Example 1
Given the equilibrium reaction:

$$N_2 + 3H_2 \rightleftharpoons 2NH_3$$

Stress: Increase in concentration of N_2:

Results of stress (dotted arrows)

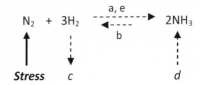

Example 2
Given the equilibrium reaction:

$$X + WY \rightleftharpoons XY + W$$

Stress: Decrease in [WY]

Results of stress (dotted arrows)

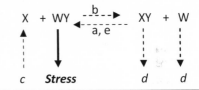

Practice 49
Given the reaction at equilibrium

$$SO_2(g) + NO_2(g) \; <======> \; SO_3(g) + NO(g)$$

As NO(g) is removed from the system, the concentration of

1) $SO_3(g)$ will increase
2) $NO_2(g)$ will increase
3) $SO_2(g)$ will increase
4) $SO_2(g)$ and $NO_2(g)$ will both be equal

Practice 50
The reaction below is at equilibrium:

$$C(s) + O_2(g) \; <=======> \; CO_2(g)$$

If the concentration of C(s) is increased, the equilibrium point will shift
1) Right, and the concentration of $O_2(g)$ will increase
2) Right, and the concentration of $O_2(g)$ will decrease
3) Left, and the concentration of $O_2(g)$ will increase
4) Left, and the concentration of $O_2(g)$ will decrease

Practice 51
Given the reaction at equilibrium:

$$N_2(g) + 3H_2(g) \; <=====> \; 2NH_3(g)$$

Increasing the concentration of $NH_3(g)$ will cause
1) A decrease in the concentration of $N_2(g)$
2) A decrease in the concentration of $H_2(g)$
3) An increase in the rate of forward reaction
4) An increase in the rate of reverse reaction

Practice 52
Given the equilibrium reaction

$$A + B \; <------> \; AB + heat$$

If the concentration of AB is decreased, the rate of forward reaction will
1) Increase, and [B] will also increase
2) Increase, and [B] will decrease
3) Decrease, and [B] will also decrease
4) Decrease, and [B] will increase

Topic 9 - Kinetics and equilibrium

28. Change in Temperature (adding or removing heat)

A change in temperature of equilibrium reaction will change the reaction to compensate for the addition or removal of heat.

Increasing temperature (by adding heat)
. *Favors* (speeds up) the endothermic reaction

In general, when temperature is increased:

a) *Rate* increases away from heat
b) *Rate* decreases toward heat
c) *Concentration* of substances on the side without heat increases
d) *Concentration* of substances on the side with heat decreases
e) Reaction *shift*s (speeds up) away from heat

Decreasing temperature (by removing heat)
. *Favors* (speeds up) the exothermic reactions

In general, when temperature is decreased:

a) *Rate* increases toward heat
b) *Rate* decreases away from heat
c) *Concentration* of substances on the side with heat increases
d) *Concentration* of substances on the side without heat decreases
e) Reaction *shift*s (speeds up) toward heat

Concept Task: Be able to determine changes to equilibrium reactions when concentration of a substance is changed.

Example 1
Given the equilibrium reaction:

$$HI + \textbf{heat} \xrightleftharpoons[\text{exo}]{\text{endo}} H_2 + I_2$$

Stress: Increase in temperature ($\uparrow$heat)

Results of stress (dotted arrows)

Example 2
Given the equilibrium reaction:

$$2 H_2(g) + O_2(g) \xrightleftharpoons[\text{endo}]{\text{exo}} 2H_2O \,(l) + \textbf{484 KJ}$$

Stress: Decrease in temperature ($\downarrow$heat)

Results of stress (dotted arrows)

Practice 53
Given the reaction at equilibrium

$$2HBr(g) + 73 \text{ KJ} \Longleftrightarrow H_2(g) + Br_2(g)$$

As the temperature decreases, the concentration of $H_2(g)$

1) Increases
2) Decreases
3) Remains the same

Practice 54
Given the equilibrium reaction

$$2A(g) + B(g) \Longleftrightarrow C(g) + 42 \text{ KJ}$$

If more heat is added to the reaction,
1) [A] and [C] will both decrease
2) [A] and [C] will both increase
3) [A] will decrease, but [C] will Increase
4) [A] will increase, but [C] will decrease

Practice 55
Given the system at equilibrium:

$$2NO_2(g) \Longleftrightarrow N_2O_4(g) + 58.1 \text{ KJ}$$

When the temperature is increased at constant pressure, the concentration of
1) N_2O_4 will increase, because the forward rate increases
2) N_2O_4 will increase, because the reverse rate increases
3) NO_2 will increase, because the forward rate increases
4) NO_2 will increase, because the reverse rate increases

Practice 56
Given the following system at equilibrium:

$$2Cl + 2H_2O + \text{energy} \Longleftrightarrow 2HCl + O_2$$

If the temperature of the system is decreased, the concentration of O_2 will
1) Decrease, and equilibrium will shift to the right
2) Increase, and equilibrium will shift to the right
3) Decrease, and equilibrium will shift to the left
4) Increase, and equilibrium will shift to the left

29. Change in Pressure

A change in pressure on equilibrium reaction in which gases are involved will change the reaction to compensate for an increased or a decreased in pressure.

Increasing pressure (by decreasing volume)

. Favors (speeds up) production of substances that are on the side with of the smaller number of moles of gases

In general, when pressure is increased

a) *Rate* increases toward the side of the smaller number of moles

b) *Rate* decreases toward the side of the greater number of moles

c) *Concentration* of substances on the side of smaller number of moles increases

d) *Concentration* of substances on the side of greater number of moles decreases

e) Reaction *shifts* (speeds up) in the direction of the smaller number of moles

Decreasing pressure (by increasing volume)
. Favors (speeds up) production of substances that are on the side of greater moles

Note: When pressure is decreased, result of stress (a-e) listed above will be opposite

Note:
In reactions in which the total moles of gases on both sides of the equation are equal, a change in pressure has no effect on equilibrium (no shift).

Concept Task: Be able to determine changes to equilibrium reactions when pressure is changed on the reaction.

Example 1
Given the equilibrium reaction below.

$$CH_4 + H_2O \underset{\text{reverse}}{\overset{\text{forward}}{\rightleftharpoons}} 3H_2 + CO$$

# of moles 1   1   3   1
total moles   2 moles   4 moles

Stress: Increase ($\uparrow$) pressure(by $\downarrow$ volume)

Results of Stress (dotted arrows)

$$CH_4 + H_2O \xleftarrow{a,\,e} \underset{b}{\dashrightarrow} 3H_2 + CO$$

$\qquad c \qquad c \qquad\qquad d \qquad d$

Stress: $\uparrow$ Pressure

Example 2
Given the equilibrium reaction below.

$$C_2(g) + D_2(g) \underset{\text{reverse}}{\overset{\text{forward}}{\rightleftharpoons}} 2\,CD(g)$$

# of moles 1   1   2
total moles   2 moles   2 moles

Stress: Increase ($\uparrow$) pressure:

Results of Stress: No change in rate, concentration or shift because the number of moles of substances are equal on both sides

Practice 57
Given the reaction: $2SO_2(g) + O_2(g) \rightleftharpoons 2SO_3(g)$

If pressure is increased on the reaction, there will be

1) A decrease in concentration of SO_3
2) An increase in concentration SO_2
3) A shift of equilibrium to right
4) A shift in equilibrium to left

Practice 58
Given the reaction at equilibrium:

$4HCl(g) + O_2(g) \rightleftharpoons 2Cl_2(g) + 2H_2O(g)$

If the volume on the system is decreased, the concentration of $Cl_2(g)$ will

1) decrease, because the reverse rate will decrease
2) decrease, because the reverse rate will increase
3) increase, because the forward rate will decrease
4) increase, because the forward rate will increase

Practice 59
Given the reaction at equilibrium
  $2HCl(g) \rightleftharpoons H_2(g) + Cl_2(g)$

As pressure is decreased at constant temperature, the concentration of HCl
1) Decreases   2) Increase   3) Remains the same

Practice 60
Given the reaction below at equilibrium

$W(g) + 3X(g) \rightleftharpoons 2Y(g) + 3Z(g)$

An increase in pressure at constant temperature will shift the equilibrium to the

1) Left, and the concentration of W(g) will increase
2) Left, and the concentration of W(g) will decrease
3) Right, and the concentration of W(g) will increase
4) Right, and the concentration of W(g) will decrease

Topic 9 - Kinetics and Equilibrium

30. Addition of a Catalyst

When a catalyst is added to a reaction at equilibrium:
. Rates of both the forward and reverse reactions increase (speed up) equally
　　　　　　As a result:
. There will be no change (no effect) on the equilibrium concentrations
. There will be no shift in either direction of the reaction

31. Chemical Equilibrium (Le Chatelier's Principle): Practice problems

Concept Task: Be able to determine stresses that will cause a certain change to a reaction

Practice 61
Given the equilibrium reaction
$$H_2 + Cl_2 + energy \longleftrightarrow 2HCl$$
Which change will cause the concentration of H_2 to decrease?
1) Decreasing Cl_2　　　　　　　　　　3) Increasing temperature
2) Decreasing pressure　　　　　　　　　4) Increasing HCl

Practice 62
Given the equilibrium reaction below:
$$2SO_2(g) + O_2(g) \longleftrightarrow 2SO_3(g) + heat$$
Which change at equilibrium will cause the rate of forward reaction to increase?
1) Decreasing concentration of $SO_2(g)$　　　3) Increasing temperature
2) Decreasing concentration of $SO_3(g)$　　　4) Decreasing pressure

Practice 63
Given the reaction
$$2C_2(g) + D_4(g) \longleftrightarrow 4CD + 20 KJ$$
Which change in the reaction will cause the equilibrium reaction to shift left?
1) Increase in pressure　　　　　　　　3) Increase in concentration of $C_2(g)$
2) Decreasing heat　　　　　　　　　　4) Adding a catalyst

Practice 64
Given the equilibrium reaction below:
$$SO_2(g) + NO_2(g) \longleftrightarrow SO_3(g) + NO(g) + heat$$
Which stress will NOT shift the equilibrium point of this reaction?
1) Decreasing pressure　　　　　　　　3) Increasing heat
2) Decreasing $SO_2(g)$ concentration　　　4) Increasing $NO(g)$ concentration

Practice 65
Given the reaction at equilibrium
$$2A(g) + 3B(g) \longleftrightarrow A_2B_3(g) + heat$$
Which change will not affect the equilibrium concentrations of $A(g)$, $B(g)$, and $A_2B_3(g)$
1) Adding more $A(g)$　　　　　　　　　3) Increase the temperature
2) Adding a catalyst　　　　　　　　　4) Increase the pressure

Practice 66
A saturated solution is represented by the equation below:
$$AgCl(s) + heat \longleftrightarrow Ag^+(aq) + Cl^-(aq)$$
Which change will cause an increase in the amount of $AgCl(s)$?
1) A decrease in pressure　　　　　　　3) A decrease in the concentration of $Ag^+(aq)$
2) An increase in temperature　　　　　4) An increase in the concentration of $Cl^-(aq)$

Topic 9 - Kinetics and Equilibrium

Concept Terms

Below is a list of vocabulary terms from Topic 9. You should know the definition and facts related to each term.

1. Kinetics
2. Rate
3. Collision Theory
4. Effective collision
5. Catalyst
6. Activation energy
7. Factors affecting reaction rate
8. Potential energy
9. Potential energy of reactants
10. Potential energy of products
11. Heat of reaction
12. Activated complex
13. Potential energy of activated complex
14. Exothermic reaction
15. Endothermic reaction
16. Potential energy diagram
17. Equilibrium
18. Physical equilibrium
19. Phase equilibrium
20. Solution equilibrium
21. Ice/water equilibrium
22. Water/steam equilibrium
23. Stress
24. Le Chatelier's Principle
25. Entropy

Concept Tasks

Below is a list of concept tasks from Topic 9. You should know how to solve problems and answer questions related to each concept task.

1. Determining which solution concentration will have the fastest or the slowest rate of reaction
2. Determining which solution temperature will produce the fastest or the slowest rate of reaction
3. Determining which pressure will cause the fastest or the slowest rate of reaction
4. Determining which solid form (different surface area) will produce the fastest or the slowest rate
5. Determining energy information of a reaction based on temperature before and after a reaction
6. Determining energy information from a given reaction equation.
7. Interpreting Table I equations with -ΔH value
8. Interpreting Table I equations with +ΔH value
9. Recognizing correct potential energy diagram as exothermic or endothermic
10. Identify line measurements on potential energy diagrams.
11. Relating equation to potential energy diagram
12. Relating potential energy diagram to ΔH of a reaction
13. Determining which phase a substance has the Highest or Lowest entropy
14. Determining which temperature a substance has the Highest or Lowest entropy
15. Determining which change equation is accompanied by an increase or a decrease in entropy
16. Determining effect on equilibrium reaction when concentration of a substance is changed
17. Determining effect of adding or removing heat (changing temperature) on equilibrium reaction
18. Determining effect of increasing or decreasing pressure (changing volume) on equilibrium reaction
19. Determining effect of adding a different salt to a solution at equilibrium
20. Determining stresses that will cause a certain change to a reaction

Topic 10 - Organic Chemistry

Topic outline

In this topic, you will learn the following concepts:

. Properties of organic compounds   . Naming and drawing organic compounds

. Classes of organic compounds   . Isomers

. Hydrocarbon compounds   . Organic reactions

. Functional group compounds

Lesson 1 – Characteristics of carbon and organic compounds

Introduction:

Organic compounds are compounds of carbon. Bonding properties of a carbon atom make it possible for carbon to bond with another carbon and with other nonmetals to form an enormous number of organic compounds that can range from one to several hundred atoms in length. Properties of organic compounds are due, in part, to chemical properties of a carbon atom.

In this lesson, you will learn about general properties of carbon and organic compounds.

1. Properties of Carbon and of Organic Compounds

Chemical and bonding properties of a carbon atom are as follow:

Concept Facts: Study to remember these properties.

. An atom of carbon has four valence electrons

. An atom of carbon must form four covalent bonds by sharing its four valence electrons

. Two adjacent carbon atoms can form a single, double or triple covalent bond

. Carbon atoms can bond to form a straight chain, side (branched) chain or ring structure

. Carbon atoms bond easily with each other, as well as with other nonmetal atoms such as H, N, O, and the halogens

$$\cdot \; \mathbf{C} \; \cdot$$

Lewis electron-dot symbol for a bonded carbon atom

4 dots = 4 valence electrons

General properties of organic compounds are as follow:

Concept Facts: Study to remember these properties of organic compounds

. Organic compounds are molecular (covalent) substances. That means they contain only nonmetal atoms

. Bonding between atoms are all covalent bonds

. General shape of basic organic molecules is tetrahedral

. Most are nonpolar or slightly polar

. Molecules of organic substances are held together by weak intermolecular forces

. Most have very low melting and low boiling points (due to weak intermolecular forces)

. Reactions of organic compounds are generally slower than those of inorganic compounds
    Reactions of organic compounds involve breaking strong covalent bonds holding the atoms together.

. Most are nonelectrolytes (do not conduct electricity well)
    Organic acids are weak electrolytes

. Most are insoluble in water (because they are nonpolar)

. Most decompose easily under heat (because they are molecular)

These properties vary among substances in the same class, as well as between the different classes.

Topic 10 - Organic Chemistry

2. Bonding in Organic Compounds

Recall that valence electrons are the electrons in the outer most electron shell of an atom. Valence electrons can be found as the last number in the electron configuration of an atom. Because of its four valence electrons, each carbon atom must form four covalent bonds.

12.001
C
6
2 – 4

$$-\overset{\textstyle |}{\underset{\textstyle |}{C}}- \qquad -\overset{\textstyle |}{\underset{\textstyle |}{C}}-\overset{\textstyle |}{\underset{\textstyle |}{C}}- \qquad -\overset{\textstyle |}{C}=\overset{\textstyle |}{C}- \qquad -C\equiv C-$$

Each C atom in the four structures shown above have four covalent bonds (–) around it. The four covalent bonds can be formed with other carbon atoms or with other nonmetal atoms.

Carbon atoms can join together to form a straight chain, branched, or ring structure as shown below.

$$-C-C-C-C-$$
straight chain

$$\overset{\textstyle CH_3}{\underset{\textstyle |}{\,}}$$
$$-C-C-C-C-$$
branched

ring (cyclic)

Concept Task: Be able to identify correctly drawn organic compound structures.

Correctly drawn structures of organic compounds must show each carbon atom with exactly four bonds.

Any organic compound structure drawn with more or less than four bonds around any of the carbon atoms is an incorrectly drawn structure.

Example 1

$$H-\overset{\textstyle H}{\underset{\textstyle H}{C}}=\overset{\textstyle H}{\underset{\textstyle H}{C}}-C-H$$

Incorrect organic structure

The Left **C** atom has only 3 bonds

The middle **C** atom has 5 bonds

$$H-\overset{\textstyle H}{C}=\overset{\textstyle H}{C}-\overset{\textstyle H}{\underset{\textstyle H}{C}}-H$$

Correct organic structure

All **C** atoms have exactly 4 bonds

Example 2

$$H-\overset{\textstyle H}{\underset{\textstyle H}{C}}-\overset{\textstyle O}{\overset{\textstyle ||}{C}}-\overset{\textstyle H}{\underset{\textstyle H}{C}}-H$$

Incorrect organic structure

The middle **C** atom has 5 bonds

$$H-\overset{\textstyle H}{\underset{\textstyle H}{C}}-\overset{\textstyle O}{\overset{\textstyle ||}{C}}-\overset{\textstyle H}{\underset{\textstyle H}{C}}-H$$

Correct organic structure

All **C** atoms have exactly 4 bonds

Practice 1

Which organic structure is correctly drawn?

1)

3)

2)

4)

Practice 2

Which structural formula is incorrect?

1) $H-\overset{\textstyle Cl}{\underset{\textstyle H}{C}}-Cl$

3) $H-C\equiv C-H$

2) $H-\overset{\textstyle O}{\overset{\textstyle ||}{C}}-OH$

4) $\overset{\textstyle H}{\underset{\textstyle H}{C}}=\overset{\textstyle H}{\underset{\textstyle H}{C}}$

3. Names of Organic Compounds

The IUPAC (International Union of Pure and Applied Chemistry) name of an organic compound has systematic components that reveal much about the compound.

Prefix (beginning root) of a name indicates the number of carbon atoms (See Reference Table P below)

Suffix (ending root) of a name indicates the class that the substance belongs (See Table below).

Numbers in a name indicate positions of side chains, multiple bonds, or functional groups.

di- or **tri-** in a name indicates the presence of two or three of the same side chain or functional group.

Three IUPAC names of organic substances are given below. The components of their names are explained under each substance. Understanding these names will help you understand names, formulas, and structures to several organic compounds given as examples as each class is explained in the next few sections of this topic.

Prop*ane*	*2*-Pentan*ol*	*2,3*-dimethyl, 1-butene
prop- : a 3 C-atom compound	pent- : a 5 C-atom compound	but-: 4 C atoms in the main chain
- ane : a compound of alkane	-ol : a compound of alcohol	-ene : a compound of an alkene
	2 : -OH functional group on carbon number 2	1 : double bond in 1st bond position
		2,3-dimethyl : 2 methyl side chains on carbon 2 and 3

Organic Prefixes: See Reference Table P

Number of Carbon	Prefix
1	meth-
2	eth-
3	prop-
4	but-
5	pent-
6	hex-
7	hept-
8	oct-
9	non-
10	dec-

Name endings : See Reference Tables Q and R

Class of compound	Name ending
Alkanes	- ane
Alkenes	- ene
Alkynes	-yne
Alcohols	-ol
Ethers	-yl
Aldehydes	-al
Ketones	-one
Organic acids	-oic
Esters	-oate
Amines	-amine
Amides	-amide

Halides are named with *halogen* prefixes:
Ex. *Chloro*butane

Concept Task: Be able to relate an organic compound name to the number of carbon atoms in the compound.

Practice 3

How many carbon atoms are in a molecule of a compound whose IUPAC name is pentanone?

1) 1   3) 3
2) 5   4) 7

Practice 4

Which is a correct name for an organic compound containing seven carbon atoms?

1) Butanol   3) Hexanal
2) Pentene   4) Heptanoic acid

Concept Task: Be able to relate IUPAC name of a substance to the class it belongs.

Practice 5

Which compound is an organic acid?

1) Pentanone   3) Hexanoic
2) Methanal   4) Propanamide

Practice 6

The compound hexanal is best classified as

1) an alkene   3) an ester
2) an aldehyde   4) a halide

Practice 7

Methyl ethanoate is classified as

1) an organic acid   3) a halide
2) an alcohol   4) an ester

Topic 10 - Organic Chemistry

Lesson 2 – Classes of Organic Compounds

Introduction:

There are enormous numbers of organic compounds. The study of these compounds are made a bit easier because they are classified into different groups. Compounds that belong in the same group share the following things in common: general formula, structural formula, molecular formula, and name ending.

Homologous series are groups of related organic compounds in which each member of the class differ from the next member by a set number of atoms. Compounds belonging to the same homologous series always share the same general formula, same molecular name ending, and similar molecular formula.

In this lesson, you will learn about the different classes of organic compounds in two sections:

I. Hydrocarbon compounds   II. Functional group compounds

Hydrocarbon Compounds

4. Saturated and Unsaturated Hydrocarbons

Hydrocarbons are classes of organic compounds that are composed of just two elements: hydrogen (H) and carbon (C). Bonding between carbon atoms in a hydrocarbon molecule could be single, double or triple covalent. Depending on the type of bond found between the carbon atoms, a hydrocarbon can be classified as saturated or unsaturated.

Saturated hydrocarbons (Alkanes)

Saturated hydrocarbons are hydrocarbons with all single covalent bonds between the carbon atoms.
A **single covalent bond** is formed between two carbon atoms when each atom contributes one electron. Since each carbon atom contributes one electron, a single covalent bond is formed by one pair of electrons (or two total electrons).
Alkanes are classified as saturated hydrocarbons.

C· ·C   C — C

1 pair (2 total) electrons   A single covalent bond

Unsaturated hydrocarbons (Alkenes and Alkynes)

Unsaturated hydrocarbons are hydrocarbons that contain one or more *multiple covalent* (double or triple) bond between two atoms.

A **double covalent bond** is formed between two carbon atoms when each atom contributes two electrons. Since each carbon atom contributes two electrons, a double covalent bond contains two pairs of electrons (or four total electrons).
Alkenes are unsaturated hydrocarbons with a double bond.

C : : C   C ═ C

2 pairs (4 total) electrons   A double covalent bond

A **triple covalent bond** is formed between two carbon atoms when each atom contributes three electrons. Since each carbon atom contributes three electrons, a triple covalent bond contains three pairs of electrons (or six total electrons).
Alkynes are unsaturated hydrocarbons with a triple bond.

C ⦂ ⦂ C   C ≡ C

3 pairs (6 total) electrons   A triple covalent bond

Practice 8
Which formula represents an unsaturated hydrocarbon?

```
  H  H                H  O
  |  |                |  ||
H–C=C–H            H–C–C–H
                     |
                     H
  1)                  3)

  H  H                H  H
  |  |                |  |
H–C–C–H            H–C–C–OH
  |  |                |  |
  H  H                H  H
  2)                  4)
```

Practice 9
What is the total number of electrons in the structure below?

```
  H            H  H
  |            |  |
H–C–C≡C–C–C–H
  |            |  |
  H            H  H
```

1) 12   3) 14
2) 24   4) 28

Topic 10 - Organic Chemistry

5. Alkanes – saturated hydrocarbons

Alkanes are saturated hydrocarbons with all single bonds between the carbon atoms. The first two members of alkane series are methane and ethane. Compounds in the alkane family share the following characteristics.

General formula	Structural formula	IUPAC name ending
C_nH_{2n+2}	all single (–) bonds	-ane

Example names and formulas of two alkanes

Molecular formula	C_3H_8	C_4H_{10}
Condensed formula	$CH_3CH_2CH_3$	$CH_3\,CH(CH_3)CH_3$

Structural formula

```
      H  H  H              H  CH₃ H
      |  |  |              |  |   |
  H – C – C – C – H    H – C – C – C – H
      |  |  |              |  |   |
      H  H  H              H  H   H
```

IUPAC name   propane   **2**-methyl prop*ane*

                           (methyl propane)

The general formula indicates the relationship between number of H atoms to C atoms. In both examples of alkanes, note how the number of H is 2 more than twice the number of C atoms.

Practice 10
Which name represents an alkane?
1) Octane   3) Propanal
2) Octene   4) Propanol

practice 11
Which formula represents an alkane?
1) $C_{10}H_{10}$ 3) $C_{11}H_{22}$
2) $C_{10}H_{20}$ 4) $C_{11}H_{24}$

Practice 12
Which compounds is a saturated hydrocarbon?
1) CH_2CH_2 3) CH_3CH_3
2) CH_3CHO 4) CH_3CH_2OH

Practice 13
Which structure is correct for an alkane?

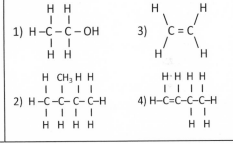

---

6. Alkenes – unsaturated hydrocarbons

Alkenes are unsaturated hydrocarbons with one double bond between two adjacent carbon atoms. The first two members of alkene series are ethene and propene. Compounds in the alkene family share the following characteristics.

General formula	Structural formula	IUPAC name ending
C_nH_{2n}	one double (=) bond	-ene

Example names and formulas of two alkenes

Molecular formula	C_3H_6	C_4H_8
Condensed formula	$CH_2\,CH\,CH_3$	$CH_3\,CH\,CH\,CH_3$

Structural formula

```
      H   H  H              H  H  H  H
      |   |  |              |  |  |  |
  H – C = C – C – H     H – C – C = C – C – H
          |                  |        |
          H                  H        H
```

IUPAC name   1-propene   2-butene
                 (propene)

The general formula indicates the relationship between number of H atoms to C atoms. In both examples of alkenes, note how the number of H atoms is twice the number of C atoms.

Practice 14
Which name represents an alkene?
1) heptyne   3) Ethane
2) Pentanol   4) Pentene

Practice 15
Which formula represents an alkene?
1) C_5H_{10} 3) C_8H_{18}
2) C_5H_{12} 4) C_8H_{14}

Practice 16
Which compound is an alkene?
1) CHCH   3) CH_3CH_2Cl
2) CH_2CH_2 4) CH_2CHCl

Practice 17
Which structure is correct for an alkene?

1) $H - C \equiv C - H$

```
                     O
                    //
          3) H – C
                    \
                     H
```

```
      H  H H  H            H  H  H  H
      |  | |  |            |  |  |  |
2) H – C – C – C – C – H   4) H – C = C – C – C – H
      |  | |  |                        |  |
      H  H H  H                        H  H
```

Topic 10 - Organic Chemistry

7. Alkynes- unsaturated hydrocarbons

Alkynes are unsaturated hydrocarbons with one triple bond between two adjacent carbon atoms. The first two members of alkyne series are ethyne and propyne. Compounds in the alkyne family share the following characteristics.

General formula	Structural formula	IUPAC name ending
C_nH_{2n-2}	one triple ($\equiv$) bond	-yne

Example names and formulas for two alkenes

Molecular formula	C_3H_4	C_4H_6
Condensed formula	CH_3CCH	$CHCCH_2CH_3$

Structural formula

$$H-\underset{\underset{H}{|}}{\overset{\overset{H}{|}}{C}}-C \equiv C - H \qquad H - C \equiv C - \underset{\underset{H}{|}}{\overset{\overset{H}{|}}{C}} - \underset{\underset{H}{|}}{\overset{\overset{H}{|}}{C}} - H$$

IUPAC name

1- propyne   1-butyne

(propyne)

The general formula indicates relationship between number of H atoms to C atoms. In both examples of alkynes, note how the number of H atoms is two fewer than twice the number of C atoms.

Practice 18
Which name represents an alkyne?
1) heptanol   3) hexane
2) Pentanoic   4) Octyne

Practice 19
Which formula could be an alkyne?
1) C_5H_{10} 3) C_6H_{14}
2) C_5H_8 4) C_6H_{12}

Practice 20
which formula correctly represents an alkyne?
1) CH_3CHCl_2 3) CHCH
2) CH_3CH_2Cl 4) CH_2CH_2

Practice 21
Which structure is correct for an alkyne?

1) $H-\underset{\underset{H}{|}}{\overset{\overset{H}{|}}{C}}=\underset{}{\overset{\overset{H}{|}}{C}}-\underset{\underset{H}{|}}{\overset{\overset{H}{|}}{C}}-\underset{\underset{H}{|}}{\overset{\overset{H}{|}}{C}}-H$ 3) $N \equiv N$

2) $H-\underset{\underset{H}{|}}{\overset{\overset{H}{|}}{C}}-C \equiv C-\underset{\underset{H}{|}}{\overset{\overset{H}{|}}{C}}-H$ 4) $O = C = O$

8. Drawing and naming hydrocarbons

Draw the following hydrocarbon compounds.

Practice 22

hexane

Practice 23

3-methyl, 2-pentene

Practice 24

$CH_3CH(CH_3)CH(CH_3)CH_3$

Name the following hydrocarbon compounds.

Practice 25

$$H-\underset{\underset{H}{|}}{\overset{\overset{H}{|}}{C}}-\underset{\underset{H}{|}}{\overset{\overset{H}{|}}{C}}-\underset{\underset{H}{|}}{\overset{\overset{H}{|}}{C}}-C=C-H$$

Practice 26

$$H-\underset{\underset{H}{|}}{\overset{\overset{H}{|}}{C}}-\underset{\underset{CH_3}{|}}{\overset{\overset{CH_3}{|}}{C}}-\underset{\underset{H}{|}}{\overset{\overset{CH_3}{|}}{C}}-\underset{\underset{H}{|}}{\overset{\overset{H}{|}}{C}}-\underset{\underset{H}{|}}{\overset{\overset{H}{|}}{C}}-\underset{\underset{H}{|}}{\overset{\overset{H}{|}}{C}}-H$$

Practice 27

$CH_3 CH_2C(CH_3)_2CH_2CH_3$

Functional Group Compounds

9. Functional Group

A **functional group** is an atom (other than hydrogen) or a group of atoms that replaces one or more hydrogen atoms of a hydrocarbon compound.

The element commonly found in most functional groups is oxygen (O). Nitrogen (N) and halogens (F, Cl, Br, or I) are also found in functional groups. Since functional group compounds contain elements other than carbon and hydrogen, they are *not* classified as hydrocarbons.

Attached functional group to a hydrocarbon chain changes the physical and chemical properties of the hydrocarbon. Properties (characteristics) of compounds with a functional group are related to the characteristics of the functional group itself.

Classes of functional group compounds that will be discussed in this section include:

Halides, alcohols, ethers, aldehydes, ketones, organic acids, esters, amines and amides.

Just as with the hydrocarbons, members of each class share similar characteristics such as general formula, molecular and structural formula, and name ending.

Below is a table summarizing classes of compounds with a functional group.

Each class of compound is further explained in the next few pages.

10. Functional Group Classes: Summary Table (Also see Reference Table R)

Class of compound		Functional group	How functional group attaches to hydrocarbon chain (R)	Example formula
1.	Halide	-Halogen	R-Halogen	$CH_3CH_2CH_2Br$
2.	Alcohol	-OH	R-OH	$CH_3CH_2CH_2OH$
3.	Ether	-O-	R-O-R'	$CH_3OCH_2CH_3$
4.	Aldehyde	$\overset{O}{\overset{\|}{-C}}-H$	$\overset{O}{\overset{\|}{R-C}}-H$	$CH_3CH_2\overset{O}{\overset{\|}{C}}-H$
5.	Ketone	$\overset{O}{\overset{\|}{-C}}-$	$\overset{O}{\overset{\|}{R-C}}-R$	$CH_3\overset{O}{\overset{\|}{C}}CH_2CH_2CH_3$
6.	Organic Acid	$\overset{O}{\overset{\|}{-C}}-OH$	$\overset{O}{\overset{\|}{R-C}}-OH$	$CH_3CH_2\overset{O}{\overset{\|}{C}}-OH$
7.	Ester	$\overset{O}{\overset{\|}{-C}}-O$	$\overset{O}{\overset{\|}{R-C}}-O-R'$	$CH_3CH_2\overset{O}{\overset{\|}{C}}OCH_3$

11. Alcohols

Alcohols are classes of organic compounds with a hydroxyl (-OH) group as the functional group. In alcohols, the −OH group replaces a hydrogen atom of a hydrocarbon. Characteristics share by all alcohols are as follows:

Functional group	General formula	IUPAC name ending
-OH	R-OH	-ol

Example name and formula of an alcohol

Molecular formula $\qquad$ C_3H_7OH

Condensed formula $\qquad$ $CH_3CH_2\,CH_2OH$

Structural formula

$$H-\overset{\displaystyle H}{\underset{\displaystyle H}{C}}-\overset{\displaystyle H}{\underset{\displaystyle H}{C}}-\overset{\displaystyle H}{\underset{\displaystyle H}{C}}-OH$$

IUPAC name $\qquad$ (1-propanol) or propanol

Types of alcohols

Monohydroxy alcohols are alcohols with one -OH group.

Depending on which C atom in a chain the one -OH is attached, a monohydroxy alcohol may also be described as primary, secondary or tertiary alcohol.

Primary alcohols are alcohols in which the **C** atom with the -OH is bonded to one other C atom.

Secondary alcohols are alcohols in which the **C** atom with the -OH is bonded to two other C atoms.

Tertiary alcohols are alcohols in which the **C** atom with the -OH is bonded to three other C atoms.

primary	secondary	tertiary
$-C-C-\underset{\underset{\displaystyle OH}{|}}{C}-$	$-C-\underset{\underset{\displaystyle OH}{|}}{C}-C-$	$-C-\underset{\overset{\displaystyle CH_3}{|}}{\underset{\underset{\displaystyle OH}{|}}{C}}-C-$
1-propanol	*2*-propanol	2-methyl, 2-propanol

Dihydroxy alcohols are alcohols with two -OH groups.

$-C-\underset{\underset{\displaystyle OH}{|}}{C}-\underset{\underset{\displaystyle OH}{|}}{C}-$ $\quad$ 1,3-dihydroxy propanol

Trihydroxy alcohols are alcohols with three -OH groups.

$-\underset{\underset{\displaystyle OH}{|}}{C}-\underset{\underset{\displaystyle OH}{|}}{C}-\underset{\underset{\displaystyle OH}{|}}{C}-$ $\quad$ 1,2,3-trihydroxy propanol (glycerol)

Practice 28

Which IUPAC name is of a compound of alcohol?

1) 2-butanal $\qquad$ 3) heptane

2) methanoic $\qquad$ 4) octanol

Practice 29

Which molecular formula represents an alcohol?

1) CH_3CH_2OH $\qquad$ 3) NH_4OH

2) CH_3CHO $\qquad$ 4) $CH_3CH_2CH_2COOH$

Practice 30

Which IUPAC name is of a primary alcohol?

1) 2-butanal $\qquad$ 3) 2-butanol

2) 1-chloropropane $\qquad$ 4) heptanol

Practice 31

Which formula represents a dihydroxy alcohol?

1) $CH_3CHOHCH_2OH$ $\qquad$ 3) CH_3COOCH_3

2) $CH_3CH_2CH_2COOH$ $\qquad$ 4) CH_3CHO

Practice 32

Which formula represents a secondary alcohol?

1)
$$H-\overset{H}{\underset{H}{C}}-\overset{CH_3}{\underset{H}{C}}-\overset{H}{\underset{OH}{C}}-\overset{H}{\underset{H}{C}}-H$$

2)
$$H-\overset{H}{\underset{H}{C}}-\overset{OH}{\underset{H}{C}}-\overset{OH}{\underset{H}{C}}-\overset{H}{\underset{H}{C}}-H$$

3)
$$H-\overset{H}{\underset{H}{C}}-\overset{H}{\underset{H}{C}}-\overset{CH_3}{\underset{OH}{C}}-\overset{H}{\underset{H}{C}}-H$$

4)
$$H-\overset{H}{\underset{H}{C}}-\overset{H}{\underset{H}{C}}-\overset{H}{\underset{H}{C}}-\overset{OH}{C}=O$$

Topic 10 - Organic Chemistry

12. Halides

Halides (halocarbons) are classes of organic compounds in which the functional group is one or more halogen atoms. Characteristics share by all halides are as follows:

Functional group	General formula	IUPAC naming
Halide	R-Halogen	-halogen prefix

Example names and formulas of halides

Molecular formula	C_3H_7F	$C_3H_6F_2$
Condensed formula	$CH_3 CH_2 CH_2F$	$CH_2FCH FCH_3$
Structural formula	H H H | | | H – C – C – C – F | | | H H H	H H H | | | H – C – C – C – H | | | F F H
IUPAC name	1- fluoropropane	1,2-difluoropropane

Practice 33

Which name represents a halide?

1) 2-butene

2) methyl proponaote

3) 2-Iodomethane

4) hexanol

Practice 34

Which molecular formula represents a halide?

1) CH_3CH_2OH

2) CH_2Cl_2

3) CH_3CHN_2

4) $HClO_3$

13. Ethers

Ethers are classes of organic compounds in which the functional group is an oxygen atom between two hydrocarbon chains. A common member of this class is diethyl ether, which was widely used as surgical anesthesia up until the 19th century.
Characteristics share by all ethers are as follows:

Functional group	General formula	IUPAC name ending
– O –	R – O – R'	-yl ending for hydrocarbons

Example name and formula of an ether:

Molecular formula	C_3H_8O
Condensed formula	$CH_3 O CH_2 CH_3$
Structural formula	H H H | | | H – C – O – C – C – H | | | H H H methyl ethyl
IUPAC name	methyl ethyl ether

Practice 35

Which molecular formula represents a member of the ether family?

1) $CH_3OCH_2CH_2CH_3$ 3) HCHO

2) $CH_3COOCH_2CH_3$ 4) $CH_2(OH)_2$

Practice 36

Which structural formula represents an ether?

1) $CH_3 - \overset{\overset{\textstyle O}{\|}}{C} - O - CH_3$

2) $CH_3 - \overset{\overset{\textstyle O}{\|}}{C} - OH$

3) $CH_3 - O - CH_3$

4) CH_3 OH

14. Aldehydes

Aldehydes are classes of organic compounds with –CHO group as the functional group. Methanal (commonly known as formaldehyde) is the first member of this class, and is commonly used as preservative of dead animals.

Characteristics share by all aldehydes are as follows:

Functional group	General formula	IUPAC ending
$\begin{array}{c} O \\ \parallel \\ -C-H \end{array}$ or $-CHO$	$\begin{array}{c} O \\ \parallel \\ R-C-H \end{array}$ or $R-CHO$	-al

Example name and formula of an aldehyde

Molecular formula	$C_2H_5\,CHO$
Condensed formula	$CH_3\,CH_2\,\textbf{CHO}$
Structural formula	$\begin{array}{c} H\ \ H\ \ \textbf{O} \\ \mid\ \ \mid\ \ \parallel \\ H-C-C-\textbf{C}-\textbf{H} \\ \mid\ \ \mid \\ H\ \ H \end{array}$
IUPAC name	Propanal

Practice 37

Which IUPAC name is a compound of aldehyde?

1) Butanol   3) Butanal

2) Butanoate   4) Butanoic

Practice 38

Which compound is an aldehyde?
1) CH_3CH_2OH 3) CH_3COOH
2) CH_3OCH_3 4) $HCHO$

Practice 39

Which structure represents an aldehyde?

15. Organic Acids

Organic acids are classes of organic compounds with -COOH (carboxyl) functional group. Organic acids, unlike other organic compounds, ionize weakly in water. They are weak electrolytes, therefore can conduct electricity. Their properties are the same as those of inorganic acids discussed in Topic 8 (acid - base topic). These properties include: producing H+ in solutions, changing litmus to red, phenolphthalein staying colorless, and pH below 7.

Characteristics share by all organic acids are as follows:

Functional group	General formula	IUPAC naming
$\begin{array}{c} O \\ \parallel \\ -C-OH \end{array}$ or $-COOH$	$\begin{array}{c} O \\ \parallel \\ R-C-OH \end{array}$	-oic

Example name and formula of an organic acid

Molecular formula	C_2H_8O
Condensed formula	$CH_3\,\textbf{COOH}$
Structural formula	$\begin{array}{c} H\ \ \textbf{O} \\ \mid\ \ \parallel \\ H-C-\textbf{C}-\textbf{OH} \\ \mid \\ H \end{array}$
IUPAC name	Ethanoic acid
Common name	(acetic acid or vinegar)

Practice 40

Which substance is an organic acid?

1) Butanoic   3) Iodomethane

2) Methylamine   4) heptanone

Practice 41

Which molecular formula is organic acid?

1) CH_3COCH_3 3) CH_3CH_2COOH

2) CH_3COOCH_3 4) $OHCH_2CH_2OH$

Practice 42

Which is a structure of an organic acid?

16. Ketones

Ketones are classes of organic compounds containing the functional group –CO–. Propanone (commonly known as acetone) is the first member of this class, and is the main chemical in most nail polish remover. Characteristics share by all ketones are as follows:

Functional group	General formula	IUPAC naming
O‖ –C– or –CO–	O‖ R–C–R'	-one

Example name and formula of a ketone

Molecular formula	C_3H_6O
Condensed formula	$CH_3 \textbf{CO}CH_3$
Structural formula	H **O** H │ ‖ │ H – C – **C** – C – H │ │ H H
IUPAC name	Propan*one*
Common name	(acetone, nail polish remover)

Practice 43

Which IUPAC name represents a compound of a ketone?

1) Chloropentane
2) Pentanoate
3) 3- hexanol
4) 3- hexanone

Practice 44

Which structure represents a ketone?

1) $CH_3CH_2CH_2COCH_3$
2) CH_3COOH
3) $CH_3CH_2OOCH_3$
4) $CH_3CH(OH)CH_3$

17. Esters

Esters are classes of organic compounds with the functional group –COO– . Ester compounds are generally responsible for characteristic smells of fruits and flowers, as well as scents of colognes and perfumes. Easters can be synthesized (made) by reacting an organic acid with an alcohol.

Characteristics share by all esters are as follows:

Functional group	General formula	IUPAC naming
O‖ –C–O– or –COO–	O‖ R–C–O–R'	-oate

Example name and formula of an ester

Molecular formula	$C_3H_6O_2$
Condensed formula	$CH_3 \textbf{COO} CH_3$
Structural formula	H **O** H │ ‖ │ H – C – **C** – **O** – C – H │ │ H H ‿ethanoate‿ ‿methyl‿
IUPAC name	methyl ethan*oate*

Practice 45

Which substance is an ester?

1) 1,2 ethanediol   3) Pentanal
2) Ethyl propanoate   4) heptanoic

Practice 46

Which formula is of an ester?

1) CH_3CH_2COOH 3) CH_3CH_2CHO
2) $CH_3COOCH_2CH_3$ 4) CH_3COCH_3

Practice 47

The formula of which compound is an ester?

1) CH_3CH_2OH

2) CH_3-O-CH_3

3) $CH_3OCH_2CH_3$ with O double bonded to the adjacent carbon

4) CH_3CCH_3 with O double bonded to the central carbon

Topic 10 - Organic Chemistry

18. Amines, Amides and Amino Acids

Amines, amides, and amino acids are classes of organic compounds containing a nitrogen atom in their functional groups.

Amines are classes of organic compounds with just a nitrogen atom, $-N-$, as the functional group.

Amides are classes of organic compounds containing both nitrogen and oxygen as part of their functional group.

Amino acids are classes of organic compounds that contain two functional groups: An amine group, $-N-$, and an acid group, -COOH.   Amino acids are joined together in polymerization chemical reactions to make proteins.

	Amine	Amide	Amino acid
Functional group	$\begin{array}{c} \mid \\ -N- \\ \mid \end{array}$	$\begin{array}{c} O \\ \parallel \ \mid \\ -C-NH- \end{array}$	$\begin{array}{c} NH_2 \\ \mid \\ -C-COOH \end{array}$
Examples			
Molecular formula	CH_5N	C_2H_5ON	
Condensed formula	$CH_3\,NH_2$	CH_3CONH_2	
Structural formula	$\begin{array}{c} H \ \ H \\ \mid \ \ \mid \\ H-C-N-H \\ \mid \\ H \end{array}$	$\begin{array}{c} H \ \ O \ \ \ \ \ \ H \\ \mid \ \ \parallel \ \ \ \nearrow \\ H-C-C-N \\ \mid \ \ \ \ \ \ \ \searrow \\ H \ \ \ \ \ \ \ \ H \end{array}$	
IUPAC name	methylamine	Ethanamide	

19. Drawing and Naming Functional Group Compounds: Practice problems

Draw the following functional group compounds.	Name the following functional group compounds.
Practice 48 3- iodohexane	**Practice 51** $\begin{array}{c} H \ \ H \ \ OH \ H \\ \mid \ \ \mid \ \ \mid \ \ \mid \\ H-C-C-C-C-H \\ \mid \ \ \mid \ \ \mid \ \ \mid \\ H \ \ H \ \ H \ \ H \end{array}$
Practice 49 dipropyl ether	**Practice 52** $\begin{array}{c} H \ \ O \ \ \ \ \ H \ \ H \\ \mid \ \ \parallel \ \ \ \ \ \mid \ \ \mid \\ H-C-C-O-C-C-H \\ \mid \ \ \ \ \ \ \ \ \ \mid \ \ \mid \\ H \ \ \ \ \ \ \ \ \ H \ \ H \end{array}$
Practice 50 $CH_3CH(NH_2)COOH$	**Practice 53** $CH_3COCH_2CH_3$

Topic 10 - Organic Chemistry

20. Isomers

Isomers are organic compounds with the same number of atoms, but different structural arrangements of the atoms.

The two compounds below are isomers.

C_3H_7Br	C_3H_7Br	*Same molecular formula*
$CH_3CH_2CH_2Br$	$CH_3CHBrCH_3$	*Same percent composition*

$$
\begin{array}{ccc}
\text{H} & \text{H} & \text{H} \\
| & | & | \\
\text{H} - \text{C} - \text{C} - \text{C} - \text{H} \\
| & | & | \\
\text{H} & \text{H} & \text{Br}
\end{array}
\qquad
\begin{array}{ccc}
\text{H} & \text{H} & \text{H} \\
| & | & | \\
\text{H} - \text{C} - \text{C} - \text{C} - \text{H} \\
| & | & | \\
\text{H} & \text{Br} & \text{H}
\end{array}
$$

Different structural formulas

1- bromopropane   **2**-bromopropane

Different names, different chemical substances

Different physical and chemical properties

Practice 54
Two isomers must have the same
1) Percent composition   3) Physical properties
2) Arrangement of atoms   4) Chemical properties

Practice 55
2-methyl butane and 2,2-dimethyl propane are isomers. Molecules of these two compounds have different
1) Number of covalent bonds   3) Molecular formulas
2) Structural formulas   4) Number of carbon

Practice 56
What is the minimum number of carbon atoms a hydrocarbon must have in other to have an isomer?
1) 1   2) 2   3) 3   4) 4

Practice 57
As the number of carbon atoms in each successive member of a homologous series of hydrocarbon series increases, the number of possible isomers
1) Increases   2) Decreases   3) Remains the same

Practice 58
Which alkane compound will have the most number of isomers?
1) C_7H_{16} 2) C_6H_{14} 3) C_5H_{12} 4) C_4H_{10}

Practice 59
Which hydrocarbon molecular formula will have the least number of isomers?
1) C_5H_8 2) C_4H_6 3) C_6H_{10} 4) C_7H_{12}

Practice 60
Which compound has no isomer?
1) C_3H_7Cl 2) C_4H_9Cl 3) C_2H_5Cl 4) $C_5H_{11}Cl$

Concept Task: Be able to determine formulas of compounds that are isomers.

Practice 61
Which two condensed formulas are isomers of each other?
1) $CH_3CH_2CH(Cl)CH_3$ and $CH_3CH(Cl)CH_2CH_3$
2) CH_2CH_2 and CH_3COCH_3
3) $CH_3CH_2CH_3$ and CH_2CHCH_3
4) $CH_3CH(OH)CH_3$ and $CH_3CH(OH)CH_2CH_3$

Practice 62
Which compound is isomer of 2-methyl butane?
1) 2,2-dimethyl propane   3) 2-methyl butene
2) 2,2-dimethyl butane   4) 3-methyl pentane

Practice 63
Which structural formula represents an isomer of the compound given below?

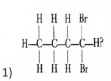

1)

3)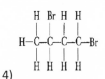

2)   4)

Topic 10 - Organic Chemistry

21. Isomers of Hydrocarbons

Every hydrocarbon with four or more carbon atoms have at least one isomer. As the number of carbon atoms increases, the number of possible isomers increases.

Alkane Isomers

Isomers of an alkane usually have different arrangements of the carbon chain, with the structures having one or more side chains (*alkyl group*).

Alkyl is a hydrocarbon group with one fewer hydrogen atom than the corresponding alkane.

CH_4 (methane, an alkane) CH_3 (methyl, an alkyl)

C_2H_6 (ethane, an alkane) C_2H_5 (ethyl, an alkyl)

Examples of alkane isomers

C_4H_{10} C_4H_{10}

$CH_3CH_2CH_2CH_3$ $CH_3\,CH(CH_3)CH_3$

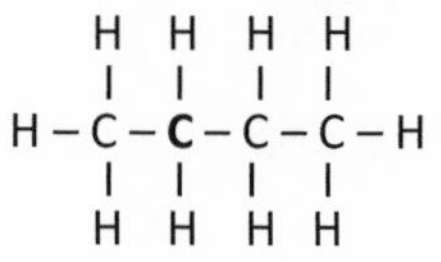

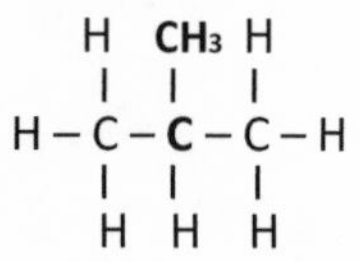

```
    H  H  H  H              H  CH₃ H
    |  |  |  |              |  |  |
H – C – C – C – C – H    H – C – C – C – H
    |  |  |  |              |  |  |
    H  H  H  H              H  H  H
```

butane   **2**-**methyl** prop*ane*

                         (methyl propane)

Alkene and alkyne isomers

Isomers of alkenes and alkynes typically have the multiple covalent (double or triple) bonds placed between different adjacent carbon atoms. Some may even have alkyl side chains along with the multiple covalent bonds.

Examples of alkene isomers

C_4H_8 C_4H_8

$CH_2CHCH_2CH_3$ $CH_3\,CHCHCH_3$

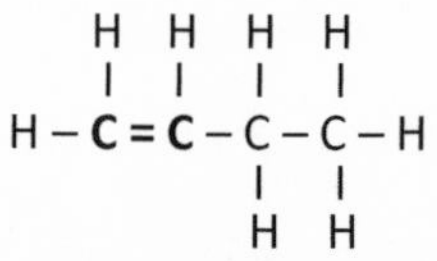

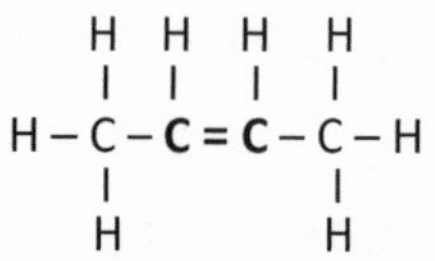

```
    H  H  H  H              H  H  H  H
    |  |  |  |              |  |  |  |
H – C = C – C – C – H    H – C – C = C – C – H
          |  |              |           |
          H  H              H           H
```

1-butene   *2*-butene

Concept Task: Be able to draw and name isomers of hydrocarbons.

Practice 64
Draw octane, and then draw and name any two isomers of octane.

Practice 65
Draw pentene, and then draw and name any two isomers of pentene.

Practice 66
Draw heptyne, and then draw and name any two isomers of heptyne.

22. Isomers of Functional Group Compounds

Isomers of functional group compounds generally have the functional group attached to different carbon atoms. In some cases, a compound from one functional group class may be an isomer of a compound from a different functional group class. For an example, a monohydroxy alcohol and an ether of the same number of carbon atoms are always isomers.

Halide isomers

C_4H_9Br	C_4H_9Br	C_4H_9Br
$CH_3CH_2CH_2CH_2Br$	$CH_3CH_2CHBrCH_3$	$CH_2(Br)CH(CH_3)CH_3$

```
  H  H  H H          H  H  H  H          H  H   H
  |  |  | |          |  |  |  |          |  |   |
H-C--C--C--C-H     H-C--C--C--C-H      H-C--C --C-H
  |  |  | |          |  |  |  |          |  |   |
  H  H  H Br         H  H  Br H          Br CH3 H
```

1- bromobutane	*2*-bromobutane	*1*-bromo, *2*-methyl propane

Alcohol and ether isomers
A monohydroxy alcohol and an ether of the same number of carbon atoms are always isomers.

C_3H_8O	C_3H_8O	C_3H_8O
$CH_3CH_2CH_2OH$	$CH_3CH(OH)CH_3$	$CH_3OCH_2CH_3$

```
  H  H  H           H  H  H          H      H  H
  |  |  |           |  |  |          |      |  |
H-C--C--C-H       H-C--C--C-H      H-C--O--C--C-H
  |  |  |           |  |  |          |      |  |
  H  H  OH          H  OH H          H      H  H
```

1-propan*ol*	2-propan*ol*	methyl ethyl ether

Ketone and aldehyde isomers
A ketone and an aldehyde of the same number of carbon atoms are always isomers.

$C_5H_{10}O$	$C_5H_{10}O$	$C_5H_{10}O$
$CH_3COCH_2CH_2CH_3$	$CH_3CH_2COCH_2CH_3$	$CH_3CH_2CH_2CH_2CHO$

```
  H  O  H H H         H  H  O  H H         H  H  H  H  O
  |  ||  | | |         |  |  ||  | |         |  |  |  |  ||
H-C--C--C--C--C-H   H-C--C--C--C--C-H   H-C--C--C--C--C-H
  |     | | |         |  |     | |         |  |  |  |
  H     H H H         H  H     H H         H  H  H  H
```

2-pentan*one*	**3**-pentan*one*	pentan*al*

Concept Task: Be able to draw and name isomers of compounds with a functional group.

Practice 67

Draw 1,1-difluoropropane, and then draw and name two isomers of 1,1-difluoropropane.

Practice 68

Draw a butanol, and then draw and name two isomers of butanol (include an ether isomer)

Practice 69

Draw 2-hexanone, and then draw and name two isomers of 2-hexanone (include an aldehyde isomer)

Lesson 5:   Reactions of Organic Compounds

Introduction:

There are many kinds of organic reactions. Organic compounds can react with each other, as well as with inorganic compounds to form a wide range of organic products. As mentioned in Lesson 1 of this topic, organic reactions are generally slower than reactions of inorganic compounds. This is due to the fact that organic reactions involve the breaking of strong covalent bonds within the organic molecules.

In this lesson, you'll learn about the different types of organic reactions.

As you study the different types of organic reactions in the next few sets, note the followings:
. A reaction name is given and defined
. The main organic reactants and products for the reaction are given
. General equation of the reaction is given
. Example equations for the different reactions are also given.

Study each reaction separately and note differences between the reactions.

23. Substitution

Substitution reactions typically involve the removing of a hydrogen atom from an alkane and replacing it with a halogen. The main organic product in a halogen substitution is a halide.

Organic reactant	*Organic product*
Alkane (saturated hydrocarbon)	Halide (with 1 halogen attached)

Example of a substitution reaction is shown below.

Alkane	+	Halogen ------ >	Halide	+	Acid

$$C_3H_8 \quad + \quad F_2 \quad ---------> \quad C_3H_7F \quad + \quad HF$$

$$\begin{array}{c} H \quad H \quad H \\ | \quad | \quad | \\ H-C-C-C-H \\ | \quad | \quad | \\ H \quad H \quad H \end{array} + \quad F-F \quad ---------> \begin{array}{c} H \quad H \quad H \\ | \quad | \quad | \\ H-C-C-C-F \\ | \quad | \quad | \\ H \quad H \quad H \end{array} + \quad H-F$$

Propane	Fluorine	Fluoropropane	Hydrogen fluoride

Practice 70

Which substance will likely undergo a substitution reaction with iodine?

1) 2-hexene   3) 2 - methyl hexyne
2) 2-pentanol   4) 2 -methyl pentane

Practice 71

Which equation represents a substitution reaction?

1) CH_2CH_2 + H_2 ------- > CH_3CH_3
2) CH_3CH_3 + O_2 ------ > CO_2 + H_2
3) CH_2CH_2 + Br_2 ------- > CH_2BrCH_2Br
4) CH_3CH_3 + Br_2 ------ > $BrCH_2CH_3$ + HBr

Practice 72

Draw and name the structural formula of the organic product.

$CH_3CH_2CH(CH_3)CH_3$ + I_2 --- > $CH_2(I)CH_2CH(CH_3)CH_3$ + HI

Practice 73

Draw and name the structural formula of the product that will form.

$$\begin{array}{c} H \quad H \quad H \quad H \quad H \\ | \quad | \quad | \quad | \quad | \\ H-C-C-C-C-C-H \\ | \quad | \quad | \quad | \quad | \\ H \quad H \quad H \quad H \quad H \end{array} + \quad Cl_2 \quad ------ > \quad HCl \quad +$$

24. Organic Reactions: **Summary Table**

Use this table for a quick a review of organic reactions.

Organic Reactions	Reactants		Products	
1. Substitution	Alkane (saturated hydrocarbon)	Halogen	1 – Halide (a one-halogen halide)	Acid (inorganic)
2. Addition **Hydrogenation**	Alkene (unsaturated hydrocarbon)	Hydrogen	Alkane	
Halogenation	Alkene	Halogen	1,2 – Halide (a two-halogen halide)	
3. Saponification	Fat	Base	1,2,3-propanetriol (glycerol)	Soap
4. Fermentation	$C_6H_{12}O_6$ (sugar)		C_2H_5OH (ethanol)	CO_2 (Carbon dioxide)
5. Combustion	Hydrocarbon	O_2	Carbon dioxide	Water
6. Esterification	Organic Acid	Alcohol	Ester	Water
7. Polymerization **Condensation Polymerization**	Alcohol (monomers)	Alcohol	Ether (a polymer)	Water
	Amino acid (monomers)	Amino acid	Protein (a polymer)	Water
Addition Polymerization	$n(CH_2=CH_2)$ (ethene monomers)		$(-CH_2-CH_2-)_n$ (polyethylene polymer)	
8. Cracking	$C_{14}H_{30}$ (long chain hydrocarbon		C_7H_{16} C_7H_{14} (shorter chains hydrocarbons)	

25. Addition

Addition reactions usually involve the breaking of a double or triple bond in unsaturated hydrocarbon, and adding hydrogen (or halogen) atoms to the free electrons. Organic reactants in addition is an alkene or alkyne. In addition reactions, one of the multiple bonds of an alkene (or an alkyne) is broken. The two free electrons from the broken bond covalently bonded with hydrogen atoms or halogens atoms.

Below are two types of addition reactions.

Hydrogen addition (hydrogenation)

In a hydrogenation, hydrogen atoms are added to a double bond of an alkene. In this reaction, an unsaturated hydrocarbon (an alkene) is changed to a saturated hydrocarbon (an alkane).

Organic reactants   *Organic products*
Alkene (unsaturated)   Alkane (saturated)

Alkene   +   Hydrogen   --------->   Alkane

C_3H_6 + H_2 ---------> C_3H_8

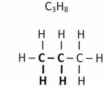

Propene   hydrogen   Propane

Halogen addition (halogenation)

In halogenation, halogen atoms are added to a double bond of an alkene. In this reaction, unsaturated hydrocarbon (alkene) is changed to a halide compound with two attached halogen atoms.

Organic reactants   *Organic product*
Alkene (unsaturated)   Halide (with 2 halogen atoms attached)

Alkene   +   Halogen   ------->   Halide

C_3H_6 + Br_2 ---------> $C_3H_6Br_2$

Propene   Bromine   1,2-dibromopropane

Practice 74

Which substance will likely undergo addition reaction with iodine?

1) 2-methyl butene   3) 2-methyl butane
2) 3-pentanone   4) 2-fluoro pentane

Practice 75

Which equation represents addition reaction?

1) C_2H_4 + H_2 -------> C_2H_6
2) C_2H_4 + O_2 ------> CO_2 + H_2
3) C_2H_6 + Cl_2 --------> C_2H_5Cl + HCl
4) $C_6H_{12}O_6$ ---------> $2C_2H_5OH$ + $2CO_2$

Practice 76

Draw and name the structural formula of the organic reactant.

$CH_3CH_2CHCH_2$ + H_2 -----> $CH_3CH_2CH_2CH_3$

Practice 77

Draw and name the structural formula of the product that will form

H H   H
  | | |
H-C-C - C = C-C-H + F_2 ----->
  | | | | |
  H H   H H H

26. Esterification

Esterification is the process of making an ester by reacting an organic acid with a primary alcohol. During esterification processes, water is also formed from H+ ion of the acid and the -OH (hydroxyl) group of the alcohol.

Example of an ester reaction is shown below. Pay attention to atoms in structures to help you see and understand how the products are formed from the reactants.

| Organic acid | + | Alcohol | ------------ > | Ester | + | Water |

$$CH_3COOH \quad + \quad HOCH_2CH_2CH_3 \quad --------- > \quad CH_3COOCH_2CH_2CH_3 \quad + \quad H_2O$$

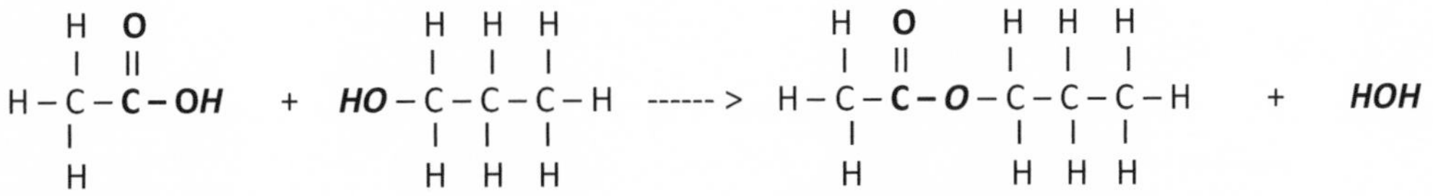

ethanoic acid   propanol   propyl ethanoate   HOH

Note:
The first part of the ester's name (*prop-*) comes from the alcohol (*prop*anol).
The second part of the ester's name (*eth-*) comes from the organic acid (*eth*anoic)

Practice 78

A structure of which organic compound is a product of a reaction between an organic acid and alcohol?

1) 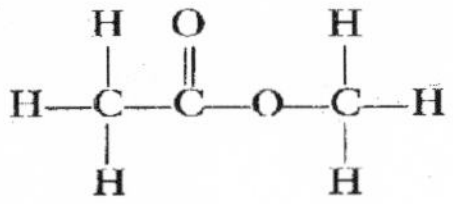   2) 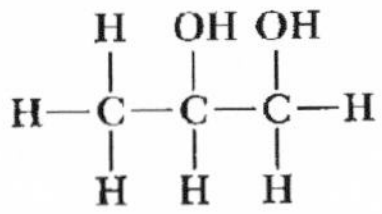   3) 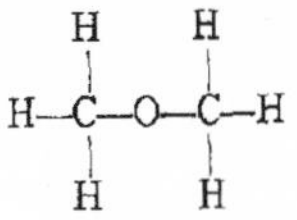   4)

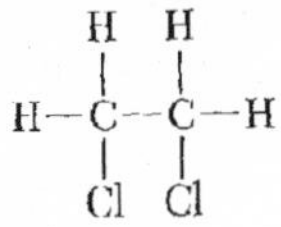

Practice 79

Which compound will react with methanol to form methyl propanoate?

1) Methyl Propyl ether   3) Propanone
2) Propanoic acid   4) Propanol

Practice 80

Draw and name the organic substance that reacts with ethanol in the reaction shown below.

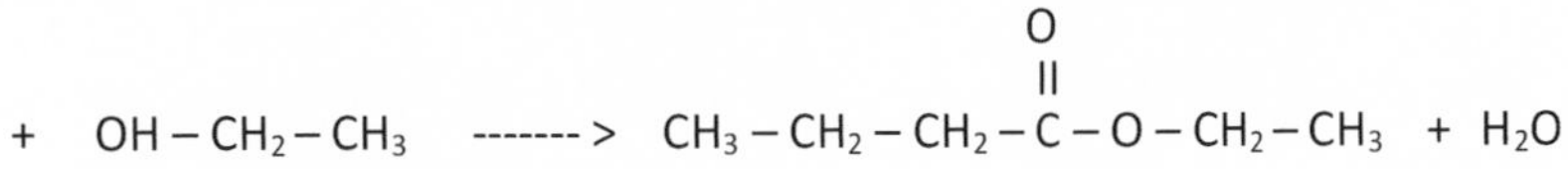

$$+ \quad OH - CH_2 - CH_3 \quad ------- > \quad CH_3 - CH_2 - CH_2 - \overset{\overset{\displaystyle O}{\|}}{C} - O - CH_2 - CH_3 \quad + \quad H_2O$$

Practice 81

Draw and name the structure of the organic product that will form in the reaction below.

27. Polymerization

Polymerization is a process of joining small organic molecules together to make a molecule with a longer chain.
Monomers are small unit molecules that are joined together by covalent bonds to form a polymer.
A *Polymer* is the large unit molecule formed by joining many (poly) monomers together in polymerization reactions.

Two types of polymerization reactions are discussed below.

Condensation polymerization

In condensation polymerization reactions, monomers with **OH** group are joined together as water is removed. *Ethers and proteins* are substances commonly produced by condensation polymerization.

Example of a condensation polymerization reaction is given below:

Monomer   +   Monomer   ----------->   Polymer   +   water

    (alcohol monomers)   *(ether polymer)*

CH_3OH + $HOCH_2CH_3$ -------------> $CH_3OCH_2CH_3$ + H_2O

```
   H                      H  H                      H        H  H
   |                      |  |                      |        |  |
H–C–O H     +     HO–C–C–H      --------->  H–C–O–C–C–H   +   HOH
   |                      |  |                      |        |  |
   H                      H  H                      H        H  H
```

    Methanol   Ethanol   Methyl   Ethyl ether   water

Addition polymerization

In addition polymerization reactions, several identical small molecules (usually double bond molecules) are joined together to create a larger polymer.

Example equation showing addition polymerization process is shown below:

    n $(CH_2=CH_2)$ ----------------> $(-CH_2-CH_2-)_n$ n represent several repeated units of the molecule.

        monomers   Polymer
    (several identical small units)   (one long unit)

Substances produced by polymerization reactions.

Familiar polymers that are produced by natural and synthetic polymerization processes are listed below.

    Natural polymers: Protein, starch, and cellulose

    Synthetic polymers: Nylon, plastic, polyethylene, and polyvinyl

---

Practice 82
Given the incomplete reaction

```
   H  H                       H  H  H  H
   |  |                       |  |  |  |
H–C–C–OH        +     OH–C–C–C–C–H      -----------> 
   |  |                       |  |  |  |
   H  H                       H  H  H  H
```

Draw and name the product of the reaction.

28. Fermentation

Fermentation is an organic process of making ethanol (an alcohol) from sugar.

. CO_2 (carbon dioxide) and water are also produced

. Enzyme, which acts as a catalyst, is required for this process

A fermentation reaction is shown below:

| sugar | | alcohol | + | carbon dioxide |

$$C_6H_{12}O_6 \quad \xrightarrow{\text{enzyme}} \quad 2C_2H_5OH \quad + \quad 2CO_2$$

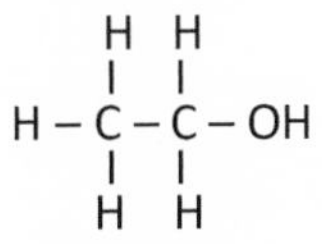

$$\begin{array}{c} \quad H \quad H \\ \quad | \quad \; | \\ H - C - C - OH \\ \quad | \quad \; | \\ \quad H \quad H \end{array}$$

ethanol

29. Saponification

Saponification is an organic process of making soap.

Glycerol, a tertiary alcohol, is also produced during a saponification process.

Saponification equation is shown below:

| Fat | + | Base | -------- > | Soap | + | Glycerol (an alcohol) |

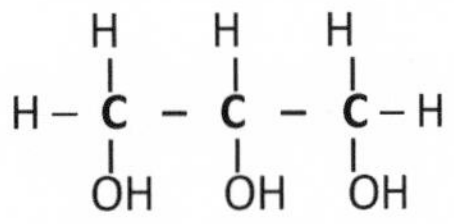

$$\begin{array}{ccc} H & H & H \\ | & | & | \\ H - C - C - C - H \\ | & | & | \\ OH & OH & OH \end{array}$$

1,2,3-propanetri*ol* (glycerol)

30. Combustion

Combustion is the process of burning organic compounds (fuel) in the presence of oxygen.

Carbon dioxide (CO_2) and water (H_2O) are the two main products of combustion reactions.

A combustion reaction is shown below.:

Organic compound + Oxygen -------> Carbon dioxide + water

$$2C_8H_{18} \quad + \quad 25O_2 \quad --------> \quad 16CO_2 \quad + \quad 18H_2O$$

Octane (car fuel)

31. Organic reactions: Practice problems

Concept Task: Be able to determine or recognize organic reaction from a given equation.

Practice 83
Which reaction is used to produce polyethylene from ethylene?
1) Addition polymerization
2) Condensation polymerization
3) Substitution
4) Combustion

Practice 84
Carbon dioxide and water are two products formed from which organic reaction?
1) Combustion
2) Esterification
3) Fermentation
4) Saponification

Practice 85
Chloromethane is likely a product of
1) Addition
2) Fermentation
3) Substitution
4) Neutralization

Practice 86
Consider the equation

$$C_5H_{10} \quad + \quad H_2 \quad \text{--------}> \quad C_5H_{12}$$

This reaction can be best described as
1) Hydrogen addition
2) Hydrogen substitution
3) polymerization
4) Combustion

Practice 87
The organic reaction
$$CH_3COOH \quad + \quad CH_3OH \quad \text{---}> \quad CH_3COOCH_3 \quad + \quad H_2O$$
can be described as

1) Addition polymerization
2) Substitution
3) Saponification
4) Esterification

Practice 88
The reaction
$$C_2H_4\,(g) \quad + \quad 3O_2(g) \quad \text{--------}> \quad H_2O(l) \quad + \quad CO_2(g)$$

is an example of

1) Substitution
2) Combustion
3) Addition
4) Saponification

Practice 89

The reaction

$$\underset{\underset{\displaystyle H\;\;H\;\;H}{|\;\;\;|\;\;\;|}}{\overset{\overset{\displaystyle H\;\;H\;\;H}{|\;\;\;|\;\;\;|}}{OH-C-C-C-H}} \quad + \quad \underset{\underset{\displaystyle H}{|}}{\overset{\overset{\displaystyle H}{|}}{H-C-OH}} \quad \text{-------}> \quad H_2O \; + \; \underset{\underset{\displaystyle H\;\;\;\;H\;\;H\;\;H}{|\;\;\;\;\;\;|\;\;\;|\;\;\;|}}{\overset{\overset{\displaystyle H\;\;\;\;H\;\;H\;\;H}{|\;\;\;\;\;\;|\;\;\;|\;\;\;|}}{H-C-O-C-C-C-H}}$$

is best classified as

1) Polymerization
2) Combustion
3) Saponification
4) Substitution

Topic 10 - Organic Chemistry

Concept Terms

Key vocabulary terms and concepts from Topic 10 are listed below. You should know definition and facts related to each term and concept.

1. Homologous Series
2. Hydrocarbon
3. Saturated hydrocarbon
4. Unsaturated hydrocarbon
5. Alkane
6. Alkene
7. Alkyne
8. Alkyl
9. Single covalent bond
10. Double covalent bond
11. Triple covalent bond
12. Halide
13. Alcohol
14. Monohydroxy alcohol
15. Primary alcohol
16. Secondary alcohol
17. Tertiary alcohol
18. Dihydroxy alcohol
19. Trihydroxy alcohol
20. Ether
21. Aldehyde
22. Ketone
23. Organic acid
24. Ester
25. Amine
26. Amide
27. Amino acid
28. Substitution
29. Addition
30. Fermentation
31. Saponification
32. Combustion
33. Esterification
34. Polymerization
35. Addition polymerization
36. Condensation polymerization

Concept Tasks

Concept tasks from Topic 10 are listed below. You should know how to solve problems and answer questions related to each concept task.

1. Relating number of carbon atoms to organic compounds names
2. Relating name ending of compound to class of organic compound
3. Determining and recognizing correctly drawn organic compound structures
4. Determining names, formulas and structures of Alkanes (saturated hydrocarbons)
5. Determining names, formulas and structures of alkenes (unsaturated hydrocarbons)
6. Determining names, formulas and structures of alkynes (unsaturated hydrocarbons)
7. Determining names, formulas and structures of halides
8. Determining names, formulas and structures of alcohols
9. Determining names, formulas and structures of primary, secondary, and tertiary alcohols
11. Determining names, formulas and structures of ethers
12. Determining names, formulas and structures of aldehydes
13. Determining names, formulas and structures of ketones
14. Determining names, formulas and structures of organic acids
15. Determining names, formulas and structures of esters
16. Determining names, formulas and structures of amines
17. Determining names, formulas and structures of amides
18. Determining names, formulas and structures of amino acids
19. Determining and recognizing formulas of compounds that are isomers.
20. Determining and recognizing names of compounds that are isomers
21. Naming structural and condense formulas of organic compounds
22. Drawing organic compounds structures from names or formulas.
23. Identify a reactant or a product of a given organic reaction
24. Determining or recognizing organic reaction name from equation
25. Determine missing reactant or product in incomplete organic reactions

Topic 11 - Redox and Electrochemistry

Topic outline

In this topic, you will learn the following concepts:

. Oxidation numbers
. Redox reactions
. Half-reactions
. Reduction
. Oxidation
. Balancing redox equations
. Writing half-reaction equations

. Electrochemistry
. Electrochemical cell
. Anode, Cathode, salt bridge
. Voltaic cell
. Electrolytic cell
. Electrolytic reductions
. Electroplating

Lesson 1 – Oxidation Numbers

Introduction:

Most chemical reactions involve the losing and gaining of electrons by substances in the reaction.   The losing and gaining of electrons in these reactions occur simultaneously (at the same time).

Oxidation is a loss of electrons by a substance in a reaction.

Reduction is a gain of electrons by a substance in a reaction.

Redox is a chemical reaction in which **red**uction and **ox**idation are occurring at the same time.

A redox reaction occurs when substances in the reaction compete for electrons. Some substances compete to lose electrons, others compete to gain electrons. Since electron has a negative charge, substances that loss and gain electrons undergo changes in oxidation states (oxidation numbers). In other words, substances in redox reactions become more positively charged or more negatively charged depending if they had lost or gained electrons. These changes in oxidation numbers of substances in redox reaction equations are used to determine which substance had lost and which one had gained electrons. A complete understanding of oxidation numbers is the key to understanding redox reactions, as well as being able to correctly answer questions related to redox reactions.

In this lesson, you will learn about oxidation numbers.

1. Oxidation Numbers

An **oxidation number** is the charge an atom has (or appears to have) when it has lost or gained electrons. An oxidation number of an atom can be 0, - (negative) or + (positive) .

Examples of oxidation numbers are given below:

The neutral atom K or K^0 has oxidation number of **0**

The ion O^{2-} has an oxidation number of **-2**

The ion Al^{3+} has an oxidation number of **+3**

In all compounds, the sum of all oxidation numbers must equal zero.

Example: In the compound Na_2SO_4 , the sum of oxidation numbers of Na, S and O is equal to **0**

In polyatomic ions, the sum of all oxidation numbers must equal the charge of the ion
Example: In the polyatomic ion CO_3^{2-} , the sum of oxidation numbers of C and O is equal to **-2.**

Topic 11 - Redox and Electrochemistry

2. Rules for Assigning Oxidation Numbers

Oxidation numbers for the elements can be found in the box of each element on the Periodic Table. In redox equations, oxidation numbers are assigned to elements to keep track of electrons lost and gained. When assigning oxidation numbers to the elements in formulas and equations, it must be done according to arbitrary rules. These rules are summarized on the table below.

Table of Rules for Assigning Oxidation Numbers

Category of element	Common oxidation states	Example formulas		
Free element	0	Na	Zn	O_2 Cl_2
Simple ion	Charge on the ion	Na^+	Zn^{2+}	O^{2-} Cl^-
Group 1 element In **ALL** compounds	+1 (see Periodic Table)	**Na**Cl	**Li**$_2$O	
Group 2 element In **ALL** compounds	+2 (see Periodic Table)	**Mg**Cl$_2$	**Ca**O	
Hydrogen In **most** compounds	+1 (see Periodic Table)	**H**Cl	**H**$_2$O	**H**$_2$SO$_4$
In **metal hydride** compounds	-1	Li**H**	Ca**H$_2$**	
Oxygen In **most** compounds	-2 (see Periodic Table)	H$_2$**O**	C**O**$_2$	HCl**O$_3$**
In **OF$_2$** (a compound with **fluorine**)	+2	**O**F$_2$		
In **Peroxide** compounds	-1	H$_2$**O$_2$**	N$_2$**O$_2$**	
Group 17 halogen In **MOST** compounds	**-1** (see Periodic Table)	Na**Cl**	Mg**Br**	Ca**I$_2$**
In compounds in which a halogen is between other elements or is a first element.	+ (see Periodic Table) The correct + value can be determined mathematically (see next page)	Na**Br**O$_3$	**Cl**O$_3$	

In the hypothetically equation below, oxidation numbers are assigned to the elements using rules stated above.

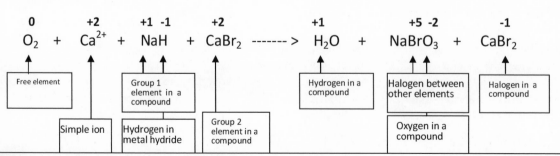

3. Oxidation Numbers

Some elements have multiple oxidation numbers. You can see this among the transition elements, halogens, nitrogen, and sulfur, etc. The oxidation number assigned to these elements in compounds depends on the oxidation numbers of the other elements in the compound. This can be done using a little math as shown in examples below.

Concept Task: Be able to determine oxidation number of an element in neutral compounds and ions.

Recall:
Sum of charges in a neutral compound is equal to 0.
Sum of charges in an ion is equal to the charge of the ion.

Example 1
What is the oxidation number of P in the compound Na_3PO_4?
1) +7   2) +5   3) -3   4) +3

Note:
P has multiple charges on the Periodic Table.
Charge of P in Na_3PO_4 must be determined mathematically.
The correct charge of P must add to the total charges from Na and O so their sum is equal to **Zero (0)**

Na = +1 charge: 3 Na = +3 total positive charges
O   = -2 charge: 4 O   = - 8 total negative charges
Total charge from **1 P** must be   **+5** for all charges to equal **0**
                                                              0

Each **P** must be a **+5** charge *(choice 2)*

Example 2
What is the oxidation number of sulfur in CaS_2O_3?
1) +2   2) +4   3) +6   4) +3

Another way to determine charge of an atom in a formula.

Count atoms in formula:	1Ca	+ 2S	+ 3O	= 0
Substitute charges *Let X be charge of S (unknown)*	1(+2)	+ 2(X)	+ 3 (-2)	= 0
Multiply out, set equal to zero	2	+ 2X	+ -6	= 0
Imply a little algebra and solve			2x	= +4
(Choice 1)			X	= +2

Example 3
What is the oxidation number of nitrogen in NH_4^+ ?
1) +1   2) -3   4) +4   4) +5

Note:
The correct charge of N must add to the total charges from H so their sum is equal to **+1** *(the charge of the ion)*

H = -1 charge: 4 H   = - 4 total negative charges
Total charge from 1N must be +5 for all charges to equal **+1.**
                                        +1
Each **N** must be a **+5** charge *(choice 3)*

Practice 1
What is the oxidation number of oxygen in ozone, O_3?
1) +1   2) 0   3) -2   4) -6

Practice 2
What is the oxidation of hydrogen in MgH_2?
1) 0   2) +1   3) +2   4) -1

Practice 3
The oxidation number of sulfur in the compound SO_3 is
1) -3   2) +3   3) +6   4) -6

Practice 4
In $Na_2Cr_2O_7$, the oxidation number of chromium is
1) +2   2) +6   3) +7   4) +11

Practice 5
Below, two compounds of chlorine are given:

Compound A: Cl_2O
Compound B: $HClO$

Which is true of the oxidation number of chlorine in Compound A and B?

1) Chlorine oxidation number is +2 in A, but a +1 in B

2) Chlorine oxidation number is +1 in A, but a +2 in B

3) Chlorine oxidation number is +2 in both A and B

4) Chlorine oxidation number is +1 in both A and B

Practice 6
The oxidation number of hydrogen in the hydronium ion, H_3O^+ is
1) +1   2) -1   3) 0   4) +3

Practice 7
What is the oxidation number of S in the ion SO_4^{2-} ?
1) -2   2) -6   3) +4   4) +6

Practice 8
In which substance does bromine has oxidation number of +3 ?
1) KBrO   3) $KBrO_2$
2) $KBrO_3$ 4) $KBrO_4$

Practice 9
In which formula does Nitrogen has the smallest oxidation number?
1) NO_2 3) NO_3
2) NO_2^- 4) NO_3^-

Topic 11 - Redox and Electrochemistry

Lesson 2 – Oxidation and reduction (redox)

Introduction

As mentioned earlier, redox reactions involve oxidation (losing of electrons) and reduction (gaining of electrons) occurring simultaneously.

In this lesson, you will learn about redox reactions, as well as oxidation and reduction.

4. Redox Reactions

All single replacement reactions are redox reactions. Most synthesis and decomposition reactions are redox reactions. All double replacement reactions are non-redox reactions. Examples of redox and non-redox reactions are given below.

⬅️ L👀KING Back Topic 5: You learned about types of reactions.

The equations below represent redox reactions

Synthesis	$N_2 + O_2 \text{---------} > 2NO$
Decomposition	$2H_2O_2 \text{----} > 2H_2O + O_2$
Single replacement	$Cu + 2AgNO_3 \text{----} > CuNO_3 + 2Ag$
Simplified redox	$Cu + 2Ag^+ \text{------} > Cu^{2+} + 2Ag$

These and similar equations represent redox because:

. Two elements in each equation have a change in oxidation number

Therefore, electrons are lost and gained in each reaction.

The equations below do not represent redox reactions.

Double replacement:	$KI + AgNO_3 \text{-----} > AgI + KNO_3$
Ions combining:	$Na^+ + Cl^- \text{--------} > NaCl$
Ionization:	$H_2O \text{------------------} > H^+ + OH^-$

These and similar equations are not redox because:

. None of the elements in each equation has a change in oxidation number

Therefore, electrons are neither lost nor gained in any of the reactions

5. Redox Equations: Practice problems

Concept Task: Be able to recognize redox and non-redox reaction equations

Use one of the following three methods to determine which equation is a redox.

. *Look* for an equation with at least one element free on one side, but in a compound on the other side (quickest)

. *Look* for an equation that represents synthesis, decomposition, or single replacement.

. *Determine* which equation has two elements changing their oxidation numbers

Practice 10

Which equation represents a redox reaction?

1) $AgNO_3 + LiBr \text{-------} > AgBr_2 + LiNO$

2) $KI \text{------------------------} > K^+ + I^-$

3) $4Na + O_2 \text{---------} > 2Na_2O$

4) $Na^+ + SO_4^{2-} \text{-------} > Na_2SO_4$

Practice 11

Which equation represents a redox reaction?

1) $PbSO_4 + Zn \text{---} > ZnSO_4 + Pb$

2) $3O_2 \text{-----------------} > 2O_3$

3) $H_3PO_4 + 3KOH \text{----} > K_3PO_4 + 3H_2O$

4) $H^+ + Cl- \text{-----------} > HCl$

Practice 12

Given the four equations below.

I: $AgNO_3 + NaCl \text{--->} AgCl + NaNO_3$

II: $Cl_2 + H_2O \text{----} > HClO + HCl$

III: $CuO + CO \text{-----} > CO_2 + Cu$

IV: $LiOH + HCl \text{----} > LiCl + H_2O$

Oxidation-reduction reactions are shown in which two equations?

1) I and II

2) II and III

3) III and I

4) IV and II

Topic 11 - Redox and Electrochemistry

6. Oxidation and Reduction

Redox reactions involve oxidation and reduction.

Oxidation:

Loss of **E**lectrons is **O**xidation **(LEO).**

An **oxidized substance** is the substance or ion that is losing (or transferring) its electrons. An oxidized substance is also known as a ***reducing agent*** because it will cause another substance in the reaction to gain electrons. Oxidation number of an oxidized substance always increases (becomes more positive) because the substance loses negative particles (electrons).

Reduction:

Gain of **E**lectrons is **R**eduction **(GER).**

A **reduced substance** is the substance or ion that is gaining (or accepting) electrons. A reduced substance is also known as an ***oxidizing agent*** because it will cause another substance in the reaction to lose electrons. Oxidation number of a reduced substance always decreases (becomes more negative) because the substance gains negative particles (electrons).

7. Half-reactions

A **half-reaction** shows either the oxidation or reduction portion of a redox reaction. A correct half- reaction must show conservation of atoms, mass, and charge.

Consider the redox reaction below:

$$2Na + Cl_2 \ ---> \ 2NaCl$$

Oxidation half-reactions show the loss of electrons by a substance in redox reactions. In the above redox reaction, sodium is the species that is losing electrons. Electrons that are lost are always shown on the right side of the half-reaction equation as represented below.

$$2Na^0 \ ----> \ 2Na^+ + 2e^- \quad \textbf{oxidation half-reaction}$$

Reduction half-reactions show the gain of electrons by a substance in redox reactions. In the above redox reaction, chlorine is the species that is gaining electrons. Electrons that are gained are always shown on the left side of the half-reaction equation as represented below.

$$Cl_2^0 + 2e^- \ ---> \ 2Cl^- \quad \textbf{reduction half-reaction}$$

Note:

Both half-reaction equations demonstrate conservation of mass, charge and atoms. This is to say that a correct half-reaction equation must be balanced.

Practice 13

Which half-reaction equation correctly represents a reduction reaction?

1) $Li^0 \ + e^- \ ---------> \ Li^+$
2) $Na^0 \ + e^- \ -----------> \ Na^+$
3) $Br_2^0 \ + 2e^- \ ---------> \ 2Br^-$
4) $Cl_2^0 \ + e^- \ --------> \ 2Cl^-$

Practice 14

Which is a correct oxidation-half equation?

1) $F_2^0 \ ---------------> \ 2F^- \ + 2e^-$
2) $Ca^0 \ ----------------> \ Ca^{2+} \ + 2e^-$
3) $Ca^{2+} \ + 2e^- \ --------> \ Ca^0$
4) $2F^- \ + 2e^- \ ---------> \ F_2^0$

Practice 15

Which half-reaction correctly represents an oxidation reaction?

1) $Nb^{5+} \ + 2e^- \ ------> \ Nb^{3+}$
2) $Mn^{4+} \ + 3e- \ ------> \ Mn^{7+}$
3) $Nb^{3+} \ ------------> \ Nb^0 \ + 3e^-$
4) $Mn^{4+} \ ----------> \ Mn^{7+} \ + 3e^-$

Practice 16

Which half-reaction correctly represents reduction?

1) $Al(s) \ ---------> \ Al^{3+}(aq) \ + 3e^-$
2) $H_2(g) \ + 2e- ------> \ 2H^+(aq)$
3) $I_2(s) \ -----------> \ 2I^-(aq) \ + 2e-$
4) $Cu^{2+}(aq) \ + e^- \ ----> \ Cu^+(s)$

8. Interpreting Half-reaction Equations

Half-reaction equations provide several information about changes that substances are going through in a redox reaction. Below, two different half-reaction equations are given. One has electrons on the left and one has electrons on the right. Each half-reaction equation is interpreted by describing changes the substance is going through.

Reduction half-reaction	**Oxidation half-reaction**
Equation with electrons on the LEFT	*Equation with electrons on the RIGHT*
$C^0 + 4e^- \text{-----------} > C^{4-}$	$Sb^{3+} \text{-----------} > Sb^{5+} + 2e^-$
C^0 atom gains 4 electrons to become C^{4-} ion	Sb^{3+} loses 2 electrons to become Sb^{5+}
C^0 oxidation number decreases from 0 to - 4	Sb^{3+} oxidation number increases from +3 to +5
C^0 is the reduced substance, and also the oxidizing agent.	Sb^{3+} is the oxidized substance, and also the reducing agent.
The oxidation number decrease of carbon is from $0 \text{-------} > - 4$. This change represents a gain of 4 electrons.	The increase oxidation number of antimony is from $+3 \text{-------} > +5$. This change represents a lost of 2 electrons
Number of electrons gained (4) is the difference between the two oxidation states: $0 - (- 4) = 4$ e-	Number of electrons lost (2) is the difference between the two oxidation states: $+5 - +3 = 2$e-

Make a scale like this one to help you determine number of electrons lost or gained.

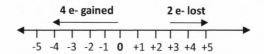

4 e- gained   **2 e- lost**

-5 -4 -3 -2 -1 **0** +1 +2 +3 +4 +5

Practice 17
Which is true of a reducing agent in oxidation-reduction reactions?
1) A reducing agent loses electrons, and is oxidized
2) A reducing agent loses electrons, and is reduced
3) A reducing agent gains electrons, and is oxidized
4) A reducing agent gains electrons, and is reduced

Practice 18
Which change in oxidation number represents oxidation?
1) 0 to -1   3) -2 to -1
2) 0 to -2   4) -2 to -3

Practice 19
In which oxidation number change would a species in a redox reaction gains the most number of electrons?
1) +3 to -1   3) 0 to +4
2) +5 to +3   4) +3 to +7

Practice 20
When Cr^{4+} changes to Cr^{2+}, there will be
1) 6 electrons gained   3) 2 electrons gained
2) 6 electrons lost   4) 2 electrons lost

Practice 21
Given the half reaction equation below
$$Fe^{3+} + 3e^- \text{----} > Fe$$
Fe^{3+} is
1) Reduced by gaining 3 electrons
2) Reduced by losing 3 electrons
3) Oxidized by gaining 3 electrons
4) Oxidized by losing 3 electrons

Practice 22
In the half-reaction equation below
$$P + 3e^- \text{-------} > P^{3-}$$
The phosphorus atom is
1) Oxidized, and becomes the oxidizing agent
2) Oxidized, and becomes the reducing agent
3) Reduced, and becomes the reducing agent
4) Reduced, and becomes the oxidizing agent

Topic 11 - Redox and Electrochemistry

9. Redox Equations

Redox equations can be given in two different forms as shown below:

REDOX EQUATION 1: Ni^0 + Fe^{2+} ----------> Ni^{2+} + Fe^+

REDOX EQUATION 2: Li + H_2SO_4 ----------> Li_2SO_4 + H_2

Both equations represent redox reactions because each equation has two substances changing their oxidation states. Again, this means that electrons are lost and gained in each reaction. For any given redox equation, you should be able to answer the followings questions:

1. What is the oxidation number change of a substance
2. How many electrons are lost or gained
3. Which substance is oxidized (or lost electrons)
4. Which substance is reduced (or gained electrons)
5. Which substance is the reducing agent
6. Which substance is the oxidizing agent
7. What is correct oxidation half-reaction
8. What is correct reduction half-reaction

Answering any of the above questions will be easier with redox equation 1 because oxidation numbers are already assigned to the elements, and changes in oxidation states are more obvious. In redox equation 2, oxidation numbers must first be correctly assigned to the elements in the equation before oxidation number changes can be considered and then be used to answer the above questions.

In the next two sets both equations will be interpreted, and you'll also learn how to answer the above eight questions for each equation.

10. Interpreting Redox Equation 1

When determining oxidized and reduced substances, consider the followings about the equation given.

Oxidized substance: The substance on the *left side* of the arrow with the *smaller charge*

Reduced substance: The substance on the *left side* of the arrow with the *larger charge*

Ni^0 + Fe^{2+} ------------> Fe^0 + Ni^{2+}

Ni^0 has a *SMALLER* charge than Fe^{2+}. *Therefore:* Ni^0 is oxidized Ni^0 loses (2) electrons Ni^0 is also the reducing agent Ni^0 oxidation number increases $\quad$ from 0 to +2 *Oxidation half-reaction:* Ni^0 -----> Ni^{2+} + 2e-	Fe^{2+} has a *LARGER* charge than Ni^0. *Therefore:* Fe^{2+} is reduced Fe^{2+} gains (2) electrons Fe^{2+} is also the oxidizing agent Fe^{2+} oxidation number decreases $\quad$ from +2 to 0 *Reduction half-reaction:* Fe^{2+} + 2e- -------> Fe^0	Substances (Fe^0 and Ni^{2+}) to the *right* of the arrow in redox equations are the results of substances on the *left* losing and gaining electrons. Therefore, these substances on the *right* are neither oxidized nor reduced, and they can never be oxidizing or reducing agent.

Topic 11 - Redox and Electrochemistry

11. Interpreting Redox Equation 1: Practice problems

Practice 23

Consider the oxidation-reaction reaction: Co^0 + Cu^{2+} --------> Co^{2+} + Cu

Which species is reduced?

1) Co^0 2) Cu^0 3) Co^{2+} 4) Cu^{2+}

Practice 24

In the oxidation-reduction reaction, Zn + Ni^{2+} ---------> Zn^{2+} + Ni ,

Which species is losing electrons?

1) Zn 2) Ni^{2+} 3) Zn^{2+} 4) Ni

Practice 25

In the oxidation-reduction reaction: $2 Fe^{3+}$ + S^{2-} ----------> $2Fe^{2+}$ + $2S^0$,
Which species acts as a reducing agent?

1) Fe^{3+} 2) Fe^{2+} 3) S^{2-} 4) S^0

Practice 26

In the oxidation-reduction reaction: $2Al$ + $3Ni^{2+}$ ---------> $2Al^{3+}$ + $3Ni$

Which species acts as an oxidizing agent?

1) Al 2) Al^{3+} 3) Ni 4) Ni^{2+}

Practice 27

Given the reaction: Pb + $2Ag^+$ --------> Pb^{2+} + $2Ag$
The lead atom is

1) Reduced by losing 1 electrons   3) Oxidized by losing 2 electrons
2) Reduced by gaining 1 electrons   4) Oxidized by gaining 2 electrons

Practice 28

Given the reaction: $2I^-(aq)$ + $Br_2(l)$ ---------> $2Br^-(aq)$ + $I_2(s)$
As the reaction takes place

1) The Br_2 is oxidized, and becomes the oxidizing agent
2) The Br_2 is reduced, and becomes the oxidizing agent
3) The $Br_2$is oxidized, and becomes the reducing agent
4) The Br_2 is reduced, and becomes the reducing agent

Practice 29

Consider the redox reaction: Mn^0 + O_2 ---------------> Mn^{4+} + $2O^{2-}$

Which half-reaction is correct for the reduction that occurs?

1) O_2 ---------------> $2O^{2-}$ + $4e^-$ 3) Mn^0 + $4e^-$ ------> Mn^{4+}
2) O_2 + $4e^-$ -----> $2O^{2-}$ 4) Mn^0 ----------------> Mn^{4+} + $4e^-$

Practice 30

In the redox reaction: $3Cu^{2+}$ + $2Al$ --------> $3Cu$ + $2Al^{3+}$

The oxidation half-reaction is

1) Cu^{2+} + $2e^-$ ------> Cu 3) Al + $3e^-$ ---> Al^{3+}
2) Cu^{2+} ----------------> Cu + $2e^-$ 4) Al ------------> Al^{3+} + $3e^-$

12. Interpreting Redox Equation 2

For redox equation 2 below:

$$Li \quad + \quad H_2SO_4 \quad \text{---------} > \quad Li_2SO_4 \quad + \quad H_2$$

Oxidation numbers must first be assigned to the elements in the equation. Oxidation number that is assigned to each element must be correct according to the arbitrary rules listed on page 202 .

Once oxidation numbers are correctly assigned to elements as shown below, only two of the elements (Li and H) in the redox equation show a change in their oxidation numbers. The oxidation number changes of these elements are then used to answer questions about the redox equation.

Just as with the previous redox equation, consider the followings about the two elements (Li and H):

Oxidized substance : The substance *left* of the arrow with the *smaller charge*

Reduced substance: The substance *left* of the arrow with the *larger charge*

$$\overset{0}{2Li} \quad + \quad \overset{+1\ +6\ -2}{H_2SO_4} \quad \text{------} > \quad \overset{+1\ +6\ -2}{Li_2SO_4} \quad + \quad \overset{0}{H_2}$$

Li has a *SMALLER* charge than H^+. *Therefore:* Li is oxidized Li loses (1) electron Li is also the reducing agent Li oxidation number increases from 0 to +1 *Oxidation half-reaction:* Li -----> Li^+ + e- *A balanced oxidation half-equation* 2Li -----> $2Li^+$ + 2e-	H+ has a *LARGER* charge than Li *Therefore* H^+ is reduced H^+ gains (1) electron H^+ is also the oxidizing agent H^+ oxidation number decreases from +1 to 0 *Reduction half-reaction:* H^+ + e- ------> H_2 *A balanced reduction half-equation* $2H^+$ + 2e- -------> H_2	Substances (Li^+ and H_2^0) to the *right* of the arrow in redox equations are the results of substances on the *left* losing and gaining electrons. Therefore, these substances on the *right* are neither oxidized nor reduced, and they can never be oxidizing or reducing agent. Also, note that the oxidation numbers of S and O did not change. Therefore, S and O are neither oxidized nor reduced .

13. Summary of Oxidation and Reduction

Below, a summary of oxidation and reduction. Use this table for quick review and comparisons of the two half-reactions.

Half-reaction	Electrons are	Oxidation number	Example equation
Oxidation Oxidized substance Reducing agent	Lost	Increases	Zn ------> Zn^{2+} + $2e^-$
Reduction Oxidized substance Reducing agent	Gained	Decreases (reduces)	Si + $4e^-$ ------> Si^{4-}

Topic 11 - Redox and Electrochemistry

14. Interpreting Redox Equation 2: Practice problems

Practice 31

Consider the oxidation-reaction reaction: Na   + H_2O --------> NaOH   + H_2

Which species is oxidized?

1) H_2 2) O^{2-} 3) H^+ 4) Na

Practice 32

In the oxidation-reduction reaction: Fe   +   2AgCl ------> 2Ag   + $FeCl_2$

Which species is gaining electrons?

1) Fe^{3+} 2) Fe^0 3) Cl^- 4) Ag^+

Practice 33

In the oxidation-reduction reaction: C(s)   + $H_2O(g)$ --------> CO(g)   + $H_2(g)$

Which species acts as a reducing agent?

1) C   2) H^+ 3) C^{2+} 4) H_2

Practice 34

In the oxidation-reduction reaction: 2KBr   + F_2 --------> 2KF   + Br_2

Which species acts as an oxidizing agent?

1) Br_2 2) K^+ 3) F_2 4) Br^-

Practice 35

Given the reaction: Zn(s)   +   2HCl(aq) -------> $ZnCl_2(aq)$ + $H_2(g)$

Which is true of hydrogen in this reaction?

1) Hydrogen is reduced, and its oxidation number increases
2) Hydrogen is reduced, and its oxidation number decreases
3) Hydrogen is oxidized, and its oxidation number increases
4) Hydrogen is oxidized , and its oxidation number decreases

Practice 36

Given the oxidation-reduction reaction: Co(s) + $PbCl_2(aq)$ ------> $CoCl_2(aq)$ +   Pb(s)

Which statement correctly describes the oxidation and reduction that occur?

1) Co(s) is oxidized and $Cl^-(aq)$ is reduced
2) Co(s) is oxidized and $Pb^{2+}(aq)$ is reduced
3) Co(s) is reduced and $Cl^-(aq)$ is oxidized
4) Co(s) is reduced and $Pb^{2+}(aq)$ is oxidized

Practice 37

In the chemical reaction: $2AgNO_3(aq)$ +   Cu(s)   ------> $Cu(NO_3)_2(aq)$ +   2Ag(s)

Which half-reaction equation correctly shows oxidation?

1) $2Ag^+(aq)$ ------------> 2 Ag(s)   + $2e^-$ 3) Cu(s) ------------> $Cu^{2+}(aq)$ + $2e^-$
2) 2Ag(s) ------------> $2Ag^+(aq)$ + $2e^-$ 4) $Cu^{2+}(aq)$ -------> Cu(s)   + $2e^-$

Practice 38

Given the following redox chemical reaction: $2KClO_3$ ----------> 2KCl   + $3O_2$

Which half-reaction equation correctly represents the reduction that occurs?

1) $2O^{2-}$ ---------------> O_2 + $4e^-$ 3) Cl^{5+} ----------------> Cl^- + $6e^-$
2) O_2 + $4e^-$ -------> $2O^{2-}$ 4) Cl^{5+} + $6e^-$ ------> Cl^-

Topic 11 - Redox and Electrochemistry

Lesson 3 - Electrochemistry

Introduction

Electrochemistry is the study of relationships between redox chemical reactions and electrical energy.

Recall from lesson 1 that redox reactions involve the loss and gain of electrons. When a substance in a redox reaction is oxidized, the electrons that are lost go to and are gained by the substance that is reduced. If a redox reaction system is set up so that there are paths for the electrons and ions to flow, electrical current can be produced.

A **battery** is a good example of a system that is set up to produce electrical energy from a redox reaction.

In Topic 9 you learned how exothermic chemical reactions release energy, and endothermic reactions absorb energy.

In this lesson of topic 11, you will learn how certain redox chemical reactions can produce (release) electrical energy, while other redox reactions require the use of (absorb) electrical energy for a reaction to occur.

15. Electrochemical Cells

For a redox reaction to produce or use electrical energy, the reaction must occur in an electrochemical cell.

An **electrochemical cell** is any device in which chemical energy is converted to electrical energy or electrical energy is converted chemical energy. The two types of electrochemical cells are described below.

A **voltaic cell** is an electrochemical cell in which a spontaneous redox reaction occurs to produce electrical energy.

In voltaic cells:
. Redox reaction is spontaneous and exothermic
. Chemical energy is converted to electrical energy
. Electrical energy produced is due to flow of electrons
. Oxidation and reduction occurs in two separate cells
. A salt bridge connects the two half cells and allows ions to flow
. A *battery* is a type of a voltaic cell

Voltaic cells

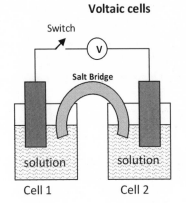

An **electrolytic cell** is an electrochemical cell in which electrical energy is used to force a nonspontaneous redox reaction to occur.

In electrolytic cells:
. Redox reaction is nonspontaneous and endothermic
. Electrical energy is converted to chemical energy
. An external electrical source (such as battery) is used to provide energy to start the redox reaction
. Oxidation and reduction occur in one (the same) cell
. Electrolytic reduction, electroplating of metals, and electrolysis of water use electrolytic cells

Electrolytic cell

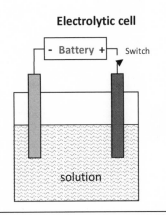

16. Anode, Cathode, and Salt Bridge

Oxidation and reduction reactions that occur in electrochemical cells take place at specific sites called electrodes.

Electrodes are sites on electrochemical cells where oxidation and reduction take place. The anode and cathode are the two electrodes on all electrochemical cells. The anode and cathode on electrochemical cells are usually labeled with − (negative) and + (positive) signs. The type of electrochemical cell determines which electrode is positive and which electrode is negative.

Anode: Oxidation

The anode is the electrode where oxidation occurs in both voltaic and electrolytic cells. The anode, therefore, is the site on any electrochemical cell where *electrons are lost*.

Signs for anode on voltaic and electrolytic cells:

Voltaic cells – **A**node is **N**egative **(-)**

Electrolytic cells – **A**node is **P**ositive **(+)**

Cathode: Reduction

The cathode is the electrode where reduction occurs in both voltaic and electrolytic cells. The cathode, therefore, is the site on any electrochemical cell where *electrons are gained*.

Signs for cathode on voltaic and electrolytic cells:

Voltaic cells – **C**athode is **P**ositive (+)

Electrolytic cells – **C**athode is **N**egative (-)

External conduit (Wire): Permits flow of electrons

Electrons lost at the anode flow to the cathode via the external conduit, which is usually any electrical wire that connects the two electrodes. The external conduit is present in both voltaic and electrolytic cells.

Salt bridge: Permits flow of ions.

The salt bridge is any porous substance that connects solutions in the two half-cells of a voltaic cell. Positive and negative ions flow (migrate) between the two cells via the salt bridge. The flow of ions is necessary to keep the two half-cells neutral, and for appropriate functioning of a voltaic cell. A salt bridge is not present in electrolytic cells.

Practice 39
A voltaic cell differs from an electrolytic cell in that a voltaic cell uses
1) Spontaneous redox reaction to produce electrical energy
2) Non-spontaneous redox reaction to produce electrical energy
3) Electrical energy to force a spontaneous redox reaction to occur
4) Electrical energy to force a non-spontaneous redox reaction to occur

Practice 40
Which is true of anode in any electrochemical cell?
1) The anode is the site for oxidation
2) The anode is the site for reduction
3) The anode is the site for both oxidation and reduction
4) The anode is the site where protons are lost and gained

Practice 41
The negative electrode in all electrolytic cells is the
1) Cathode, at which oxidation occurs
2) Cathode, at which reduction occurs
3) Anode, at which oxidation occurs
4) Anode, at which reduction occurs

Practice 42
An electrochemical cell setup consists of two half cells connected by an external conductor and a salt bridge. The function of the salt bridge is to
1) Block a path for the flow of electrons
2) Block a path for the flow of ions
3) Provide a path for the flow of electrons
4) Provide a path for the flow of ions

Use these codes to help you remember key information:

LEO :   Loss of Electrons is Oxidation

GER: Gain of Electrons is Reduction.

An Ox: **An**ode is for **Ox**idation

Red Cat: **Red**uction at **Cat**hode

APE: **A**node is **P**ositive in **E**lectrolytic

VAN: **V**oltaic, **A**node is **N**egative

CVP: **C**athode in **V**oltaic is **P**ositive

CEN: **C**athode in **E**lectrolytic is **N**egative

Topic 11 - Redox and Electrochemistry

17. Voltaic Cells

Below is a diagram representing a voltaic cell. Note the different components of the cell diagram. An equation representing the reaction taking place in this cell is given at the bottom of the diagram.

Reference Table J (Activity Series) may be used in identifying components of a voltaic cell.

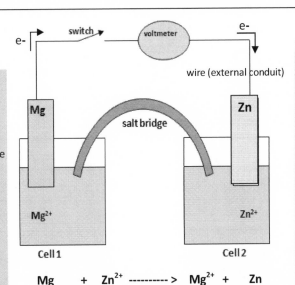

According to Table J

Mg is more active than Zn
> *Therefore*

Mg is the Anode (oxidation site)

Mg is the negative (-) electrode

Mg is also oxidized (loses e-)

Mg is also the reducing agent

Mg will lose mass

Oxidation half-reaction

Mg ------> Mg^{2+} + 2e-

According to Table J

Zn is Less active than Mg.
> *Therefore*

Zn is the Cathode (reduction site)

Zn is the positive (+) electrode

Zn will gain mass

Zn^{2+} is the ion of the less active of the two metals.
> *therefore*

Zn^{2+} is reduced (gains e-)

Zn^{2+} is the oxidizing agent

Reduction half-reaction

Zn^{2+} + 2e- ----> Zn

$$Mg + Zn^{2+} ----------> Mg^{2+} + Zn$$

The equation of the reaction taking place in the cell is sometimes given. You can use the equation to determine the oxidized and reduced substances.

18. How the Voltaic Cell Works

When the switch is closed:

In Cell 1: The more active of the two metals, **Mg** , will be oxidized by losing its electrons.
  The *oxidation-half* reaction at the anode is: Mg ----------> Mg^{2+} + 2e$^-$

The wire (external conduit) carries electrons from Mg (anode) to Zn (cathode).

In Cell 2: The ion of the less active metal, **Zn^{2+}** , will be reduced by gaining electrons lost by Mg.
  Note: Although reduction occurs at Zn (cathode), it is the Zn^{2+} that is reduced.
  The *reduction-half* reaction at the cathode is: Zn^{2+} + 2e- -----> Zn

Electrical energy produced is the flow of electrons from the anode to cathode.

The voltmeter registers the amount of electrical potential energy (voltage) produced by the reaction.

The salt bridge allows ions in the solutions to flow back and forth between Cell 1 and Cell 2 to maintain neutrality of the cells. This is necessary for the voltaic cell to operate .

19. Voltaic Cell: Practice problems

Concept Task: Be able to interpret voltaic cell diagrams

Answer practice questions 43 - 49 based on the diagram below

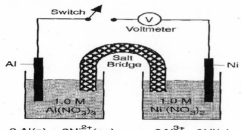

$$2 Al(s) + 3Ni^{2+}(aq) \longrightarrow 2Al^{3+} + 3Ni(s)$$

43. The cathode in this electrochemical cell is
1) Al atoms
2) Al^{3+} ions
3) Ni atoms
4) Ni^{2+} ions

44. Which particles in this electrochemical cell undergo reduction?
1) Al^{3+}
2) Ni^{2+}
3) Al
4) Ni

45. The loss of electrons occurs at
1) Aluminum electrode, because it is the anode
2) Aluminum electrode, because it is the cathode
3) Nickel electrode, because it is the anode
4) Nickel electrode, because it is the cathode

46. Which is true of the electrochemical cell when the switch is closed?
1) Electrons will flow from Ni^{2+} to Ni
2) Electrons will flow from Al^{3+} to Al
3) Electrons will flow from Ni to Al
4) Electrons will flow from Al to Ni

47. The salt bridge in the electrochemical cell connects
1) Al atom to Ni atom
2) Al^{3+} ions to Ni^{2+} ions
3) Ni atom to Ni^{2+} ion
4) Ni^{2+} ion to Al atom

48. When the switch is closed, which correctly shows the reduction process that takes place?
1) $Al + 3e^- \longrightarrow Al^{3+}$
2) $Al \longrightarrow Al^{3+} + 3e^-$
3) $Ni^{2+} + 2e^- \longrightarrow Ni$
4) $Ni^{2+} \longrightarrow Ni + 2e^-$

49. Which is true of this cell as the redox reaction is taking place?
1) The mass of Al electrode will increase, and the mass of Ni electrode will decrease
2) The mass of Al electrode will decrease, and the mass of Ni electrode will increase
3) The mass of Al electrode will increase, and the mass of Ni electrode will remain the same
4) The mass of Al electrode will remain the same, and the mass of Ni electrode will increase

Answer practice questions 50 – 55 based on the diagram below

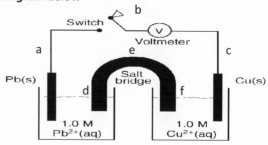

50. This reaction that will occur in this cell is
1) Redox, and non-spontaneous
2) Redox, and spontaneous
3) Non-redox and spontaneous
4) Non-redox and nonspontaneous

51. In the electrochemical diagram, Pb (s) is the
1) Cathode, where oxidation occurs
2) Cathode, where reduction occurs
3) Anode, where oxidation occurs
4) Anode, where reduction occurs

52. In the given electrochemical diagram, the Cu^{2+} ions
1) Gain protons
2) Lose protons
3) Gains electrons
4) Lose electrons

53. Which is true of Pb in this cell?
1) Pb is the oxidizing agent, because it gains electrons
2) Pb is the oxidizing agent, because it loses electrons
3) Pb is the reducing agent, because it gains electrons
4) Pb is the reducing agent, because it loses electrons

54. Which is true of the Pb^{2+} ion in this cell?
1) It is reduced
2) It is oxidized
3) It migrate across the salt bridge
4) it migrate across the external conductor

55. When the switch is closed, which letters show the path and direction of the electrons?
1) abc
2) def
3) cba
4) fed

20. Electrolytic Cells

An electrolytic cell is setup to use electrical energy to force a nonspontaneous chemical reaction. The setup of the cell depends on the type of process that is occurring in the cell. Three electrolytic processes are described below.

Electrolysis of water is a reaction by which water molecules split to produce oxygen and hydrogen.

$$2H_2O(l) \quad + \quad electricity \quad \text{--------} > \quad 2H_2(g) \quad + \quad O_2(g)$$

Electrolytic reduction is a reaction by which very reactive metals are obtained from their fused salts. Elements in Group 1 and Group 2 of the Periodic Table, because of their high reactivity, are generally obtained from this process.

$$2NaBr(aq) \quad + \quad electricity \quad \text{--------} > \quad 2Na(s) \quad + \quad Br_2(g)$$

fused salt   *high reactive*
                                            element obtained

Electroplating is a process by which ion of a desired metal is reduced to produce the metal. The metal produced winds up on the surface of another object.

$$Au^+(aq) \quad + \quad e- \quad \text{--------} > \quad Au(s)$$

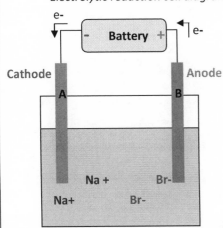

Electrolytic reduction cell diagram

Cathode   Anode

2NaBr(aq) + electricity ------ > 2Na + Br₂

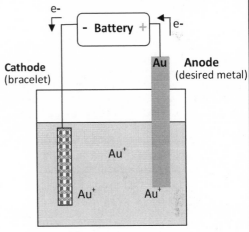

Electroplating cell diagram

Cathode
(bracelet)   Anode
                             (desired metal)

Au⁺   + e- ------ > Au

In any given electrolytic cell, you should be able to identify the different components of the cell. You should also be able to identify the oxidized and reduced substance based on the elements and ions taking parts in the reaction.

Anode (object that loses mass):   Metal or object connected to +end of the battery

Cathode (object that gains mass):   Metal or object connected to –end of the battery

Oxidized substance (loses electrons)

      Electrolytic Reduction: The negative nonmetal ion (Br⁻) $2Br^- \text{ -----} > Br_2 + 2e^-$

      Electroplating: Metal connected to +end of battery (Au) $Au \text{ ------} > Au^+ + e-$

Reduced substance (gains electrons)

      Electrolytic Reduction: The Positive metal ion (Na⁺) $2Na^+ + 2e^- \text{ -----} > 2Na$

      Electroplating: Ion of the metal (Au⁺) $Au^+ + e- \text{ -----} > Au$

21. Electrolytic Cells: Practice problems

Concept Task: Be able to interpret electrolytic diagrams

Answer Practice questions 56 - 61 based on the cell diagram below.

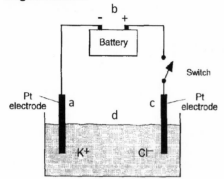

56. Which is reduced?
1) K^+ 2) Cl^- 3) K 4) Pt

57. The cathode in this diagram is the
1) Positive electrode, where oxidation occurs
2) Negative electrode, where oxidation occurs
3) Positive electrode, where reduction occurs
4) Negative electrode, where reduction occurs

58. When the switch is closed in this cell, the
1) Cl^- ions migrate toward the cathode, where they will lose electrons
2) Cl^- ions migrate toward the cathode, where they will gain electrons
3) Cl^- ions migrate toward the anode, where they will lose electrons
4) Cl^- ions migrate toward the anode, where they will gain electrons

59. Which equation best represents the reaction at the negative electrode?
1) $K^+(aq) \text{---------------} > K(s) + e^-$
2) $K^+(aq) + e^- \text{-------} > K(s)$
3) $2Cl^-(aq) \text{------------} > Cl_2(g) + 2e^-$
4) $2Cl^-(aq) + 2e^- \text{---}> Cl_2(g)$

60. The redox reaction that occurs in this cell is best described as
1) Spontaneous and endothermic
2) Spontaneous and exothermic
3) Non-spontaneous and endothermic
4) Non-spontaneous and exothermic

61. When the switched is closed in the cell, what will be the direction of electrons flow?
1) abc   3) adc
2) cba   4) cda

Base your answers to questions 62 - 67 on the cell diagram below.

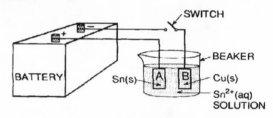

62. Which species are oxidized and reduced in this cell?
1) Sn^{2+} is oxidized, and Sn is reduced
2) Sn is oxidized, and Sn^{2+} is reduced
3) Cu is oxidized, and Sn is reduced
4) Sn is oxidized, and Cu is reduced

63. When the switch is closed, Sn^{2+} is
1) Oxidized, and Sn will be coated with Cu
2) Reduced, and Sn will be coated with Cu
3) Oxidized, and Cu will be coated with Sn
4) Reduced, and Cu will be coated with Sn

64. Which best explains why the mass of electrode B increases as a redox reaction occurs in this cell?
1) Electrode B is oxidized
2) Electrode B is losing electrons
3) Electrode B is coated with more copper
4) Electrode B is coated with tin

65. Which statement is true of electrode A when the switch is closed in this cell diagram?
1) A is the cathode, where oxidation is occurring
2) A is the cathode, where reduction is occurring
3) A is the anode, where oxidation is occurring
4) A is the anode, where reduction is occurring

66. When the switch is closed, the half-reaction that occurs at electrode B is represent by which equation?
1) $Sn(s) + 2e^- \text{-------} > Sn^{2+}(aq)$
2) $Sn^{2+}(aq) + 2e^- \text{-------} > Sn(s)$
3) $Sn(s) \text{---------------} > Sn^{2+}(aq) + 2e^-$
4) $Sn^{2+}(aq) \text{---------------} > Sn(s) + 2e^-$

67. The battery in this cell acts as the
1) External conduit   3) Salt bridge
2) External energy source   4) Voltmeter

22. Electrochemical Cells: Summary Table

Below is a summary of voltaic and electrolytic cells. Use this table for a quick review and comparisons of the two electrochemical cells.

Concept Facts: Study to remember

		Voltaic	Electrolytic
	Diagrams		
D i f f e r e n c e s	**Example redox equation**	Pb + Cu^{2+} ----> Pb^{2+} + Cu	H$_2$O + electricity --> H$_2$ + O$_2$
	Type of reaction	Spontaneous redox Exothermic	Non-spontaneous redox Endothermic
	Energy conversion	Chemical to electrical energy	Electrical to chemical energy
	Anode (site for oxidation)	Negative (-) electrode	Positive (+) electrode
	Cathode (site for reduction)	Positive (+) electrode	Negative (-) electrode
	Half-Reactions occur in	Two separate cells	One cell
	Salt bridge present?	Yes (connects the two half-cells and permits the flow of ions)	No
	Usages and examples	Battery	Electroplating Electrolytic reduction Electrolysis
S i m i l a r i t i e s	**Oxidation** (losing of electrons) at	Anode (-) (loses mass)	Anode (+) (loses mass)
	Reduction (gaining of electrons) at	Cathode (+) (gains mass)	Cathode (-) (gains mass)
	Direction of electron flow	Anode to Cathode	Anode to Cathode

Lesson 4 – Spontaneous Reactions

Introduction

> A **spontaneous reaction** is a reaction that will take place (occur) under a specific set of conditions.
>
> *In Topic 8 (the acid-base)* you learned that certain metals will react spontaneously with acids to produce hydrogen gas.
>
> *In Topic 9 (kinetics and equilibrium)*, you learned that a reaction is spontaneous if the reaction will lead to a lower energy and higher entropy products.
>
> In this lesson, you will learn how to use the Activity Series Reference Table J to predict which reactions will occur spontaneous.

23. Spontaneous and Non-spontaneous Reactions

Spontaneous redox reactions

Recall that a single replacement reaction is a redox reaction. A single replacement reaction will occur spontaneously when the **single (free) element** reactant is more reactive than the **similar element** of the compound.

Examples of spontaneous redox reactions.

$$\underset{\text{free element}}{\textbf{Zn}} \quad + \quad \underset{\underset{\text{similar element}}{\downarrow}}{\textbf{Fe(NO}_3)_2} \text{ --------> } \textbf{Zn(NO}_3)_2 \quad + \quad \textbf{Fe}$$

$$\underset{\text{free element}}{\textbf{Cl}_2} \quad + \quad \underset{\underset{\text{similar element}}{\downarrow}}{\textbf{SnBr}_2} \text{ --------> } \textbf{SnCl}_2 \quad + \quad \textbf{Br}_2$$

In each reaction, the free element is more reactive (higher up on Table J) than the similar element it is replacing. These reactions will occur under normal conditions.

Nonspontaneous redox reactions

A reaction is nonspontaneous if the free element is less reactive than the element it is suppose to replace. These types of reactions will not occur under normal conditions.

Example of nonspontaneous reactions

$$\underset{\text{free element}}{\textbf{Fe}} \quad + \quad \underset{\underset{\text{similar element}}{\downarrow}}{\textbf{Zn(NO}_3)_2} \text{ --------> } \textbf{Fe(NO}_3)_2 \quad + \quad \textbf{Zn}$$

$$\underset{\text{free element}}{\textbf{Br}_2} \quad + \quad \underset{\underset{\text{similar element}}{\downarrow}}{\textbf{SnCl}_2} \text{ --------> } \textbf{SnBr}_2 \quad + \quad \textbf{Cl}_2$$

In each reaction, the free element is less reactive (lower down on Table J) than the similar element (lower down on Table J) it is replacing. These reactions *will not* occur under normal conditions.

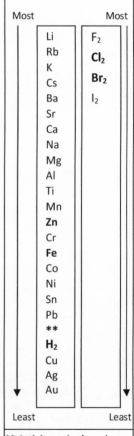

**Reference Table J
Activity Series**

Most		Most
	Li	F_2
	Rb	Cl_2
	K	Br_2
	Cs	I_2
	Ba	
	Sr	
	Ca	
	Na	
	Mg	
	Al	
	Ti	
	Mn	
	Zn	
	Cr	
	Fe	
	Co	
	Ni	
	Sn	
	Pb	
	**	
	H_2	
	Cu	
	Ag	
	Au	
Least		Least

** Activity series based on Hydrogen standard

Topic 11 - Redox and Electrochemistry

24. Spontaneous Redox: Practice problems

Be able to predict spontaneous and nonspontaneous reactions based on activity series

Practice 68

Based on Reference Table J, which reaction will take place spontaneously?

1) $Ni^{2+}(aq) + Pb(s) ----> Ni(s) + Pb^{2+}(aq)$
2) $Sr^{2+}(aq) + Sn(s) ---> Sr(s) + Sn^{2+}(aq)$
3) $Au^{3+}(aq) + Al(s) ---> Au(s) + Al^{3+}(aq)$
4) $Fe^{2+}(aq) + Cu(s) ---> Fe(s) + Cu^{2+}(aq)$

Practice 69

According to information from Reference Table J, which redox reaction occurs spontaneously?

1) $Cu(s) + 2H^{+}(aq) ----> Cu^{2+}(aq) + H_2(g)$
2) $Mg(s) + 2H^{+}(aq) ----> Mg^{2+}(aq) + H_2(g)$
3) $2Ag(s) + 2H^{+}(aq) ----> 2Ag^{+}(aq) + H_2(g)$
4) $2Au(s) + 2H^{+}(aq) ----> 2Au^{+}(aq) + H_2(g)$

Practice 70

Based on Reference Table J, which redox reaction will occur spontaneously?

1) $Br_2 + KI ----> KBr + I_2$
2) $I_2 + KCl ----> KI + Cl_2$
3) $Cl_2 + KF ----> KCl + F_2$
4) $I_2 + KBr ----> KI + Br_2$

Practice 71

Referring to the Activity Series on Reference Table J, which reaction will not occur spontaneously under standard conditions?

1) $Sn(s) + 2HF(aq) ----> SnF_2(aq) + H_2(g)$
2) $Mg(s) + 2HF(aq) ----> MgF_2(aq) + H_2(g)$
3) $Ba(s) + 2HF(aq) ----> BaF_2(aq) + H_2(g)$
4) $2Cu(s) + 2HF(aq) ----> CuF_2(aq) + H_2(g)$

Practice 72

Which metal, according to Reference Table J, will react spontaneously with $Al^{3+?}$

1) Ca(s)   2) Cu(s)   3) Cr(s)   4) Co(s)

25. Most easily Oxidized or Reduced using Activity Table J

Some elements are more easily oxidized, others are more easily reduced. The Activity Series Table J can be used to determine which element or ion is most likely to be oxidized or reduced. On the information below, the element or ion in parentheses is in comparison to all the elements listed on Table J.

Metals

Most easily oxidized: Metal closest to top (Li)

Most easily reduced: Ion of metal closest to bottom (Au^{+})

An element on the top will cause an ion of an element below it to reduce. For example, Ca will cause Na+ to reduce to Na .

An ion of an element on the bottom will cause any element above it to oxidize. For example, Na+ will cause Ca to oxidize to Ca^{2+} .

Nonmetals

Most easily oxidized: Ion of nonmetal closest to bottom (I^{-})

Most easily reduced: Nonmetal closest to top (F_2)

Practice 73

According to Reference Table J, which of these ions is most easily reduced?

1) Ca^{2+} 2) Cr^{3+} 3) Co^{2+} 4) Cs^{+}

Practice 74

Based on Reference Table J, which most easily oxidized?

1) Ba   2) Sr   3) Ca   4) Mg

Practice 75

According to Table J, which ion is least easily oxidized?

1) Br^{-} 2) Cl^{-} 3) F^{-} 4) I^{-}

Practice 76

Which metal will reduce Zn^{2+} to Zn?

1) Mn   2) Cr   3) H_2 4) Ag

Practice 77

Which ion is most likely to oxidize K to K^{+}?

1) Li^{+} 2) Rb^{+} 3) Cs^{+} 4) Ba^{2+}

Topic 11 – Redox and Electrochemistry

Concept Terms

Key vocabulary terms and concepts from Topic 11 are listed below. You should know definition and facts related to each term and concept.

1. Oxidation number
2. Redox
3. Oxidation
4. Reduction
5. Oxidized substance
6. Reduced substance
7. Oxidizing agent
8. Reducing agent
9. Half-reaction
10. Electrochemical cell
11. Voltaic cell
12. Electrolytic cell
13. Electrolytic reduction
14. Electrolysis
15. Electroplating
16. Electrode
17. Anode
18. Cathode
19. Salt bridge
20. External conduit
21. Battery
22. Most easily oxidized or reduced
23. Least easily oxidized or reduced

Concept Tasks

Concept tasks from Topic 11 are listed below. You should know how to solve problems and answer questions related to each concept task.

1. Determine oxidation numbers of elements in a neutral formula
2. Determining oxidation numbers of elements in polyatomic ions
3. Recognizing equations that are REDOX
4. Describing and interpreting half-reaction equation for oxidation and reduction
5. Recognizing half-reaction equation for oxidation
6. Recognizing half-reaction equation for reduction
7. Determining oxidation number change for oxidation
8. Determining oxidation number change for reduction
9. Determining oxidation number change showing greatest or least number of electrons lost or gained
10. Determining number of electrons lost or gained based on a change in oxidation number.
11. Determining oxidized substance (reducing agent, substance losing electrons) in redox equation
12. Determining reduced substance (oxidizing agent, substance gaining electrons) in redox equation
13. Recognizing the correct oxidation half-reaction equation for a given redox
14. Recognizing the correct reduction half-reaction equation for a given redox reaction
15. Writing oxidation and reduction half-equation for a given redox reaction
16. Identifying components of a voltaic cell
17. Answering question related to voltaic cells
18. Describing how a voltaic cell works
19. Identifying components of an electrolytic cell
20. Answering questions related to electrolytic reduction cell diagram
21. Answering questions related to electroplating cell diagrams
22. Describing how an electrolytic reduction cell works
23. Describing how an electroplating cell
24. Determining spontaneous and nonspontaneous reactions using Table J
25. Determining most easily oxidized or reduced substance
26. Determining least easily oxidized or reduced substance

Topic 12 - Nuclear Chemistry

Topic outline

In this topic, you will learn the following concepts:

. Transmutations

. Nuclear stability

. Nuclear equations

. Nuclear particles and radiations

. Separation of particles

. Balancing nuclear equations

. Natural transmutation

. Alpha decay, beta decay, positron emission

. Artificial transmutation

. Nuclear energy processes

. Fission and Fusion

. Half-life

. Radioisotopes usages and wastes

Lesson 1 – Nuclear Transmutations

Introduction:

Nuclear chemistry is the study of changes that occur in the nucleus of atoms.

 L**OO**KING Back: Topic 3: Atomic structure, you had learned about nucleus of atom.

Recall the following important facts about the nucleus, and about particles found in the nucleus:

. Protons and neutrons are found in the nucleus of atoms

.The number of protons (atomic number) identifies each element

.The number of neutrons determines mass number of atoms

Any change to the nucleus of an atom likely involves a change to the number of protons and/or neutrons. Any change to the nucleus of an atom will always change that atom to a different atom.

Transmutation is the changing (converting) of one atom to another by ways of nuclear changes.

In this lesson, you will learn about the different types of nuclear transmutations, and ways of representing them by nuclear equations.

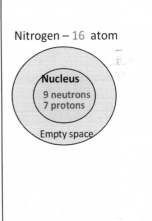

Nitrogen – 16 atom

Nucleus
9 neutrons
7 protons

Empty space

1. Nuclear Transmutations: Ways that a nucleus can change

Transmutation occurs when one nucleus is changed into another. There are several ways that a nucleus of an atom can be changed to a different nucleus.

For examples:

. A nucleus can release a particle (proton, neutron, alpha, positron, and/or electron)

. A nucleus can absorb a particle

. A nucleus can absorb one particle, and release another

. A nucleus can split into smaller nuclei

. A nucleus can join with another nucleus to form a larger nucleus.

Any of the above changes to the nucleus of an atom will result in the formation of a different atom. Nuclear equations are used to show these changes.

2. Nuclear Equation

A **nuclear equation** is used to show changes taking place during a nuclear reaction.

Recall that information about a nucleus of an atom can be represented using a nuclear symbol.

⬅️ L👀KING Back: Topic 3 - Atomic structure: You learned about nuclear symbols

Below, nuclear symbol for an atom of strontium (Sr) is given.

$$^{90}_{38}Sr$$

90 = mass number = number of protons + neutrons

Sr = symbol for strontium

38 = Atomic number = number of protons

Nuclear symbols are used in nuclear change equations. You will be seeing a lot of these symbols in this topic.

Nuclear change equation: $\quad ^{90}_{38}Sr \ ------> \ ^{86}_{36}Rn \ + \ ^{4}_{2}He$

Chemical change equation: $\quad 2KClO_3(s) \ ----> \ 2KCl(s) \ + \ 3O_2(g)$

Physical change equation: $\quad CO_2(s) \ ------> \ CO_2(g)$

Concept Task: Be able to recognize nuclear equations

Practice 1

Which of the these equation represents a nuclear change?

1) $H^+ \ + \ OH^- \ ---> \ H_2O$

2) $H_2O \ + \ Na \ --> \ NaOH \ + \ H_2$

3) $NaCl \ (s) \ ----> \ Na^+(aq) \ + \ Cl^-(aq)$

4) $^{4}_{2}He \ + \ ^{12}_{6}C \ --> \ ^{16}_{7}N \ + \ ^{0}_{1}n$

Practice 2

Which equation is an example of a transmutation?

1) $^{9}Be \ + \ ^{4}He \ ---> \ ^{12}C \ + \ ^{1}n$

2) $U \ + 3F_2 \ ----> \ UF_6$

3) $Mg(OH)_2 \ + \ 2HCl \ ---> 2H_2O \ + \ MgCl_2$

4) $Ca \ + 2H_2O \ ---> \ Ca(OH)_2 \ + \ H_2$

3. Nuclear Particles

During nuclear transmutations and radioactivity, particles are absorbed and released by the nucleus. The change (or transmutation) depends on the type of particles absorbed and /or released.

Radiation (or radioactivity) describes particles and energy related to nuclear changes.

Particles and radiations most commonly involved in nuclear changes are given on the Table below. Some information on this table can also be found on Reference Table O. More information about each particle is given on the next page.

Nuclear Particle	Symbol	Mass	Charge	Penetrating power	Able to be accelerated
Alpha	$^{4}_{2}He$, α	4 amu	+2	Low (weakest)	Yes
Beta	$^{0}_{-1}e$, -β	0 amu	-1	Medium	Yes
Positron	$^{0}_{+1}e$, +β	0 amu	+1	Medium	Yes
Gamma	$^{0}_{0}y$	0 amu	0	High (strongest)	No
Neutron	$^{1}_{0}n$	1 amu	0	------	No

Topic 12: Nuclear Chemistry

4. Nuclear Chemistry Particles and Radiations

Alpha particles $^{4}_{2}He$ or α

Alpha particles are similar to helium nuclei.
Alpha particles have a mass of 4 amu and a charge of +2
Alpha particles have the lowest penetrating power of
all radiations

Beta particles $^{0}_{-1}e$ or $\beta-$

Beta particles are similar to a high speed electron.
Beta particles have a mass of 0 and a charge of -1.
Beta particles are produced when a neutrons are converted to
protons.

Positrons: $^{0}_{+1}e$ or $\beta+$

Positrons have a mass of 0 and a charge of +1.
Positrons are produced when protons are converted neutrons.

Gamma rays $^{0}_{0}\gamma$

Gamma rays (radiation) are similar to high energy x-rays.
Gamma rays have a mass of 0 and a charge of 0.
Gamma rays have the highest penetrating power of
all radiations.

Neutron: $^{1}_{0}n$

Neutrons have a mass of 1 amu and a charge of 0.

An **accelerator** is a device that moves
charged particles to a high speed.
Only charged particles (alpha,
beta, and positron) can be
accelerated.

Penetrating power refers to the
strength of a particle to go
through an object.

Alpha particles (α) has the weakest
penetrating power. It can be
stopped by a sheet of paper.

Gamma radiation (γ) has the strongest
penetrating power. Gamma rays can
only be stopped by metals of very high
density like lead.

properties.

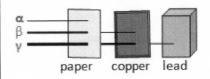

paper   copper   lead

5. Separation of Particles

Nuclear emanations (particles) released from a radioactive source can be separated through an electric or a
magnetic field.

An **electric field** contains two charged plates; A positive and negative charged plate as shown below.

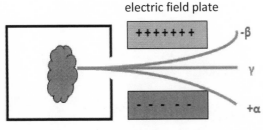

electric field plate

+ + + + + + +   -β

γ

- - - - - - -   +α

electric field plate

Radioactive substance
in a lead box

As particles are released from a radioactive source:

. Negative (-) particles will attract (are deflected)
  toward the positive plates (+) of the electric field

. Particles with no charge will be unaffected (not
  deflected) by the electric field, and will go straight
  through

. Positive (+) particles will attract (are deflected)
  toward the negative plates (-) of the electric field.

6. Nuclear Particles: Practice problems

Practice 3
Which nuclear radiation is similar to high energy X-ray?
1) Beta   3) Alpha
2) Gamma   4) Neutron

Practice 4
Alpha particles and beta particles differ in
1) Mass only   3) Both mass and charge
2) Charge only   4) Neither mass nor charge

Practice 5
Which nuclear emission has neither mass nor charge?
1) α 3) $\beta+$
2) $\beta-$ 4) γ

Practice 6
Which list of particles is in order of increasing mass?
1) Proton ------> Beta --------> Alpha
2) Alpha------- > Beta -------- > Proton
3) Beta -------- > Proton ----- > Alpha
4) Proton -----> Alpha ------> Beta

Practice 7
Which list is showing the particles arranged in order of increasing penetrating power?
1) Gamma -----> Beta ----------> Alpha
2) Alpha-------- > Beta -------- > Gamma
3) Beta --------- > Gamma ---- > Alpha
4) Gamma -----> Alpha -------> Beta

Practice 8
which list can all particles be accelerated by electric field?
1) Alpha, beta, and neutrons
2) Alpha, protons, and neutrons
3) Alpha, beta, and protons
4) Beta, protons, and neutrons

Practice 9
Which nuclear emission moving through an electric field would be attracted toward a positive electrode?
1) Proton   3) Gamma radiation
2) Beta Particle   4) Alpha particle

Practice 10
Given the diagram below

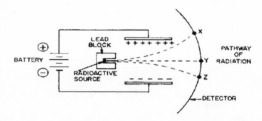

Which correctly list the radiations in order of increasing charge?
1) z , y, x   3) y, x, z
2) x, y, z   4) z, x, y

7. Nucleus Stability

Most nuclei are stable (do not undergo spontaneous decay) in their natural state. A few of the elements have no stable nuclei at all. *The ratio of neutrons to protons* in the nucleus determines stability of a nucleus.

. Nuclei of elements with equal amounts of neutrons and protons (ratio of 1 : 1) are generally stable and will not undergo radioactive decay

. All radioactive nuclei have more neutrons than protons

. *All nuclei of elements with atomic number 83 and above are unstable because of their high neutron to proton ratios.* As a result, all elements with atomic number higher than 82 are naturally radioactive.

For example, Francium (#87) has no stable isotope.

Below, a comparison of two carbon isotopes.

Carbon-12   Carbon-14
^{12}C ^{14}C

Stable isotope   *Unstable isotope*

A carbon-14 nucleus contains two extra neutrons that make it unstable and radioactive.

Topic 12: Nuclear Chemistry

8. Radioisotopes and Decay Modes

Decay mode refers to the type of radiation that a radioisotope will release as it decays. *Reference Table N* lists selected radioisotopes and their decay modes.

A **radioisotope** is any radioactive isotope of an element. A radioisotope can be described as one of the followings depending on its decay mode.

An **alpha emitter** is a radioisotope that decays by releasing an alpha particle.

Radioisotopes with atomic number 83 and above tend to be alpha emitters.

Ex. Francium–220 and uranium–238 are alpha emitters.

A **beta emitter** is a radioisotope that decays by releasing a beta particle.

Ex. Cobalt–60 and strontium–90 are beta emitters.

A **positron emitter** is a radioisotope that decays by releasing a positron.

Ex. Iron–53 and neon–19 are positron emitters.

Radioisotopes of small atomic numbers tend to be beta and positron emitters.

Concept Task: Be able to match a radioisotope to its decay mode

Practice 11
Which radioisotope decays by releasing a particle with a mass of 4 ?

1) ^{32}P 3) ^{14}C

2) ^{239}Pu 4) ^{3}H

Practice 12
Which particle is spontaneously emitted in the nucleus of Calcium - 37?

1) Alpha   3) Beta

2) Positron   4) Electron

Practice 13
Which notation of a radioisotope is correctly paired with the notation of its emission particle?

1) ^{37}K and β-   3) ^{222}Rn and α

2) ^{16}N and β+   4) ^{99}Tc and β-

Practice 14
Which two radioisotopes have the same decay mode?

1) ^{37}K and ^{42}K 3) ^{220}Fr and ^{222}Rn

2) ^{232}Th and ^{32}P 4) ^{233}U and ^{99}Tc

9. Types of Transmutations

Transmutation is the changing (converting) of one atom to a different atom. Transmutation can be natural or artificial.

Natural transmutation occurs when a single unstable radioactive nucleus spontaneously changes by decaying (breaking down).

. Alpha decay, beta decay, and positron emission are all types of natural transmutation

Artificial transmutation occurs when a stable nonradioactive nucleus is hit (bombarded) with a high speed particle and is changed to an unstable nucleus.

10. Alpha Decay : a natural transmutation

Alpha decay occurs when a radioactive nucleus spontaneously breaks down to emit an alpha particle.

Example of an alpha decay

$$^{238}_{92}U \text{ -------------} > \quad ^{4}_{2}He \quad + \quad ^{234}_{90}Th$$

Alpha emitter   alpha particle   new atom
(Unstable radioactive nucleus)   emitted

After an alpha decay, numbers of particles of the new atom are different from those of the radioactive atom. Below, a comparison for the alpha decay equation given above.

	Radioactive atom $^{238}_{92}U$	New atom $^{234}_{90}Th$
Mass number	238	234
protons (atomic #)	92	90
neutrons (mass # - atomic #)	146	144

. Mass number is decreased by 4
. Number of protons (atomic number) is decreased by 2
. Number of neutrons is decreased by 2

Practice 15
Compared to an atom before an alpha decay, the number of protons of the atom after alpha decay will be

1) Greater by 4
2) Greater by 2
3) Lesser by 2
4) The same

Practice 16
Which of the following equations represents an alpha decay?

1) $^{19}_{10}Ne$ -----> $^{19}_{11}Na$ + $^{0}_{-1}e$

2) $^{228}_{89}Ac$ ----> $^{228}_{88}Ra$ + $^{0}_{+1}e$

3) $^{232}_{90}Th$ -----> $^{4}_{2}He$ + $^{228}_{88}Ra$

4) $^{220}_{87}Fr$ + $^{4}_{2}He$ ---> $^{224}_{89}Ac$

11. Beta Decay: a natural transmutation

Beta decay occurs when a radioactive nucleus converts a neutron to a proton and an electron. The electron is then released from the nucleus.

Example of a beta decay

$$^{14}_{6}C \text{ -------------} > \quad ^{0}_{-1}e \quad + \quad ^{14}_{7}N$$

beta emitter   beta particle   new atom
(unstable radioactive nucleus)   emitted

After a beta decay, numbers of particles of the new atom are different from those of the radioactive atom. Below, a comparison for the beta decay equation given above.

	Radioactive atom $^{14}_{6}C$	New atom $^{14}_{7}N$
Mass number	14	14
protons (atomic #)	6	7
neutrons (mass # - atomic #)	8	7

. Mass number remains the same *(b/c the electron created has no mass)*
. Number of protons is increased by 1 *(b/c a proton was created)*
. Number of neutrons is decreased by 1 *(b/c a neutron was converted)*

Practice 17
As a radioactive isotope undergoes a beta decay, the mass number of the atom

1) Increases by 2
2) Increases by 1
3) Decreases by 1
4) Remains unchanged

Practice 18
Which of the following equations represents a beta decay?

1) $^{220}_{87}Fr$ + $^{4}_{2}He$ ------> $^{224}_{89}Ac$

2) $^{43}_{21}Sc$ -------------> $^{43}_{20}Ca$ + $^{0}_{+1}e$

3) $^{198}_{79}Au$ ----------> $^{198}_{80}Hg$ + $^{0}_{-1}e$

4) $^{42}_{19}K$ + $^{0}_{-1}e$ ------> $^{42}_{18}Ar$

Topic 12: Nuclear Chemistry

12. Positron Emission: a natural transmutation

A **positron emission** occurs when a radioactive nucleus converts a proton to a neutron and a positron. The positron is released from nucleus.

Example of a positron emission

$$^{37}_{20}\text{Ca} \quad \text{-----------} > \quad ^{0}_{+1}e \quad + \quad ^{37}_{19}\text{K}$$

positron emitter   positron   new atom
(Unstable radioactive nucleus)   emitted

After a positron emission, the numbers of particles of the new atom are different from those of the radioactive atom. Below, a comparison for the positron emission equation given above.

	Radioactive atom $^{37}_{20}\text{Ca}$	New atom $^{37}_{19}\text{K}$
Mass number	37	37
protons (atomic #)	20	19
neutrons (mass # - atomic #)	17	18

. Mass number remains the same *(b/c the positron created has no mass)*
. Number of protons is decreased by 1 *(b/c a proton was converted)*
. Number of neutrons is increased by 1 *(b/c a neutron was created)*

Practice 19
Compared to an atom after a positron emission, the number of protons of the atom before the decay is

1) 1 more
2) 1 fewer
3) 2 fewer
4) the same

Practice 20
Which of the following equations represents an alpha decay?

1) $^{19}_{10}\text{Ne} \; \text{-----} > \; ^{19}_{11}\text{Na} \; + \; ^{0}_{-1}e$

2) $^{228}_{89}\text{Ac} \; \text{----} > \; ^{228}_{88}\text{Ra} \; + \; ^{0}_{+1}e$

3) $^{232}_{90}\text{Th} \; \text{-----} > \; ^{4}_{2}\text{He} \; + \; ^{228}_{88}\text{Ra}$

4) $^{220}_{87}\text{Fr} \; + \; ^{4}_{2}\text{He} \; \text{---} > \; ^{224}_{89}\text{Ac}$

13. Decay Series

During a decay series, a radioactive nucleus continuously decays by releasing alpha and beta particles until a stable nucleus is produced.

Uranium-238 decay series is one of the most common decay series. At the end of the decay series uranium-238 will decay to lead-206 (a stable nucleus).

The graph below is showing the decay series of Th-230. Each decay by alpha or beta leads to a new isotope until a stable Pb-206 isotope is produced.

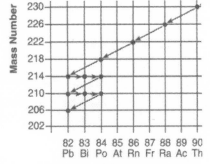

Sections of the graph where arrows drop down indicate alpha decays.

Sections where arrows stay straight indicate beta decays.

Practice 21

The chart below shows the spontaneous decay of U-238 to Th-234 to Pa-234 to U-234.

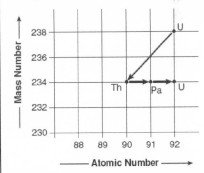

What is the correct order of nuclear decay modes for the change from U-238 to U-234?

1) β- decay, γ decay, β-decay

2) β-decay, β-decay, α decay

3) α decay, α decay, β-decay

4) α decay, β-decay, β-decay

Topic 12: Nuclear Chemistry

14. Artificial Transmutation

Artificial transmutation occurs when a stable non-radioactive nucleus is bombarded (hit) with a high speed particle, and is changed (transmuted) into a different atom.

Example of artificial transmutation:

$$^{4}_{2}He \quad + \quad ^{9}_{4}Be \quad ----------> \quad ^{12}_{6}C \quad + \quad ^{1}_{0}n$$

accelerated high speed particles   *stable and non-radioactive*   *unstable radioisotope*   *neutron released*

Practice 22	**Practice 23**
Which equation is an example of artificial transmutation?	Artificial transmutation is represented by which equation?
1) $^{1}_{0}n + ^{14}_{7}N ------> ^{14}_{6}C + ^{1}_{1}H$	1) $^{43}_{21}Sc ------------> ^{43}_{20}Ca + ^{0}_{+1}e$
2) $^{38}_{19}K -------------> ^{37}_{18}Ar + ^{1}_{1}p$	2) $^{10}_{4}Be -------------> ^{10}_{5}B + ^{0}_{-1}e$
3) $^{212}_{84}Po ---------------> ^{208}_{82}Pb + ^{4}_{2}He$	3) $^{235}_{92}U + ^{1}_{0}n -----> ^{139}_{56}Ba + ^{94}_{36}Kr + 3^{1}_{0}n$
4) $^{2}_{1}H + ^{2}_{1}H -----> ^{3}_{2}He$	4) $^{32}_{16}S + ^{1}_{0}n --------> ^{32}_{15}P + ^{1}_{1}H$

Lesson 2 – Nuclear Energy: Fission and Fusion Reactions

Introduction

During certain nuclear processes, it is known that the total mass of the products is slightly less than that of the reactants. The result of this is called the **mass defect.** The relationship between the missing mass and the tremendous amount of energy produced from nuclear reactions is given by this well known equation:

$$E = mc^2$$

Where **E** is energy produced

m is the mass defect (missing mass)

c is the speed of light

Concept Facts: Study to remember the relationship between mass and energy during nuclear reactions.

According to the above equation, it can be concluded that during a nuclear reaction:

. Energy is converted from mass (or mass is converted to energy)

. Energy released is extremely high in comparison to that of ordinary chemical reactions

Fission and fusion reactions are two types of nuclear reactions that can produce high amounts of energy.

In this lesson, you will learn more about nuclear fission and fusion reactions.

15. Fission – a nuclear energy reaction

Fission is a nuclear reaction in which a large nucleus is split into smaller nuclei.

The diagram and the equation below are showing a nuclear fission reaction. In the reaction, a neutron hits a uranium nucleus, causing it to break into two smaller nuclei fragments. Three neutrons and a tremendous amount of energy and radiation are also produced.

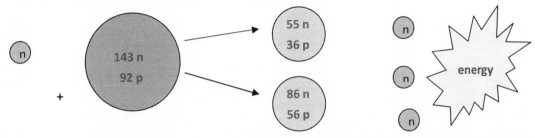

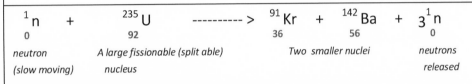

$$_{0}^{1}n \ + \ _{92}^{235}U \ ---------> \ _{36}^{91}Kr \ + \ _{56}^{142}Ba \ + \ 3_{0}^{1}n$$

| neutron | A large fissionable (split able) | Two smaller nuclei | neutrons |
| (slow moving) | nucleus | | released |

Concept Facts: Study to remember the following facts about fission reactions

. A large fissionable (splittable) nucleus absorbs slow moving neutrons
   The large nucleus is split into smaller fragments, with release of more neutrons.

.Tons of nuclear energy is released. Energy is converted from mass
   Energy released is less than that of fusion reactions.

. In nuclear power plants, the fission process is well controlled.
   Energy produced is used to produce electricity

. In nuclear bombs, the fission process is uncontrolled
   Energy and radiations released are used to cause destruction.

. Nuclear wastes are also produced
   Nuclear wastes are dangerous and pose serious health and environmental problems.
   Nuclear wastes must be stored and disposed of properly.

Practice 24
The amount of energy released from a fission reaction is much greater than the energy from a chemical reaction because in a fission reaction
1) Energy is converted to mass
2) Ionic bonds are broken
3) Mass is converted to energy
4) Covalent bonds are broken

Practice 25
Which nuclear equation represents fission reaction?

1) $_{0}^{1}n \ + \ _{7}^{14}N \ ------> \ _{6}^{14}C \ + \ _{1}^{1}H$

2) $_{92}^{238}U \ + \ _{2}^{4}He \ -----> \ _{94}^{241}Pu \ + \ _{0}^{1}n$

3) $_{19}^{38}K \ --------------> \ _{18}^{37}Ar \ + \ _{1}^{1}p$

4) $_{94}^{239}Pu \ + \ _{0}^{1}n \ ------> \ _{38}^{91}Br \ + \ _{56}^{146}La \ + \ 3_{0}^{1}n$

Topic 12: Nuclear Chemistry

16. Fusion – a nuclear energy reaction

Fusion is a nuclear reaction in which small nuclei are joined (fused) to create a larger nucleus.

Only small atoms like those of hydrogen and helium can be fused (joined) in a nuclear fusion reaction.

The diagram and equation below are showing a nuclear fusion reaction. In the reaction, two small hydrogen nuclei join (fuse) to produce a larger helium nucleus. A tremendous amount of energy is also produced.

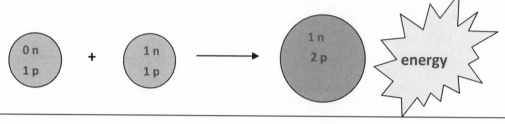

$$^{1}_{1}\text{H} \quad + \quad ^{2}_{1}\text{H} \quad \text{-----------} > \quad ^{3}_{2}\text{He} \quad + \quad \text{energy}$$

small nuclei   *Larger nucleus*

Concept Facts: Study to remember facts about fusion reactions

. Two small nuclei are brought together under extremely high temperature and pressure
   The two nuclei are fused (joined) to create a slightly larger nucleus.

.Tons of nuclear energy are released. Energy is converted from mass.
   Energy released is much greater than that of fission reaction.

. Fusion produces no nuclear waste, unlike fission.

. Energy from the sun is due to fusion reactions that occur in the core of the sun.

. High temperature and high pressure are required for a fusion reaction to occur
   High temperature and pressure are necessary to overcome the repelling force of the two positive nuclei that are to be fused.
   Recall that the nucleus is positively charged. In fusion, two positive nuclei must be brought (joined) together. Opposites attract, BUT similar charges repel. Therefore, extremely high temperature and pressure are needed to make two positively charged nuclei join together in a fusion reaction.

Practice 26
Which statement explains why fusion reactions are difficult to start?
1) Positive nuclei attract each other   3) Negative nuclei attract each other
2) Positive nuclei repel each other   4) Negative nuclei repel each other

Practice 27
Which nuclear equation represents a fusion reaction?

1) $^{14}_{7}\text{N} + ^{1}_{0}\text{n} \text{ -----} > ^{14}_{6}\text{C} + ^{1}_{1}\text{H}$ 3) $^{1}_{1}\text{H} + ^{3}_{2}\text{He} \text{ -----} > ^{4}_{2}\text{He} + ^{0}_{+1}\text{e}$

2) $^{238}_{92}\text{U} + ^{4}_{2}\text{He} \text{ -----} > ^{241}_{94}\text{Pu} + ^{1}_{0}\text{n}$ 4) $^{235}_{92}\text{U} + ^{1}_{0}\text{n} \text{ ------} > ^{87}_{35}\text{Br} + ^{146}_{57}\text{La} + 3\,^{1}_{0}\text{n}$

Topic 12 - Nuclear Chemistry

17. Nuclear Equations: Summary Table

Below is a summary of the five types of nuclear processes discussed in the last few pages.

Use this table for quick studying and for comparing the five nuclear reactions.

Nuclear process and equation	Important facts to remember		
	Mass number after decay	Protons (atomic number) after decay	Neutrons after decay
Alpha decay (natural transmutation) $^{226}_{88}Ra$ ------> $^{222}_{86}Rn$ + $^{4}_{2}He$	$\downarrow 4$	$\downarrow 2$	$\downarrow 2$
Beta decay (natural transmutation) $^{14}_{6}C$ ------> $^{14}_{7}N$ + $^{0}_{-1}e$	same	$\uparrow 1$	$\downarrow 1$
Positron emission (natural transmutation) $^{226}_{88}Ra$ ------> $^{226}_{87}Fr$ + $^{0}_{+1}e$	same	$\downarrow 1$	$\uparrow 1$
Artificial Transmutation $^{40}_{18}Ar$ + $^{1}_{1}H$ ----> $^{40}_{19}K$ + $^{1}_{0}n$	Bombarding nucleus with high speed particles		
Fission (nuclear energy) $^{235}_{92}U$ + $^{1}_{0}n$ ---> $^{142}_{56}Ba$ + $^{91}_{36}Kr$ + $3^{1}_{0}n$	Nucleus splits into smaller nuclei. Mass is converted to energy. More energy then chemical reactions. *Problems:* Produces dangerous radioactive wastes.		
Fusion (nuclear energy) $^{2}_{1}H$ + $^{2}_{1}H$ -----> $^{4}_{2}He$ + energy	Nuclei join to make a larger nucleus. Mass is converted to energy. Energy is more than that of fission. Produces no radioactive waste. *Problems:* High energy and high pressure to overcome repelling nuclei.		

Topic 12: Nuclear Chemistry

18. Balancing Nuclear Equations

A nuclear equation is balanced when the sum of masses (top numbers) and sum of charges (bottom numbers) are equal on both sides of the equation.

Example of a balanced nuclear equation is demonstrated below:

$$^{222}_{86}Rn \quad ----------> \quad ^{4}_{2}He \quad + \quad ^{218}_{84}Po$$

This nuclear equation is balanced because:

The mass (top) number on the *left* (*222*) is equal to the sum of the masses on the *right (4 + 218 = 222)*.

The charge (bottom) number on the *left* (*86*) is equal to the sum of charges on the *right (2 + 84 = 86)*

An unbalanced nuclear equation is usually given as an incomplete equation in which the missing particle (X) must be determined.

Example of an unbalanced nuclear equation is given below:

$$^{37}_{18}Ar \quad + \quad ^{0}_{-1}e \quad ------> \quad X \qquad \text{The X can be determine with a simple math}$$

$$^{37}_{18}Ar \quad + \quad ^{0}_{-1}e \quad ------> \quad ^{37}_{17}X \qquad \begin{array}{l}\text{Top (mass) number of X (37) must equal sum of 0 + 37}\\ \text{Bottom (charge) number of X (17) must equal sum of 18 + -1}\end{array}$$

$$X \text{ is } ^{37}_{17}Cl \qquad \begin{array}{l}\text{Bottom number of X is determined to be 17}\\ \text{17 is the atomic number for chlorine (Cl)}\end{array}$$

Concept Task: **Be** able to complete and balance nuclear equations

---

Practice 28
In the nuclear equation:

$$^{234}_{91}Pa \quad ------------> \quad X \quad + \quad ^{0}_{-1}e$$

Which particle is represented by the X?

1) $^{234}_{92}U$ 2) $^{234}_{93}Np$ 3) $^{235}_{92}U$ 4) $^{235}_{93}Np$

Practice 29
Which particle is represented by X in the nuclear equation below?

$$^{75}_{33}As \quad + \quad X \quad ------> \quad ^{78}_{35}Br \quad + \quad ^{1}_{0}n$$

1) $^{1}_{1}H$ 2) $^{1}_{0}n$ 3) $^{0}_{+1}e$ 4) $^{4}_{2}He$

Practice 30
Given the nuclear reaction:

$$^{241}_{95}Am \quad -----------> \quad ^{237}_{93}Np \quad + \quad X$$

Which particle is represented by X?
1) Alpha   3) Beta
2) Positron   4) Proton

Practice 31
Consider the equation below:

$$^{235}_{92}U \quad + \quad ^{1}_{0}n \quad ------> \quad X \quad + \quad ^{146}_{57}La \quad + \quad 3^{1}_{0}n$$

X in the equation represents

1) Br-35   3) Ge-32
2) Br-87   4) Ge-85

Practice 32
Which nuclear reaction involves the emission of a positron?

$$1) \quad ^{9}_{4}Be \quad + \quad ^{1}_{1}H \quad ------> \quad ^{6}_{3}Li \quad + \quad X$$

$$2) \quad ^{18}_{9}F \quad ---------------> \quad ^{18}_{8}O \quad + \quad X$$

$$3) \quad ^{234}_{90}Th \quad -----------> \quad ^{234}_{91}Pa \quad + \quad X$$

$$4) \quad ^{14}_{7}N \quad + \quad ^{1}_{0}n \quad ------> \quad ^{14}_{6}C \quad + \quad X$$

19. Writing Decay Equations

On Reference Table N, you are given radioisotope symbols and their decay mode.

Concept Task: Be able to write or determine a balance nuclear equation for a radioisotope if its decay mode is known.

Note: This is generally done by piecing together information from Reference Tables N, O, and the Periodic Table.

Examples

Write nuclear equations for the decay of plutonium-239 and iodine-131.

Study the steps below to learn how to do the same for any radioisotope whose decay mode is known.

Step 1: Write	*Step 2: Write*	*Step 3 : Determine missing*
Nuclide symbol -----> (Use Table N)	Decay mode symbol + (Use Table N and O)	Top #, bottom #, and atom's symbol (numbers must make for a balanced equation)

					Note:
Plutotonium-239	$^{239}_{94}Pu$	----->	$^{4}_{2}He$ +	$^{235}_{92}U$	The bottom # of each symbol is the atomic number (from the
Iodine-131	$^{131}_{53}I$	------>	$^{0}_{-1}e$ +	$^{131}_{54}Xe$	Periodic Table)

For Practice questions 33 - 37

Use information provided in Reference Table N to write balanced nuclear equations for the decay of following radioisotopes.

33. Krypton – 85

34. Uranium – 233

35. Neon - 19

36. Radon – 222

37. Gold – 198

For practice questions 38 - 44

Write a balanced nuclear equation for each reaction based on the information provided.

38. Alpha emission of ^{214}Po

39. Electron absorption of ^{116}Sb

40. Proton emission of ^{41}K

41. Neutron emission of ^{107}Ag

42. Positron absorption of ^{40}Ar

43. Alpha absorption by ^{14}N with neutron emission

44. Neutron absorption by ^{209}Bi with alpha emission

Lesson 3 – Half-life

20. Half-life

Half-life is the length of time it takes for a radioactive substance to decay to half its original mass. During a radioactive decay, the radioisotope is converted to a different substance. Over time, less and less of the radioactive substance remains, while more of the new substance is formed. At a certain time in the decay process, exactly half of the original mass (or atoms) of the radioactive substance will remain unchanged. The time (seconds, minutes, hours, or years) it takes the substance to decay to half its original mass is the half-life of the substance.

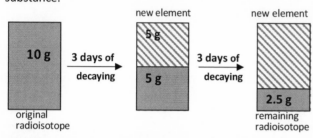

This diagram shows a 10-gram sample of a radioisotope decaying to 5 grams after 3 days, and to 2.5 grams in another 3 days.

The half-life of the radioisotope is 3 days.
The number of half-life periods (how many times it halved) is 2.
The total length of time is 6 days.

. Decaying of a radioisotope is at a constant rate, therefore, half-life of a radioisotope is constant.

. Temperature, pressure, and amount do not change the half-life of a radioisotope.

. Each radioisotope has its own half-life.

Reference Table N list selected radioisotopes, their decay modes, and their half-lives.

Table N
Selected Radioisotopes

Nuclide	Half-Life	Decay Mode	Nuclide Name
^{198}Au	2.695 d	β^-	gold-198
^{14}C	5715 y	β^-	carbon-14
^{37}Ca	182 ms	β^+	calcium-37
^{60}Co	5.271 y	β^-	cobalt-60
^{137}Cs	30.2 y	β^-	cesium-137
^{53}Fe	8.51 min	β^+	iron-53
^{220}Fr	27.4 s	α	francium-220
^{3}H	12.31 y	β^-	hydrogen-3
^{131}I	8.021 d	β^-	iodine-131
^{37}K	1.23 s	β^+	potassium-37
^{42}K	12.36 h	β^-	potassium-42
^{85}Kr	10.73 y	β^-	krypton-85
^{16}N	7.13 s	β^-	nitrogen-16
^{19}Ne	17.22 s	β^+	neon-19
^{32}P	14.28 d	β^-	phosphorus-32
^{239}Pu	2.410×10^4 y	α	plutonium-239
^{226}Ra	1599 y	α	radium-226
^{222}Rn	3.823 d	α	radon-222
^{90}Sr	29.1 y	β^-	strontium-90
^{99}Tc	2.13×10^5 y	β^-	technetium-99
^{232}Th	1.40×10^{10} y	α	thorium-232
^{233}U	1.592×10^5 y	α	uranium-233
^{235}U	7.04×10^8 y	α	uranium-235
^{238}U	4.47×10^9 y	α	uranium-238

Source: CRC Handbook of Chemistry and Physics, 91st ed., 2010–2011, CRC Press

Practice 45
As a sample of Iodine-131 decays, its half-life
1) increases   2) decreases   3) remains the same

Practice 46
Which of the following radioisotope has the longest half-life?
1) Fr-220   2) K -37   3) N-16   4) Ne-19

Practice 47
Which radioisotope has a half-life that is less than 1 minute?
1) K – 37   2) K – 42   3) P-32   4) Fe-53

Practice 48
Compared to K-37, the isotope of K-42 has a
1) Shorter half-life and the same decay mode
2) Longer half-life and the same decay mode
3) Shorter half-life and a different decay mode
4) Longer half-life and a different decay mode

Practice 49
Compared to U – 238, U – 235 has a
1) Shorter half-life and the same decay mode
2) Shorter half-life and a different decay mode
3) longer half-life and the same decay mode
4) longer half-life and a different decay mode

Topic 12: Nuclear Chemistry

There are many different types of half-life related questions. How well and easily you can solve a half-life problem depend on your understanding of the concept. Multiple choice questions can be answered with little or no setup if you have a clear understanding of half-life concept. Short answer problems can be setup and solve in a few simple steps with clear understanding of the concept. In the next few sets, you will learn how solve different types of half-life related problems.

21. Number of Half-life Period Calculations

The **number of half-life periods** of a decay is the number of times a radioactive substance decays in half to go from one mass to another. In all half-life problems the number of half-life periods must be known in order to solve the problem. Determining the number of half-life periods depends on the information that is given in the question.

If the original mass (OM) and remaining mass (RM) are given

Number of half-life periods = The number of times OM is halved (or is divided by 2) to get to RM

or

= The number of times RM is doubled (or is multiplied by 2) to get to OM.

Example 1
How many half-life periods does it take for a 12-gram sample of radioactive substance to decay to just 0.75 grams ?

Use arrow method to determine (each arrow cuts the grams in half).

12 g ---------- > 6 g --------- > 3g -------- > 1.5 --------> **0.75 g**

Start with   Stop with
  OM   *4 arrows = **4 Half-life periods***   RM

Use another method to determine
12 g ÷ 2 = 6 ÷ 2 = 3 ÷ 2 = 1.5 ÷ = **0.75 g**

       *Four division signs = **Four half-life periods***

If the length of time and half-life of a radioisotope are known

Number of half-life periods =	$\dfrac{\text{Length of time}}{\text{Half-life}}$

Example 2
The half-life of a radioisotope is 15 minutes. In 75 minutes, how many half-life periods would the substance had gone through?

Number of half-life periods = $\dfrac{75 \text{ min.}}{15 \text{ min.}}$ = **5**

                               setup   *calculated result*

Practice 50
How many half-life periods would it take for a sample of Co-60 to decay from 200 mg to 50 mg?
1) 1   3) 3
2) 2   4) 4

Practice 51
A 30 gram sample of uranium-235 will decay to approximately 1.88 grams in how many half-life periods?
1) 16   3) 15
2) 4   4) 3

Practice 52
A radioisotope has a half-life of 25 years. How many half-life period will it take for 1000-g to decay to 31.25 grams?
1) 5   3) 10
2) 40   4) 6

Practice 53
A sample of francium-220 was allowed to decay for 165 seconds. How many half-life periods did the sample decayed?
1) 1.33   3) 5
2) 2   4) 6

Practice 54
A 20-gram sample of ^{99}Tc decaying for 6.4×10^5 years will undergo how many life-periods?
1) 1   3) 3
2) 2   4) 4

Practice 55
A 10-gram sample of Cs-137 was accidently left in a laboratory that was closed in 1940. It was found in 2000 when the laboratory was set to be demolished. How many half-life period of decaying did this sample undergo?
1) 6   3) 3
2) 2   4) 5

Topic 12: Nuclear Chemistry

22. Length of Time and Half-life Calculations

Length of time of a decaying process is the time it takes for a radioisotope to decay from one mass to another. **Half-life** is the time it takes for just half the amount of the substance to decay to a new substance. Either of the two can be determined if certain information is known about the decaying process of a radioisotope.

Length of time from number of half-life period and half-life

Length of Time = Number of half-life periods x half-life

Example 1
Approximately how long will it take for a radioactive ^{42}K to undergo 6 half-life periods?

Use equation above to setup and solve
Note: half-life of ^{42}K is on Table N

Length of Time = 6 x 12.4 hours = **74.4 hours**
                        setup   *calculated result*

Half-life from number of half-life periods and length of time

Half-life = $\dfrac{\text{Length of time}}{\text{Number of half-life periods}}$

Example 2
What is the half-life of an unknown radioisotope if takes 12 years for the radioisotope to undergo 5 half-life periods?

Half-life = $\dfrac{12 \text{ years}}{5}$ = **2.4 years**
                  setup   *calculated result*

Length of Time and Half-life from masses

Step 1: Determine number of half-life periods from masses (see previous page)

Step 2: Use number of half-life periods in equations above

Example 3
How long will it take for potassium–42 to decay from 100 g to 12.5 g?

Step 1: 100 g ---> 50 g ---> 25 g -----> 12.5 g
                  3 arrows = 3 half-life periods

Step 2: Length of time = 3 x 12.4 hrs = **37.2 hrs** *(answer)*

Practice 56
^{131}I will go through 4 half-life periods in approximately how many days?
1) 32 days   3) 2 days
2) 24 days   4) 12 days

Practice 57
The half life of a radioisotope X is 30 days. In how many days will X undergo 3 half –life periods?
1) 3 days   3) 33 days
2) 10 days   4) 90 days

Practice 58
How many days are required for a 200-gram sample of Radon-222 to decay to 50.0-gram?
1) 1.91   3) 7.64
2) 3.82   4) 11.5

Practice 59
The half-life of a radioisotope is 30 seconds. Which set up is correct for calculating the total length of time it takes for a 50 g sample of this isotope to decay to 3.125 g?
1) 30 x 3.125   3) 30 x 4
2) 30 ÷ 3.125   4) 30 ÷ 4

Practice 60
A radioisotope undergoes 2 half-life periods in 180 ms. What is the half life of this radioisotope?
1) 90 ms   3) 180 ms
2) 360 ms   4) 2 ms

Practice 61
An unknown substance decays undergoes 5 half-life periods in 1.5 x 10^3 years. What is the half-life of this substance?
1) 2.8 x 10^3 y   3) 3.00 x 10^2 y
2) 3.00 x 10^3 y   4) 2.34 x 10^1 y

Practice 62
In 6.20 h, a 100 gram sample of Ag-112 decays to 25.0 gram. What is the half-life of Ag-112?
1) 1.60 h   3) 6.20 h
2) 3.10 h   4) 12.4 h

Practice 63
A 1.00-g sample of ^{25}Na decays to 16.00 g in 237 seconds. Which setup is correct for calculating the half-life of ^{25}Na ?
1) 237 x 16   3) 237 x 4

2) $\dfrac{237}{16}$ 4) $\dfrac{237}{4}$

23. Original and Remaining Masses Calculations

Original mass of a radioisotope is the amount of the radioisotope that was present at the beginning of a decaying process.
Remaining mass is the amount that remained after a given length of time of decaying. Either of the two masses can be determined if certain information is known about the decaying process of a substance.

Original mass (OM) from number of half-life periods and remaining mass (RM)

Original mass = Double the remaining mass as many times as the number of half-life periods given

Example 1

After 6 half-life periods, 15 grams of an unknown radioisotope remains. What was the original mass of the unknown radioisotope?

(answer)

15g ----> 30 ----> 60 ----> 120 ----> 240 ----> 480 ----> **960 g**
start   stop
with RM given   after 6 doubling-arrows

Remaining mass (RM) from number of half-life periods and original mass (OM)

Remaining mass = halve the original mass as many times as the number of half-life periods given

Example 2

After 4 half-life periods, how many grams of a 12 mg sample of a radioisotope will remain unchanged?

12 mg ------ > 6 ------ > 3 --------- > 1.5 ------ > **0.75** mg *(answer)*
start   stop
with OM given   after 4 halving-arrows

Original and remaining masses from length of time and half-life

Step 1: Determine number of half-life periods = $\dfrac{\text{length of time}}{\text{half-life}}$

Step 2: Use number of half-life periods as shown in above two examples

Example 3

In approximately 4800 years, how many grams of a 100-gram sample of Radon – 226 will remain unchanged?

Step 1: Number of half-life periods = $\dfrac{4800 \text{ yrs}}{1600 \text{ yrs}}$ = 3
(see Table N)

Step 2: Halve 100 grams 3 times

100g -------> 50 g -------> 25 g -------> **12.5 g** *(answer)*

Practice 64
After 4 half-life periods, 1.5 mg of a radioactive isotope remained. What was the mass of the original sample of the isotope?
1) 6.0 mg   3) 3.0 mg
2) 0.375 mg   4) 24 mg

Practice 65
If 10.0 grams of P-32 remains after 3 half-life periods, what was the original mass of P-32?
1) 60.0 g   3) 20.0 g
2) 30.0 g   4) 3.33 g

Practice 66
What was the original mass of ^{198}Au if only 4 grams of the isotope remained after about 8 days?
1) 2 g   3) 8 g
2) 4 g   4) 32 g

Practice 67
A sample of ^{99}Tc decays to 0.5 grams in 1.49 x 10^6 years. What was the mass of the original sample?
1) 64 g   3) 32 g
2) 128 g   4) 8 g

Practice 68
What is the total mass of a 50-gram sample of a radioisotope remaining after 3 half-life periods?
1) 150 grams   3) 12.5 grams
2) 6.25 grams   4) 16.7 grams

Practice 69
What amount of a 48 g sample of K-37 will remain after 5 half-life periods?
1) 1.5 g   3) 5.1 g
2) 3.0 g   4) 6.0 g

Practice 70
Approximately how many grams of a 50 g sample of radium-226 will remain unchanged after 6400 years?
1) 25 g   3) 128 g
2) 6.25 g   4) 3.13 g

Practice 71
A radioisotope of element X has a half-life of 1.5 days. How many grams of a 5 gram sample of this isotope will remain unchanged after 3.0 days?
1) 1.25 grams   3) 2.5 grams
2) 7.5 grams   4) 4.5 grams

Topic 12: Nuclear Chemistry

24. Fraction Remaining Calculations

Fraction remaining expresses the remaining mass of a radioisotope in terms of ratio.

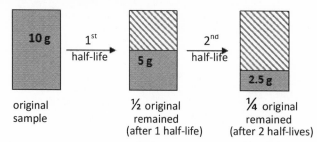

| original sample | ½ original remained (after 1 half-life) | ¼ original remained (after 2 half-lives) |

Fraction remaining of a radioisotope can be calculated when certain information is known of a decaying process.

Fraction remaining from number of half-life periods (n)

$$\text{Fraction remaining} = \frac{1}{2^n} \quad n = \text{number of half-life}$$

Example 1
What fraction of Au-198 will remain unchanged after 4 half-life periods?

1) $^1/_8$ 2) $^1/_2$ 3) $^1/_{16}$ 4) $^1/_4$

$$\text{Fraction remaining} = \frac{1}{2^n} = \frac{1}{2^4} = \frac{1}{2 \times 2 \times 2 \times 2} = \frac{1}{16}$$

choice 3

Fraction remaining from length of time (t) and half-life (T)

$$\text{Fraction remaining} = \frac{1}{(2)^{t/T}}$$

t = length of time
T = half-life
$t/T = n = $ # of half-life periods

Example 2
What fraction of ^{19}Ne will remain unchanged after 86 seconds?

1) $^1/_{32}$ 2) $^1/_5$ 3) $^1/_2$ 4) $^1/_{16}$

$$\text{Fraction remaining} = \frac{1}{(2)^{86/17.2}} = \frac{1}{2^5} = \frac{1}{2 \times 2 \times 2 \times 2 \times 2}$$

$$\text{Fraction remaining} = \frac{1}{32} \quad \textit{choice 1}$$

Practice 72
What fraction of a radioactive substance will remain after 3 half-life periods?
1) $^1/_8$ 3) $^1/_3$
2) $^1/_4$ 4) $^1/_2$

Practice 73
What fraction of the radioactive waste Strontium-90 will remain unchanged after 5 half-life periods of decaying?
1) $^1/_{32}$ 3) $^1/_{16}$
2) $^1/_8$ 4) $^1/_5$

Practice 74
A radioactive element has a half-life of 2 days. Which fraction represents the amount of an original sample of this element remaining after 6 days?
1) $^1/_6$ 3) $^1/_2$
2) $^1/_3$ 4) $^1/_8$

Practice 75
If the half-life of a radioactive element is 2.5 years, what fraction of this element will remain unchanged after 15 years?
1) $^1/_{32}$ 3) $^1/_2$
2) $^1/_{16}$ 4) $^1/_{64}$

Practice 76
After 1.42×10^9 years, what fraction of a 6 gram sample of U-235 will remain unchanged?
1) $^1/_4$ 3) $^1/_2$
2) $^1/_6$ 4) $^1/_8$

Practice 77
What is the total number of half-life periods it will take for any sample of Co-60 to decay to $^1/_{16}$th of its original mass?
1) 1   3) 3
2) 2   4) 4

Practice 78
A sample of a radioisotope Cr-51 decays to $^1/_8$th in 84 days, what is the half-life of Cr-51?
1) 14 days   3) 56 days
2) 28 days   4) 84 days

Practice 79
A radioisotope has a half-life of 16 years. In how many years would a given sample of this isotope decays leaving only $^1/_{32}$th of this isotope remaining?
1) 8 years   3) 80 years
2) 2 years   4) 512 years

Topic 12: Nuclear Chemistry

25. Identifying radioisotopes

When certain information about a decaying process is known, you can identify which radioisotope on Table N the information is referring.

keep the following in mind when comparing the isotopes given as choices

Decays to greatest extent	**Decays to least extent**
- Shortest half-life	- Longest half-life

Smallest remaining %	**Greatest remaining %**
- Shortest half-life	- Longest half-life
- Smallest mass	- Greatest mass

Practice 80
A 10-gram sample of which radioisotope will decay to the greatest extent in 50 years?
1) Kr-85   3) Cs-137
2) H-3   4) Sr-90

Practice 81
Which radioisotope sample will have the smallest amount remaining after 10 years?
1) 2.0 g of Au-198   3) 4.0 g of P-32
2) 2.0 g of K-42   4) 4.0 g of Co-60

Practice 82
According to Reference Table N, which radioisotope will retain only $\frac{1}{8}^{th}$ its original mass after approximately 43 days?
1) Phosphorus-32   3) Radon-222
2) Gold-198   4) Iron-53

26. Decay data, tables and graphs

The decaying process of a radioisotope can be shown with a graph, diagram or data table.

The graph and data below are both showing the mass of a radioisotope remaining as it decays over time.

Time (days)	Mass of radioisotope sample remaining (g)
0	160
4	120
8	80 (half original mass)
12	60
16	40
20	30
24	20
28	15
32	10

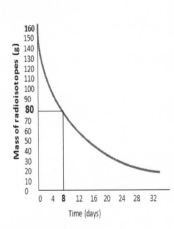

The half-life of the radioisotope is 8 days.
This is the number of days half (80 g) of the original (160 g) of the radioisotope is unchanged.

The radioisotope is likely iodine-131 .
According to Reference Table N, the half-life of I-131 is 8.07 day.

The graph below represents the decay of a radioactive material X into a stable decay product?

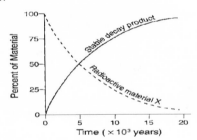

Practice 83
What is the half-life of radioactive material X?
1) 50 x 10^3 y   3) 20 x 10^3 y
2) 5 x 10^3 y   4) 10 x 10^3 y

Practice 84
Which graph best represents the relative percentages of the radioactive material X and its stable product after 15,000 years? (shaded area represents radioactive material while the non-shaded area represents stable products)

1)   3)

2)   4)

27. Radioactivity Applications and Wastes

Radioactivity applications and benefits

Some radioisotopes listed on Reference Table N have common usages in areas such as medicine, research, and geological (rock) and archeological (fossil) dating.

A **tracer** is a radioisotope that is used to follow path of a chemical reaction.

Radioisotope tracers in medical treatments and **diagnoses** must have short half-lives and be quickly eliminated from the body.

Radioisotopes for dating usually have very long half-lives.

The table below gives a list of radioisotopes and their common applications.

Radioisotope name	Radioisotope symbol	Common applications and benefits	Field of application
Iodine-131	^{131}I	Thyroid disorder; diagnosis and treatment	Medical
Technetium-99	^{99}Tc	Cancer tumor diagnosis	Medical
Cobalt-60	^{60}Co	Cancer treatment	Medical
Iron-56	^{56}Fe	Blood disorder treatment	Medical
Carbon-14 *(alone)*	^{14}C	Tracer for chemical reactions	Research
Carbon-14 *with* Carbon-12	^{14}C ^{12}C	Fossilized dating	Archeological dating
Uranium – 238 *with* Lead - 206	^{238}U ^{206}Pb	Rock dating	Geological dating

Radioactive waste and radiation problems
Radiations and wastes produced from nuclear reactors are very dangerous to life on earth.
Prolonged and high dose exposures to radiation can cause serious health issues, and sometimes death.
. *Radiation* from nuclear power plants must be well contained to protect humans and other living things.
. *Nuclear wastes* are equally dangerous because they are highly radioactive.
. *Nuclear wastes* have to be stored in safe areas to protect the public from being exposed to them.

Solid Wastes (Highly radioactive): Sr-90   Cs-137   **Gaseous Wastes:** Rn-222   Kr-85   N-16

Practice 85
A radioisotope is called a tracer when it is used to
1) Determine the age of animal skeletal remains
2) Determine the course of a chemical reaction
3) Kill cancerous tissue
4) Kill bacteria in food

Practice 86
Which procedure is based on the half-life of a radioisotope?
1) Accelerating to increase kinetic energy
2) Counting to determine a level of radioactivity
3) Dating to determine age
4) Radiating to kill cancer cells

Practice 87
Iodine-131 is used in diagnosing thyroid disorders because it is absorbed by the thyroid gland and
1) Has a very short half-life
2) Has a very long half-life
3) Emits alpha particle
4) Emits gamma radiation

Practice 88
A radioisotope that is sometimes used in pinpointing brain tumor is
1) Technetium – 99   3) Lead – 206
2) Uranium – 238   4) Carbon – 12

Topic 12: Nuclear Chemistry

Concept Terms

Key vocabulary terms and concepts from Topic 12 are listed below. You should know definition and facts related to each term and concept.

1. Transmutation
2. Natural transmutation
3. Artificial transmutation
4. Alpha particle
5. Beta particle
6. Gamma ray
7. Positron
8. Neutron
9. Separation of particles
10. Penetrating power
11. Accelerator

12. Alpha emitter
13. Beta emitter
14. Positron emitter
15. Alpha decay
16. Beta decay
17. Positron emission
18. Decay series
19. Fission
20. Fusion
21. Tracer

21. Half-life
22. Number of half-life period
23. Radioisotope

Concept Tasks

Concept tasks from Topic 12 are listed below. You should know how to solve problems and answer questions related to each concept task.

1. Recognizing a nuclear change equation
2. Determining the decay mode of a radioisotope
3. Recognizing natural transmutation equations
4. Recognizing alpha decay equations
5. Recognizing beta decay equations
6. Recognizing positron emission equations
7. Recognizing artificial transmutation equations
8. Recognizing fission equations.
9. Recognizing fusion equations.
10. Determining the missing particle in an incomplete nuclear equation
11. Calculating number of half-life periods from original and remaining mass
12. Calculating number of half-life periods from length of time and half-life
13. Calculating length of time of decaying from half-life and half-life periods
14. Calculating length of time of decaying from half-life and original and remaining masses
15. Calculating half-life of a radioisotope from length of time and half-life periods
16. Calculating half-life of a radioisotope from length of time , original and remaining masses
17. Calculate original mass from number of half-life periods and remaining mass
18. Calculate original mass from length of time, half-life, and remaining mass
19. Calculate remaining mass from number of half-life periods and original mass
20. Calculate remaining mass from length of time, half-life, and original mass
21. Calculating fraction remaining from number of half-life period
22. Calculating fraction remaining from length of time and half-life
23. Determining name or symbol of radioisotope from half-life information
24. Determining a radioisotope that decays to the greatest or least extent
25. Determining a radioisotope that has the greatest or the smallest percentage remaining
26. Interpreting data and graph of a decay

Topic 13: Lab safety, equipment and measurements

1. Lab Safety

During lab experiments appropriate safety procedures must be followed and observed.

Some important lab safety guidelines are listed below.

Wear protective goggles at all time.

No eating or drinking in lab, or out of lab equipment.

No running in the lab.

Tie back long hair.

Roll up long sleeves.

Know locations of lab safety equipment and how to use them properly.

When lighting a Bunsen burner, strike a match first, and then turn on the gas.

When mixing acid with water, pour acid slowly into water while stirring.

Always pay attention and follow the instructions of your lab instructor.

2. Lab Equipment

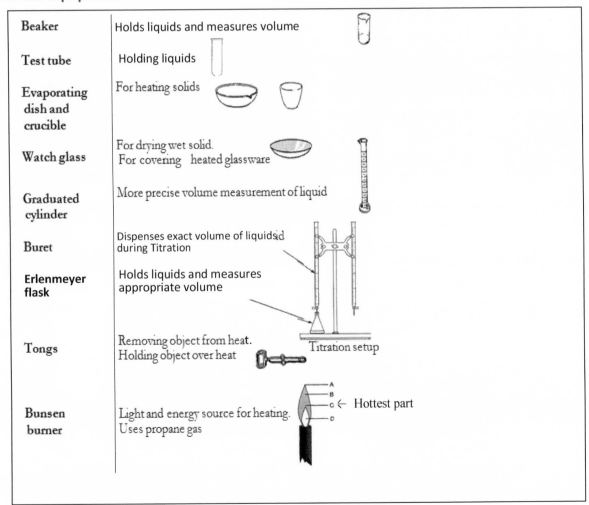

Beaker	Holds liquids and measures volume
Test tube	Holding liquids
Evaporating dish and crucible	For heating solids
Watch glass	For drying wet solid. For covering heated glassware
Graduated cylinder	More precise volume measurement of liquid
Buret	Dispenses exact volume of liquids d during Titration
Erlenmeyer flask	Holds liquids and measures appropriate volume
Tongs	Removing object from heat. Holding object over heat
Bunsen burner	Light and energy source for heating. Uses propane gas

Titration setup

A
B
c ← Hottest part
D

Topic 13: Lab and measurements

3. Lab Safety and Procedure: Practice problems

Practice 1
Which of the following statements contained in a student's laboratory report is a conclusion?
1) A gas is evolved   3) The gas is hydrogen
2) The gas is insoluble in water   4) The gas burns in air

Practice 2
Which of the following statements in a student's laboratory report is an observation?
1) Metal A will also react with an acid   3) Metal A is an alkali metal
2) Metal A has luster   4) Metal A will be good for electrical wiring

Practice 3
During a laboratory activity, a student combined two solutions. In the laboratory report, the student wrote " A yellow color appeared." The statement represents the student's recorded
1) Conclusion   3) Hypothesis
2) Observation   4) Inference

Practice 4
A student investigated the physical and chemical properties of a sample of an unknown gas and then identified the gas. Which statement represents a conclusion rather than an experimental observation?
1) The gas is colorless
2) The gas is carbon dioxide
3) When the gas is bubbled into limewater, the liquid becomes cloudy
4) When placed in the gas, a flaming splint stops burning

Practice 5
Flame tests are used to identify
1) Polar molecules   3) Nonmetal ions
2) Nonpolar molecules   4) Metal ions

Practice 6
What is the safest method for diluting concentrated sulfuric acid with water?
1) Add the acid to the water quickly   3) Add the acid to the water slowly while stirring
2) Add the water to the acid quickly   4) Add the water to the acid slowly while stirring

Practice 7
A student wishes to prepare approximately 100 mL of an aqueous solution of 6 M HCl using 12 M HCl. Which procedure is correct?
1) Adding 50 mL of 12 M HCl to 50 mL of water while stirring the mixture steadily
2) Adding 50 mL of 12 M HCl to 50 mL of water, and then stir the mixture steadily
3) Adding 50 mL of water to 50 mL of 12 M HCl while stirring the mixture steadily
4) Adding 50 mL of water to 50 mL of 12 M HCl , and then stir the mixture steadily

Practice 8
Which activity is considered a proper laboratory technique

1) Heating the contents of an open test tube held vertically over a flame

2) Heating the content of a test tube that has been closed with a stopper

3) Adding water to a concentrated acids

4) Striking a match first before turning on the gas valve to light a Bunsen burner

4. Percent Error

During a lab activity, collected data and measured results are often different from what are expected. Errors in lab results can be attributed to factors such as faulty equipment and human mistakes.

Percent error is the relative difference between the measured value and the accepted value of a lab result .

$$\text{Percent error} = \frac{\text{measured value} - \text{accepted value}}{\text{accepted value}} \times 100$$

The lower the percent error, the more accurate a lab result.

Reference Table T equation

Practice 9
A student determined the percentage of water of hydration in $BaCl_2 \cdot 2H_2O$ by using the data in the table below.

Quantity Measured	Value Obtained
Mass of $BaCl_2 \cdot 2H_2O$	3.80 grams
Mass of $BaCl_2$	3.20 grams
% of water calculated	15.79 %

The accepted percent of water of hydration is 14.75 %. What is the student's percent error?
1) 1.04 %   2) 6.00 %   3) 6.59 %   4) 7.05 %

Practice 10
A student determined in the laboratory that the percent by mass of water in $CuSO_4 \cdot 5H_2O$ is 40.0%. If the accepted value is 36%, what is the percent error?
1) 0.11 %   2) 1.1 %   3) 11 %   4) 4.0 %

Practice 11
A student found the boiling point of a liquid to be $80.4^{\circ}C$. If the liquid's actual boiling point is $80.6^{\circ}C$, the experimental percent error is equal to

1) $\dfrac{80.6 - 80.4}{80.6} \times 100$

2) $\dfrac{80.6 - 80.4}{80.4} \times 100$

3) $\dfrac{80.5 - 80.4}{80.5} \times 100$

4) $\dfrac{80.5 - 80.4}{80.4} \times 100$

5. Lab Measurements

Practice 12

The diagram below represents a Celsius thermometer recording a certain temperature.

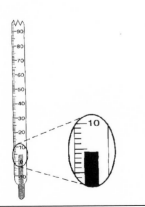

What is the correct reading of the thermometer?

1) $5^{\circ}C$

2) $0.3^{\circ}C$

3) $4.3^{\circ}C$

4) $4^{\circ}C$

Practice 13
The diagram below represents a section of a buret containing acid used in acid-base titration

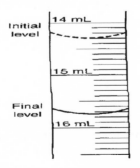

What is the total volume of acid that was used?
1) 1.10 mL   2) 1.30 mL   3) 1.40 mL   4) 1.45 mL

6. Significant Figures

Significant figures in a number include all digits that are known for certain, plus one estimated digit.

Rules for determining number of significant figures

Significant figures in a number can be determined using Atlantic – Pacific rule.

If a decimal is <u>Absent</u> in a number (whole number)
. Start counting with the first nonzero from <u>A</u>tlantic (right) side of the number

. Count toward the left

. Stop counting with the last non zero digit..

How many you counted is the number of significant figure in that number.

If a decimal is <u>Present</u> in a number (decimal fraction)
. Start counting with the first nonzero from <u>Pacific</u> (left) side of the number

. Count toward right and count all numbers (including zeros) once you have started counting
How many you counted is the number of significant figure in that number.

NOTE:
All zeros between two non-zero are always counted as being significant.

All zeros to start a number are never counted as being significant.

Examples:

405	has **3** significant figures
4050	has **3** significant figures
200	has **1** significant figure
02	has **1** significant figure
0.0036	has **2** significant figures
0.0936	has **3** significant figures
0.09360	has **4** significant figures
200.	has 3 significant figures
1.04	has **3** significant figures
01.0	has **2** significant figures

Practice 14
Which mass measurement contains four significant figures?
1) 0.086 g   2) 0.431 g   3) 1003 g   4) 3870 g

Practice 15
Which measurement contains three significant figures?
1) 0.03 g   2) 0.030 g   3) 0.035 g   4) 0.0351 g

Practice 16
Which volume measurement is expressed in two significant figures?
1) 20 mL   2) 202 mL   3) 220 mL   4) 0.2 mL

Practice 17
Which measurement has the greatest number of significant figures?
1) 44000 g   2) 404 g   3) 40.44 g   4) 0.40004 g

Practice 18
Which pressure measurement has the least number of significant figures?
1) 84 kPa   2) 34.1 kPa   3) 70.88 kPa   4) 90 kPa

7. Significant Figures in Calculations

Rules for leaving (or limited) a calculated result to the right number of significant figures vary depending on the type of mathematical operation that is involved in the calculation. These rules are described below.

When multiplying or dividing

Limit or round the calculated result so it has the same number of significant figures as the factor with the *least number of significant figures.*

Example 1

How much heat is absorbed by a 17 gram sample of ice to melt? *Leave answer in the correct number of significant figures.*

Heat = mass x H_f

Heat = 17 x 334

Heat = 5678 J

Heat = **5700 J**

17	factor with least number of sig fig.: 2
5678	(calculator result) has 4 sig fig. It must be rounded to 2 sig. fig
5700	(answer) is rounded to 2 sig fig.

Example 2

What is the density of an unknown substance if a 42.6 cm^3 sample has a mass of 22.43 g?

Density = $\dfrac{mass}{volume}$

Density = $\dfrac{22.43\ g}{42.6\ cm^3}$ = **0.527 $\dfrac{g}{cm^3}$**

42.6	factor with the least number of sig fig: 3
0.527	(answer) also has 3 significant figures

When adding or subtracting

Limit or round the calculated result so it has the same number of decimal places as the factor with the *least number of decimal places (numbers after the decimal point)*

Example 3

What is the sum of 0.31 , 1.310 and 1.3205 to the correct number of significant figures?

0.31 + 1.310 + 1.3205 = 2.9405 = **2.94**

0.31	Factor with the least number of decimal places: 2
2.9405	(calculator result) has 4 decimal places. It must be rounded and limited to 2 decimal places.
2.94	(answer) has 2 decimal places.

Practice 19

The mass of a solid is 3.60 g and its volume is 1.8 cm^3. What is the density of the solid, expressed to the correct number of significant figures?

1) 12 g/cm^3 3) 0.5 g/cm^3

2) 2.0 g/cm^3 4) 0.50 g/cm^3

Practice 20

Which quantity expresses the sum of 22.1 g + 375.66 g + 5400.132 g to the correct number of significant figures?

1) 5800 g   3) 5797.9 g

2) 5798 g   4) 5797.892 g

Practice 21

The volume of a gas sample is 22 L at STP. The density of the gas is 1.35 g/L. What is the mass of the gas sample, expressed to the correct number of significant figures?

1) 30. g   3) 16.7 g

2) 30.0 g   4) 2.56 g

Practice 22

A student calculates the density of an unknown solid. The mass is 10.04 grams, and the volume is 8.21 cubic centimeters. How many significant figures should appear in the final answer?

1) 1   3) 3

2) 2   4) 4

Practice 23

The density of a solid is 1.9 g/mL and its volume is 40.2 mL. A student calculating the mass of the solid should have how many significant figures in the final answer?

1) 1   3) 3

2) 2   4) 4

14 Days of Questions for
Regents and Final Exams Practice

The following section contains day-by-day practice question sets for preparing for any end-of-the-year chemistry exam.

14 *Days* of Questions for Regents and Final Exams Practice

Day 1: Matter and Energy - Multiple Choices

1. Which of these terms refers to matter that could be heterogeneous?
   1) Element   2) Mixture   3) Compound   4) Solution

2. One similarity between all mixtures and compounds is that both
   1) Are heterogeneous   3) Combine in definite ratios
   2) Are homogeneous   4) Consist of two or more substances

3. Which correctly describes particles of a substance in the gas phase?
   1) Particles are arranged in a regular geometric pattern and are far apart
   2) Particles are in a fixed rigid position and are close together
   3) Particles move freely in a straight path
   4) Particles move freely and are close together.

4. When a substance evaporates, it is changing from
   1) Liquid to gas   2) Gas to liquid   3) Solid to gas   4) Gas to solid

5. Energy that is stored in chemical substances is called
   1) Potential energy   2) Activation energy   3) Kinetic energy   4) Ionization energy

6. The specific heat capacity of water is 4.18 J/ g •°C. Adding 4.18 Joules of heat to a 1-gram sample of water will cause the water to
   1) Change from solid to liquid   3) Change its temperature 1 degree Celsius
   2) Change from liquid to solid   4) Change its temperature 4.18 degree Celsius

7. Real gases differ from ideal gases because the molecules of real gases have
   1) Some volume and no attraction for each other
   2) Some attraction and some attraction for each other
   3) No volume and no attraction for each other
   4) No volume and some attraction for each other

8. Under which two conditions do real gases behave most like an ideal gas?
   1) High pressure and low temperature   3) High pressure and high temperature
   2) Low pressure and high temperature   4) Low pressure and low temperature

9. At constant pressure, the volume of a confined gas varies
   1) Directly with the Kelvin temperature   3) Directly with the mass of the gas
   2) Indirectly with the Kelvin temperature   4) Indirectly with the mass of the gas

10. Under which conditions would a volume of a given sample of a gas decrease?
    1) Decrease pressure and increase temperature   3) Increase pressure and decrease temperature
    2) Decrease pressure and decrease temperature   4) Increase pressure and increase temperature

11. Which statement describes a chemical property of iron?
    1) Iron can be flattened into sheets.
    2) Iron conducts electricity and heat.
    3) Iron combines with oxygen to form rust.
    4) Iron can be drawn into a wire.

12. Which sample at STP has the same number of molecules as 5 liters of $NO_2(g)$ at STP?
    1) 5 grams of $H_2(g)$ 3) 5 moles of $O^2(g)$
    2) 5 liters of $CH_4(g)$ 4) 5×10^{23} molecules of $CO_2(g)$

Day 1: Matter and Energy - Multiple Choices

13. Which substance can be decomposed by a chemical change?
   1) Ammonia
   2) Potassium
   3) Aluminum
   4) Helium

14. The graph below represents the relationship between temperature and time as heat is added at a constant rate to a substance. starting when the substance is a solid below its melting point

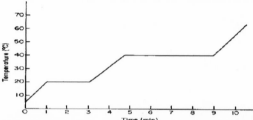

During which time period (in minutes) does the substance's average kinetic energy remain the same?
   1) $0-1$
   2) $1-3$
   3) 3 - 5
   4) $9-10$

15. Molecules of which substance have the lowest average kinetic energy?
   1) NO at $20^{o}C$
   2) NO_2 at $-30^{o}C$
   3) NO_2 at 35 K
   4) N_2O_3 at 110 K

16. At STP, the difference between the boiling point and the freezing point of water in the Kelvin scale is
   1) 373
   2) 273
   3) 180
   4) 100

17. How much heat is needed to change a 5.0 gram sample of water from $65^{o}C$ to $75^{o}C$?
   1) 210 J
   2) 14 J
   3) 21 J
   4) 43 J

18. A real gas will behave most like an ideal gas under which conditions of temperature and pressure?
   1) $0^{o}C$ and 1 atm
   2) $0^{o}C$ and 2 atm
   3) $273^{o}C$ and 1 atm
   4) $273^{o}C$ and 2 atm

19. A 2.0 L sample of $O_2(g)$ at STP had its volume changed to 1.5 L. If the temperature of the gas was held constant, what is the new pressure of the gas in kilopascals?
   1) 3.0 kPa
   2) 152 kPa
   3) 101.3 kPa
   4) 135 kPa

20. A gas occupies a volume of 6 L at 3 atm and $70^{o}C$. Which setup is correct for calculating the new volume of the gas if the temperature is changed to $150^{o}C$ and the pressure is dropped to 1.0 atm?

   1) $6 \times \dfrac{3 \times 150}{1 \times 70}$

   2) $6 \times \dfrac{3 \times 80}{1 \times 150}$

   3) $6 \times \dfrac{3 \times 423}{1 \times 343}$

   4) $6 \times \dfrac{3 \times 343}{1 \times 423}$

21. Given the balanced particle-diagram equation:

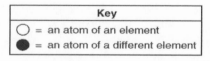

Key	
○ = an atom of an element	
● = an atom of a different element	

Which statement describes the type of change and the chemical properties of the product and reactants?

1) The equation represents a physical change, with the product and reactants having different chemical properties.
2) The equation represents a physical change, with the product and reactants having identical chemical properties.
3) The equation represents a chemical change, with the product and reactants having different chemical properties.
4) The equation represents a chemical change, with the product and reactants having identical chemical properties.

14 Days of Questions for Regents and Final Exams Practice

Day 1: Matter and Energy - Constructed Response

Base your answers to questions 22 to 25 on the diagram of a molecule of nitrogen shown below.

 represents one molecule of nitrogen.

Write your answers here

22. Draw a particle model that shows at least six molecules of nitrogen gas.

22.

23. Draw a particle model that shows at least six molecules of liquid nitrogen.

23.

24. Describe, in terms of particle arrangement, the difference between nitrogen gas and liquid nitrogen.

24.

25. Good models should reflect the true nature of the concept being represented. What is the limitation of two-dimensional models?

25.

Base your answer to questions 26 through 28 on the information and diagrams below.

Cylinder A contains 22.0 grams of $CO_2(g)$ and Cylinder B contains $N_2(g)$. The volumes, pressures, and temperatures of the two gases are indicated under each cylinder.

A

CO_2

V = 12.3 L
P = 1.0 atm
T = 300. K

B

N_2

V = 12.3 L
P = 1.0 atm
T = 300. K

Show work and answers here

26. How does the number of molecules of $CO_2(g)$ in cylinder A compare to the number of molecules of $N_2(g)$ in container B? Your answer must include both $CO_2(g)$ and $N_2(g)$.

26.

27. The temperature of $CO_2(g)$ is increased to 450. K and the volume of cylinder A remains constant. Show a correct numerical setup for calculating the new pressure of $CO_2(g)$ in cylinder A.

27.

28. Calculate the new pressure of $CO_2(g)$ in cylinder A based on your setup.

28.

Day 1: Matter and Energy - Constructed Response

Base your answers to questions 29 through 33 on the information below.

A substance is a solid at 15°C . A student heated a sample of the substance and recorded the temperature at one-minute intervals in the data table below.

Time (min)	0	1	2	3	4	5	6	7	8	9	10	11	12
Temperature (°C)	15	32	46	53	53	53	53	53	53	53	53	60	65

Heating Curve

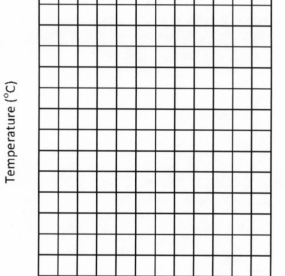

Temperature (°C)

0 1 2 3 4 5 6 7 8 9 10 11 12

Time (min)

29. On the grid , mark an appropriate scale on the axis labeled " Temperature (°C) ." An appropriate scale is one that allows a trend to be seen.

30 . Plot the data from the data table. Circle and connect the points

Write your answers on this side.

31. Based on the data table, what is the melting point of the substance?   31.

32. What is the evidence that the average kinetic energy of the particles of the substance is increasing during the first three minutes?   32.

33. The heat of fusion for this substance is 122 joules per gram. How many joules of heat are needed to melt 7.50 grams of this substance at its melting point?   33.

14 Days of Questions for Regents and Final Exams Practice

Day 2: The Periodic Table - Multiple Choices

1. Which determines the order of placement of the elements on the modern Periodic Table?
   1) Atomic mass
   2) Atomic number
   3) The number of neutrons, only
   4) The number of neutrons and protons

2. The elements located in the lower left corner of the Periodic Table are classified as
   1) Metals
   2) Nonmetals
   3) Metalloids
   4) Noble gases

3. The strength of an atom's attraction for the electrons in a chemical bond is measured by
   1) density
   2) ionization energy
   3) heat of reaction
   4) electronegativity

4. What is a property of most metals?
   1) They tend to gain electrons easily when bonding.
   2) They tend to lose electrons easily when bonding.
   3) They are poor conductors of heat.
   4) They are poor conductors of electricity.

5. A metal, M, forms an oxide compound with the general formula M_2O. In which group on the Periodic Table could metal M be found?
   1) Group 1
   2) Group 2
   3) Group 16
   4) Group 17

6. Which halogen is correctly paired with its phase at STP?
   1) Br is a liquid
   2) F is a solid
   3) I is a gas
   4) Cl is a liquid

7. As the elements in Group 1 of the Periodic Table are considered in order of increasing atomic number, the atomic radius of each successive element increases. This is primarily due to an increase in the number of
   1) Neutrons in the nucleus
   2) Unpaired electrons
   3) Valence electrons
   4) Electron shells

8. When elements within Period 3 are considered in order of decreasing atomic number, ionization energy of each successive element generally
   1) Increases due to an increase in atomic size
   2) Increases due to a decrease in atomic size
   3) Decreases due to an increase in atomic size
   4) Decreases due to a decrease in atomic size

9. Which set of characteristics is true of elements in Group 2 of the Periodic Table?
   1) They all have two energy levels and have different chemical characteristics
   2) They all have two energy levels and share similar chemical characteristics
   3) They all have two valence electrons and share similar chemical properties
   4) They all have two valence electrons and have different chemical properties

10. At STP, solid carbon can exist as graphite or as diamond. These two forms of carbon have
    1) the same properties and the same crystal structures
    2) the same properties and different crystal structures
    3) different properties and the same crystal structures
    4) different properties and different crystal structures

11. Which grouping of circles, when considered in order from the top to the bottom, best represents the relative size of the atoms of Li, Na, K, and Rb, respectively?

1)　　　　　　2)　　　　　　3)　　　　　　4)

Day 2: The Periodic Table - Multiple Choices

12. Elements strontium and beryllium both form a bond with fluorine with similar chemical formulas. The similarity in their formulas is due to
    1) Strontium and beryllium having the same number of kernel electrons
    2) Strontium and beryllium having the same number of valence electrons
    3) Strontium and beryllium having the same number of protons
    4) Strontium and beryllium having the same molecular structure

13. The element Antimony is a
    1) Metal   2) Nonmetal   3) Metalloid   4) Halogen

14. Which of these elements in Period 2 is likely to form a negative ion?
    1) Oxygen   2) Boron   3) Ne   4) Li

15. Which of these characteristics best describes the element sulfur at STP?
    1) It is brittle   2) It is malleable   3) It has luster   4) It is ductile

16. Which of these elements has the highest thermal and electrical conductivity
    1) Iodine   2) Carbon   3) Phosphorus   4) Iron

17. Chlorine will bond with which metallic element to form a colorful compound?
    1) Aluminum   2) Sodium   3) Strontium   4)Manganese

18. According to the Periodic Table, which sequence correctly places the elements in order of increasing atomic size?
    1) Na ----- > Li ------ > H ----- > K   3) Te ----- > Sb ------- > Sn ------ > In
    2) Ba ----- > Sr ----- >Ca ----- > Mg   4) H ------ > He ------- > Li ------ > Be

19. Which of these elements has stronger metallic characteristics than aluminum?
    1) He   2) Mg   3) Ga   4) Si

20. Which element has a greater tendency to attract electrons than phosphorus?
    1) Silicon   2) Arsenic   3) Boron   4) Sulfur

21. Which element has the greatest density at STP?
    1) barium   2) magnesium   3) beryllium   4) radium

22. An element that is malleable and a good conductor of heat and electricity could have an atomic number of
    1) 16   2) 18   3) 29   4) 35

23. Sodium atoms, potassium atoms, and cesium atoms have the same
    1) Atomic radius   3) First ionization energy
    2) Total number of protons   4) Oxidation state

24. When the elements in Group 1 are considered in order from top to bottom, each successive element at standard pressure has
    1) a higher melting point and a higher boiling point
    2) a higher melting point and a lower boiling point
    3) a lower melting point and a higher boiling point
    4) a lower melting point and a lower boiling point

25. Elements Q, X, and Z are in the same group on the Periodic Table and are listed in order of increasing atomic number. The melting point of element Q is −219°C and the melting point of element Z is −7°C. Which temperature is closest to the melting point of element X?
    1) −7°C   2) −101°C   3) −219°C   4) −226°C

Day 2: The Periodic Table - Constructed Response

Base your answer to questions 26 through 29 on the information below.

A metal, M, was obtained from compound in a rock sample. Experiments have determined that the element is a member of Group 2 on the Periodic Table of the Elements.

Write answers here.

26. What is the phase of element M at STP?   26.

27. Explain, in terms of electrons, why element M is   27.
   a good conductor of electricity.

28. Explain why the radius of a positive ion of element   28.
   M is smaller than the radius of an atom of element M.

29. Using the element symbol M for the element, write   29.
   the chemical formula for the compound that forms
   when element M reacts with Iodine?

The table below shows the electronegativity of selected elements of the Periodic Table.

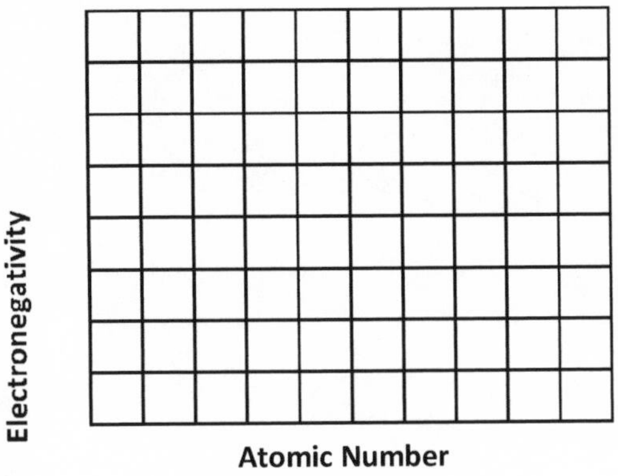

Element	Atomic Number	Electronegativity
Beryllium	4	1.6
Boron	5	2.0
Carbon	6	2.6
Fluorine	9	4.0
Lithium	3	1.0
Oxygen	8	3.4

Electronegativity

Atomic Number

30. On the grid, set up a scale for electronegativity on the y-axis and atomic number on the x-axis.
   Plot the data by drawing a best-fit line.

Write answers here.

31. Using the graph, predict the electronegativity of nitrogen.   31. _____

32. For these elements, state the trend in electronegativity in   32.
   terms of atomic number.

Day 3: The Atomic Structure - Multiple Choices

1. Which conclusion was a direct result of the gold foil experiment?
   1) An atom is composed of at least three types of subatomic particles.
   2) An atom is mostly empty space with a dense, positively charged nucleus.
   3) An electron has a positive charge and is located inside the nucleus.
   4) An electron has properties of both waves and particles.

2. In the wave-mechanical model of the atom, orbitals are regions of the most probable locations of
   1) protons   2) positrons   3) neutrons   4) electrons

3. What is the charge and mass of an electron?
   1) Charge of +1 and a mass of 1 amu
   2) Charge of -1 and a mass of 1 amu
   3) Charge of +1 and a mass of 1/1836 amu
   4) Charge of -1 and a mass of 1/1836 amu

4. Which phrase describes an atom?
   1) a positively charged electron cloud surrounding a positively charged nucleus
   2) a positively charged electron cloud surrounding a negatively charged nucleus
   3) a negatively charged electron cloud surrounding a positively charged nucleus
   4) a negatively charged electron cloud surrounding a negatively charged nucleus

5. Which total mass is the smallest?
   1) the mass of 2 electrons
   2) the mass of 2 neutrons
   3) the mass of 1 electron plus the mass of 1 proton
   4) the mass of 1 neutron plus the mass of 1 electron

6. Which statement concerning elements is true?
   1) Different elements must have different numbers of isotopes.
   2) Different elements must have different numbers of neutrons.
   3) All atoms of a given element must have the same mass number.
   4) All atoms of a given element must have the same atomic number.

7. Which value of an element is calculated using both the mass and the relative abundance of each of the naturally occurring isotopes of this element?
   1) Atomic number   2) Atomic mass   3) Half-life   4) Molar volume

8. Which sequence represents a correct order of historical developments leading to the modern model of the atom?
   1) Atom is a hard sphere → atom is mostly empty space → electrons exist in orbitals outside the nucleus
   2) Atom is a hard sphere → electrons exist in orbitals outside the nucleus → atom is mostly empty space
   3) Atom is mostly empty space → atom is a hard sphere → electrons exist in orbitals outside the nucleus
   4) Atom is empty space → electrons exist in orbitals outside the nucleus → atom is a hard sphere

9. An atom is electrically neutral because the
   1) number of protons equals the number of electrons
   2) number of protons equals the number of neutrons
   3) ratio of the number of neutrons to the number of electrons is 1:1
   4) ratio of the number of neutrons to the number of protons is 2:1

10. How do the energy and the most probable location of an electron in the third shell of an atom compare to the energy and the most probable location of an electron in the first shell of the same atom?
    1) In the third shell, an electron has more energy and is closer to the nucleus.
    2) In the third shell, an electron has more energy and is farther from the nucleus.
    3) In the third shell, an electron has less energy and is closer to the nucleus.
    4) In the third shell, an electron has less energy and is farther from the nucleus.

11. During a flame test, ions of a specific metal are heated in the flame of a gas burner. A characteristic color of light is emitted by these ions in the flame when the electrons
    1) gain energy as they return to lower energy levels
    2) gain energy as they move to higher energy levels
    3) emit energy as they return to lower energy levels
    4) emit energy as they move to higher energy levels

Day 3: The Atomic Structure - Multiple Choices

12. A particle of an atom contains 26 protons, 23 electrons, and 56 neutrons. What will be the correct atomic number for this particle?

    1) 26   2) 23   3) 56   4) 33

13. An atom with 21 neutrons and 40 nucleons has

    1) A nuclear charge of +19   3) A mass number of 61
    2) A nuclear charge of +40   4) A mass number of 19

14. Which element could have a mass number of 86 atomic mass units and 49 neutrons in its nucleus?

    1) In   2) Rb   3) Rn   4) Au

15. Which correctly represents two isotopes of element X?

    1) $^{226}_{91}X$ and $^{226}_{91}X$ 3) $^{227}_{91}X$ and $^{227}_{90}X$

    2) $^{226}_{91}X$ and $^{227}_{91}X$ 4) $^{226}_{90}X$ and $^{227}_{91}X$

16. Which atom is an isotope of oxygen?

    1) $^{14}_{7}N$ 2) $^{16}_{8}N$ 3) $^{14}_{7}O$ 4) $^{17}_{8}O$

17. What is the total number of nucleons in the nuclide $^{65}_{30}Zn$?

    1) 65   2) 30   3) 35   4) 95

18. In which pair of atoms do the nuclei contain the same number of neutrons?

    1) Calcium-40 and Calcium-42   3) Bromine – 83 and Krypton - 83
    2) Chlorine-35 and Sulfur- 34   4) Iodine – 127 and Bromine – 80

19. Which is a ground state electron configuration of an atom in the fourth period of the periodic table

    1) $2 – 8 – 4$ 3) $2 – 8 – 18 – 18 – 4$
    2) $2 – 8 – 18 – 4$ 4) $2 – 4$

20. The total number of electrons found in the electron configuration of a neutral chromium atom is

    1) 24   2) 6   3) 13   4) 52

21. The highest amount of energy will be emitted by an electron when it moves from the

    1) 4th to 1st electron shell   3) 1st to 5th electron shell
    2) 1st to 4th electron shell   4) 5th to 4th electron shell

22. What is the total number of electrons in a Cr^{3+} ion?

    1) 3   2) 21   3) 24   4) 27

23. Which symbol represents a particle with a total of 10 electrons?

    1) N   2) Al   3) N^{3+} 4) Al^{3+}

24. Which electron configuration represents an atom of aluminum in an excited state?

    1) 2-7-4   2) 2-8-3   3) 2-7-7   4) 2-8-6

25. Element X has two isotopes. If 72.0% of the element has an isotopic mass of 84.9 amu, and 28.0% of the element has an isotopic mass of 87.0 amu, the average atomic mass of element X is numerically equal to

    1) (72.0 + 84.9) x (28.0 + 87.0)   3) $\dfrac{(72.0 \times 84.9)}{100} + \dfrac{(28.0 \times 87.0)}{100}$

    2) (72.0 - 84.9) x (28.0 + 87.0)   4) $\dfrac{(72.0 \times 84.9)}{100} - \dfrac{(28.0 \times 87.0)}{100}$

26. the diagram below represents the nucleus of an atom	What are the atomic number and mass number of this atom?
Key ● = proton ○ = neutron 	1) The atomic number is 9 and the mass number is 19. 2) The atomic number is 9 and the mass number is 20. 3) The atomic number is 11 and the mass number is 19. 4) The atomic number is 11 and the mass number is 20.

Day 3: The Atomic Structure – Constructed Response

Base your answers to questions 27 through 29 on the information below.

In the modern model of the atom, each atom is composed of three major subatomic (or fundamental) particles.

Write your answers here.

27. Name the subatomic particles contained in the nucleus.

27.

28. State the charge associated with each type of subatomic particle contained in the nucleus of the atom.

28.

29. What is the sign of the net charge of the nucleus?

29.

Base your answers to questions 30 through 32 on the data table below, which shows three isotopes of neon.

Isotope	Atomic Mass (atomic mass units)	Percent Natural Abundance
^{20}Ne	19.99	90.9 %
^{21}Ne	20.99	0.3 %
^{22}Ne	21.99	8.8 %

Write your answers here.

30. Based on the atomic mass and the natural abundances shown in the data table show a correct numerical set-up for calculating the average atomic mass of neon.

30.

31. Based on natural abundances, the average atomic mass of neon is closest to which whole number?

31.

32. In terms of atomic particles, state one difference between these three isotopes of neon.

32.

Day 3: The Atomic Structure – Constructed Response

Base your answers to questions 33 and 34 on the diagram below, which shows bright-line spectra of selected elements.

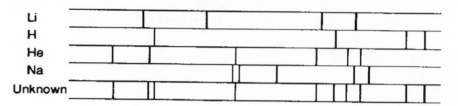

Li
H
He
Na
Unknown

Write your answers here.

33. Explain, in terms of excited state, energy transition, and ground state, how a bright-line spectrum is produced.

33.

34. Identify the two elements in the unknown spectrum.

34.

Base your answers to questions 35 and 36 on the diagram below, which represents an atom of magnesium-26 in the ground state.

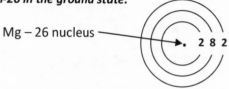

Mg – 26 nucleus ——————▶ 2 8 2

Write your answers here.

35. Write an appropriate number of electrons in each shell to represent a Mg – 26 atom in an excited state. Your answer may include additional shells.

35.

36. What is the total number of valence electrons in an atom of Mg-26 in the ground state?

36.

14 Days of Questions for Regents and Final Exams Practice

Day 4: Chemical bonding - Multiple Choices

1. Atoms bond due to the interaction between
   1) Protons and neutrons
   2) Protons and electrons
   3) Neutrons and electrons
   4) Neutrons and positrons

2. Which statement describes what occurs as two atoms of bromine combine to become a molecule of bromine?
   1) Energy is absorbed as a bond is formed.
   2) Energy is absorbed as a bond is broken.
   3) Energy is released as a bond is formed.
   4) Energy is released as a bond is broken.

3. Which particles may be gained, lost, or shared by an atom when it forms a chemical bond?
   1) protons
   2) electrons
   3) neutrons
   4) nucleons

4. The amount of potential energy in chemical bonds of substances depends on
   1) The composition of the substances only
   2) The structure of the substances only
   3) Both the composition and the structure of the substances
   4) Neither the composition nor the structure of the substances

5. Which type of bond results when one or more valence electrons are transferred from one atom to another?
   1) a hydrogen bond
   2) an ionic bond
   3) a nonpolar covalent bond
   4) a polar covalent bond

6. Which type of bonding is found in all molecular substances?
   1) covalent bonding
   2) hydrogen bonding
   3) ionic bonding
   4) metallic bonding

7. Two nonmetal atoms of the same element share electrons equally. The resulting molecule is
   1) Polar, only
   2) Nonpolar, only
   3) Either polar or nonpolar
   4) Neither polar nor nonpolar

8. Which best describes the shape and charge distribution in polar molecules?
   1) Asymmetrical shape with equal charge distribution
   2) Asymmetrical shape with unequal charge distribution
   3) Symmetrical shape with equal charge distribution
   4) Symmetrical shape with unequal charge distribution

9. Which characteristic is a property of molecular substances?
   1) Good heat conductivity
   2) Good electrical conductivity
   3) Low melting point
   4) High melting point

10. The degree of polarity of a chemical bond in a molecule of a compound can be predicted by determining the difference in the
    1) melting points of the elements in the compound
    2) densities of the elements in the compound
    3) electronegativities of the bonded atoms in a molecule of the compound
    4) atomic masses of the bonded atoms in a molecule of the compound

11. A solid substance is an excellent conductor of electricity. The chemical bonds in this substance are most likely
    1) ionic, because the valence electrons are shared between atoms
    2) ionic, because the valence electrons are mobile
    3) metallic, because the valence electrons are stationary
    4) metallic, because the valence electrons are mobile

14 Days of Questions for Regents and Final Exams Practice

Day 4: Chemical bonding - Multiple Choices

12. Given the reaction at 101.3 kilopascals and 298 K:

 hydrogen gas + iodine gas $\rightarrow$ hydrogen iodide gas .
 This reaction is classified as

 1) endothermic, because heat is absorbed   3) exothermic, because heat is absorbed
 2) endothermic, because heat is released   4) exothermic, because heat is released

13. Atom X and atom Y bond to form a compound. The electron configuration of X and Y are 2 – 8. Which two atoms could be X and Y ?
 1) X could be magnesium and Y could be sulfur
 2) X could be magnesium and Y could be oxygen
 3) X could be calcium and Y could be sulfur
 4) X could be calcium and Y could be oxygen

14. Atoms in which compound are held together by ionic bonds?
 1) CH_4 2) $AlCl_3$ 3) H_2O 4) NH_3

15. Which formula contains nonpolar covalent bonds?
 1) NH_3 2) H_2O 3) O_2 4) $NaCl$

16. The atoms of which substance are held together by metallic bonds?
 1) $H_2(g)$ 2) $H_2O(l)$ 3) $SiC(s)$ 4) $Fe(s)$

17. Which compound contains both ionic and covalent bonds?
 1) Ammonia   3) Methane
 2) Lithium sulfate   4) Potassium chloride

18. The C – Cl bond in CCl_4 is best described as
 1) Ionic, because electrons are transferred   3) Covalent, because electrons are transferred
 2) Ionic, because electrons are shared   4) Covalent, because electrons are shared

19. Which structural formula represents a polar molecule?
 1) H – H   2) Na – H   3) H – Br   4) O = O

20. Which pair of atoms forms a bond that is the least covalent?
 1) Ba and I   2) Br and Cl   3) K and Cl   4) P and I

21. An atom of nitrogen is most stable when it bonds with
 1) One sodium atom   3) One aluminum atom
 2) One magnesium atom   4) One calcium atom

22. Based on bond type, which compound has the highest melting point?
 1) CH_3OH 2) C_6H_{14} 3) $CuCl_2$ 4) CCl_4

23. Which of the following has the lowest boiling point?
 1) He   2) Xe   3) Ne   4) Kr

24. Which electron-dot symbol represents a nonpolar molecule?

 1) $H:\overset{\displaystyle H}{\underset{\displaystyle H}{\ddot{C}}}\!:\!\ddot{C}\!l\!:$ 2) $H:\ddot{C}\!l\!:$ 3) $H:\overset{\displaystyle H}{\underset{\displaystyle H}{\ddot{C}}}\!:\!H$ 4) $H:\overset{\displaystyle \ddot{O}:}{\underset{\displaystyle H}{}}$

25. Molecules in a sample of $NH_3(g)$ are held closely together by intermolecular forces
 1) existing between ions   3) caused by different numbers of neutrons
 2) existing between electrons   4) caused by unequal charge distribution

26. Which Lewis electron-dot diagram correctly represents a hydroxide ion?

 1) $\left[:\ddot{O}:H\right]^-$ 2) $\left[:O:H:\right]^-$ 3) $\left[:\ddot{O}::H\right]^-$ 4) $\left[:O:\ddot{H}:\right]^-$

Day 4: Chemical bonding - Constructed Response

Base your answers to questions 27 through 31 on your knowledge of chemical bonding and on the Lewis electron-dot diagrams of H_2S, CO_2, and F_2 below.

$$H:\ddot{\underset{\cdot\cdot}{S}}: \qquad :\ddot{O}::C::\ddot{O}: \qquad :\ddot{F}:\ddot{F}:$$
$$H$$

27. Which atom, when bonded as shown, has the same electron configuration as an atom of argon?

    27.

28. Explain, in terms of structure and/or distribution of charge, why CO_2 is a nonpolar molecule:

    28.

29 . Explain, in terms of electronegativity, why a C = O bond in CO_2 is more polar than an F – F bond in F_2

    29.

30. What is the total number of covalent bonds in a molecule of CO_2?

    30.

31. What is the shape and molecular polarity of H_2S?

    31 . Shape:

          Molecular Polarity:

Base your answers to questions 32 through 34 on the information below.

Carbon and oxygen are examples of elements that exist in more than one form in the same phase.

  Graphite and diamond are two crystalline arrangements for carbon. The crystal structure of graphite is organized in layers. The bonds between carbon atoms within each layer of graphite are strong. The bonds between carbon atoms that connect different layers of graphite are weak because the shared electrons in these bonds are loosely held by the carbon atoms. The crystal structure of diamond is a strong network of atoms in which all the shared electrons are strongly held by the carbon atoms. Graphite is an electrical conductor, but diamond is not. At 25°C, graphite has a density of 2.2 g/cm^3 and diamond has a density of 3.51 g/cm^3.

  The element oxygen can exist as diatomic molecules, O_2, and as ozone, O_3. At standard pressure the boiling point of ozone is 161 K.

32. Explain, in terms of electrons, why graphite is an electrical conductor and diamond is *not*. Your response must include information about *both* graphite and diamond.

    32.

33. Calculate the volume, in cm^3, of a diamond at 25°C that has a mass of 0.200 grams. Your response must include *both* a correct numerical setup and the calculated result.

    33.

34. Explain, in terms of intermolecular forces, the difference in the boiling points of O_2 and O_3 at standard pressure. Your response must include information about *both* O_2 and O_3.

    34.

Day 4: Chemical bonding - Constructed Response

Base your answers to question 35 and 36 on the table and information below.

The table below shows some properties of three solids: X, Y, and Z

Properties	X	Y	Z
Melting Point ($^{\circ}$C)	800	80	1200
Soluble in water	yes	no	no
Solid state conducts electricity	no	no	Yes
Liquid state conduct electricity	yes	no	yes

35. Classify solids X, Y, and Z as the following:

      metallic, ionic, or molecular

35.   Solid X :_____

         Solid Y: _____

         Solid Z: _____

36. Explain, in terms of ions, why solid X would be able to conduct electricity when it dissolves in water.

36.

37. Explain, in terms of intermolecular forces, why pure hydrogen has a lower boiling point than hydrogen bromide.

37.

38. Explain, in terms of electronegativity difference, why the bond in H – Cl is more polar than the bond in H – I.

38.

39. Explain, in terms of molecular polarity, why pure hydrogen chloride is more soluble than hydrogen in water under the same conditions of temperature and pressure.

39.

Day 5: Chemical formulas and equations - Multiple Choices

1. A chemical formula is an expression of
   1) Qualitative composition, only
   2) Quantitative composition, only
   3) Both qualitative and quantitative composition
   4) Neither qualitative nor quantitative composition

2. A type of formula showing the simplest ratio in which atoms are combined is called
   1) A molecular formula
   2) An empirical formula
   3) A structural formula
   4) A condensed formula

3. Given the balanced equation representing a reaction:
   $$H^+(aq) \quad + \quad OH^-(aq) \rightarrow \quad H_2O(l) \quad + \quad 55.8 \, kJ$$
   In this reaction there is conservation of
   1) mass, only
   2) mass and energy, only
   3) mass and charge, only
   4) mass, charge, and energy

4. Given a balanced chemical equation, it is always possible to determine
   1) Whether a reaction will or will not take place
   2) The conditions necessary for the reaction to take place
   3) The relative number of moles taking place in the reaction
   4) The physical state of the products and reactants

5. Which list consists of types of chemical formulas?
   1) atoms, ions, molecules
   2) empirical, molecular, structural
   3) metals, nonmetals, metalloids
   4) synthesis, decomposition, neutralization

6. Which list is composed only of types of chemical reactions?
   1) Synthesis, decomposition, single replacement
   2) Decomposition, evaporation, and double replacement
   3) Synthesis, decomposition, freezing
   4) Decomposition, melting, combustion

7. In the compound, $Ca_3(PO_4)_2$, what is the total number of phosphate ions in the formula?
   1) 3   2) 2   3) 8   4) 4

8. The total number of atoms in the hydrate $CuSO_4 \cdot 3H_2O$ is
   1) 9   2) 12   3) 15   4) 24

9. What is the ratio of ammonium ions to sulfate ions in the formula $(NH_4)_2SO_4$?
   1) 2 : 1   2) 1 : 2   3) 8 : 4   4) 4 : 1

10. Which formula is an empirical formula?
    1) H_2CO_3 2) $H_2C_2O_4$ 3) CH_3COOH 4) CH_2OHCH_2OH

11. Which two compounds have the same empirical formula?
    1) C_2H_2 and C_2H_4 2) CH_2 and C_3H_8 3) HO and H_2O 4) NO_2 and N_2O_4

12. Which is the correct formula for iron(II) sulfide?
    1) FeS 2) Fe_5O_3 3) Fe_2S_3 4) $Fe_2(SO_4)_2$

13. The correct name for $NaClO_4$ is sodium
    1) Chloride   2) Chlorate   3) Perchlorate   4) chlorite

14. Which formula is a binary compound?
    1) KOH 2) $NaClO_3$ 3) Al_2S_3 4) $Bi(NO_3)_3$

Day 5: Chemical formulas and equations - Multiple Choices

15. What is the formula of titanium(II) oxide?
    1) TiO   2) Ti_2O 3) TiO_2 4) Ti_2O_3

16. What is the simplest ratio of nitrogen to oxygen atoms in the compound nitrogen(IV) oxide?
    1) $1:2$ 2) $2:1$ 3) $2:4$ 4) $4:2$

17. Which substance has a chemical formula with the same ratio of metal ions to nonmetal ions as in potassium sulfide?
    1) sodium oxide   3) sodium chloride
    2) magnesium oxide   4) magnesium chloride

18. A single replacement reaction is shown in which equation?
    1) $Ca(OH)_2 + 2HCl \rightarrow CaCl_2 + 2H_2O$
    2) $Ca + 2H_2O \rightarrow H_2 + Ca(OH)_2$
    3) $2H_2 + O_2 \rightarrow 2H_2O$
    4) $2H_2O_2 \rightarrow 2H_2O + O_2$

19. Which of these equations shows conservation of atoms?
    1) $2KBr \rightarrow K + Br_2$ 3) $CuCO_3 \rightarrow CuO + CO_2$
    2) $2KClO_3 \rightarrow 2KCl + 2O_2$ 4) $CaCO_3 \rightarrow CO_2 + 2CaO$

20. Which chemical equation is correctly balanced?
    1) $H_2(g) + O_2(g) \rightarrow H_2O(g)$ 3) $2KCl(s) \rightarrow 2K(s) + Cl_2(g)$
    2) $N_2(g) + H_2(g \rightarrow NH_3(g)$ 4) $2NaCl(s) \rightarrow Na(s) + Cl_2(g)$

21. Given the equation:
    $$X + Cl_2 \rightarrow C_2H_5Cl + HCl$$
    Which molecule is represented by X?
    1) C_2H_4 2) C_2H_6 3) C_3H_6 4) C_3H_8

22. Given the unbalanced equation:
    $$\_Fe_2O_3 + \_CO \rightarrow \_Fe + \_CO_2$$

    When the equation is correctly balanced using the smallest whole-number coefficients, what is the coefficient of CO?
    1) 1   2) 2   3) 3   4) 4

23. What is the chemical formula for sodium sulfate?
    1) Na_2SO_3 2) Na_2SO_4 3) $NaSO_3$ 4) $NaSO_4$

24. Given the structural formula:

    ```
         H  H  H  H
         |  |  |  |
    HO − C − C − C − C − OH
         |  |  |  |
         H  H  H  H
    ```

    What is the empirical formula of this compound?

    1) CH_3O 2) $C_4H_{10}O_2$ 3) C_2H_5O 4) $C_8H_{20}O_4$

25. Which polyatomic ion contains the greatest number of oxygen atoms?
    1) acetate   2) carbonate   3) hydroxide   4) peroxide

Day 5: Chemical Formulas and Equations - Constructed Response

26. What is the correct formula for ammonium dichromate?   26.

27. What is the correct IUPAC name for the formula BeO ?   27.

Base your answers to questions 28 through 30 on the equation below.

$$\_\_\_ \ C_4H_6 \ + \ \_\_\_ \ O_2 \ \text{---------} > \ \_\_\_ \ CO_2 \ + \ \_\_\_ \ H_2O$$

28. Balance the equation above, using the smallest whole number coefficients.

29. What is the sum of all coefficients when the equation is balanced?   29.

30. What type of chemical reaction is represented by the equation?   30.

Base your answers to questions 31 through 34 on the information below.

Arsenic is often obtained by heating the ore arsenopyrite, FeAsS. The decomposition of FeAsS is represented by the balanced equation below.

$$FeAsS(s) \ \text{--------} > \ FeS(s) \ + \ As(g)$$

In the solid phase, arsenic occurs in two forms. One form, yellow arsenic, has a density of 1.97 g/cm^3 at STP. The other form, gray arsenic, has a density of 5.78 g/cm^3 at STP. When arsenic is heated rapidly in air, arsenic(III) oxide is formed.

Although arsenic is toxic, it is needed by the human body in very small amounts. The body of a healthy human adult contains approximately 5 milligrams of arsenic.

31. Convert the mass of arsenic found in the body of a healthy human adult to grams.   31.

32. When heated, a 125.0-kilogram sample of arsenopyrite yields 67.5 kilograms of FeS. Determine the total mass of arsenic produced in this reaction.   32.

33. Write the formula for the compound produced when arsenic is heated rapidly in air.   33.

34. Explain, in terms of the arrangement of atoms, why the two forms of arsenic have different densities at STP.   34.

Day 5: Chemical formulas and equations - Constructed Response

Base your answers to questions 35 through 37 on the information below.

Antacids can be used to neutralize excess stomach acid.

Brand A antacids contain the acid-neutralizing agent magnesium hydroxide, $Mg(OH)_2$. It reacts with HCl(aq) in the stomach according to the following equation:

$$HCl(aq) \ + \ Mg(OH)_2\,(aq) \ \text{--------}> \ MgCl_2(aq) \ + \ H_2O(l)$$

Brand B antacids contain the acid-neutralizing agent sodium hydrogen carbonate.

35. Write the chemical formula for sodium hydrogen carbonate.   35.

36. What type of reaction is shown in the above balanced equation?   36.

37. Balance the equation below using the smallest whole-number coefficients.

   ___ HCl(aq) + ___ $Mg(OH)_2$ (aq) --------> ____ $MgCl_2$(aq) + ___ $H_2O(l)$

14 Days of Questions for Regents and Final Exams Practice

Day 6: Stoichiometry: Mole Interpretation and Calculations - Multiple Choices

1. What is the total number of moles of hydrogen atoms in 4 moles of $(NH_4)_2SO_4$?
   - 1) 8
   - 2) 10
   - 3) 16
   - 4) 32

2. How many different types of atoms are in the formula $Ba(OH)_2 \cdot 8H_2O$?
   - 1) 3
   - 2) 2
   - 3) 5
   - 4) 8

3. What is the gram-formula mass of $Ca_3(PO_4)_2$?
   - 1) 248 g/mole
   - 2) 263 g/mole
   - 3) 279 g/mole
   - 4) 310. g/mole

4. What is the approximate mass in grams of 0.5 moles of Co?
   - 1) 27
   - 2) 29
   - 3) 12
   - 4) 59

5. The number of moles of H_2SO_4 that weighs 245 grams is equal to
   - 1) 0.4 mole
   - 2) 1 mole
   - 3) 2.5 moles
   - 4) 3 moles

6. The number of moles of the element lead that will have a mass of 311 grams is equal to
   - 1) 2 moles
   - 2) 1.5 moles
   - 3) 0.67 mole
   - 4) 1.0 mole

7. What is the total mass in grams of 0.75 moles of SO_2?
   - 1) 16 g
   - 2) 24 g
   - 3) 32 g
   - 4) 48 g

8. The mass in grams of two moles of $(NH_4)_2CO_3$ is equal to
   - 1) 96 x 2
   - 2) 108 x 2
   - 3) $\frac{96}{2}$
   - 4) $\frac{2}{96}$

9. What is the percent composition of nitrogen in the compound NH_4NO_3?
   - 1) 35 %
   - 2) 29 %
   - 3) 18 %
   - 4) 5.7 %

10. What is the approximate percent composition of $CaCO_3$?
    - 1) 48% Ca, 12% C and 40% O
    - 2) 12% Ca, 48% C, and 40% O
    - 3) 40% Ca , 12% C and 48% O
    - 4) 40% Ca , 48% C, and 12% O

11. In which compound is the percent by mass of oxygen greatest?
    - 1) BeO
    - 2) MgO
    - 3) CaO
    - 4) SrO

12. A sample of a substance containing only magnesium and chlorine was tested in the laboratory and was found to be composed of 74.5% chlorine by mass. If the total mass of the sample was 190.2 grams, what was the mass of the magnesium?
    - 1) 24.3 g
    - 2) 48.5 g
    - 3) 70.9 g
    - 4) 142 g

13. A student measured an 8.24 g sample of a hydrated salt and heated it until it had a constant mass of 6.20 g. What was the percent by mass of water in the hydrated salt?
    - 1) 14.1 %
    - 2) 24.8 %
    - 3) 32.9 %
    - 4) 75.2 %

14. A compound has an empirical formula of CH_2Br and a molecular mass of 188 grams per mole. What is the molecular formula of this compound?
    - 1) CH_2Br
    - 2) $C_2H_4Br_2$
    - 3) $C_3H_6Br_3$
    - 4) $CHBr_2$

15. A compound has a molar mass of 90. grams per mole and the empirical formula CH_2O. What is the molecular formula of this compound?
    - 1) CH_2O
    - 2) $C_2H_4O_2$
    - 3) $C_3H_6O_3$
    - 4) $C_4H_8O_4$

Day 6: Stoichiometry: Mole interpretations and Calculation - Multiple Choices

16. Acetic acid has a formula of $HC_2H_3O_2$. What is the ratio by mass of hydrogen to carbon to oxygen in this formula?
    1) $2 : 1 : 1$ 2) $2 : 3 : 3$ 3) $1 : 6 : 8$ 4) $1 : 2 : 4$

17. A sample of a compound contains 65.4 grams of zinc, 12.0 grams of carbon, and 48.0 grams of oxygen. What is the mole ratio of zinc to carbon to oxygen in this compound?
    1) $1 : 1 : 2$ 2) $1 : 1 : 3$ 3) $1 : 4 : 6$ 4) $5 : 1 : 4$

18. Given the reaction;

    $$2C_2H_6 \ + \ 7O_2 \ \rightarrow \ 4CO_2 \ + \ 6H_2O$$

    What is the ratio of moles of CO_2 produced to moles of C_2H_6 consumed?
    1) 2 to 1   2) 1 to 1   3) 3 to 2   4) 7 to 2

19. Given the balanced equation representing a reaction:

    $$F_2(g) \ + \ H_2(g) \ \rightarrow \ 2HF(g)$$

    What is the mole ratio of $H_2(g)$ to $HF(g)$ in this reaction?
    1) $1 : 1$ 2) $1 : 2$ 3) $2 : 1$ 4) $2 : 3$

20. Given the balanced equation representing the reaction between propane and oxygen:

    $$C_3H_8 \ + \ 5O_2 \ \rightarrow \ 3CO_2 \ + \ 4H_2O$$

    According to this equation, which ratio of oxygen to propane is correct?

    1) $\dfrac{5 \text{ grams } O_2}{1 \text{ grams } C_3H_8}$
    2) $\dfrac{5 \text{ moles } O_2}{1 \text{ mole } C_3H_8}$
    3) $\dfrac{10 \text{ grams } O_2}{11 \text{ grams } C_3H_8}$
    4) $\dfrac{10 \text{ moles } O_2}{11 \text{ moles } C_3H_8}$

21. Given the reaction:

    $$4Fe \ + \ 3O_2 \ \rightarrow \ 2Fe_2O_3$$

    To produce 3 moles of Fe_2O_3, how many moles of Fe must be reacted?
    1) 1.5 moles   2) 3 moles   3) 4 moles   4) 6 moles

22. Given the balanced equation representing a reaction:

    $$C_3H_8(g) \ + \ 5O_2(g) \ \rightarrow \ 3CO_2(g) \ + \ 4H_2O(g)$$

    What is the total number of moles of $O_2(g)$ required for the complete combustion of 1.5 moles of $C_3H_8(g)$?
    1) 0.30 mol   2) 1.5 mol   3) 4.5 mol   4) 7.5 mol

23. According to the reaction below:

    $$2SO_2(g) \ + \ O_2(g) \ \rightarrow \ 2SO_3(g)$$

    What is the total number of liters of $O_2(g)$ that will react completely with 89.6 liters of SO_2 at STP?

    1) 44.8 L   2) 22.4 L   3) 1.0 L   4) 0.500 L

24. Given the reaction:

    $$4Al(s) \ + \ 3O_2(g) \ \rightarrow \ 2Al_2O_3(s)$$

    What is the minimum number of grams of O_2 gas required to produce 102 grams of Al_2O_3?
    1) 32.0 g   2) 192 g   3) 96.0 g   4) 48.0 g

Day 6: Stoichiometry: Mole Interpretations and Calculations - Constructed Response

---

Base your answers to questions 25 through 27 on the information below.

Gypsum is a mineral that is used in the construction industry to make drywall (sheetrock). The chemical formula for this hydrated compound is $CaSO_4 \cdot 2H_2O$. A hydrated compound contains water molecules within the crystalline structures. Gypsum contains 2 moles of water for each 1 mole of calcium sulfate.

Show work and answers here.

25. What is the gram-formula mass of $CaSO_4 \cdot 2H_2O$?   25.

26. Show a correct numerical setup for calculating the percent composition by mass of water in this compound and record your result.   26.

27. What is the IUPAC name for gypsum, $CaSO_4 \cdot 2H_2O$?   27.

Base your answers to questions 28 through 30 on the information below.

The decomposition of sodium azide, $NaN_3(s)$, is used to inflate airbags. On impact, $NaN_3(s)$ is ignited by an electrical spark, producing $N_2(g)$ and Na. The $N_2(g)$ inflates the airbag.

Show work and answers here.

28. An inflated airbag has a volume of $5.00 \times 10^4 \, cm^3$ at STP. The density of $N_2(g)$ at STP is $0.00125 g/cm^3$. What is the total number of grams of $N_2(g)$ in the bag?   28.

29. What is the total number of moles present in a 52.0 gram sample of NaN_3. (Gram-formula mass = 65.0 grams/mole)   29.

30. Balance the equation to the right using the smallest whole number coefficients.   30. ___ NaN_3 -----> ___ Na + ___N_2

Base your answers to questions 31 and 32 on the balanced chemical equation below.

$$2H_2O \quad \text{-----------} > \quad 2H_2 \; + \; O_2$$

Show work and answers here.

31. What is the total number of moles of O_2 produced when 8 moles of H_2O is completely consumed?   31.

32. How does the balanced chemical equation show the Law of Conservation of Mass?   32.

Day 6: Stoichiometry: Mole Interpretations and Calculations - Constructed Response

---

Base your answers to questions 33 through 37 on the information below.

A hydrate is a compound that has water molecules within its crystal structure. The formula for the hydrate $CuSO_4 \cdot 5H_2O(s)$ shows that there are five moles of water for every one mole of $CuSO_4(s)$. When $CuSO_4 \cdot 5H_2O(s)$ is heated, the water within the crystals is released, as represented by the balanced equation below.

$$CuSO_4 \cdot 5H_2O(s) \rightarrow CuSO_4(s) + 5H_2O(g)$$

A student first masses an empty crucible (a heat-resistant container). The student then masses the crucible containing a sample of $CuSO_4 \cdot 5H_2O(s)$. The student repeatedly heats and masses the crucible and its contents until the mass is constant. The student's recorded experimental data and calculations are shown below.

Data and calculation before heating:

mass of $CuSO_4 \cdot 5H_2O(s)$ and crucible	21.37 g
− mass of crucible	19.24 g
mass of $CuSO_4 \cdot 5H_2O(s)$	2.13 g

Data and calculation after heating to a constant mass:

mass of $CuSO_4(s)$ and crucible	20.61 g
− mass of crucible	19.24 g
mass of $CuSO_4(s)$	1.37 g

Calculation to determine the mass of water:

mass of $CuSO_4 \cdot 5H_2O(s)$	2.13 g
− mass of $CuSO_4(s)$	1.37 g
mass of $H_2O(g)$	0.76 g

33. Identify the total number of significant figures   33.
    recorded in the calculated mass of $CuSO_4 \cdot 5H_2O(s)$.

34. In the space to the right, use the student's data to   34
    show a correct numerical setup for calculating the
    percent composition of water by mass in the hydrate.

35. Explain why the sample in the crucible must be   35.
    heated until the constant mass is reached.

36. How many moles of $CuSO_4$ is represented by the   36.
    mass of $CuSO_4$ calculated by the student?

37. How many moles of water is represented by the   37.
    mass of H_2O calculated by the student?

Day 7: Solutions - Multiple Choices

1. The process of recovering a salt from a solution by evaporating the solvent is known as
   1) Decomposition
   2) Crystallization
   3) Reduction
   4) Filtration

2. Which changes will increase the solubility of a gas in water?
   1) Increase in pressure and increase in temperature
   2) Increase in pressure and decrease in temperature
   3) Decrease in pressure and increase in temperature
   4) Decrease in pressure and decrease in temperature

3. The solubility of a salt in a given volume of water depends largely on the
   1) Surface area of the salt crystals
   2) Pressure on the surface of the water
   3) Rate at which the salt and water are stirred
   4) Temperature of the water

4. A solution in which equilibrium exists between dissolved and undissolved particles is also a
   1) Saturated solution
   2) Concentrated solution
   3) Supersaturated solution
   4) Dilute solution

5. A student adds solid KCl to water in a flask. The flask is sealed with a stopper and thoroughly shaken until no more solid KCl dissolves. Some solid KCl is still visible in the flask. The solution in the flask is
   1) saturated and is at equilibrium with the solid KCl
   2) saturated and is not at equilibrium with the solid KCl
   3) unsaturated and is at equilibrium with the solid KCl
   4) unsaturated and is not at equilibrium with the solid KCl

6. Which phrase describes the molarity of a solution?
   1) liters of solute per mole of solution
   2) liters of solution per mole of solution
   3) moles of solute per liter of solution
   4) moles of solution per liter of solution

7. As a solute is added to a solvent, what happens to the freezing point and the boiling point of the solution?
   1) The freezing point decreases and the boiling point decreases
   2) The freezing point decreases and the boiling point increases
   3) The freezing point increases and the boiling point decreases
   4) The freezing point increases and the boiling point increases

8. As water is added to a solution, the number of dissolved ions in the solution
   1) Increases, and the concentration of the solution remains the same
   2) Decreases, and the concentration of the solution increases
   3) Remains the same, and the concentration of the solution decreases
   4) Remains the same, and the concentration of the solution remains the same

9. The depression of the freezing point is dependent on
   1) The nature of the solute
   2) The concentration of dissolved particles
   3) Hydrogen bonding
   4) The formula of the solute

10. The vapor pressure of H_2O is less than that of CS_2. The best explanation for this is that H_2O has
    1) Larger molecules
    2) A larger molecular mass
    3) Stronger ionic bonds
    4) Stronger intermolecular forces

11. A dilute, aqueous potassium nitrate solution is best classified as a
    1) homogeneous compound
    2) homogeneous mixture
    3) heterogeneous compound
    4) heterogeneous mixture

Day 7: Solutions - Multiple Choices

12. What happens when $Ca(NO_3)_2(s)$ is dissolved in water?
    1) NO_3^- ions are attracted to the oxygen atoms of water
    2) Ca^{2+} ions are attracted to the oxygen atoms of water
    3) Ca^{2+} ions are attracted to the hydrogen atoms of water
    4) No attractions are involved; the crystal just falls apart

13. A decrease in water temperature will increase the solubility of
    1) $C_6H_{12}O_6(s)$ 2) $NH_3(g)$ 3) $KCl(s)$ 4) $Br_2(l)$

14. Under which two conditions would water contain the least number of dissolved $SO_2(g)$ molecules?
    1) 101.3 kPa and 273 K   3) 60 kPa and 273 K
    2) 101.3 kPa and 546 K   4) 60 kPa and 546 K

15. According to Reference Table F, which of these compounds is soluble in water at STP?
    1) $ZnSO_4$ 2) $BaSO_4$ 3) $ZnCO_3$ 4) $BaCO_3$

16. At STP, which aqueous solution will contain the least amount of dissolved ions?
    1) $NaNO_3$ 2) Na_2SO_4 3) $Pb(NO_3)_2$ 4) $PbSO_4$

17. What is the mass of NH_4Cl that must dissolve in 200. grams of water at 50.°C to make a saturated solution?
    1) 104 g   2) 84 g   3) 42 g   4) 26 g

18. According to Reference Table G, which solution is a saturated solution at 30°C?
    1) 30 grams of $KClO_3$ in 100 grams of water   3) 76 grams of NaCl in 100 grams of water
    2) 30 grams of $KClO_3$ in 200 grams of water   4) 76 grams of NaCl in 200 grams of water

19. What amount of potassium chloride must be added to a solution made by dissolving 80 g of the solute in 200 grams of H_2O at 60°C to produce a saturated solution?
    1) 45 g   2) 160 g   3) 100 g   4) 10 g

20. One hundred grams of water is saturated with NH_4Cl at 50°C. If the temperature of the solution is decreased to 10°C, what amount of the solute will precipitate?
    1) 5 g   2) 17 g   3) 30 g   4) 50 g

21. Based on Reference Table G, a solution of $NaNO_3$ that contains 120 g of solute dissolved in 100 grams of H_2O at 50 °C is best described as
    1) Saturated   2) Unsaturated   3) Supersaturated

22. A solution containing 140 grams of potassium iodide in 100 grams of water at 20°C is best classified as
    1) Unsaturated and dilute   3) Saturated and dilute
    2) Unsaturated and concentrated   4) Supersaturated and concentrated

23. A saturated solution of which compound will be the least concentrated solution in 100 g of water at 40°C?
    1) SO_2 2) NaCl   3) $KClO_3$ 4) NH_4Cl

24. A 3.0 M HCl(aq) solution contains a total of
    1) 3.0 grams of HCl per liter of water   3) 3.0 moles of HCl per liter of solution
    2) 3.0 grams of HCl per mole of solution   4) 3.0 moles of HCl per mole of water

25. When 5 grams of KCl are dissolved in 50. grams of water at 25°C, the resulting mixture can be described as
    1) heterogeneous and unsaturated   3) homogeneous and unsaturated
    2) heterogeneous and supersaturated   4) homogeneous and supersaturated

Day 7: Solutions - Multiple Choices

26. According to Reference Table G, how does a decrease in temperature from $40^{\circ}C$ to $20^{\circ}C$ affect the solubility of $NH_3(g)$ and that of NH_4Cl?
    1) The solubility of NH_3 increases, and the solubility of NH_4Cl increases
    2) The solubility of NH_3 decreases, and the solubility of NH_4Cl increases
    3) The solubility of NH_3 increases, and the solubility of NH_4Cl decreases
    4) The solubility of NH_3 decreases, and the solubility of NH_4Cl decreases

27. A solution of NaCl contains 1.8 moles of the solute in 600 mL of solution. What is the concentration of the solution?
    1) 333 M   2) 0.003 M   3) 3 M   4) 0. 05 M

28. A student dissolved 48 grams of $(NH_4)_2CO_3$ in 2000 mL of water. What will be the molarity of this solution?
    1) 1 M   2) 2 M   3) 0.25 M   4) 0.5 M

29. How many moles of KNO_3 are required to make .50 liter of a 2 molar solution of KNO_3?
    1) 1.0   2) 2.0   3) 0.50   4) 4.0

30. What is the total mass of solute in 1000 grams of a solution having a concentration of 5 parts per million?
    1) 0.005 g   2) 0.05 g   3) 0.5 g   4) 5 g

31. If 0.025 grams of $Pb(NO_3)_2$ is dissolved in 100. grams of H_2O, what is the concentration of the resulting solution, in parts per million?
    1) 2.5×10^{-4} ppm   2) 4.0×10^{3} ppm   3) 250 ppm   4) 2.5 ppm

32. The vapor pressure of a liquid is 0.92 atm at $60^{\circ}C$. The normal boiling point of the liquid could be
    1) $35^{\circ}C$ 2) $45^{\circ}C$ 3) $55^{\circ}C$ 4) $65^{\circ}C$

33. Which sample, when dissolved in 1.0 liter of water, produces a solution with the lowest freezing point?
    1) 0.1 mol of C_2H_5OH 3) 0.2 mol of $C_6H_{12}O_6$
    2) 0.1 mol of LiBr   4) 0.2 mol of $CaCl_2$

34. A student prepares four aqueous solutions, each with a different solute. The mass of each dissolved solute is shown in the table below.

**Mass of Dissolved Solute
for Four Aqueous Solutions**

Solution Number	Solute	Mass of Dissolved Solute (per 100. g of H_2O at $20.^{\circ}C$)
1	KI	120. g
2	$NaNO_3$	88 g
3	KCl	25 g
4	$KClO_3$	5 g

Which solution is saturated?
1) 1   2) 2   3) 3   4) 4

14 Days of Questions for Regents and Final Exams Practice

Day 7: Solutions - Constructed Response

Base your answers to questions 35 and 36 on the information below.

A student is instructed to make 0.250 liter of a 0.200 M aqueous solution of $Ca(NO_3)_2$.

35. In order to prepare the described solution in the laboratory, two quantities must be measured accurately. One of these quantities is the volume of the solution. What other quantity must be measured to prepare this solution?

35.

36. Show a correct numerical setup for calculating the total number of moles of $Ca(NO_3)_2$ needed to make 0.250 liter of the 0.200 M calcium nitrate solution.

36.

Base your answers to questions 37 through 39 on the information below.

When cola, a type of soda pop, is manufactured, $CO_2(g)$ is dissolved in it.

On the set of axes to the right.

37. Label one of them "Solubility" and the other "Temperature."

38. Draw a line to indicate the solubility of $CO_2(g)$ versus temperature.

39. A capped bottle of soda contains $CO_2(g)$ under high pressure. When the cap is removed, how does pressure affect the solubility of the dissolved $CO_2(g)$?

39.

Given the balanced equation for the dissolving of $NH_4Cl(s)$ in water:

$$NH_4Cl(s) \ ----\underline{H_2O}---- > NH_4^+(aq) \ + \ Cl^-(aq)$$

40. A student is holding a test tube containing 5.0 milliliters of water. When a sample of $NH_4Cl(s)$ is placed in the test tube, the test tube feels colder to the student's hand. Describe the direction of heat flow between the test tube and the hand.

40.

41.

41. Using the key to the right, draw at least two water molecules in the box showing the correct orientation of each water molecule when it is near the Cl^- ion in the aqueous solution

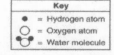

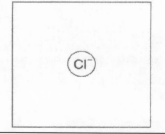

Day 7: Solutions - Constructed Response

Base your answers to questions 42 through 45 on the information below.

Scientists who study aquatic ecosystems are often interested in the concentration of dissolved oxygen in water. Oxygen, O_2, has a very low solubility in water, and therefore its solubility is usually expressed in units of milligrams per 1000. grams of water at 1.0 atmosphere pressure. The graph below shows a solubility curve of oxygen in water.

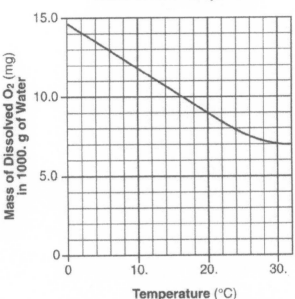

42. A student determines that 8.2 milligrams of oxygen is dissolved in a 1000. gram sample of water at 15°C and 1.0 atmosphere of pressure. In terms of saturation, what type of solution is this sample?

42.

43. Explain, in terms of molecular polarity, why oxygen gas has a low solubility in water. Your response must include both oxygen and water.

43.

44. A student prepared a solution of oxygen by dissolving 6.0 mg of oxygen in 1000 grams of water at 20°C. Determine how many more milligrams of oxygen must be added to the solution to make it a saturated solution.

44.

45. An aqueous solution has 0.007 grams of oxygen dissolved in 1000 grams of water. In the space to the right, calculate the dissolved oxygen concentration of this solution in parts per million. Your response should include both a correct numerical setup and calculated result.

45

Day 8: Acids, Bases and Salts - Multiple Choices

1. When a solution of an acid is tested with pH paper, the result will be a pH
   1) Above 7, and the solution will conduct electricity
   2) Above 7, and the solution will not conduct electricity
   3) Below 7, and the solution will conduct electricity
   4) Below 7, and the solution will not conduct electricity

2. When a base is dissolved in water, it produces
   1) OH^- as the only negative ions in solution
   2) NH_4^+ as the only positive ions in solution
   3) CO_3^{2-} as the only negative ions in solution
   4) H^+ as the only positive ions in solution

3. As water is added to a 0.10 M NaCl aqueous solution, the conductivity of the resulting solution
   1) decreases because the concentration of ions decreases
   2) decreases, but the concentration of ions remains the same
   3) increases because the concentration of ions decreases
   4) increases, but the concentration of ions remains the same

4. A substance is classified as an electrolyte because
   1) it has a high melting point
   2) it contains covalent bonds
   3) its aqueous solution conducts an electric current
   4) its aqueous solution has a pH value of 7

5. The Arrhenius theory explains the behavior of
   1) acids and bases
   2) alcohols and amines
   3) acids and salts
   4) metals and nonmetals

6. Which statement describes an alternate theory of acids and bases?
   1) Acids and bases are both H^+ acceptors.
   2) Acids and bases are both H^+ donors.
   3) Acids are H^+ acceptors, and bases are H^+ donors.
   4) Acids are H^+ donors, and bases are H^+ acceptors.

7. According to the Arrhenius theory, an acid is a substance that
   1) changes litmus from red to blue
   2) changes phenolphthalein from colorless to pink
   3) produces hydronium ions as the only positive ions in an aqueous solution
   4) produces hydroxide ions as the only negative ions in an aqueous solution

8. Which substance is always produced in a reaction between an acid and a base?
   1) Water
   2) Hydrogen gas
   3) Oxygen gas
   4) A precipitate

9. The compound KOH(s) dissolves in water to yield
   1) hydroxide ions as the only negative ions
   2) hydroxide ions as the only positive ions
   3) hydronium ions as the only negative ions
   4) hydronium ions as the only positive ions

10. Which word equation represents a neutralization reaction?
    1) base + acid $\rightarrow$ salt + water
    2) base + salt $\rightarrow$ water + acid
    3) salt + acid $\rightarrow$ base + water
    4) salt + water $\rightarrow$ acid + base

11. Given the equation: $HCl(g)$ + $H_2O(l)$ $\rightarrow$ $X(aq)$ + $Cl^-(aq)$
    Which ion is represented by X?
    1) hydroxide
    2) hydronium
    3) hypochlorite
    4) perchlorate

Day 8: Acids, Bases and Salts - Multiple Choices

12. Which two formulas represent Arrhenius acids?
    1) CH_3COOH and CH_3CH_2OH
    2) $HC_2H_3O_2$ and H_3PO_4
    3) $KHCO_3$ and $KHSO_4$
    4) $NaSCN$ and $Na_2S_2O_3$

13. Which compound releases hydroxide ions in an aqueous solution?
    1) CH_3COOH　　　2) HCl　　　3) CH_3OH　　　4) LiOH

14. Which aqueous solution could have a pH of 3?
    1) $H_2O(l)$　　　2) KOH(aq)　　　3) $CH_3OH(aq)$　　　4) $H_2SO_4(aq)$

15. Which compound when dissolved in water will turn blue litmus red?
    1) CH_3OH　　　2) HBr　　　3) $C_6H_{12}O_6$　　　4) $Ca(OH)_2$

16. Which is true of an aqueous solution of NH_4OH?
    1) It contains more OH^- ions than H^+ ions, and is a nonelectrolyte
    2) It contains more OH^- ions that H^+ ions, and is an electrolyte
    3) It contains more H^+ than OH^-, and is a nonelectrolyte
    4) It contains more H^+ than OH^-, and is an electrolyte

17. An example of a nonelectrolyte is
    1) $C_{12}H_{22}O_{11}(aq)$　　　2) $K_2SO_4(aq)$　　　3) $NH_4Cl(aq)$　　　4) HCl(aq)

18. Which pH of a solution indicates the strongest base?
    1) 6　　　2) 7　　　3) 8　　　4) 9

19. When phenolphthalein is added to a solution, the solution stays colorless. What could be the pH of this solution?
    1) 2　　　2) 9　　　3) 11　　　4) 13

20. In a solution with a pH of 13, phenolphthalein will be
    1) pink, and litmus will be red
    2) pink , and litmus will be blue
    3) colorless, and litmus will be red
    4) colorless, and litmus will be blue

21. Which of these metals will not produce a reaction with sulfuric acid ?
    1) Ca　　　2) Au　　　3) Zn　　　4) Li

22. The pH of an aqueous solution changes from 4 to 3 when the hydrogen ion concentration in the solution is
    1) decreased by a factor of $^4/_3$
    2) decreased by a factor of 10
    3) increased by a factor of $^3/_4$
    4) increased by a factor of 10

23. In the diagram below, which solution will cause the light bulb to glow?

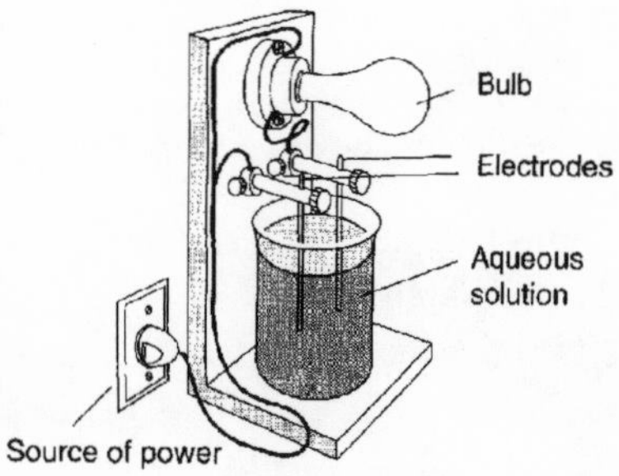

1) $C_6H_{12}O_6(aq)$　　　2) $CO_2(aq)$　　　3) $Cu(NO_3)_2(aq)$　　　4) $C_2H_5OH(aq)$

24. Which equation represents a neutralization reaction?
1) $4Fe(s) + 3O_2(g) \rightarrow 2Fe_2O_3(s)$
2) $2H_2(g) + O_2(g) \rightarrow 2H_2O(l)$
3) $HNO_3(aq) + KOH(aq) \rightarrow KNO_3(aq) + H_2O(l)$
4) $AgNO_3(aq) + KCl(aq) \rightarrow KNO_3(aq) + AgCl(s)$

25. In the neutralization reaction:

$$HC_2H_3O_2 + NH_4OH \rightarrow NH_4C_2H_3O_2 + H_2O$$

The salt is
1) NH_4OH 2) $HC_2H_3O_2$ 3) $NH_4C_2H_3O_2$ 4) H_2O

26. If 20 mL of 2.0 M KOH is exactly neutralized by 10 mL of HCl, the molarity of the HCl is
1) 0.50 M   2) 2.0 M   3) 1.0 M   4) 4.0 M

27. How many milliliters of 3.0 M HCl are neutralized by 60 mL of 0.5 M $Ca(OH)_2$?
1) 20 mL   2) 30 mL   3) 40 mL   4) 60 mL

Day 8: Acids, Bases and Salts - Constructed Response

Base your answers to questions 28 through 30 on the information below.

A student was studying the pH difference in samples from two Adirondack streams. The student measured a pH of 4 in stream A and a pH of 6 in stream B.

28. Identify one compound that could be used to neutralize the sample from stream A.   28.

29. What is the color of bromthymol blue in the sample from stream A?   29.

30. Compare the hydronium ion concentration in stream A to the hydronium ion concentration in stream B.   30.

Base your answers to questions 31 through 33 on the information below.

A student titrates 60.0 mL of $HNO_3(aq)$ with 0.30 M NaOH(aq). Phenolphthalein is used as the indicator. After adding 42.2 mL of NaOH(aq), a color change remains for 25 seconds, and the student stops the titration.

31. What color change does phenolphthalein undergo during this titration?   31.

32. What is the concentration of the HNO_3 that was titrated?   32.

33. Complete the equation below for the reaction that occurs during the titration.

$HNO_3(aq) + NaOH(aq) \;----\!\!>$ _____ + _____

Day 8: Acids, Bases and Salts - Constructed Response

Base your answers to questions 34 through 37 on the graph below. The graph shows the relationship between pH value and hydronium ion concentration for common aqueous solutions and mixtures.

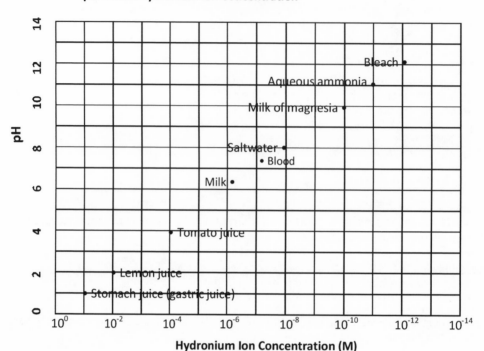

pH Versus Hydronium Ion Concentration

	Write your answers here.
34. According to this graph, which mixture is approximately 100 times more acidic than milk of magnesia?	34.
35. According to the graph, which mixture is approximately 10 times less acidic than aqueous ammonia?	35.
36. What color is thymol blue when added to milk of magnesia?	36.
37. What is the hydronium concentration of tomato juice?	37.

14 Days of Questions for Regents and Final Exams Practice

Day 9: Kinetic and Equilibrium - Multiple Choices

1. Energy needed to start a chemical reaction is called
   1) Kinetic energy
   2) Activation energy
   3) Potential energy
   4) Ionization energy

2. Two particles collide with proper orientation. The collision will be effective if the particles have
   1) High activation energy
   2) High electronegativity
   3) Sufficient kinetic energy
   4) Sufficient potential energy

3. Which information about a chemical reaction is provided by a potential energy diagram?
   1) the oxidation states of the reactants and products
   2) the average kinetic energy of the reactants and products
   3) the change in solubility of the reacting substances
   4) the energy released or absorbed during the reaction

4. A catalyst works by
   1) increasing the potential energy of the reactants
   2) increasing the energy released during a reaction
   3) decreasing the potential energy of the products
   4) decreasing the activation energy required for a reaction

5. Why can an increase in temperature lead to more effective collisions between reactant particles and an increase in the rate of a chemical reaction?
   1) The activation energy of the reaction increases.
   2) The activation energy of the reaction decreases.
   3) The number of molecules with sufficient energy to react increases.
   4) The number of molecules with sufficient energy to react decreases.

6. A 1.0-gram sample of powdered Zn reacts faster with HCl than a single 1.0-gram piece of Zn because the surface atoms in powdered Zn have
   1) higher average kinetic energy
   2) lower average kinetic energy
   3) more contact with the H^+ ions in the acid
   4) less contact with the H^+ ions in the acid

7. In a reversible reaction, chemical equilibrium is attained when the
   1) rate of the forward reaction is greater than the rate of the reverse reaction
   2) rate of the reverse reaction is greater than the rate of the forward reaction
   3) concentration of the reactants reaches zero
   4) concentration of the products remains constant

8. The net energy released or absorbed during a reversible chemical reaction is equal to
   1) the activation energy of the endothermic reaction
   2) the activation energy of the exothermic reaction
   3) the difference between the potential energy of the products and the potential energy of the reactants
   4) the sum of the potential energy of the products and the potential energy of the reactants

9. Systems in nature tend to undergo changes toward
   1) Lower energy and higher entropy
   2) Lower energy and lower entropy
   3) Higher energy and lower entropy
   4) Higher energy and higher entropy

10. Increasing temperature on equilibrium reactions favors
    1) Exothermic reactions, only
    2) Endothermic reactions, only
    3) Both exothermic and endothermic reactions
    4) Neither exothermic nor endothermic reactions

Day 9: Kinetic and Equilibrium - Multiple Choices

11. In each of the four beakers shown below, a 2.0-centimeter strip of magnesium ribbon reacts with 100 milliliters of HCl(aq) under the conditions shown.

A

0.1 M HCl
20°C

B

1.0 M HCl
20°C

C

0.1 M HCl
50°C

D

1.0 M HCl
50°C

In which beaker will the reaction occur at the fastest rate?
1) A   2)   3) C   4) D

12. Based on the nature of the reactants in each equation, which reaction at 25°C will occur at the fastest rate?
1) $KI(aq)$ + $AgNO_3(aq)$ → $AgI(s)$ + $KNO_3(aq)$
2) $2C(s)$ + $O_2(g)$ → $2CO(g)$
3) $2SO_2(g)$ + $O_2(g)$ → $2SO_3(g)$
4) $NH_3(g)$ + $HCl(g)$ → $NH_4Cl(s)$

13. Given the reaction:
I   +   I   → I_2 +   energy
This reaction has
1) $+\Delta H$ because the products have less energy than the reactants
2) $+\Delta H$ because the products have more energy than the reactants
3) $-\Delta H$ because the products have less energy than the reactants
4) $-\Delta H$ because the products have more energy than the reactants

14. Given the chemical change
$2H_2O(l)$ + 572 kJ   → $2H_2(g)$ + $O_{2(g)}$

This reaction
1) Is endothermic and releases 572 kJ of heat energy
2) Is endothermic and absorbs 572 kJ of heat energy
3) Is exothermic and releases 572 kJ of heat energy
4) Is exothermic and absorbs 572 kJ of heat energy

15. Given the balanced equation:
$I_2(s)$ + energy → $I_2(g)$

As a sample of $I_2(s)$ sublimes to $I_2(g)$, the entropy of the sample
1) increases because the particles are less randomly arranged
2) increases because the particles are more randomly arranged
3) decreases because the particles are less randomly arranged
4) decreases because the particles are more randomly arranged

16. Which balanced equation represents a phase equilibrium?
1) $H_2(g)$ + $I_2(g)$ ↔ $2HI(g)$
2) $2NO_2(g)$ ↔ $N_2O_4(g)$
3) $Cl_2(g)$ ↔ $Cl_2(l)$
4) $3O_2(g)$ ↔ $2O_3(g)$

Day 9: Kinetic and Equilibrium - Multiple Choices

17. A potential energy diagram for a chemical reaction is given below.

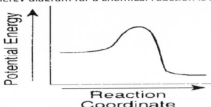

According to Reference Table I, which reaction could be represented by this potential energy diagram?

1) $2C(s) + 3H_2(g) \rightarrow C_2H_6(g)$
2) $2C(s) + 2H_2(g \rightarrow C_2H_4(g)$
3) $N_2(g) + O_2(g) \rightarrow 2NO(g)$
4) $NH_4Cl(s) \rightarrow NH_4^+(aq) + Cl^-(aq)$

18. The potential energy diagram for a chemical reaction is shown below.

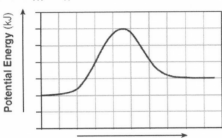

Each interval on the axis labeled "Potential Energy (kJ)" represents 40 kilojoules.
What is the heat of reaction?

1) –120 kJ   2) –40 kJ   3) +40 kJ   4) +160 kJ

19. Given the equilibrium reaction below

$$N_2O_4 + 58.1 kJ \leftrightarrow 2NO_2(g)$$

If heat is decreased on the reaction,
1) the rate of the forward reaction will increase, and equilibrium will shift to the right
2) the rate of the forward reaction will increase, and equilibrium will shift to the left
3) the rate of the reverse reaction will increase, and equilibrium will shift to the right
4) the rate of the reverse reaction will increase, and equilibrium will shift to the left

20. Given the reaction:
$$N_2(g) + O_2(g) + 182.6 kJ \leftrightarrow 2NO(g)$$

Which change would cause an immediate increase in the rate of the forward reaction?
1) increasing the concentration of $NO(g)$
2) increasing the concentration of $N_2(g)$
3) decreasing the reaction temperature
4) decreasing the reaction pressure

21. Given the system at equilibrium:
$$2POCl_3(g) + energy \leftrightarrow 2PCl_3(g) + O_2(g)$$
Which changes occur when $O_2(g)$ is added to this system?
1) The equilibrium shifts to the right and the concentration of $PCl_3(g)$ increases.
2) The equilibrium shifts to the right and the concentration of $PCl_3(g)$ decreases.
3) The equilibrium shifts to the left and the concentration of $PCl_3(g)$ increases.
4) The equilibrium shifts to the left and the concentration of $PCl_3(g)$ decreases

Day 9: Kinetic and Equilibrium - Constructed Response

Base your answer to questions 22 through 25 on the potential energy diagram below.

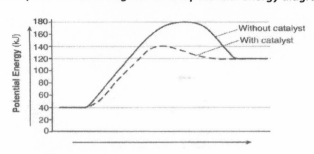

22. Explain, in terms of the function of a catalyst, why the curves on the potential energy diagram for the catalyzed and uncatalyzed reactions are different.

22.

23. What is the activation energy for the forward reaction with the catalyst?

23.

24. What is the heat of reaction for the reverse reaction without the catalyst?

24.

25. What is the heat of the activated complex for the reaction with the catalyst?

25.

Base your answers to questions 26 through 29 on the information below.

An investigation was conducted to study the effect of the concentration of a reactant on the total time needed to complete a chemical reaction. Four trials of the same reaction were performed. In each trial the initial concentration of the reactant was different. The time needed for the chemical reaction to be completed was measured. The data for each of the four trials are shown in the data table below.

Reactant Concentration and Reaction Time

Trial	Initial Concentration (M)	Reaction Time (s)
1	0.020	11
2	0.015	14
3	0.010	23
4	0.005	58

26. On the grid, mark an appropriate scale on the axis labeled "Reaction Time (s)." An appropriate scale is one that allows a trend to be seen.

27. On the same grid, plot the data from the table. Circle and connect the points .

28. State the effect of the concentration of the reactant on the rate of the chemical reaction.

29. In a different experiment involving the same reaction, it was found that an increase in temperature increased the rate of the reaction. Explain this result in terms of collision theory.

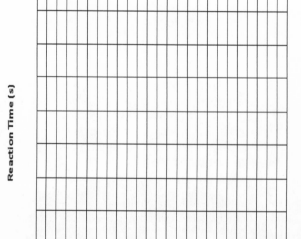

Reaction Time Versus Initial Concentration

Day 9: Kinetic and Equilibrium - Constructed Response

Base your answers to questions 30 through 32 on the information below.

Nitrogen gas, hydrogen gas, and ammonia gas are in equilibrium in a closed container at constant temperature and pressure. The equation below represents this equilibrium.

$$N_2(g) + 3H_2(g < ====== > 2NH_3(g)$$

The graph below shows the initial concentration of each gas, the changes that occur as a result of adding $H_2(g)$ to the system, and the final concentration when equilibrium is reestablished.

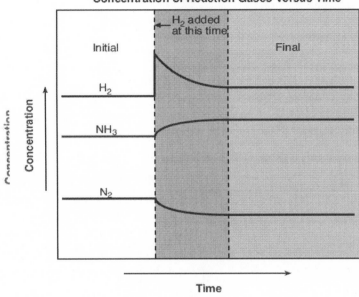

Concentration of Reaction Gases Versus Time

30. What information on the graph indicates that the system was initially at equilibrium?

    30.

31. Explain, in terms of Le Chatelier's Principle, why the final concentration of $NH_3(g)$ is greater than the initial concentration of $NH_3(g)$.

    31.

32. Explain, in terms of collision theory, why the concentration of $H_2(g)$ begins to decrease immediately after more $H_2(g)$ is added to the system.

    32.

Day 10: Organic Chemistry - Multiple Choices

1. A compound that is classified as organic must contain the element
   1) Carbon
   2) Nitrogen
   3) Oxygen
   4) Hydrogen

2. Compared with the rate of an inorganic reaction, the rate of an organic reaction is usually
   1) Faster, because organic compounds are ionic substances
   2) Faster, because organic compounds are molecular substances
   3) Slower, because organic compounds are ionic substances
   4) Slower, because organic compounds are molecular substances

3. A series of hydrocarbons in which each member of a group differs from the preceding member by one carbon is called
   1) A periodic series
   2) A homologous series
   3) An actinide series
   4) A lanthanide series

4. The total number of electrons shared between two adjacent carbon atoms in a saturated hydrocarbon is
   1) 1
   2) 2
   3) 3
   4) 4

5. Which series of hydrocarbons contain unsaturated molecule, only?
   1) Alkane and benzene series
   2) Alkyl and alkene series
   3) Alkene and alkyne series
   4) Alkane and alkyne series

6. Each molecule of butane will contain a total of how many carbon atoms?
   1) 2
   2) 4
   3) 6
   4) 8

7. The total number of electrons shared between two carbon atoms in a triple bond is
   1) 2
   2) 3
   3) 5
   4) 6

8. As the length of the chain of carbon atoms in molecules of alkene series increases, the number of double bonds per molecule
   1) Increases
   2) Decreases
   3) Remains the same

9. The general formula for all alkyne molecules is
   1) C_nH_{2n}
   2) C_nH_{2n+2}
   3) C_nH_{2n-2}
   4) C_nH_{2n+6}

10. Which functional group is found in all alcohols?
    1) $-OH$
    2) $-COOH$
    3) $-CHO$
    4) $-O-$

11. Which IUPAC name ending is common for the class of organic compounds called aldehydes?
    1) $-yl$
    2) $-al$
    3) $-ol$
    4) $-one$

12. Which is true of organic acids?
    1) They are non-electrolytes
    2) They are weak electrolytes
    3) They turn litmus blue
    4) They turn phenolphthalein pink

13. Two isomers must have the same
    1) Percent composition
    2) Arrangement of atoms
    3) Physical properties
    4) Chemical properties

14. The formation of large molecules from smaller molecules is an example of
    1) Saponification
    2) Decomposition
    3) Substitution
    4) Polymerization

15. What type of organic reaction describes the burning of a hydrocarbon in the presence of oxygen?
    1) Addition
    2) Decomposition
    3) Combustion
    4) Substitution

Day 10: Organic Chemistry - Multiple Choices

16. Each molecule of pentyne will contain a total of how many hydrogen atoms?
    1) 5   2) 8   3) 10   4) 12

17. Given the organic structure below,

$$H-\overset{\displaystyle H}{\underset{\displaystyle H}{C}}-\overset{\displaystyle H}{\underset{\displaystyle H}{C}}-OH$$

    Which IUPAC name is possible for a compound with this structure?
    1) Methane   2) Ethanol   3) Propene   4) Butanol

18. Which two formulas are of compounds belonging to the alkane series?
    1) C_4H_6 and C_4H_8 3) C_2H_4 and C_4H_6
    2) $C_{11}H_{22}$ and $C_{11}H_{24}$ 4) C_8H_{18} and C_9H_{20}

19. Which set of IUPAC names are of compounds that are classified as alkenes?
    1) Methyl and ethyl   3) Ethane and pentene
    2) Ethene and decene   4) Ethyne and ethane

20. Which is an IUPAC name of a secondary alcohol?
    1) 1,2,-ethandiol   3) 1,2,3-propanetriol
    2) Propanol   4) 2-butanol

21. The formula of which compound represents an alcohol?
    1) CH_3CHO 2) CH_3CH_2OH 3) CH_3COOH 4) CH_3COOCH_3

22. A formula of which compound is an organic halide?
    1) $CH_3CH_2NH_2$ 3) $CH_3CH_2CH_2Br$
    2) CH_3OCH_3 4) HCl

23. A compound of which IUPAC name represents an aldehyde?
    1) Pentane   2) Butanoic   3) Propanol   4) Hexanal

24. The structure

$$H-\overset{\displaystyle H}{\underset{\displaystyle H}{C}}-\overset{\displaystyle}{\underset{\displaystyle OH}{C}}=O$$

is classified as an organic acid because it contains

    1) –OH groups   2) –COOH group   3) $-C-C-$ bonds   4) $C = O$ bond

25. The structure of which compound contains the functional group $-O-$
    1) Dimethyl ether   3) Propanone
    2) Methyl Butanoate   4) Ethanoic acid

26. The condensed formula that represents methyl propanoate is
    1) $CH_3CH_2COOCH_3$ 3) CH_3CH_2CHO
    2) CH_3COOH 4) CH_3CHO

27. Which compound is an isomer of butanoic acid, $CH_3CH_2CH_2COOH$?
    1) $CH_3CH_2CH_2CH_2OH$ 3) $CH_3CH_2CH_2CH_2COOH$
    2) $CH_3CH_2COOCH_3$ 4) $CH_3CH_2OCH_3$

28. Given the reaction below:
$$C_4H_8 \quad + \quad Cl_2 \text{ ---------> } C_4H_8Cl_2$$
    What type of reaction is represented by the equation.

    1) Combustion   2) Substitution   3) Polymerization   4) Addition

29. Which formula correctly represents a compound formed from a reaction between C_2H_4 and Br_2?
    1) Bromoethene   3) Bromoethane
    2) 1,2-dibromoethane   4) 1,2-dibromoethene

30. Given the equation
$$C_2H_6 \quad + \quad F_2 \text{ ---------> } X \quad + \quad HF$$

    What is the name of compound X produced?
    1) Ethene   2) Fluoroethane   3) 1,2-difluoroethane   4) Fluoropropane

Day 10: Organic Chemistry - Constructed Response

Base your answers to questions 31 through 33 on the information below.

Ethene (common name ethylene) is a commercially important organic compound. Millions of tons of ethene are produce by the chemical industry each year. Ethene is used in the manufacture of synthetic fibers for carpeting and clothing, and it is widely used in the making of polyethylene. Low-density polyethylene can be stretched into a clear, thin film that is used for wrapping food products and consumer goods. High-density polyethylene is molded into bottles for milk and other liquids. Ethene can also be oxidized to produce ethylene glycol, which is widely used in antifreeze for automobiles. The structural formula for ethylene glycol is:

```
       H   H
       |   |
   H – C – C – H
       |   |
      OH  OH
```

At standard atmosphere pressure, the boiling point of ethylene glycol is $198^{\circ}C$, compared to ethene that boils at $-104^{\circ}C$.

31. Explain, in terms of bonding, why ethene is an   31.
    unsaturated hydrocarbon.

32. According to the information in the reading passage,   32.
    state two consumer products manufactured from ethene.

33. Identify the type of organic reaction by which ethene is   33.
    made into polyethylene.

Day 10: Organic Chemistry - Constructed Response

Base your answers to questions 34 through 37 on the information and diagram below, and on your knowledge of chemistry.

Crude oil is a mixture of many hydrocarbons that have different numbers of carbon atoms. The use of fractionating towers allows the separation of this mixture bases on the boiling points of the hydrocarbons.

To begin the separation process, the crude oil is heated to about 400°C in a furnace, causing many of the hydrocarbons of the crude oil to vaporize. The vaporized mixture is pumped into a fractionating tower that is usually more than 30 meters tall. The temperature of the tower is highest at the bottom. As vaporized samples of hydrocarbons travel up the tower, they cool and condense. The liquid hydrocarbons are collected on trays and removed from the tower. The diagram below illustrates the fractional distillation of the crude oil and the temperature ranges in which the different hydrocarbons condense.

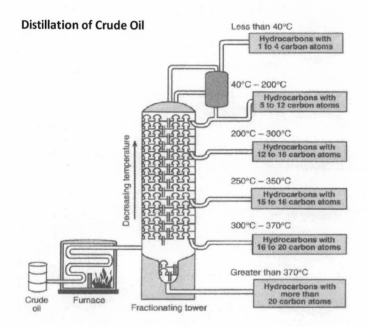

34. State the trend between the boiling point of the hydrocarbons contained in the crude oil and the number of carbon atoms in these molecules.

34.

35. Describe the relationship between the strength of the intermolecular forces and the number of carbon atoms in the different hydrocarbon molecules.

35.

36. Write the IUPAC name of one of the saturated hydrocarbon that leaves the fractionating tower at less than 40°C.

36.

37. How many hydrogen atoms are present in one molecule of octane.

37.

Day 11: Redox and Electrochemistry - Multiple Choices

1. Which particles are gained and lost during a redox reaction?
   1) Protons   2) Electrons   3) Neutrons   4) Positrons

2. Which statement correctly describes a redox reaction?
   1) The oxidation half-reaction and the reduction half-reaction occur simultaneously
   2) The oxidation half-reaction occurs before the reduction half-reaction
   3) The oxidation half-reaction occurs after the reduction half-reaction
   4) The oxidation half-reaction occurs spontaneously but the reduction half-reaction does not

3. The sum of all oxidation numbers of atoms in a chemical formula must equal
   1) -1   2) 0   3) 1   4) 2

4. In an oxidation-reduction chemical reaction, reduction is a
   1) Gain of protons   3) Gain of electrons
   2) Loss of protons   4) Loss of electrons

5. What kind of reaction occurs in a voltaic cell?
   1) Non-spontaneous oxidation-reduction
   2) Spontaneous oxidation-reduction
   3) Non-spontaneous oxidation, only
   4) Spontaneous reduction, only

6. An electrolytic cell is different from a voltaic cell because in an electrolytic cell
   1) An electrical current is produced
   2) An electrical current causes a chemical reaction
   3) A redox reaction occurs
   4) A spontaneous reaction occurs

7. The negative electrode in a voltaic cell is the
   1) Cathode, where electrons are gained
   2) Cathode, where electrons are lost
   3) Anode, where electrons are gained
   4) Anode, where electrons are lost

8. What type of chemical reaction occurs in all electrochemical cells?
   1) Neutralization   3) Redox
   2) Double replacement   4) Hydrolysis

9. In any redox reaction, the substance that undergoes reduction will
   1) lose electrons and have a decrease in oxidation number
   2) lose electrons and have an increase in oxidation number
   3) gain electrons and have a decrease in oxidation number
   4) gain electrons and have an increase in oxidation number

10. In all redox reactions, there is conservation of
    1) Mass, but not charge   3) Both mass and charge
    2) Charge, but not mass   4) Neither mass nor charge

11. Which is true of a reducing agent in oxidation-reduction reactions?
    1) A reducing agent loses electrons, and is oxidized
    2) A reducing agent loses electrons, and is reduced
    3) A reducing agent gains electrons, and is oxidized
    4) A reducing agent gains electrons, and is reduced

Day 11: Redox and Electrochemistry - Multiple Choices

12. What is the oxidation number of nitrogen in HNO_3?
    1) +5   2) +4   3) -3   4) -1

13. What is the oxidation number of hydrogen in LiH?
    1) 0   2) +1   3) +2   4) -1

14. What is the oxidation number of Cr in the polyatomic ion, $Cr_2O_7^{2-}$?
    1) +7   2) +6   3) -2   4) +2

15. In which substance does phosphorus have an oxidation number of +3?
    1) P_4O_{10} 2) PCl_5 3) $Ca_3(PO_4)_2$ 4) KH_2PO_3

16. Which equation represents an oxidation – reduction reaction?
    1) SO_2 + H_2O $\rightarrow$ H_2SO_3
    2) SO_3^{2-} + $2H^+$ $\rightarrow$ H_2SO_4
    3) O_2 + $2H_2$ $\rightarrow$ $2H_2O$
    4) OH^- + H^+ $\rightarrow$ H_2O

17. In which oxidation number change would a species in a redox reaction gain the most number of electrons?
    1) +3 to -1   3) 0 to +4
    2) +6 to +3   4) +3 to +7

18. Which half-reaction equation correctly represents a reduction reaction?
    1) Li^0 + e^- $\rightarrow$ Li^+
    2) Na^0 + e^- $\rightarrow$ Na^+
    3) Br_2^0 + $2e^-$ $\rightarrow$ $2Br^-$
    4) Cl_2^0 + e^- $\rightarrow$ $2Cl^-$

19. Consider the half-reaction equation below:
    $$Li^0 \rightarrow Li^+ + e^-$$
    The Li^0 is
    1) Oxidized, and is the reducing agent
    2) Oxidized, and is the oxidizing agent
    3) Reduced, and is the reducing agent
    4) Reduced, and is the oxidizing agent

20. In the oxidation-reduction reaction below,

    $$2Al + 3Ni^{2+} \rightarrow 2Al^{3+} + 3Ni$$

    Which species acts as an oxidizing agent?
    1) Al   2) Al^{3+} 3) Ni   4) Ni^{2+}

21. In the reaction,

    $$Mg + ZnCl_2 \rightarrow MgCl_2 + Zn$$

    Which is true of the magnesium?
    1) It is oxidized by losing electrons
    2) It is oxidized by gaining electrons
    3) It is reduced by losing electrons
    4) It is reduced by gaining electrons

Day 11: Redox and Electrochemistry - Multiple Choices

22. Given the cell diagram below

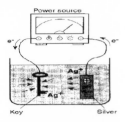

Which statement best describes the key in this diagram?
1) It acts as the anode, and is negative
2) It acts as the anode, and is positive
3) It acts as the cathode, and is negative
4) It acts as the cathode, and is positive

23. Given the reaction:

$$Mg(s) \ + \ FeSO_4(aq) \ \rightarrow \ Fe(s) \ + \ MgSO_4(aq)$$

The reaction would most likely occur in
1) A voltaic cell, and will produce energy
2) An electrolytic cell, and will produce energy
3) A voltaic cell, and will absorb energy
4) An electrolytic cell, and will absorb energy

24. Given a cell diagram below:

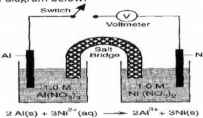

$$2\,Al(s) + 3Ni^{2+}(aq) \longrightarrow 2Al^{3+} + 3Ni(s)$$

When the switch is closed, which species will be oxidized in this electrochemical cell?
1) Al^{3+} ions   2) Al atoms   3) Ni^{2+} ions   4) Ni atoms

25. Consider the reaction below:

$$2H_2O \ + \ electricity \ \rightarrow \ 2H_2 \ + \ O_2$$

In which type of cell would this reaction most likely occur?
1) A voltaic, because it releases energy
2) An electrolytic, because it releases energy
3) A voltaic, because it absorbs energy
4) An electrolytic, because it absorbs energy

26. Which ion is most easily reduced?
1) Zn^{2+} 2) Mg^{2+} 3) Pb^{2+} 4) Na^+

27. Which element is likely to be obtained from the electrolytic process of the fused salt?
1) Br   2) Cu   3) H   4) K

28. In an electrolytic cell, which ion would migrate through solution to the positive electrode?
1) a hydrogen ion
2) a fluoride ion
3) an ammonium ion
4) a hydronium ion

Day 11: Redox and Electrochemistry - Constructed Response

Base your answers to questions 29 through 31 on the diagram and balanced equation below, which represents the electrolysis of molten NaCl.

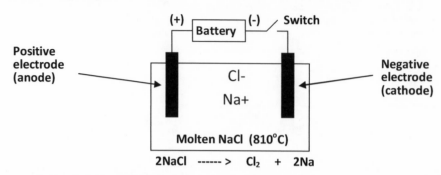

29. Write the balanced half-reaction for the reduction   29.
    that occurs in this electrolytic cell.

30. What is the purpose of the battery in this   30.
    electrolytic cell?

31. When the switch is closed, which electrode   31.
    will attract the sodium ions?

Base your answers to questions 32 and 33 on the equation below.

$$4\,Al(s) \quad + \quad 3O_2(g) \quad ------> \quad 2\,Al_2O_3\,(s)$$

32. Write a balanced oxidation half-reaction equation   32.
    for this reaction.

33. What is the oxidation number of oxygen in Al_2O_3?   33.

Base your answers to questions 34 through 39 on the following redox reaction, which occurs spontaneously.

$$Zn \quad + \quad Cr^{3+} \quad -------> \quad Zn^{2+} \quad + \quad Cr$$

34. State what happens to the number of protons in a   34.
    Zn atom when it changes to Zn^{2+} as the redox
    reaction occurs.

35. Which half-reaction occurs at the anode?   35.

36. Which species loses electrons and which species   36. Loses:
    gains electrons?
                                                        Gains:

37. Write the half-reaction for the oxidation that occurs.   37.

38. Write the half-reaction for the reduction that occurs.   38.

39. Balance the redox equation using the smallest   39. __Zn + __Cr^{3+} ----> __Zn^{2+} + __Cr
    whole-number coefficients.

Day 12: Nuclear Chemistry - Multiple Choices

1. Which process converts an atom from one element to another when the nucleus of an atom is bombarded with high-energy particles?
   1) Artificial transmutation
   2) Addition polymerization
   3) Natural transmutation
   4) Condensation polymerization

2. Spontaneous decay of certain elements in nature occurs because these elements have a
   1) Disproportionate ratio of electrons to protons
   2) Disproportionate ratio of neutrons to protons
   3) High reactivity with oxygen
   4) Low reactivity with oxygen

3. The energy released by a nuclear reaction results primarily from
   1) Breaking of bonds between atoms
   2) Formation of bonds between atoms
   3) Conversion of mass into energy
   4) Conversions of energy into mass

4. An electron has a charge identical to that of
   1) A positron
   2) A beta particle
   3) An alpha particle
   4) A proton

5. Which nuclear emission symbol has neither mass nor charge?
   1) α
   2) $\beta-$
   3) $\beta+$
   4) γ

6. Which list is showing the particles arranged in order of decreasing penetrating power?
   1) Gamma $\rightarrow$ Beta $\rightarrow$ Alpha
   2) Beta $\rightarrow$ Gamma $\rightarrow$ Alpha
   3) Alpha $\rightarrow$ Beta $\rightarrow$ Gamma
   4) Gamma $\rightarrow$ Alpha $\rightarrow$ Beta

7. Which nuclear emission moving through an electric field would be attracted toward a positive electrode?
   1) Gamma radiation
   2) Proton
   3) Beta Particle
   4) Alpha particle

8. When an alpha particle is emitted by an atom, the atomic number of the atom
   1) Increases by 2
   2) Increases by 4
   3) Decreases by 2
   4) Decreases by 4

9. Cobalt-60 and Iodine-131 are radioactive isotopes that are used in
   1) Dating geologic formations
   2) Industrial measurements
   3) Medical procedures
   4) Nuclear power

10. One benefit of nuclear fission reactions is
    1) Nuclear reaction meltdowns
    2) Storage of waste materials
    3) Biological exposure
    4) Production of energy

11. Diagnostic injections of radioisotopes used in medicine normally have
    1) Short half-lives and are quickly eliminated from the body
    2) Short half-lives and are slowly eliminated from the body
    3) Long half-lives and are quickly eliminated from the body
    4) Long half-lives and are slowly eliminated from the body

12. A beta or an alpha particle may be spontaneously emitted from
    1) A ground-state atom
    2) A stable nucleus
    3) An excited electron
    4) An unstable nucleus

13. Which Group 18 element is naturally radioactive and has no known stable isotope?
    1) Ar
    2) Po
    3) Xe
    4) Kr

14. Which notation of a radioisotope is correctly paired with the notation of its emission particle?

    1) $^{32}_{15}P$ and $^{0}_{+1}e$
    2) $^{226}_{88}Ra$ and $^{0}_{-1}e$
    3) $^{239}_{90}Pu$ and $^{4}_{2}He$
    4) $^{3}_{1}H$ and $^{0}_{+1}e$

Day 12: Nuclear Chemistry - Multiple Choices

15. Artificial transmutation is represented by which nuclear equation?

1) $^{238}_{92}U + ^{4}_{2}He \longrightarrow ^{241}_{94}Pu + ^{1}_{0}n$

3) $^{235}_{92}U + ^{1}_{0}n \longrightarrow ^{87}_{35}Br + ^{146}_{57}La + 3^{1}_{0}n$

2) $^{16}_{7}N \longrightarrow ^{16}_{8}O + ^{0}_{-1}e$

4) $^{2}_{1}H + ^{1}_{1}H \longrightarrow ^{3}_{2}He$

16. Given the nuclear reaction

$$^{19}_{10}Ne \longrightarrow ^{0}_{+1}e + ^{19}_{9}F$$

The reaction is an example of
1) Fission
2) Natural transmutation
3) Fusion
4) Artificial transmutation

17. Given the nuclear equation below

$$^{121}_{53}I \rightarrow X + ^{121}_{52}Te$$

The reaction is best described as
1) Beta decay
2) Artificial transmutation
3) Positron emission
4) Alpha decay

18. Exactly how much time elapses before 16 grams of potassium-42 decays, leaving 2 grams of the original isotope?
1) 98.88 hours
2) 24.72 hours
3) 37.08 hours
4) 49.44 hours

19. A radioactive isotope of an element decays from 20 grams to 5 grams in 8 minutes. What is the half-life of this radioisotope?
1) 15 minutes
2) 4 minutes
3) 10 minutes
4) 20 minutes

20. The half-life of a radioisotope is 20.0 minutes. What is the total amount of a 10 g sample of this isotope remaining after 1 hour?
1) 1.25 g
2) 2.50 g
3) 3.33 g
4) 5.00 g

21. Approximately what fraction of an original ^{60}Co sample remains unchanged after 21 years?
1) $^{1}/_{2}$
2) $^{1}/_{4}$
3) $^{1}/_{8}$
4) $^{1}/_{16}$

22. A sample of which radioisotope will have the greatest remaining amount after 100 years of decaying?
1) 5 g of Co-60
2) 5 g of H-3
3) 5 g of Kr-85
4) 5 g of Sr-90

23. Radioactive dating of the remains of organic materials can be done by comparing the ratio of which two isotopes?
1) Uranium -235 to Uranium -238
2) Carbon-14 to Carbon-12
3) Nitrogen-14 to Nitrogen-16
4) Hydrogen-2 to Hydrogen-3

24. If 8.0 grams of a sample of ^{60}Co existed in 1990, in what year was the remaining amount of ^{60}Co in the sample 0.50 grams?
1) 1995
2) 2000
3) 2006
4) 2011

25. If 3.0 grams of ^{90}Sr in a rock sample remained in 1989, approximately how many grams of ^{90}Sr were present in the original rock sample in 1931?
1) 9.0g
2) 12. g
3) 3.0 g
4) 6.0 g

14 _Days_ of Questions for Regents and Final Exams Practice

Day 12: Nuclear Chemistry - Constructed Response

Base your answers to questions 26 through 29 on the information below, which relates the numbers of neutrons and protons for specific nuclides of C, N, Ne, and S.

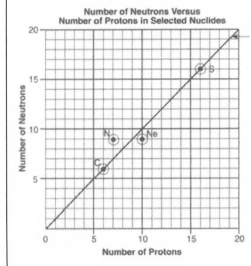

Number of Neutrons Versus Number of Protons in Selected Nuclides

This line connects the points where the neutron to proton ratio is 1 : 1

26. Based on your Reference Tables, complete the nuclear decay equation for Ne-19.

$$^{19}\text{Ne} \text{ ------} > \text{\_\_\_\_\_} + \text{_____}$$

27. Using the point plotted on the graph for nitrogen, what is the neutron-to-proton ratio of this nuclide?

28. Explain, in terms of atomic particles, why S-32 is a stable nuclide.

29. What is the mass number of the carbon isotope represented on the graph?

Base your answers to questions 30 to 32 on the information and table below.

Some radioisotopes use tracers to make it possible for doctors to see the images of internal body parts and observe their functions. The table below lists information about three radioisotopes and their body part each radioisotope is used to study.

Medical uses of Some Radioisotopes

Radioisotope	Half-life	Decay Mode	Body Part
^{24}Na	15 hours	Beta	Circulatory system
^{59}Fe	44.5 days	Beta	Red blood cells
^{131}I	8.1 days	Beta	Thyroid

30. It could take up to 60. hours for a radioisotope to be delivered to the hospital from the laboratory where it is produced. What fraction of an original sample of ^{24}Na remains unchanged after 60 hours?

30.

31. Complete the equation for the nuclear decay of the radioisotope used to study red blood cells. Include both atomic number and the mass number for each missing particle.

31. $^{59}\text{Fe} \text{ ------} > \text{\_\_\_\_\_} + \text{\_\_\_\_\_}$

32. A patient at a clinic was injected with a 100 mg sample of Iodine-131 during a routine thyroid function test. How much of the original iodine-131 will remain in the patient's body after approximately 48 hours?

32.

Day 13 and 14 questions comprise a full actual Regents Exam practice.

Day 13: Practice Regents Exam - Part A and B-1

Part A: Answer all questions in this part

Directions (1 – 30): For each statement or question, write on the separate answer sheet the number of the word or expression that, of those given, best completes the statement or answer the question. Some questions may require the use of the Reference tables for Physical Setting/Chemistry.

1. What is the total number of valence electrons in a calcium atom in the ground state?
(1) 8
(2) 2
(3) 18
(4) 20

2. Which subatomic particles are located in the nucleus of an He-4 atom?
(1) electrons and neutrons
(2) electrons and protons
(3) neutrons and protons
(4) neutrons, protons, and electrons

3. In the late 1800s, experiments using cathode ray tubes led to the discovery of the
(1) electron
(2) neutron
(3) positron
(4) proton

4. The atomic mass of titanium is 47.88 atomic mass units. This atomic mass represents the
(1) total mass of all the protons and neutrons in an atom of Ti
(2) total mass of all the protons, neutrons, and electrons in an atom of Ti
(3) weighted average mass of the most abundant isotope of Ti
(4) weighted average mass of all the naturally occurring isotopes of Ti

5. An atom of which element has the largest atomic radius?
(1) Fe
(2) Mg
(3) Si
(4) Zn

6. Which element requires the least amount of energy to remove the most loosely held electron from a gaseous atom in the ground state?
(1) bromine
(2) calcium
(3) sodium
(4) silver

7. A balanced equation representing a chemical reaction can be written using
(1) chemical formulas and mass numbers
(2) chemical formulas and coefficients
(3) first ionization energies and mass numbers
(4) first ionization energies and coefficients

8. Every water molecule has two hydrogen atoms bonded to one oxygen atom. This fact supports the concept that elements in a compound are
(1) chemically combined in a fixed proportion
(2) chemically combined in proportions that vary
(3) physically mixed in a fixed proportion
(4) physically mixed in proportions that vary

9. The percent composition by mass of nitrogen in NH_4OH (gram- formula mass = 35 grams/mole) is equal to

(1) $\dfrac{4}{35} \times 100$

(2) $\dfrac{14}{35} \times 100$

(3) $\dfrac{35}{14} \times 100$

(4) $\dfrac{35}{4} \times 100$

10. Which Group 15 element exists as diatomic molecules at STP?
(1) phosphorus
(2) nitrogen
(3) bismuth
(4) arsenic

11. What is the total number of electrons shared in a double covalent bond?
(1) 1
(2) 2
(3) 3
(4) 4

12. Given the balanced equation representing a reaction:
$$Br_2 + \text{energy} \longrightarrow Br + Br$$
Which statement describes the energy change and bonds in this reaction?
(1) Energy is released as bonds are broken.
(2) Energy is released as bonds are formed.
(3) Energy is absorbed as bonds are broken.
(4) Energy is absorbed as bonds are formed.

13. Which substance can not be broken down by a chemical change?
(1) methane
(2) propanal
(3) tungsten
(4) water

Day 13: Practice Regents Exam - Part A and B-1

14. Object A at 40.°C and object B at 80.°C are placed in contact with each other. Which statement describes the heat flow between the objects?
    (1) Heat flows from object A to object B.
    (2) Heat flows from object B to object A.
    (3) Heat flows in both directions between the objects.
    (4) No heat flow occurs between the objects.

15. Which unit can be used to express the concentration of a solution?
    (1) L/s   (3) ppm
    (2) J/g   (4) kPa

16. Which formula represents a mixture?
    (1) $C_6H_{12}O_6(\ell)$ (3) LiCl(aq)
    (2) $C_6H_{12}O_6(s)$ (4) LiCl(s)

17. Which sample has particles with the lowest average kinetic energy?
    (1) 1.0 g of I_2 at 50.°C
    (2) 2.0 g of I_2 at 30.°C
    (3) 7.0 g of I_2 at 40.°C
    (4) 9.0 g of I_2 at 20.°C

18. Which gas sample at STP has the same total number of molecules as 2.0 liters of $CO_2(g)$ at STP?
    (1) 5.0 L of $CO_2(g)$ (3) 3.0 L of $H_2S(g)$
    (2) 2.0 L of $Cl_2(g)$ (4) 6.0 L of He(g)

19. Petroleum can be separated by distillation because the hydrocarbons in petroleum are
    (1) elements with identical boiling points
    (2) elements with different boiling points
    (3) compounds with identical boiling points
    (4) compounds with different boiling points

20. Which compound is insoluble in water?
    (1) KOH   (3) Na_3PO_4
    (2) NH_4Cl (4) $PbSO_4$

21. A gas sample is at 25°C and 1.0 atmosphere. Which changes in temperature and pressure will cause this sample to behave more like an ideal gas?
    (1) decreased temperature and increased pressure
    (2) decreased temperature and decreased pressure
    (3) increased temperature and increased pressure
    (4) increased temperature and decreased pressure

22. The isotopes K-37 and K-42 have the same
    (1) decay mode
    (2) bright-line spectrum
    (3) mass number for their atoms
    (4) total number of neutrons in their atoms

23. Which element is present in all organic compounds?
    (1) carbon   (3) nitrogen
    (2) hydrogen   (4) oxygen

24. Each of four test tubes contains a different concentration of HCl(aq) at 25°C. A 1-gram cube of Zn is added to each test tube. In which test tube is the reaction occurring at the fastest rate?

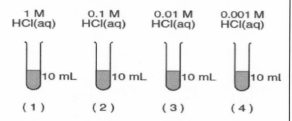

25. Which energy conversion occurs during the operation of an electrolytic cell?
    (1) chemical energy to electrical energy
    (2) electrical energy to chemical energy
    (3) nuclear energy to electrical energy
    (4) electrical energy to nuclear energy

26. Which compound is an Arrhenius acid?
    (1) CaO   (3) K_2O
    (2) HCl   (4) NH_3

27. Based on the results of testing colorless solutions with indicators, which solution is most acidic?
    (1) a solution in which bromthymol blue is blue
    (2) a solution in which bromcresol green is blue
    (3) a solution in which phenolphthalein is pink
    (4) a solution in which methyl orange is red

28. According to one acid-base theory, water acts as an acid when an H_2O molecule
    (1) accepts an H^+ (3) accepts an H^-
    (2) donates an H^+ (4) donates an H^-

Day 13: Practice Regents Exam - Part A and B-1

29. In which type of reaction is an atom of one element converted to an atom of a different element?
(1) decomposition (3) saponification
(2) neutralization (4) transmutation

30. Which nuclide is listed with its half-life and decay mode?
(1) K-37, 1.24 h, α
(2) N-16, 7.2 s, $\beta-$
(3) Rn-222, 1.6 x 10^3 y, α
(4) U-235, 7.1 x 10^8 y, $\beta-$

Part B-1: Answer all questions in this part.

Directions (31 – 50): For each statement or question, write on the separate answer sheet the number of the word or expression that, of those given, best completes the statement or answer the question. Some questions may require the use of the Reference tables for Physical setting/Chemistry

31. Which formula represents copper(I) oxide?
(1) CuO (3) Cu_2O
(2) CuO_2 (4) Cu_2O_2

32. At STP, a 7.9-gram sample of an element has a volume of 1.69 cubic centimeters. The sample is most likely
(1) Ta (3) Te
(2) Tc (4) Ti

33. Which element, represented by X, reacts with fluorine to produce the compound XF_2?
(1) aluminum (3) magnesium
(2) argon (4) sodium

34. Each diagram below represents nucleus of a different atom.

| 1p | 1p 1n | 1p 2n | 2p 2n |
| D | E | Q | R |

Which diagrams represents nuclei of the same element?
(1) D and E, only (3) Q and R, only
(2) D, E, and Q (4) Q, R, and E

35. As atomic number increases within Group 15 on the Periodic Table, atomic radius
(1) decreases, only
(2) increases, only
(3) decreases, then increases
(4) increases, then decreases

36. Given the balanced equation representing a reaction:

$$CaO(s) + CO_2 ---> CaCO_3(s) + heat$$

What is the total mass of CaO(s) that reacts completely with 88 grams of $CO_2(g)$ to produce 200. grams of $CaCO_3(s)$?
(1) 56 g (3) 112 g
(2) 88 g (4) 288 g

37. What is the empirical formula of a compound that has a carbon-to-hydrogen ratio of 2 to 6?
(1) CH_3 (3) C_3H
(2) C_2H_6 (4) C_6H_2

38. Given the balanced equation representing a reaction:

$$H_2(g) + Cl_2(g) ---> 2HCl(g) + energy$$

Which statement describes the energy changes in this reaction?
(1) Energy is absorbed as bonds are formed, only.
(2) Energy is released as bonds are broken, only
(3) Energy is absorbed as bonds are broken, and energy is released as bonds are formed.
(4) Energy is absorbed as bonds are formed, and energy is released as bonds are broken.

39. Which solution has the highest boiling point at standard pressure?
(1) 0.10 M KCl(aq)
(2) 0.10 M K_2SO_4(aq)
(3) 0.10 M K_3PO_4(aq)
(4) 0.10 M KNO_3(aq)

Day 13: Practice Regents Exam - Part A and B-1

40. What is the Molarity of 1.5 liters of an aqueous solution that contains 52 grams of lithium fluoride, LiF (gram-formula mass = 26 grams/mole)?
    (1) 1.3 M   (3) 3.0 M
    (2) 2.0 M   (4) 0.75 M

41. What occurs when a 35-gram aluminum cube at 100°C is placed in 90. grams of water at 24°C in an insulated cup?
    (1) Heat is transferred from the aluminum to the water, and the temperature of the water decreases.
    (2) Heat is transferred from the aluminum to the water, and the temperature of the water increases.
    (3) Heat is transferred from the water to the aluminum, and the temperature of the water decreases.
    (4) Heat is transferred from the water to the aluminum, and the temperature of the water increases.

42. Which temperature is equal to 120. K?
    (1) -153°C   (3) +293°C
    (2) -120.°C   (4) +393°C

43. A rigid cylinder contains a sample of gas at STP. What is the pressure of this gas after the sample is heated to 410 K?
    (1) 1.0 atm   (3) 0.67 atm
    (2) 0.50 atm   (4) 1.5 atm

44. Given the balanced equation representing a phase change?

    $C_6H_4Cl_2(s)$ + energy ---> $C_6H_4Cl_2(g)$

    Which statement describes this change?
    (1) It is endothermic, and entropy decreases
    (2) It is endothermic, and entropy increases
    (3) It is exothermic, and entropy decreases
    (4) It is exothermic, and entropy increases

45. In a biochemical reaction, an enzyme acts as a catalyst, causing the
    (1) activation energy of the reaction to decrease
    (2) potential energy of the reactants to decrease
    (3) kinetic energy of the reactant to increase
    (4) heat of the reaction to increase

46. Given the formula for an organic compound:

    $$H - \overset{\overset{\displaystyle H}{|}}{C} - \overset{\overset{\displaystyle H}{|}}{C} - \overset{\overset{\displaystyle H}{|}}{C} - \overset{\overset{\displaystyle H}{|}}{C} - \overset{\overset{\displaystyle O}{||}}{C} - OH$$

    This compound is classified as an
    (1) aldehyde   (3) ester
    (2) amine   (4) organic acid

47. Butanal and butanone have different chemical and physical properties primarily because of differences in their
    (1) functional groups
    (2) molecular masses
    (3) molecular formula
    (4) number of carbon atoms per molecule

48. Which salt is produced when sulfuric acid and calcium react completely?
    (1) CaH_2 (3) CaS
    (2) CaO   (4) $CaSO_4$

49. Which radioisotope is used to treat thyroid disorders?
    (1) Co-60   (3) C-14
    (2) I-131   (4) U-238

Day 13: Practice Regents Exam - Part A and B-1

50. The diagram below represents an operating electrochemical cell and the balanced ionic equation for the reaction occurring in the cell.

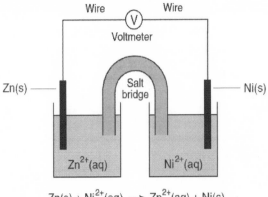

$$Zn(s) + Ni^{2+}(aq) \longrightarrow Zn^{2+}(aq) + Ni(s)$$

Which statement identifies the part of the cell that conducts electrons and describes the direction of electron flow as the cell operates?

(1) Electrons flow through the salt bridge from Ni(s) to the Zn(s)
(2) Electrons flow through the salt bridge from Zn(s) to the Ni(s)
(3) Electrons flow through the wire from Ni(s) to the Zn(s)
(4) Electrons flow through the wire from Zn(s) to the Ni(s)

Day 14: Practice Regents Exam – Constructed Response Part B-2 and C

Part B-2: **Answer all questions in this part**

Directions (51-63): Record your answers in the spaces provided in your answer booklet. Some questions may require the use of the Reference Tables for Physical Setting/Chemistry.

---

51. *In your answer booklet*, write an electron configuration for a silicon atom in an excited state. [1]

Base your answers to questions 52 and 53 on the information below.

Densities of Group 14 Elements

Element	Density at STP (g/cm³)
C	3.51
Si	2.33
Ge	5.32
Sn	7.31
Pb	11.35

52. Identify *one* element from this table for *each* type of element: metal, metalloid, and nonmetal. [1]

53. Calculate the volume of a tin block that has a mass of 95.04 grams at STP. Your response must include *both* a numerical setup and the calculated result. [2]

Base your answers to questions 54 through 56 on the elements in Group 2 on the Periodic Table.

54. State the general trend in first ionization energy for the elements in Group 2 as these elements are considered in order from top to bottom in the group. [1]

55. State, in terms of the number of electron shells, why the radius of a strontium atom in the ground state is larger than the radius of a magnesium atom in the ground state. [1]

56. Explain, in terms of atomic structure, why the elements in Group 2 have similar chemical properties. [1]

14 Days of Questions for Regents and Final Exams Practice

Day 14: Practice Regents Exam – Constructed Response Part B-2 and C

Base your answers to questions 57 and 58 on the information below.

Heat is added to a sample of liquid water, starting at 80.°C, until the entire sample is a gas at 120.°C. This process, occurring at standard pressure, is represented by the balanced equation below.

$$H_2O(\ell) + heat \quad \text{--------}> \quad H_2O(g)$$

57. In the box *in your answer booklet*, using the key, draw a particle diagram to represent *at least five* molecules of the product of this physical change at 120.°C. [2]

58. On the diagram *in your answer booklet*, complete the heating curve for this physical change. [1]

Base your answers to questions 59 and 60 on the information below.

In the gold foil experiment, a thin sheet of gold was bombarded with alpha particles. Almost all the alpha particles passed straight through the foil. Only a few alpha particles were deflected from their original paths.

59. State *one* conclusion about atomic structure based on the observation that almost all alpha particles passed straight through the foil. [1]

60. Explain, in terms of charged particles, why some of the alpha particles were deflected. [1]

Base your answers to questions 61 through 63 on the information below.

Some Properties of Three Compounds at Standard Pressure

Compound	Boiling Point (°C)	Solubility in 100. Grams of H_2O at 20.°C (g)
ammonia	−33.2	56
methane	−161.5	0.002
hydrogen chloride	−84.9	72

61. Convert the boiling point of hydrogen chloride at standard pressure to kelvins. [1]

62. Explain, in terms of molecular polarity, why hydrogen chloride is more soluble than methane in water at 20.°C and standard pressure. [1]

63. Explain, in terms of intermolecular forces, why ammonia has a higher boiling point than the other compounds in the table. [1]

Day 14: Practice Regents Exam – Constructed Response Part B-2 and C

Part C: Answer all questions in this part.

Directions (64-81): Record your answer in the spaces provided in your answer booklet. Some questions may require the use of the Reference tables for Physical Setting/Chemistry.

Base your answers to questions 64 through 66 on the information below.

The diagram below represents an operating voltaic cell at 298 K and 1.0 atmosphere in a laboratory investigation. The reaction occurring in the cell is represented by the balanced ionic equation below.

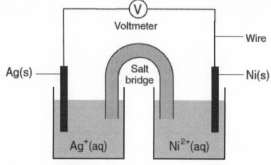

$$2Ag^+(aq) + Ni(s) \longrightarrow 2Ag(s) + Ni^{2+}(aq)$$

64. Identify the anode in this cell. [1]

65. Determine the total number of moles of Ni^{2+}(aq) ions produced when 4.0 moles of Ag^+(aq) ions completely react in this cell. [1]

66. Write a balanced half-reaction equation for the reduction that occurs in this cell. [1]

Base your answers to questions 67 through 69 on the information below.

Gasoline is a mixture composed primarily of hydrocarbons such as isooctane, which is also known as 2,2,4-trimethylpentane.

Gasoline is assigned a number called an octane rating. Gasoline with an octane rating of 87 performs the same as a mixture that consists of 87% isooctane and 13% heptane. An alternative fuel, E-85, can be used in some automobiles. This fuel is a mixture of 85% ethanol and 15% gasoline.

67. State the octane rating of a gasoline sample that performs the same as a mixture consisting of 92% isooctane and 8% heptane. [1]

68. In the space _in your answer booklet,_ draw a structural formula for a molecule of 2,2,4-trimethylpentane. [1]

69. Identify the functional group in a molecule of ethanol in the alternative fuel E-85. [1]

14 Days of Questions for Regents and Final Exams Practice

Day 14: Practice Regents Exam – Constructed Response Part B-2 and C

Base your answers to questions 70 through 72 on the information below.

Hydrogen peroxide, H_2O_2, is a water-soluble compound. The concentration of an aqueous hydrogen peroxide solution that is 3% by mass H_2O_2 is used as an antiseptic. When the solution is poured on a small cut in the skin, H_2O_2 reacts according to the balanced equation below.

$$2H_2O_2 \;\;----\!\!-->\;\; 2H_2O + O_2$$

70. Identify the type of chemical reaction represented by the balanced equation. [1]

71. Calculate the total mass of H_2O_2 in 20.0 grams of an aqueous H_2O_2 solution that is used as an antiseptic. Your response must include *both* a numerical setup and the calculated result. [2]

72. Determine the gram-formula mass of H_2O_2. [1]

Base your answers to questions 73 and 74 on the information below.

The catalytic converter in an automobile changes harmful gases produced during fuel combustion to less harmful exhaust gases. In the catalytic converter, nitrogen dioxide reacts with carbon monoxide to produce nitrogen and carbon dioxide. In addition, some carbon monoxide reacts with oxygen, producing carbon dioxide in the converter. These reactions are represented by the balanced equations below.

Reaction 1: $2NO_2(g) + 4CO(g) ------\!\!-> N_2(g) + 4CO_2(g) + 1198.4$ kJ

Reaction 2: $2CO(g) + O_2(g) ----------\!\!-> 2CO_2(g) + 566.0$ kJ

73. The potential energy diagram *in your answer booklet* represents reaction 1 without a catalyst. On the same diagram, draw a dashed line to indicate how potential energy changes when the reaction is catalyzed in the converter. [1]

74. Determine the oxidation number of carbon in *each* carbon compound in reaction 2. Your response must include *both* the sign and value of *each* oxidation number. [1]

Day 14: Practice Regents Exam – Constructed Response Part B-2 and C

Base your answers to questions 75 through 78 on the information below.
In one trial of an investigation, 50.0 milliliters of HCl(aq) of an unknown concentration is titrated with 0.10 M NaOH(aq). During the titration, the total volume of NaOH(aq) added and the corresponding pH value of the reaction mixture are measured and recorded in the table below.

Titration Data

Total Volume of NaOH(aq) Added (mL)	pH Value of Reaction Mixture
10.0	1.6
20.0	2.2
24.0	2.9
24.9	3.9
25.1	10.1
26.0	11.1
30.0	11.8

75. On the grid _in your answer booklet_, plot the data from the table. Circle and connect the points. [1]

76. Determine the total volume of NaOH(aq) added when the reaction mixture has a pH value of 7.0. [1]

77. Write a balanced equation that represents this neutralization reaction. [1]

78. In another trial, 40.0 milliliters of HCl(aq) is completely neutralized by 20.0 milliliters of this 0.10 M NaOH(aq). Calculate the Molarity of the titrated acid in this trial. Your response must include _both_ a numerical setup and the calculated result. [2]

Base your answers to questions 79 through 81 on the information below.

The radioisotope uranium-238 occurs naturally in Earth's crust. The disintegration of this radioisotope is the first in a series of spontaneous decays. The sixth decay in this series produces the radioisotope radon-222. The decay of radon-222 produces the radioisotope polonium-218 that has a half life of 3.04 minutes. Eventually, the stable isotope lead-206 is produced by the alpha decay of an unstable nuclide.

79. Explain, in terms of electron configuration, why atoms of the radioisotope produced by the sixth decay in the U-238 disintegration series do not readily react to form compounds. [1]

80. Complete the nuclear equation _in your answer booklet_ for the decay of the unstable nuclide that produces Pb-206, by writing a notation for the missing nuclide. [1]

81. Determine the original mass of a sample of Po-218, if 0.50 milligram of the sample remains unchanged after 12.16 minutes. [1]

Day 14 Answer Booklet

Part	Maximum Score	Student's Score
A	30	
B–1	20	
B–2	15	
C	20	

Total Written Test Score
(Maximum Raw Score: 85)

Final Score
(from conversion chart)

PHYSICAL SETTING
CHEMISTRY

Practice Regents Exam

Day 14 Answer Booklet

Student . . . . Sex: ☐ Male ☐ Female

Teacher . . . .

School . . . . Grade . . . .

Answer all questions in this examination. Record your answers in this booklet.

Raters' Initials:

Rater 1 . . . . Rater 2 . . . .

Part A

1 . . . . 11 . . . . 21 . . . .

2 . . . . 12 . . . . 22 . . . .

3 . . . . 13 . . . . 23 . . . .

4 . . . . 14 . . . . 24 . . . .

5 . . . . 15 . . . . 25 . . . .

6 . . . . 16 . . . . 26 . . . .

7 . . . . 17 . . . . 27 . . . .

8 . . . . 18 . . . . 28 . . . .

9 . . . . 19 . . . . 29 . . . .

10 . . . . 20 . . . . 30 . . . .

Part A Score

Part B–1

31 . . . . 41 . . . .

32 . . . . 42 . . . .

33 . . . . 43 . . . .

34 . . . . 44 . . . .

35 . . . . 45 . . . .

36 . . . . 46 . . . .

37 . . . . 47 . . . .

38 . . . . 48 . . . .

39 . . . . 49 . . . .

40 . . . . 50 . . . .

Part B–1 Score

The declaration below must be signed when you have completed the examination.

I do hereby affirm, at the close of this examination, that I had no unlawful knowledge of the questions or answers prior to the examination and that I have neither given nor received assistance in answering any of the questions during the examination.

_____

Signature

Part B–2

For Raters Only

51 _____

51 ☐

52 Metal: _____

Metalloid: _____

52 ☐

Nonmetal: _____

53

53 ☐

_____ cm^3

54 _____

_____

54 ☐

55 _____

_____

55 ☐

56 _____

_____

56 ☐

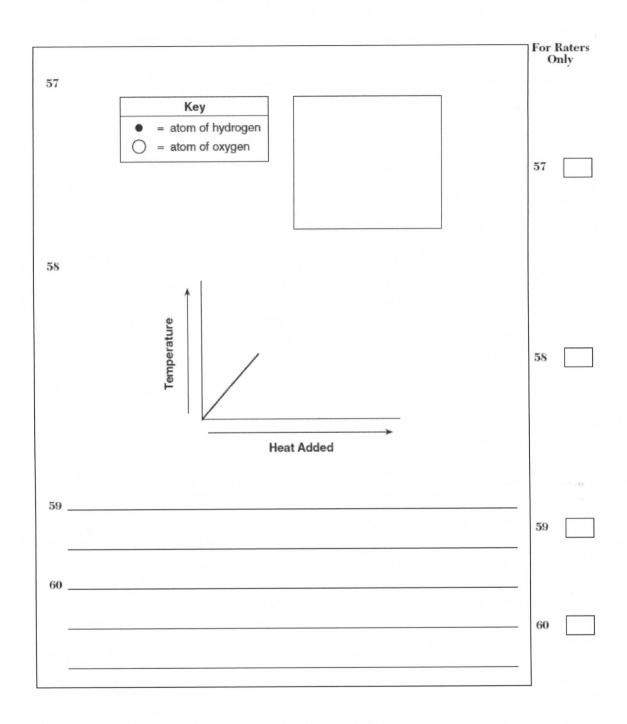

For Raters Only

61 ______________________ K

61 [ ]

62 ____

____

____

62 [ ]

63 ____

____

____

63 [ ]

[ ]

Total Score for Part B–2

Part C	For Raters Only
64 ____________________	64
65 ____________ mol	65
66 ____	66
67 ____________	67
68	68
69 ____________	69
70 ____________________	70
71 ____________ g	71
72 ____________ g/mol	72

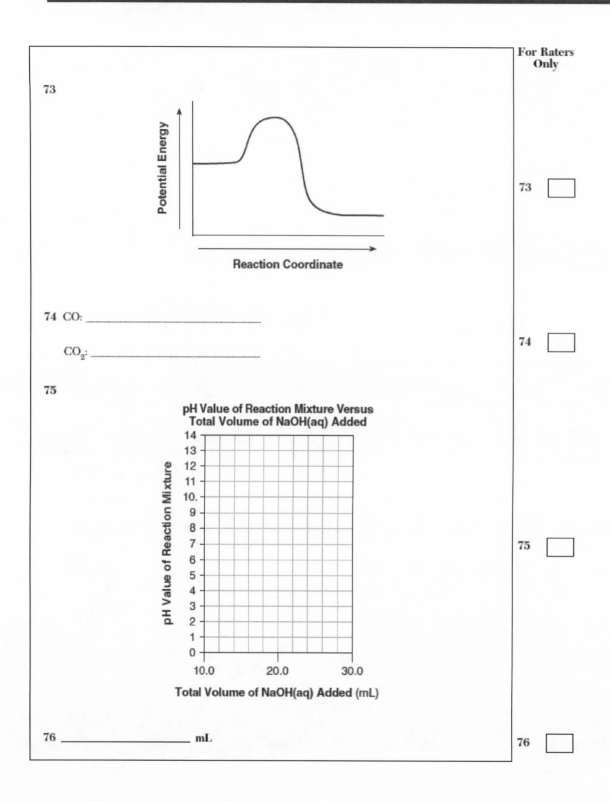

73

73 ☐

74 CO: _____

   CO$_2$: _____

74 ☐

75

**pH Value of Reaction Mixture Versus
Total Volume of NaOH(aq) Added**

75 ☐

76 _____ mL

76 ☐

	For Raters Only
77 ______________________________	77 ☐
78	
	78 ☐
______________ M	
79 ______________________________	
______________________________	79 ☐
______________________________	
80 ____________ → $^{4}_{2}He + ^{206}_{82}Pb$	80 ☐
81 ______________ mg	81 ☐

Total Score for Part C

Table A
Standard Temperature and Pressure

Name	Value	Unit
Standard Pressure	101.3 kPa 1 atm	kilopascal atmosphere
Standard Temperature	273 K 0°C	kelvin degree Celsius

Table B
Physical Constants for Water

Heat of Fusion	334 J/g
Heat of Vaporization	2260 J/g
Specific Heat Capacity of $H_2O(\ell)$	4.18 J/g•K

Table C
Selected Prefixes

Factor	Prefix	Symbol
10^3	kilo-	k
10^{-1}	deci-	d
10^{-2}	centi-	c
10^{-3}	milli-	m
10^{-6}	micro-	μ
10^{-9}	nano-	n
10^{-12}	pico-	p

Table D
Selected Units

Symbol	Name	Quantity
m	meter	length
g	gram	mass
Pa	pascal	pressure
K	kelvin	temperature
mol	mole	amount of substance
J	joule	energy, work, quantity of heat
s	second	time
min	minute	time
h	hour	time
d	day	time
y	year	time
L	liter	volume
ppm	parts per million	concentration
M	molarity	solution concentration
u	atomic mass unit	atomic mass

Table E
Selected Polyatomic Ions

Formula	Name	Formula	Name
H_3O^+	hydronium	CrO_4^{2-}	chromate
Hg_2^{2+}	mercury(I)	$Cr_2O_7^{2-}$	dichromate
NH_4^+	ammonium	MnO_4^-	permanganate
$C_2H_3O_2^-$ } CH_3COO^- }	acetate	NO_2^-	nitrite
		NO_3^-	nitrate
CN^-	cyanide	O_2^{2-}	peroxide
CO_3^{2-}	carbonate	OH^-	hydroxide
HCO_3^-	hydrogen carbonate	PO_4^{3-}	phosphate
$C_2O_4^{2-}$	oxalate	SCN^-	thiocyanate
ClO^-	hypochlorite	SO_3^{2-}	sulfite
ClO_2^-	chlorite	SO_4^{2-}	sulfate
ClO_3^-	chlorate	HSO_4^-	hydrogen sulfate
ClO_4^-	perchlorate	$S_2O_3^{2-}$	thiosulfate

Table F
Solubility Guidelines for Aqueous Solutions

Ions That Form *Soluble* Compounds	Exceptions	Ions That Form *Insoluble* Compounds*	Exceptions
Group 1 ions (Li^+, Na^+, etc.)		carbonate (CO_3^{2-})	when combined with Group 1 ions or ammonium (NH_4^+)
ammonium (NH_4^+)		chromate (CrO_4^{2-})	when combined with Group 1 ions, Ca^{2+}, Mg^{2+}, or ammonium (NH_4^+)
nitrate (NO_3^-)			
acetate ($C_2H_3O_2^-$ or CH_3COO^-)		phosphate (PO_4^{3-})	when combined with Group 1 ions or ammonium (NH_4^+)
hydrogen carbonate (HCO_3^-)		sulfide (S^{2-})	when combined with Group 1 ions or ammonium (NH_4^+)
chlorate (ClO_3^-)		hydroxide (OH^-)	when combined with Group 1 ions, Ca^{2+}, Ba^{2+}, Sr^{2+}, or ammonium (NH_4^+)
halides (Cl^-, Br^-, I^-)	when combined with Ag^+, Pb^{2+}, or Hg_2^{2+}		
sulfates (SO_4^{2-})	when combined with Ag^+, Ca^{2+}, Sr^{2+}, Ba^{2+}, or Pb^{2+}		

*compounds having very low solubility in H_2O

Table G
Solubility Curves at Standard Pressure

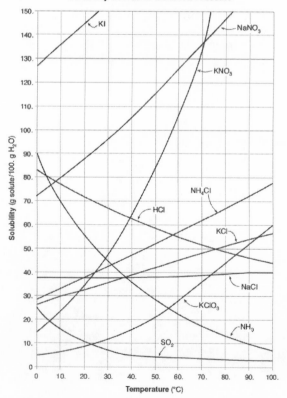

Table H
Vapor Pressure of Four Liquids

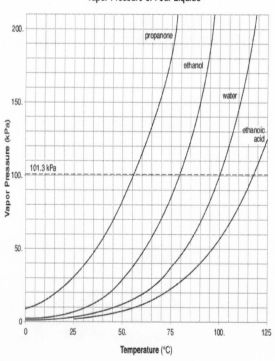

Table I
Heats of Reaction at 101.3 kPa and 298 K

Reaction	ΔH (kJ)*
$CH_4(g) + 2O_2(g) \longrightarrow CO_2(g) + 2H_2O(\ell)$	−890.4
$C_3H_8(g) + 5O_2(g) \longrightarrow 3CO_2(g) + 4H_2O(\ell)$	−2219.2
$2C_8H_{18}(\ell) + 25O_2(g) \longrightarrow 16CO_2(g) + 18H_2O(\ell)$	−10943
$2CH_3OH(\ell) + 3O_2(g) \longrightarrow 2CO_2(g) + 4H_2O(\ell)$	−1452
$C_2H_5OH(\ell) + 3O_2(g) \longrightarrow 2CO_2(g) + 3H_2O(\ell)$	−1367
$C_6H_{12}O_6(s) + 6O_2(g) \longrightarrow 6CO_2(g) + 6H_2O(\ell)$	−2804
$2CO(g) + O_2(g) \longrightarrow 2CO_2(g)$	−566.0
$C(s) + O_2(g) \longrightarrow CO_2(g)$	−393.5
$4Al(s) + 3O_2(g) \longrightarrow 2Al_2O_3(s)$	−3351
$N_2(g) + O_2(g) \longrightarrow 2NO(g)$	+182.6
$N_2(g) + 2O_2(g) \longrightarrow 2NO_2(g)$	+66.4
$2H_2(g) + O_2(g) \longrightarrow 2H_2O(g)$	−483.6
$2H_2(g) + O_2(g) \longrightarrow 2H_2O(\ell)$	−571.6
$N_2(g) + 3H_2(g) \longrightarrow 2NH_3(g)$	−91.8
$2C(s) + 3H_2(g) \longrightarrow C_2H_6(g)$	−84.0
$2C(s) + 2H_2(g) \longrightarrow C_2H_4(g)$	+52.4
$2C(s) + H_2(g) \longrightarrow C_2H_2(g)$	+227.4
$H_2(g) + I_2(g) \longrightarrow 2HI(g)$	+53.0
$KNO_3(s) \xrightarrow{H_2O} K^+(aq) + NO_3^-(aq)$	+34.89
$NaOH(s) \xrightarrow{H_2O} Na^+(aq) + OH^-(aq)$	−44.51
$NH_4Cl(s) \xrightarrow{H_2O} NH_4^+(aq) + Cl^-(aq)$	+14.78
$NH_4NO_3(s) \xrightarrow{H_2O} NH_4^+(aq) + NO_3^-(aq)$	+25.69
$NaCl(s) \xrightarrow{H_2O} Na^+(aq) + Cl^-(aq)$	+3.88
$LiBr(s) \xrightarrow{H_2O} Li^+(aq) + Br^-(aq)$	−48.83
$H^+(aq) + OH^-(aq) \longrightarrow H_2O(\ell)$	−55.8

*The ΔH values are based on molar quantities represented in the equations.
A minus sign indicates an exothermic reaction.

Table J
Activity Series**

Most Active	Metals	Nonmetals	Most Active
	Li	F_2	
	Rb	Cl_2	
	K	Br_2	
	Cs	I_2	
	Ba		
	Sr		
	Ca		
	Na		
	Mg		
	Al		
	Ti		
	Mn		
	Zn		
	Cr		
	Fe		
	Co		
	Ni		
	Sn		
	Pb		
	H_2		
	Cu		
	Ag		
Least Active	Au		Least Active

**Activity Series is based on the hydrogen standard. H_2 is *not* a metal.

Table K
Common Acids

Formula	Name
HCl(aq)	hydrochloric acid
HNO_2(aq)	nitrous acid
HNO_3(aq)	nitric acid
H_2SO_3(aq)	sulfurous acid
H_2SO_4(aq)	sulfuric acid
H_3PO_4(aq)	phosphoric acid
H_2CO_3(aq) or CO_2(aq)	carbonic acid
CH_3COOH(aq) or $HC_2H_3O_2$(aq)	ethanoic acid (acetic acid)

Table L
Common Bases

Formula	Name
NaOH(aq)	sodium hydroxide
KOH(aq)	potassium hydroxide
$Ca(OH)_2$(aq)	calcium hydroxide
NH_3(aq)	aqueous ammonia

Table M
Common Acid–Base Indicators

Indicator	Approximate pH Range for Color Change	Color Change
methyl orange	3.1–4.4	red to yellow
bromthymol blue	6.0–7.6	yellow to blue
phenolphthalein	8–9	colorless to pink
litmus	4.5–8.3	red to blue
bromcresol green	3.8–5.4	yellow to blue
thymol blue	8.0–9.6	yellow to blue

Table N
Selected Radioisotopes

Nuclide	Half-Life	Decay Mode	Nuclide Name
^{198}Au	2.695 d	β^-	gold-198
^{14}C	5715 y	β^-	carbon-14
^{37}Ca	182 ms	β^+	calcium-37
^{60}Co	5.271 y	β^-	cobalt-60
^{137}Cs	30.2 y	β^-	cesium-137
^{53}Fe	8.51 min	β^+	iron-53
^{220}Fr	27.4 s	α	francium-220
^{3}H	12.31 y	β^-	hydrogen-3
^{131}I	8.021 d	β^-	iodine-131
^{37}K	1.23 s	β^+	potassium-37
^{42}K	12.36 h	β^-	potassium-42
^{85}Kr	10.73 y	β^-	krypton-85
^{16}N	7.13 s	β^-	nitrogen-16
^{19}Ne	17.22 s	β^+	neon-19
^{32}P	14.28 d	β^-	phosphorus-32
^{239}Pu	2.410×10^4 y	α	plutonium-239
^{226}Ra	1599 y	α	radium-226
^{222}Rn	3.823 d	α	radon-222
^{90}Sr	29.1 y	β^-	strontium-90
^{99}Tc	2.13×10^5 y	β^-	technetium-99
^{232}Th	1.40×10^{10} y	α	thorium-232
^{233}U	1.592×10^5 y	α	uranium-233
^{235}U	7.04×10^8 y	α	uranium-235
^{238}U	4.47×10^9 y	α	uranium-238

Table O
Symbols Used in Nuclear Chemistry

Name	Notation	Symbol
alpha particle	^4_2He or $^4_2\alpha$	α
beta particle	$^0_{-1}e$ or $^0_{-1}\beta$	β^-
gamma radiation	$^0_0\gamma$	γ
neutron	^1_0n	n
proton	^1_1H or ^1_1p	p
positron	$^0_{+1}e$ or $^0_{+1}\beta$	β^+

Table Q
Homologous Series of Hydrocarbons

Name	General Formula	Examples	
		Name	Structural Formula
alkanes	C_nH_{2n+2}	ethane	H H | | H—C—C—H | | H H
alkenes	C_nH_{2n}	ethene	H H \ / C=C / \ H H
alkynes	C_nH_{2n-2}	ethyne	H—C≡C—H

Note: n = number of carbon atoms

Table P
Organic Prefixes

Prefix	Number of Carbon Atoms
meth-	1
eth-	2
prop-	3
but-	4
pent-	5
hex-	6
hept-	7
oct-	8
non-	9
dec-	10

Table R
Organic Functional Groups

Class of Compound	Functional Group	General Formula	Example
halide (halocarbon)	—F (fluoro-) —Cl (chloro-) —Br (bromo-) —I (iodo-)	$R—X$ (X represents any halogen)	$CH_3CHClCH_3$ 2-chloropropane
alcohol	—OH	$R—OH$	$CH_3CH_2CH_2OH$ 1-propanol
ether	—O—	$R—O—R'$	$CH_3OCH_2CH_3$ methyl ethyl ether
aldehyde	$\overset{O}{\underset{\|\|}{\ }}$ —C—H	$R—\overset{O}{\overset{\|\|}{C}}—H$	$CH_3CH_2\overset{O}{\overset{\|\|}{C}}—H$ propanal
ketone	$—\overset{O}{\overset{\|\|}{C}}—$	$R—\overset{O}{\overset{\|\|}{C}}—R'$	$CH_3CCH_2CH_2CH_3$ 2-pentanone
organic acid	$—\overset{O}{\overset{\|\|}{C}}—OH$	$R—\overset{O}{\overset{\|\|}{C}}—OH$	$CH_3CH_2\overset{O}{\overset{\|\|}{C}}—OH$ propanoic acid
ester	$—\overset{O}{\overset{\|\|}{C}}—O—$	$R—\overset{O}{\overset{\|\|}{C}}—O—R'$	$CH_3CH_2COCH_3$ methyl propanoate
amine	$—\overset{\|}{N}—$	$R—\overset{R'}{\underset{\|}{N}}—R''$	$CH_3CH_2CH_2NH_2$ 1-propanamine
amide	$—\overset{O}{\overset{\|\|}{C}}—\overset{\|}{N}H$	$R—\overset{O}{\overset{\|\|}{C}}—\overset{R'}{\underset{\|}{N}}H$	$CH_3CH_2\overset{O}{\overset{\|\|}{C}}—NH_2$ propanamide

Note: R represents a bonded atom or group of atoms.

Periodic Table of the Elements

KEY

Atomic Mass →	12.011
Symbol →	C
Atomic Number →	6
Electron Configuration →	2-4
Selected Oxidation States ←	−4 +2 +4

Relative atomic masses are based on $^{12}C = 12$ (exact)

Note: Numbers in parentheses are mass numbers of the most stable or common isotope.

Period	Group 1	2	3	4	5	6	7	8	9	10	11	12	13	14	15	16	17	18
1	1.00794 +1 −1 H 1 1																	4.00260 0 He 2 2
2	6.941 +1 Li 3 2-1	9.01218 +2 Be 4 2-2											10.81 +3 B 5 2-3	12.011 −4 +2 +4 C 6 2-4	14.0067 −3 −2 −1 +1 +2 +3 +4 +5 N 7 2-5	15.9994 −2 O 8 2-6	18.9984 −1 F 9 2-7	20.180 0 Ne 10 2-8
3	22.98977 +1 Na 11 2-8-1	24.305 +2 Mg 12 2-8-2											26.98154 +3 Al 13 2-8-3	28.0855 −4 +2 +4 Si 14 2-8-4	30.97376 −3 +3 +5 P 15 2-8-5	32.065 −2 +4 +6 S 16 2-8-6	35.453 −1 +1 +5 +7 Cl 17 2-8-7	39.948 0 Ar 18 2-8-8
4	39.0983 +1 K 19 2-8-8-1	40.08 +2 Ca 20 2-8-8-2	44.9559 +3 Sc 21 2-8-9-2	47.867 +2 +3 +4 Ti 22 2-8-10-2	50.9415 +2 +3 +4 +5 V 23 2-8-11-2	51.996 +2 +3 +6 Cr 24 2-8-13-1	54.9380 +2 +3 +4 +7 Mn 25 2-8-13-2	55.845 +2 +3 Fe 26 2-8-14-2	58.9332 +2 +3 Co 27 2-8-15-2	58.693 +2 +3 Ni 28 2-8-16-2	63.546 +1 +2 Cu 29 2-8-18-1	65.409 +2 Zn 30 2-8-18-2	69.723 +3 Ga 31 2-8-18-3	72.64 −4 +2 +4 Ge 32 2-8-18-4	74.9216 −3 +3 +5 As 33 2-8-18-5	78.96 −2 +4 +6 Se 34 2-8-18-6	79.904 −1 +1 +5 Br 35 2-8-18-7	83.798 0 +2 Kr 36 2-8-18-8
5	85.4678 +1 Rb 37 2-8-18-8-1	87.62 +2 Sr 38 2-8-18-8-2	88.9059 +3 Y 39 2-8-18-9-2	91.224 +4 Zr 40 2-8-18-10-2	92.9064 +3 +5 Nb 41 2-8-18-12-1	95.94 +6 Mo 42 2-8-18-13-1	(98) +4 +6 +7 Tc 43 2-8-18-13-2	101.07 +3 Ru 44 2-8-18-15-1	102.906 +3 Rh 45 2-8-18-16-1	106.42 +2 +4 Pd 46 2-8-18-18	107.868 +1 Ag 47 2-8-18-18-1	112.41 +2 Cd 48 2-8-18-18-2	114.818 +3 In 49 2-8-18-18-3	118.71 +2 +4 Sn 50 2-8-18-18-4	121.760 −3 +3 +5 Sb 51 2-8-18-18-5	127.60 −2 +4 +6 Te 52 2-8-18-18-6	126.904 −1 +1 +5 +7 I 53 2-8-18-18-7	131.29 0 +2 +4 +6 Xe 54 2-8-18-18-8
6	132.905 +1 Cs 55 2-8-18-18-8-1	137.33 +2 Ba 56 2-8-18-18-8-2	138.9055 +3 La 57 2-8-18-18-9-2	178.49 +4 Hf 72 *18-32-10-2	180.948 +5 Ta 73 -18-32-11-2	183.84 +6 W 74 -18-32-12-2	186.207 +4 +6 +7 Re 75 -18-32-13-2	190.23 +3 +4 Os 76 -18-32-14-2	192.217 +3 +4 Ir 77 -18-32-15-2	195.08 +2 +4 Pt 78 -18-32-17-1	196.967 +1 +3 Au 79 -18-32-18-1	200.59 +1 +2 Hg 80 -18-32-18-2	204.383 +1 +3 Tl 81 -18-32-18-3	207.2 +2 +4 Pb 82 -18-32-18-4	208.980 +3 +5 Bi 83 -18-32-18-5	(209) +2 +4 Po 84 -18-32-18-6	(210) At 85 -18-32-18-7	(222) 0 Rn 86 -18-32-18-8
7	(223) +1 Fr 87 -18-32-18-8-1	(226) +2 Ra 88 -18-32-18-8-2	(227) +3 Ac 89 -18-32-18-9-2	(261) +4 Rf 104	(262) Db 105	(266) Sg 106	(272) Bh 107	(277) Hs 108	(276) Mt 109	(281) Ds 110	(280) Rg 111	(285) Cn 112	(284) Uut 113**	(289) Uuq 114	(288) Uup 115	(292) Uuh 116	(?) Uus 117	(294) Uuo 118

140.116 +3 +4 Ce 58	140.908 +3 Pr 59	144.24 +3 Nd 60	(145) +3 Pm 61	150.36 +2 +3 Sm 62	151.964 +2 +3 Eu 63	157.25 +3 Gd 64	158.925 +3 Tb 65	162.500 +3 Dy 66	164.930 +3 Ho 67	167.259 +3 Er 68	168.934 +3 Tm 69	173.04 +2 +3 Yb 70	174.9668 +3 Lu 71
232.038 +4 Th 90	231.036 +4 +5 Pa 91	238.029 +3 +4 +5 +6 U 92	(237) +3 +4 +5 +6 Np 93	(244) +3 +4 +5 +6 Pu 94	(243) +3 +4 +5 +6 Am 95	(247) +3 Cm 96	(247) +3 +4 Bk 97	(251) +3 Cf 98	(252) +3 Es 99	(257) +3 Fm 100	(258) +2 +3 Md 101	(259) +2 +3 No 102	(262) +3 Lr 103

*denotes the presence of (2-8-) for elements 72 and above

**The systematic names and symbols for elements of atomic numbers 113 and above will be used until the approval of trivial names by IUPAC.

Source: *CRC Handbook of Chemistry and Physics*, 91st ed., 2010–2011, CRC Press

Table S
Properties of Selected Elements

Atomic Number	Symbol	Name	First Ionization Energy (kJ/mol)	Electro-negativity	Melting Point (K)	Boiling Point* (K)	Density** (g/cm³)	Atomic Radius (pm)
41	Nb	niobium	652	1.6	2750	5017	8.57	156
42	Mo	molybdenum	684	2.2	2896	4912	10.2	146
43	Tc	technetium	702	2.1	2430	4538	11	138
44	Ru	ruthenium	710	2.2	2606	4423	12.1	136
45	Rh	rhodium	720	2.3	2237	3968	12.4	134
46	Pd	palladium	804	2.2	1828	3236	12.0	130
47	Ag	silver	731	1.9	1235	2435	10.5	136
48	Cd	cadmium	868	1.7	594	1040	8.69	140
49	In	indium	558	1.8	430	2345	7.31	142
50	Sn	tin (white)	709	2.0	505	2875	7.287	140
51	Sb	antimony (gray)	831	2.1	904	1860	6.68	140
52	Te	tellurium	869	2.1	723	1261	6.232	137
53	I	iodine	1008	2.7	387	457	4.933	136
54	Xe	xenon	1170	2.6	161	165	0.005366	136
55	Cs	cesium	376	0.8	302	944	1.873	238
56	Ba	barium	503	0.9	1000	2170	3.62	206
57	La	lanthanum	538	1.1	1193	3737	6.15	194
							Elements 58–71 have been omitted	
72	Hf	hafnium	659	1.3	2506	4876	13.3	164
73	Ta	tantalum	728	1.5	3290	5731	16.4	158
74	W	tungsten	759	1.7	3695	5828	19.3	150
75	Re	rhenium	756	1.9	3458	5869	20.8	141
76	Os	osmium	814	2.2	3306	5285	22.587	136
77	Ir	iridium	865	2.2	2719	4701	22.562	132
78	Pt	platinum	864	2.3	2041	4098	21.5	130
79	Au	gold	890	2.4	1337	3129	19.3	130
80	Hg	mercury	1007	1.9	234	630	13.536	132
81	Tl	thallium	589	1.8	577	1746	11.8	144
82	Pb	lead	716	1.8	600	2022	11.3	145
83	Bi	bismuth	703	1.9	544	1837	9.79	150
84	Po	polonium	812	2.0	527	1235	9.20	142
85	At	astatine	—	2.2	575	—	—	148
86	Rn	radon	1037	—	202	211	0.009074	146
87	Fr	francium	393	0.7	300	—	—	242
88	Ra	radium	509	0.9	969	—	5	211
89	Ac	actinium	499	1.1	1323	3471	10.	201

Elements 90 and above have been omitted.

*boiling point at standard pressure
**density of solids and liquids at room temperature and density of gases at 298 K and 101.3 kPa
— no data available
Source: CRC Handbook for Chemistry and Physics, 91st ed., 2010–2011, CRC Press

Atomic Number	Symbol	Name	First Ionization Energy (kJ/mol)	Electro-negativity	Melting Point (K)	Boiling Point* (K)	Density** (g/cm³)	Atomic Radius (pm)
1	H	hydrogen	1312	2.2	14	20	0.00008	32
2	He	helium	2372	—	—	4	0.000164	37
3	Li	lithium	520	1.0	454	1615	0.534	130
4	Be	beryllium	900	1.6	1560	2744	1.85	99
5	B	boron	801	2.0	2348	4273	2.34	84
6	C	carbon	1086	2.6	—	—	—	75
7	N	nitrogen	1402	3.0	63	77	0.001145	71
8	O	oxygen	1314	3.4	54	90	0.001308	64
9	F	fluorine	1681	4.0	53	85	0.001553	60
10	Ne	neon	2081	—	24	27	0.000825	62
11	Na	sodium	496	0.9	371	1156	0.97	160
12	Mg	magnesium	738	1.3	923	1363	1.74	140
13	Al	aluminum	578	1.6	933	2792	2.70	124
14	Si	silicon	787	1.9	1687	3538	2.336	114
15	P	phosphorus (white)	1012	2.2	317	554	1.823	109
16	S	sulfur (monoclinic)	1000	2.6	388	718	2.00	104
17	Cl	chlorine	1251	3.2	172	239	0.002898	100
18	Ar	argon	1521	—	84	87	0.001633	101
19	K	potassium	419	0.8	337	1032	0.89	200
20	Ca	calcium	590	1.0	1115	1757	1.54	174
21	Sc	scandium	633	1.4	1814	3109	2.99	159
22	Ti	titanium	659	1.5	1941	3560	4.506	148
23	V	vanadium	651	1.6	2183	3680	6.0	144
24	Cr	chromium	653	1.7	2180	2944	7.15	130
25	Mn	manganese	717	1.6	1519	2334	7.3	129
26	Fe	iron	762	1.8	1811	3134	7.87	124
27	Co	cobalt	760	1.9	1768	3200	8.86	118
28	Ni	nickel	737	1.9	1728	3186	8.90	117
29	Cu	copper	745	1.9	1358	2835	8.96	122
30	Zn	zinc	906	1.7	693	1180	7.134	120
31	Ga	gallium	579	1.8	303	2477	5.91	123
32	Ge	germanium	762	2.0	1211	3106	5.3234	120
33	As	arsenic (gray)	944	2.2	1090	—	5.75	120
34	Se	selenium (gray)	941	2.6	494	958	4.809	118
35	Br	bromine	1140	3.0	266	332	3.1028	117
36	Kr	krypton	1351	—	116	120	0.003425	116
37	Rb	rubidium	403	0.8	312	961	1.53	215
38	Sr	strontium	549	1.0	1050	1655	2.64	190
39	Y	yttrium	600	1.2	1795	3618	4.47	176
40	Zr	zirconium	640	1.3	2128	4682	6.52	164

Table T
Important Formulas and Equations

Density	$d = \dfrac{m}{V}$	d = density m = mass V = volume
Mole Calculations	number of moles = $\dfrac{\text{given mass}}{\text{gram-formula mass}}$	
Percent Error	% error = $\dfrac{\text{measured value} - \text{accepted value}}{\text{accepted value}} \times 100$	
Percent Composition	% composition by mass = $\dfrac{\text{mass of part}}{\text{mass of whole}} \times 100$	
Concentration	parts per million = $\dfrac{\text{mass of solute}}{\text{mass of solution}} \times 1\,000\,000$	
	molarity = $\dfrac{\text{moles of solute}}{\text{liter of solution}}$	
Combined Gas Law	$\dfrac{P_1 V_1}{T_1} = \dfrac{P_2 V_2}{T_2}$	P = pressure V = volume T = temperature
Titration	$M_A V_A = M_B V_B$	M_A = molarity of H^+ M_B = molarity of OH^- V_A = volume of acid V_B = volume of base
Heat	$q = mC\Delta T$ $q = mH_f$ $q = mH_v$	q = heat H_f = heat of fusion m = mass H_v = heat of vaporization C = specific heat capacity ΔT = change in temperature
Temperature	$K = {}^\circ C + 273$	K = kelvin ${}^\circ C$ = degree Celsius

---

NOTE: The important decay equations below *are not* parts of the new 2011 Reference Table Edition.

Radioactive Decay	fraction remaining = $\left(\dfrac{1}{2}\right)^{\frac{t}{T}}$ number of half-life periods = $\dfrac{t}{T}$	t = total time elapsed T = half-life

Glossary and Index

Glossary and Index

C

Calorimeter   (11)
a device used in measuring heat energy change during a physical and a chemical process.

Catalyst   (154, 157)
a substance that speeds up a reaction by providing an alternate, lower activation energy pathway.

Cathode   (212)
an electrode (site) where reduction occurs in electrochemical (Voltaic and electrolytic) cells.
In voltaic cells, the cathode is positive.
In electrolytic cells, the cathode is negative.

Cathode ray experiment   (46)
experiment conducted by J.J. Thompson that confirms the existence of negative particles in atoms

Charles' Law   (23)
describes behavior of gases at constant pressure: At constant pressure, the volume of a gas is directly proportional to its Kelvin (absolute) temperature.

Chemical bonding   (69)
the simultaneous attraction of two nuclei to electrons.

Chemical change   (26, 99)
the changing of composition of one or more substances during chemical reactions.

Chemical equation   (99)
a way of using chemical symbols to show changes in chemical composition of substances

Chemical formula   (91)
expression of qualitative and quantitative composition of pure substances.

Chemical property   (26)
a characteristic of a substance based on its interaction with other substances.

Chemical Change   (26)
any change that leads to a change in composition of a substance

Chemistry   (1)
the study of the composition, properties, changes, and energy of matter.

Coefficient   (99)
a number (usually a whole number) in front of a formula that indicates how many moles (or unit) of that substance.

Collision Theory   (154)
for a chemical reaction to occur, reacting particles must collide effectively.

Combustion   (100, 197)
an exothermic reaction of a substance with oxygen to release energy and produce CO_2 and H_2O

Compound   (2, 6)
a substance composed of two or more different elements chemically combined in a definite ratio
a substance that can be separated (decomposed) only by chemical methods.

Concentrated solution   (131)
a solution containing a large amount of dissolved solute relative to the amount of solvent.

Condensation   (8)
exothermic phase change of a substance from gas (vapor) to a liquid.

Condensation polymerization   (193, 196)
the joining of monomers (small unit molecules) into a polymer (a large unit molecule) by the removal of water.

Conductivity   (31)
ability of an electrical current to flow through a substance.
conductivity of electrolytes (soluble substances) in aqueous and liquid phase is due to mobile ions.
Conductivity of metallic substances is due to mobile valence electrons.

Covalent bond   (71)
a bond formed by the sharing of electrons between nonmetal atoms.

Cracking   (193
the breaking of a large hydrocarbon molecule into smaller molecules.

Crystallization   (124)
a process of recovering a solute from a solution (mixture) by evaporation (or boiling).

Glossary and Index

D

Decomposition (100)
a chemical reaction in which a compound is broken down into simpler substances.

Density (31)
mass per unit volume of a substance ;   Density = $\dfrac{Mass}{Volume}$

Deposition (8)
an exothermic phase change by which a gas changes to a solid.

Diatomic molecules (element)
a molecule consisting of two identical atoms (ex. O_2)

Dihydroxy alcohol (184)
an alcohol with two attached –OH (hydroxyl) groups

Dilute solution (131)
a solution containing very little dissolved solute in comparison to the amount of solvent.

Dipole (aka polar) (83)
a molecule with positive and negative ends due to uneven charge distributions.

Distillation (4)
a process by which components of a homogeneous mixture can be separated by differences in boiling points.

Double covalent bond (=) (180, 181)
the sharing of two pairs of electrons (four total electrons) between two atoms.

Double replacement (100)
a chemical reaction that involves the exchange of ions.

Dynamic equilibrium
a state of a reaction by which the forward and reverse reactions are equal, while the concentration (amount) of substances remains constant.

Ductile (31)
ability (property) of a metal to be drawn into a thin wire.

E

Effective collision (154)
a collision in which the particles collide with sufficient kinetic energy, and at appropriate angles.

Electrochemical cell (211)
a system in which there is a flow of electrical current while a chemical reaction is taking place. Voltaic and Electrolytic cells are the two most common types of electrochemical cells.

Electrode (212)
a site at which oxidation or reduction can occur in electrochemical cells.
the anode (oxidation site) and cathode (reduction site) are the two electrodes of electrochemical cells.

Electrolysis (215)
a process by which electrical current forces a nonspontaneous redox reaction to occur.
Electrolysis of water: $2H_2O$ + electricity ------- > $2 H_2$ + O_2

Electrolyte (150)
a substances that dissolves in water to produce an aqueous solution that conducts electricity. Conductivity of an electrolyte is due to the mobile ions in solutions.

Electrolytic cell (211, 215)
an electrochemical cell that requires an electrical current to cause a nonspontaneous redox reaction to occur.

Electron (49)
a negatively charged subatomic particle found surrounding the nucleus (in orbitals) of an atom.

Electron configuration (580
distribution of electrons in electron shells (energy levels) of an atom.

Electron-dot diagram (81)
a diagram showing the symbol of an atom and dots equal to the number of valence electrons.

Glossary and Index

Glossary and Index

Filtration   (4, 124)
 a process that is used to separate a heterogeneous mixture that is composed of substances with different particle sizes.

Flame test   (63)
 a lab procedure used for identifying metallic ions in compounds

Fission   (229)
 the splitting of a large nucleus into smaller nuclei fragments in a nuclear reaction.
 Mass is converted to huge amounts of energy during fission.

Formula   (91)
 symbols and subscripts used to represent the composition of a substance.

Formula mass   (107)
 the total mass of all the atoms in one unit of a formula.

Freezing (solidification)   (8)
 an exothermic phase change by which a liquid changes to a solid.

Freezing point (solid/liquid equilibrium)
 the temperature at which both solid and liquid phases of a substance can exist at equilibrium
 The freezing point and melting point of a substance are the same.

Functional group   (183)
 an atom or a group of atoms that replaces a hydrogen atom in a hydrocarbon .

Fusion (nuclear change)   (230)
 the joining of two small nuclei to make a larger nucleus in a nuclear reaction.
 Mass is converted to a tremendous amount of energy during fusion.

Fusion (melting) phase change   (8)
 endothermic phase change by which a solid changes to a liquid.

G

Gamma ray   (223)
 high-energy rays similar to X-rays that are released during nuclear decay.
 A gamma ray has zero mass and zero charge ($^0_0\gamma$).

Gaseous phase   (7)
 a phase of matter with no definite shape and no definite volume.

Gay-Lussac's Law   (24)
 describes behavior of a gas at constant volume: At constant volume, pressure of a gas varies directly with the Kelvin temperature

Geological dating   (240)
 determining the age of a rock or mineral by comparing amounts of Uranium-238 to Lead-206 in a sample.

Gold Foil experiment   (46)
 an experiment conducted by Earnest Rutherford that led him to proposed the "Empty Space" theory of atoms

Gram-formula mass   (107)
 Mass of one mole of a substance expressed in grams.
 the total mass of all atoms in one mole of a substance.

Ground state   (61)
 a state of an atom in which all electrons of the atom occupy the lowest available electron shell.

Group (family)   (30, 36 – 38)
 the vertical column of the Periodic Table.

H

Haber process   (170)
 a chemical reaction that produces ammonia from nitrogen and hydrogen.
 N_2 + $3H_2$ ---------- > $2NH_3$ (Haber process equation).

Half-life   (234)
 the length of time it takes for a sample of a radioisotope to decay to half its original mass (or atoms)

Glossary and Index

Half-reaction   (205)
a reaction that shows either the oxidation or the reduction part of a redox reaction.

Halide   (185)
a compound that contains a halogen (Group 17) atom.

Halogen   (37)
an element found in Group 17 of the Periodic Table.

Heat   (14 - 18)
a form of energy that can flow (or transfer) from one substance (or area) to another
Joules and calories are two units commonly used to measure the quantity of heat.

Heat of fusion   (16, 17)
the amount of heat needed to change a unit mass of a solid to a liquid at its melting point.
Heat of fusion for water is 334 Joules per gram.

Heat of reaction (Δ H)   (159)
the amount of heat absorbed or released during a reaction.
the difference between the heat energy of the products and the heat energy of the reactants.
ΔH = heat of products   −   heat of reactants.

Heat of vaporization   (16, 17)
the amount of heat needed to change a unit mass of a liquid to vapor (gas) at its boiling point.
Heat of vaporization for water is 2260 Joules per gram.

Heterogeneous   (3, 123)
a type of mixture in which substances in the mixture are not uniformly or evenly mixed.

Homogeneous   (3, 123)
a type of mixture in which substances in the mixture are uniformly and evenly mixed.
Solutions are homogeneous mixtures.
Pure substances (compounds and elements) always have homogeneous properties.

Homologous series   (180)
a group of related compounds in which one member differs from the next member by a set
number of atoms.

Hydrate   (115)
an ionic compound containing a set number of water molecules within its crystal structures.

$CuSO_4 \cdot 5H_2O$ is an example formula of a hydrate. This hydrate contains five moles of water.

Hydrocarbon   (180)
an organic compound containing only hydrogen and carbon atoms.

Hydrogen bond   (85)
the attraction of a hydrogen atom to oxygen, nitrogen, or fluorine atom of another molecule.
hydrogen bonding exists (or is strongest) in H_2O (water), NH_3 (ammonia), and HF (hydrogen
fluoride).

Hydrogen ion (H^+)   (142)
a hydrogen atom that has lost its only electron. H^+ is similar to a proton.
The only positive ion produced by all Arrhenius acids in solutions.

Hydrolysis
a reaction of a salt in water to produce a solution that is either acidic, basic, or neutral.

Hydronium ion (H_3O^+)   (142)
a polyatomic ion formed when H_2O (a water molecule) combines with H^+ (hydrogen ion).
Ion formed by all Arrhenius acids in solutions.

Hydroxide ion (OH $^-$)   (142)
the only negative ion produced by Arrhenius bases in solutions.

Hydroxyl group (–OH)   (184)
a functional group found in compounds of alcohols. NOTE: Hydroxyl groups do not ionize in water.

Glossary and Index

Ideal gas (19)
a theoretical gas that possesses all the characteristics described by the kinetic molecular theory

Immiscible liquids (126)
two liquids that do not mix well with each other

Indicator (144)
any substance that changes color in the presence of another substance.
An indicator can also be used to determine the completion of a chemical reaction.
Acid-base indicators are used to determine if a substance is an acid or a base.

Inert gas (noble gas) (38)
elements in Group 18 of the Periodic Table.

Insoluble (126, 129)
a solute substance with low solubility (doesn't dissolve well) in a given solvent.

Intermolecular forces (85)
weak forces holding molecules together in the solid and liquid states

Ion (64)
a charged (+ or -) particle.

Ionic bond (71)
a bond formed by the transfer of one or more electrons from one atom to another.
An ionic bond is formed by the electrostatic attraction of a positive ion to a negative ion.

Ionic compound (substance) (76, 95)
compounds that are composed of positive and negative particles.
$NaCl$, $NaNO_3$, and ammonium chloride are examples of ionic substances.

Ionic radius (65)
the size of an ion as measured from the nucleus to the outer energy level of that ion.

Ionization energy (31, 42)
the amount of energy needed to remove the most loosely bound valence electron from an atom.

Isomers (189-191)
organic compounds with the same molecular formula but different structural formulas.
isomers also have different properties.

Isotopes (52)
atoms of the same element with the same number of protons but different numbers of neutrons.
atoms of the same element with the same atomic number but different mass numbers.

J

Joules (14)
a unit for measuring the amount of heat energy.

K

Kelvin (K) (9)
a unit for measuring temperature.
a Kelvin temperature unit is always 273 higher than the equivalent temperature in Celsius.
$K = {}^{o}C + 273$

Ketone (187)
an organic compound containing $-\overset{\overset{O}{\|}}{C}-$ ($-CO-$), a carbonyl group) as the functional group.

Kinetic energy (9, 12)
energy due to motion or movement of particles in a substance.
Average kinetic energy of particles in a substance determines temperature of the substance.

Kinetic molecular theory (of an ideal gas) (19)
a theory that is used to explain behavior of gas particles.

Kinetics (153
the study of rates and mechanisms of reactions

Glossary and Index

L

Law of conservation (101)
In a chemical reaction, mass, atoms, charges, and energy are conserved (neither created nor destroyed).

Law of definite composition (2)
atoms of a compound are in a fixed ratio.

Le Chatelier's principle (170)
a chemical or physical process will shift at equilibrium to compensate for added stress

Lewis electron-dot diagram (81 – 84)
a diagram showing the symbol of an atom and dots equal to the number of its valence electrons.

Liquid phase (7)
a phase of matter with definite volume but no definite shape (takes the shape of the container).

Luster (31)
a property that describes the shininess of a metallic element

M

Malleable (31)
ability (or property) of a metal to be hammered into a thin sheet.

Mass number (50)
the total number of protons and neutrons in the nucleus of an atom.

Matter (1)
anything that has mass and volume (occupied space).

Melting point (solid/liquid equilibrium) (9)
the temperature at which both the solid and the liquid phases of a substance can co-exist.
The melting point of water is 0°C or 273 K.

Metal (32, 76)
an element that tends to lose electrons and form a positive ion during chemical reactions.
The majority of the elements (about 75%) are metals.

Metallic bond (73)
a bond due to the attraction of valence electrons of a metallic atom to its positive nucleus.
metallic bonding is described as "positive ions immersed in a sea of mobile electrons."

Metalloid (32)
an element with both metallic and nonmetallic properties (characteristics).

Mixture (2, 6)
a physical (not chemically bonded) combination of two or more substances.
a type of matter that can be separated by a physical method.
a type of matter that can be either homogeneous or heterogeneous.

Molar mass (107)
the mass in grams of one mole of a substance

Molarity (134)
concentration of a solution expressed in moles of solute per liter of solution.

$$\text{Molarity} = \frac{\text{moles of solute}}{\text{liter of solution}}$$

Mole (105)
a unit for measuring the number of particles (atoms, molecules, ions, electrons) in a substance.

Molecular formula (93)
a formula showing the actual composition (or ratio of atoms) in a substance

Molecule (77)
the smallest unit of a covalent (molecular) substance that has all properties of the substance

Molecular substance (covalent substance) (77, 78, 98)
a substance composed of molecules

Glossary and Index

Monohydroxy alcohol (184)

an alcohol with one attached –OH (hydroxyl) group

Monomer (196)

an individual unit of a polymer.

Multiple covalent bond (180)

a double or a triple covalent bond formed by the sharing of more than two electrons.

N

Negative ion (64)

a charged atom with more electrons than protons

Network covalent (72, 75)

a bond in network solid substances with absence of discrete particles

Neutral atom (64)

an atom with equal number of protons to electrons

Neutralization (148)

a reaction of an acid with a base to produce water and a salt.

Neutron (48)

a subatomic particle with no charge, found in the nucleus of an atom

Noble gas (inert gas) (38)

an element found in Group 18 of the Periodic Table

Nonmetal (32)

an element that tends to gain electrons and forms negative ions, or shares electrons to form a covalent bond.

Nonpolar covalent bond (72)

a bond formed by the equal sharing of electrons between two identical nonmetal atoms (or atoms with the same electronegativity)

Nonpolar substance (78, 83)

a type of molecular substance with symmetrical charge distribution within its molecules

Nucleons (50)

particles in the nucleus of atoms. Protons and neutrons.

Nucleus (48)

the small, dense, positive core of an atom containing protons and neutrons.

O

Octet of electrons (69)

when an atom has a stable electron configuration with eight electrons in the valence shell.

Orbital (45, 58)

a region in an atom where electrons are likely to be found (or located).

Organic acid (186)

a compound containing –COOH or $-\overset{\overset{\displaystyle O}{\|}}{C}-OH$ as its functional group.

Organic compounds (177)

carbon based compounds.

Oxidation (201, 205)

the loss of electrons by an atom during a redox reaction.
Oxidation leads to an increase in oxidation state (number) of a substance.

Oxidized substance (Reducing agent) (205)

a substance that loses electrons in a redox reaction.
a substance whose oxidation number (state) increases after a redox reaction

Oxidizing agent (Reduced substance) (205)

a substance that is reduced (gains electrons) in a redox reaction.
a substance whose oxidation number (state) decreases after a redox reaction

Oxidation number/ Oxidation state (201, 203)

a charge an atom has or appears to have during a redox reaction

Ozone (43)

O_3, an allotrope (a different molecular form) of oxygen

P

Parts per million   (135)
concentration of a solution expressed as the ratio of mass of solute per million parts of a solution.

$$\text{Part per million (ppm)} = \frac{\text{mass of solute}}{\text{mass of solution}} \times 1\ 000\ 000$$

Percent composition   (114)
composition of a compound as the percentage by mass of each element compared to the total mass of the compound.

$$\text{Percent composition} = \frac{\text{mass of parts}}{\text{mass of whole}} \times 100$$

Period   (30)
the horizontal row of the Periodic Table
Elements within a Period have the same number of occupied electron shells (or energy levels).

Periodic law   (30)
states that properties of elements are periodic functions of their atomic numbers.

pH   (143)
values that indicate the strength of an acid or a base. pH value ranges from 0 – 14.
pH value is determined from how much H^+ ions are in a solution.

Phase equilibrium   (168)
a state of balance when the rates of two opposing (opposite) phase changes are equal.

Physical change   (26)
a change that does not change the composition of a substance.
Phase changes and dissolving are examples of physical changes.

Physical properties   (26)
characteristics of a substance that can be observed or measured without changing the chemical composition of the substance

Polar covalent bond   (72)
a bond formed by the unequal sharing of electrons between two different nonmetal atoms.

Polar substance   (78, 83)
a type of molecular substance with asymmetrical charge distribution within its molecules

Polyatomic ion   (76, 95)
a group of two or more atoms with excess positive or negative charges (See Reference Table E).

Polymer   (196)
an organic compound composed of chains of monomers (smaller units).

Polymerization   (193, 196)
an organic reaction by which monomers (small units of molecules) are joined together to make a polymer (a larger unit molecule).

Positron   (223)
a positively charge particle similar in mass to an electron. $^{\ 1}_{0}e$

Positive ion   (65)

a charged atom containing more protons than electrons

Positron decay (emission)   (227)
a nuclear decay that releases a positron

Potential energy   (159)
stored energy in chemical substances.
Amount of potential energy depends on composition and the structure of a substance.

Potential energy diagram   (163-164)
a diagram showing the changes in potential energy of substances during a reaction.

Precipitate   (133)
a solid that forms out of a solution

Primary alcohol   (184)
an alcohol with an –OH functional group attached to an end carbon

337

Glossary and Index

Glossary and Index

T

Temperature   (12, 20)
the measure of the average kinetic energy of particles in a substance
Temperature and average kinetic energy are directly related. As one increases, so does the other.

Tertiary alcohol   (184)
an alcohol in which the –OH is bonded to a carbon atom that is already bonded to three other carbon atoms.

Titration   (149)
a process used in determining the concentration of an unknown solution by reacting it with a solution of known concentration.

Thompson, JJ   (45, 46)
conducted "Cathode Ray" experiment that confirmed the existence of negative particles in atoms

Tracer   (240)
a radioisotope used to track a chemical reaction.

Transition element   (37)
an element found in Groups 3 – 12 of the Periodic Table

Transmutation   (221, 225)
the changing or converting of a nucleus of one atom into a nucleus of a different atom

Trihydroxy alcohol   (184)
an alcohol with three –OH (hydroxyl) groups

Triple covalent bond   (180)
a covalent bond resulting from the sharing of three pairs of electrons (six total electrons).

U

Unsaturated hydrocarbon   (180)
organic compound containing double or triple bonded carbon atoms.

Unsaturated solution   (131)
a solution containing less dissolved solute than can be dissolved at a given temperature.

V

Valence electrons   (65)
the electrons in the outermost electron shell (energy level) of an atom.

Vapor   (136)
a gas form of a substance that is normally a liquid at room temperature.

Vapor pressure   (136 – 137)
the pressure exerted by vapor (evaporated particles) on the surface of the liquid

Vaporization (evaporation).   (8)
endothermic phase change of a substance from liquid to gas at its boiling point.

Voltaic cell   (211, 213)
an electrochemical cell in which electrical energy is produced from a spontaneous redox chemical reaction.

W

Wave-mechanical model (electron-cloud model)   (45)
the current model of an atom that places electrons in orbital.
The orbital is described as the most probable location (region) of finding electrons in an atom.

Surviving Chemistry eBooks

Student and teacher friendly supplemental instructional books and exam preps for high school chemistry and biology

WHICH OF OUR BOOKS IS RIGHT FOR YOUR STUDENTS?

Let them choose

from our

eBook School-license Deals

As low as

$1

per book

Take additional
10-40% off

Our eBook Platform

- ✓ Online based; no downloading and no software to install.
- ✓ Quick and easy access for your students anytime, anywhere.
- ✓ Compatible with all brands of computers and browsers.
- ✓ Mobile eBook format for on-the-go access with iPad, tablet or phone.
- ✓ Visually stunning digital flipbook for students.
- ✓ Easy to browse, read, search and print pages.
- ✓ No screen advertisements to annoy and distract students.
- ✓ Customized specifically for your school.

Surviving Chemistry
School-license
Deals

Study anywhere, anytime.

Unlimited access to one or more eBooks for as low as

$1 per book

Take additional 10-40% off depending on school size

Easy to Order

from

SurvivingChem.com

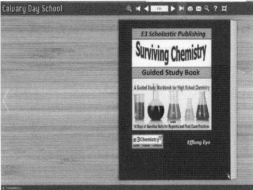

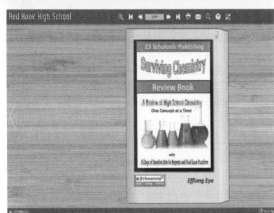

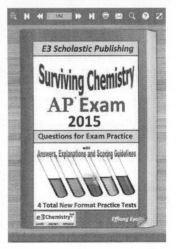

84922413R00210

Made in the USA
Middletown, DE
22 August 2018